Namedropping
In The Wings

DAVID COLLISON

Copyright © 2012 David Collison

All rights reserved.

ISBN: 979-8-5763-8187-6

DEDICATION

This book is dedicated to the many people who helped shape my career in the theatre. In particular: Robert Baty, Peter Hall, Michael Elliott, Sean Kenny and Richard Pilbrow.

Particular thanks are due to my sister Penelope Plas for her diligent proof reading and to my wife Alison for her skills as an editor and for persuading me to write the book in the first place.

Cover design by Christopher Brown

CONTENTS

Prologue 1
    Early Trauma
    The School Years
    Benjamin Britten
    The Blythe-Collison Opera Company
    A Job in the Theatre

Getting Started 30
    The Arts Theatre Club
    Peter Hall
    How To Ruin A Performance
    Ronnie Barker and Maggie Smith
    A Hostile Audience
    Your Country Needs You
    Leo McKern and Hugh Griffith
    A Memorable Experience
    Promotion
    About To Get The Sack

The Big Time 70
    Into The Commercial Theatre
    Resting

1957 79
    Zuleika
    Kenneth Williams
    Who Needs A Lighting Designer?
    Cat On A Hot Tin Roof

1958 94
    Peter Sellers and *Brouhaha*

1959 106
    The Pigalle
    Michael Elliott
    Richard Pilbrow

1960 123
    Struggling To Make A Living

1961 125
    Suddenly in Demand

1962   **131**
    Lionel Bart And *Blitz!*
    Tony Horder
    Final Season Of The Old Vic

1963   **156**
    The Wars Of The Roses
    Half A Sixpence
    Harry Secombe And *Pickwick*
    A Funny Thing Happened On The Way To The Forum
    The National Theatre Company
    New York
    Las Vegas

1964   **186**
    Shakespeare's Birthday
    She Loves Me
    Sammy Davis Junior Again
    Maggie May

1965   **203**
    Becoming A Guru
    The Horrors of *Twang!*
    Sir Donald Wolfit

1966   **215**
    On The Level
    Madame Tussauds

1967   **223**
    Heroes Live
    Fiddler On The Roof
    Harry Secombe as D'Artagnan
    Expo 67 Montreal
    Consultants To The National Theatre

1968   **244**
    Judi Dench and *Cabaret*
    Forty Years On
    The Ruling Class

1969   **249**
    Ginger Rogers and *Mame*

1970   **252**
    Who Do We Have In The Studio Today?
    The Library
    Tommy Steele
    Carol Channing Disaster
    The Great Waltz
    Jacques Brel
    Kiss Me Kate

1971   **273**
    A Rival On The Scene
    Paris And Peter Brook
    Working With Dolphins
    The Consultancy Company

1972   **285**
    Company
    Stitched Up
    Jesus Christ Superstar
    John Schlesinger
    Lauren Bacall
    Pete And Dud
    South Africa

1973   **313**
    The Amazing Technicolor Dreamcoat
    Grease
    Pippin
    The Raymond Revuebar

1974   **325**
    Michael Crawford And Ghosts
    Hair
    The Good Companions
    The Beatles
    More Nudes and More Dolphins
    Rocky Horror Show
    A Brush With The Musician's Union

1975   **344**
    Stagesound
    A Little Night Music
    Jeeves
    Dad's Army
    Pilgrim
    Bernard Miles

Namedropping in the Wings

1976   **355**
Summoned To The Palace
Side By Side By Sondheim
Stars At The Palladium
Another Stinker
Opening Of The National Theatre - 25th October 1976
Becoming An Author
South Africa Again

1977   **373**
Serious Opposition
Denmark
Musical Nightmare
A Brush With Max Bygraves
Return To Canada

1978   **386**
The Soundman Is Deaf
Bruce Forsythe
Kismet
Not Much Fun Anymore

1979   **394**
Strange Bedfellows
The Threepenny Opera

1980   **401**
Worrying Times
Cameron Mackintosh
Son et Lumiére

1981   **404**
Where Has The Money Gone?
Final Meeting With A Great Talent

1982   **407**
Elizabeth Taylor
Another Royal Occasion

1983   **410**
Crisis Upon Crisis
Boardroom Drama

1984   **416**
Skullduggery In Holland
Leonard Bernstein Approves
Hazards of the Job

1985 _____ **418**
   Too Many Balls In The Air

1986 _____ **420**
   Collapse Of Stout Party
   Frankie Howerd Again
   A Fairy Tale

1987 _____ **426**
   Anthony Hopkins Is Not Pleased
   Horse Racing Across America

1988 _____ **432**
   Back To Reality

AUTHOR'S NOTE

I have included a few anecdotes that appear in some form or another in my book *The Sound of Theatre.* I have also drawn heavily upon Richard Pilbrow's book *A Theatre Project* to which I was a contributor.

PROLOGUE

"David dear," - Laurence Olivier tended to call everyone dear - "I have been thinking; in the scene where Hamlet talks to the ghost of his father, if we record the voice, could you somehow make it magically move around the stage? What do you think? We could combine it with a lighting effect," he added excitedly. "It would be really thrilling if the ghost addresses Hamlet from one side of the stage, then suddenly appears from the other side of the stage." His voice rose in pitch. "Hamlet is confused. The spectre is upstage and then down. It moves to and fro. Hamlet is spinning round. He does not know which way to turn. He is totally disorientated..." He paused for a dramatic moment before murmuring with a shy smile, "I would love that." Then, placing a hand on my arm and gazing into my eyes, he almost pleaded, "Do you think you could do that for me?"

For my benefit only, I had just been treated to a master class in acting.

In his wildest dreams, the painfully shy thirteen-year-old boy, putting on a puppet show with his school friends in Ipswich, could never have imagined that by the time he was twenty-six, he would be chatting to such a towering presence in the theatre, a legendary movie star and the man renowned as the greatest Shakespearean actor of the day.

Yet here I was, discussing the inaugural production of the National Theatre Company at the Old Vic, the theatre that was to be their home for the next twelve years until the opening of the new building on the South Bank. It was 1963 and Sir Laurence Olivier, the artistic director of the company, was rehearsing "Hamlet" with Peter O'Toole in the title role. I was engaged to design a completely new sound system for the theatre and record all the sound effects for the production.

None of this had been planned. There was no history of show business in my family, but for some reason the theatre had always held a fascination. Not acting - perish the thought - it was the magic created by the people backstage that was so intriguing.

It was only because of a series of complete flukes that I was here at all....

Stage Struck

Early Trauma

I was born in 1937, two years before the outbreak of World War Two. We lived in a pleasantly situated three-bedroom house on the outskirts of Ipswich. My father was a sales rep covering the whole of East Anglia for a clothes-manufacturing company. The last time I saw my mother was when I was four. She arrived home one day in tears, obviously in pain, and my brother ushered me upstairs while the doctor was called. Later I learned that she was in hospital, but nobody ever actually mentioned that she had died. When I asked if I could see her, my grandmother said, "Your mummy has been very ill and she won't be coming back." That was it. The family did not mention her in my presence until I was much older. Even as an adult, I never asked my father about her. The subject had always been taboo, so I thought this was the way he wanted it.

When the tragedy struck, my grandmother and my mother's younger sister arrived from London to look after us. My father was doing his bit for the war effort as a volunteer Special Constable in the police force. He was also trying to keep his business ticking over, and there was now the worrying responsibility for two young boys. When grandma returned to London, it was decided that my mother's sister should stay on to help out. She and my father were both attractive people and they seemed to get on well. Time passed and one day they announced that they were getting married. Apart from anything else, it was a practical arrangement, but was probably not the best idea in the long run for either of them.

My brother and I saw little of my father during the war years. Even when it ended, he was absent a great deal of the time. Normally working six days a week, his job as a sales rep often entailed staying away for a few days. The transition of aunt to mother was handled seamlessly and, as children do, we accepted the inevitable; although being four years older, I believe that it was more difficult for my brother. Under less than ideal circumstances, our step-mother looked after us well, but relationships in the household were often under strain.

The School Years

My first theatrical experiences were not until after the end of the War in 1945. I had never really experienced peacetime and the war years had been pretty drab, so there was great excitement when the Ipswich Hippodrome opened its doors once again and began to stage variety shows. What a revelation to be confronted with so much sparkle and glitter! I had only just got over the surprise of seeing streetlights lit up for the first time.

As the name 'variety' suggests, the shows presented a mixed bag of performers including comedians, dancers, acrobats, jugglers, magicians, and other speciality acts. These were listed by number in the programme and to keep one abreast during the performance, the relevant numbers would light up on gold framed panels positioned either side of the proscenium.

Topping the bill at the end of the evening would be one of the famous orchestras or musicians of the day. We saw the world renowned singer "Hutch" (Leslie Hutchinson), the dazzling duo Rawicz and Landauer playing back to back on two grand pianos, "Two-Ton Tessie" (Tessie O'Shea singing and plunking away at her banjolele) and Winfred Atwell playing melodies on a concert grand before moving to an old beat-up honky-tonk piano to set our toes tapping with her ragtime hits.

I was enthralled by the big dance bands of Lew Stone and Bert Ambrose. There was the Billy Reid orchestra with singer Dorothy Squires, Troise and his Banjoliers and the zany Professor Crock and his Crackpots. At home, I would fantasize about being a band leader, and spend ages conducting imaginary orchestras whenever anything suitable came on the radio. But by far my favourites were the bands that came with exotic costumes and stage sets. Felix Mendelssohn and his Hawaiian Serenaders with garlands of flowers around their necks played in a jungle, while dusky maidens in grass skirts sang and swayed to the music. Then there was Big Bill Campbell and His Rocky Mountaineers. Wow! Real cowboys playing their instruments in front of a genuine timber shack in the prairie with the Bunkhouse Boys chorus and Big Bill himself, looking and sounding a bit like John Wayne, occasionally asking the lovely Miss Peggy to "give us a song". What more could a nine year-old boy wish for? To me, it was complete magic.

That was until my illusions were shattered by an incident in one of the shows; a comedy dance duo attempting a difficult lift at the back of the set, toppled backwards into a curtain bringing it down on top of them. The falling curtain revealed a brick wall at the back of the stage and two startled stagehands hurriedly scuttling out of sight. I was horrified - until the audience laughter made me realise that this was not some terrible accident. More importantly, it dawned upon me for the first time that there were things going on behind the scenes. People back there were making all this happen - people were creating the magic.

I acquired glove puppets and staged Punch and Judy shows for my long-suffering family, moving on to collecting string-puppets to stage marionette shows. Always staying behind the scenes.

By the time I was twelve, with a few friends, we formed a puppet club at my school (the Ipswich School). One of the teachers foolishly suggested a one-act play that we should perform. As the whole thing took place in a drawing room and was totally lacking in action, it was entirely unsuitable for puppets. Nevertheless, our classmates sat through it and duly applauded at the end.

The school had little interest in any form of artistic endeavour. In fact, they actively discouraged a musical I later attempted to write with my friend David Blythe. This came about because David had a natural aptitude for playing the piano and an extraordinary gift for writing melodies, so I suggested that we should write a musical entertainment together. I came up with a rough script that was a kind of fairy tale with songs. Then, with the blind enthusiasm of 14-years olds, as soon as I had produced a couple of lyrics to which David wrote some music, we began to think about casting. If we could get one or two of the teaching staff involved, then surely we would be allowed to stage the show in the school hall. We knew from an end of term concert that one of the maths teachers had a rich bass voice, so we approached him with the suggestion that he might like to play the villain. Surprisingly, he showed interest indicating that, subject to seeing the finished piece, he could be persuaded.

Unfortunately, he must have related the incident in the masters' common room - no doubt to the amusement of other member of staff - because, a few days later, we were summoned to appear before the Head. This was serious. What had we done? It never crossed our minds that it could be anything to do with our musical.

The 'Bonce' (as he was un-fondly known) was seated behind an imposing desk, entirely clear except for a large leather-bound blotter before him and a couple of family photographs in silver frames to one side. I could not help noticing the swishy cane hanging on the oak-panelled wall behind. Following a lengthy pause during which he studied us with an expression of mild distaste, he spoke:

"It has been brought to my attention that you two boys are being diverted from your studies by spending time on some sort of theatrical enterprise when all your efforts should be directed towards the forthcoming 'O' Level examinations. Is that correct?" Receiving no response, he repeated more firmly: "Is that correct?"

"Yes, sir." we both mumbled.

"Whilst I am always happy to encourage interesting hobbies, from your record of achievement in most subjects, I hardly think you can afford *any* form of distraction. So I strongly advise that, out of school hours, your entire concentration should be directed towards your homework. That is, if you wish for good exam results. I presume that you do wish for good exam results?"

"Yes, sir."

"Yes, sir. That is correct. I think we understand each other."

"Yes, sir."

"Thank you. That is all." And we were dismissed.

As soon as we had recovered from this traumatic experience, we agreed to accept the Bonce's advice. We would abandon our little musical. Instead, we would write an 'operetta' and have it performed outside the school. Exactly how, and by whom, was a small detail to be resolved in the fullness of time. Thus, much of our spare time during the following eighteen months leading up to the dreaded 'O' Level (equivalent to today's GSCE) was spent with me writing lyrics and David producing some wonderful music.

The not very original story, set in a mythical European country called "Divadikov" (clever play on word!) was entitled *"The Physician's Folly"*.

That summer, my father rented a cottage in Aldeburgh on the Suffolk coast for a two-week family holiday. David and I were now well into the writing process and it was inconvenient being out of contact. So David bicycled the 25 miles from Ipswich and pitched a tent on the beach so that we could spend a weekend discussing the Great Work.

And this is when I had my first brush with celebrity.

Benjamin Britten

The most famous resident in Aldeburgh was Benjamin Britten, often seen in the town or walking on the beach. Everyone knew the house on the seafront that he shared with the tenor Peter Pears.

Being a fellow composer, David suggested that we should pay him a call and have a chat. It seemed a reasonable idea. So, that evening, we knocked on the door and were not at all surprised when it was answered by the great man himself. He had a glass of wine in his hand and there seemed to be a number of people in the house.

"Hello. Can I help you?"

David spoke up: "Yes, we are writing an opera and wondered if we could talk to you about it. Perhaps you might have some advice."

He did not turn a hair. "That sounds very interesting. But, as you can see, I am entertaining at the moment. Would it be convenient to come round tomorrow morning, say around eleven?"

"Yes, that would be fine. Thank you very much."

"Very good. I look forward to having a little chat then."

The following morning found us sitting at a table in the garden, each with a glass of cider, discussing the pros and cons of writing an opera. Considering that our only experience of any form of opera had been a school production of *HMS Pinafore* and seeing an amateur production of *The Pirates of Penzance* in Felixtowe, one hates to think what sort of impression we made. As the interview drew to a close, Britten invited us to attend a run-through of his latest opera in the Jubilee Hall that evening, soon to be premiered at the annual Aldeburgh Festival.

Thus, we became the first members of the public to witness a performance of *The Turn of the Screw* with Peter Pears singing the part of Quint and a young David Hemmings as the boy Miles. It was a rehearsal without scenery or costume and we found it very interesting, but I thought David wrote much better tunes.

Back home in Ipswich, David asked me one day if I was aware that my father had telephoned his father shortly after our encounter with Benjamin Britten.

"But they don't know each other, and hardly have anything in common," I said. "What on earth could they be talking about?"

"Apparently your father was concerned because Britten is a homosexual."

"Homosexual? What does that mean?"

"It's when a man likes men more than women".

Having been in an all-boys environment since leaving kindergarten, I had hardly spoken to a girl since. All my friends were boys. So, somewhat puzzled, I replied: "What's wrong with that? I think I prefer boys". A statement that probably set him wondering.

The Blythe-Collison Opera Company

We decided to form an amateur company to put on our operetta. An advertisement was placed in the local paper inviting anyone who could sing to join. There was little interest. However, an opportunity for publicity came up when we noticed that the Odeon cinema was holding a talent contest. It was bound to get press coverage, so David decided that he would enter, play the cinema organ and, of course, win!

The manager of the cinema was sceptical, pointing out that it took years of experience to handle a Mighty Wurlitzer organ. But if he would like to come along at eleven thirty the following morning before the films started, he could have a go. Although David had only played the small two-manual organ for a few services in the school chapel, he was quietly confident.

Getting to the Odeon at that hour of the morning meant bunking off school. We arranged that he would sneak out during the mid-morning break and I would do my best to cover if necessary. Unfortunately, during the next lesson his absence was noticed. The master addressed the class, "Blythe is missing. Has anyone seen him?" To forestall further investigation, I volunteered that he was feeling poorly during the break and perhaps he gone home. This was strictly against the rules and did not go down at all well, but we got away with it.

At the competition the following Sunday morning, the standard of talent was not very high, except for a young girl dancer who received an enthusiastic ovation from the audience. When David's turn came, he pressed a button and the Mighty Wurlitzer rose majestically from the depths as he played a current hit tune called "Little Red Monkey". During the rendition, his hands darted over all four of the manuals and everyone could see his feet pumping away at the bass keyboard. He had discovered how to add drums and cymbals and vary the sound by pulling out different stops and, half way through the piece, he set all the coloured lights flashing in the organ's glass surround. Building to a crescendo, he ended with a flourish. The audience burst into wild applause.

Before the compère could stop him, David began playing a second piece. This was a song from our Great Work where the hero expresses his love to the heroine. It was a beautiful melody with a lyric that ran: *There are moonbeams in your eyes and stardust in your hair, I will love you all my life with a love most rare.* Fortunately, no one was subjected to the words on this occasion.

At the end of the competition, David was proclaimed the winner and the compère asked the name of the last piece he had played. In reply, David took the opportunity to plug the operetta and mention that we were looking for singers. The compère, impressed, asked the audience if they would like to hear the tune again and they signified their approval with another enthusiastic round of applause.

Because of the ensuing publicity in the local press, I received a letter from Cliff Michelmore at the BBC asking to see some samples of our work. A few months later, we found ourselves appearing on television in a programme called "The Under 21 Club".

On the appointed day, two nervous sixteen year olds travelled from Ipswich to London and presented themselves at the BBC building in Lime Grove. The studio was on an upper floor and the first of several surreal moments was to find ourselves sharing a lift with the show's Star Guest, Richard Burton.

Hosted by musician Steve Race, our item began with a painfully stilted interview. As was the custom in those days, a script had been sent to us, which we were supposed to have learned. Apparently we both looked like frightened rabbits. Following the interview, two of our songs were performed by professional singers. At least that bit went well.

The TV appearance occurred some months after our 'O' Levels had been completed — less than impressive results in my case — and our schooldays were thankfully behind us. Consequently, it was a great surprise to receive a letter from our erstwhile headmaster, the man who had been so dismissive of our musical ambitions, congratulating us on our "wonderful achievement". He went on to express great pride in the fact that we were the first 'Old Ipswichians' to appear on television. I do not have the letter. I tore it up in disgust.

David Blythe at 16

Out in the real world, I had no idea what I was going to do with my life. It was 1953, and in those days school leavers were expected to get a job. I approached the local repertory company and offered my services, but was told that, with no experience, I would just be a nuisance.

My father encouraged me to enter the rag trade. In addition to his job as a sales rep, he was now part-owner of a small ladies outfitters shop in Ipswich. My older brother had gone into farming, so my father was hoping that I might enter the family business. Since my aunt had become a stepmother, I now had a three-quarters sister and a three-quarters brother, aged seven and five respectively. But who knew what career paths they might choose?

I began my working life as a junior sales assistant in the linen department of Footman and Pretty, the largest store in Ipswich and one of my father's major clients. I hated it. The days dragged on interminably. I was far too shy to be a successful salesman and I loathed standing behind a counter trying to sell towels and sheets.

There was only one bright spot in the week: the Saturday evening rehearsals for our operetta. Although these had been going on for some months, David was still teaching our group of performers the songs from Act One. When one of them asked when they could start working on the next act, David replied sternly that he was not prepared to move on until he was entirely happy with the way they were performing the current songs. This from a boy of sixteen addressing nineteen people, all of whom were his elders, with some old enough to be his parents. Such was his confidence and sense of authority that they took it.

Of course he could not admit that the real reason the rehearsals were so protracted was because we had not yet got round to writing the second act. It took several more weeks before we were able to produce the full score.

By the time the piece was finally written and a director had come on board to pull it all together, I had already moved to London to take up my first job in the theatre; about which more later.

The Physician's Folly was launched on an unsuspecting public at the Art Gallery in Ipswich that happened to have a decent stage and a couple of dodgy spotlights. The production was a complete sell-out during its entire run (four nights!) and one member of the local press hailed us as the new Gilbert and Sullivan.

The programme even had a foreword written by Benjamin Britten that began by "welcoming most warmly into the exciting world of opera my young colleagues, Blythe and Collison."

David Blythe had an extraordinary talent but, sadly, did not pursue a musical career. I will never understand how one can be blessed with such a gift and not wish to use it. However, one good thing did come out of our musical enterprise. Four years later, he married our leading lady with me in attendance as Best Man. Sixty plus years later and they are still going strong.

Some months before the Grand Premiere of *The Physician's Folly* a possible escape route from life in the linen department had presented itself. The mother of a school friend overheard me complaining about my job and wishing I could find a way into the theatre. She suggested that her husband might be able to help. Formerly the Town Clerk of Ipswich, he had recently taken up a position with the London County Council, which was involved with the Royal Festival Hall. Perhaps he could ask the man who ran it for some advice to help me with my ambition.

A Job In The Theatre

When I told my father that I had been given the opportunity to travel up to London and talk to the manager of the Festival Hall about a career in the theatre, he expressed neither surprise nor disappointment. Probably suspecting that nothing would come it, he offered to accompany me, so long as I also agreed to be interviewed for an apprenticeship at the big John Lewis department store in Oxford Street while we were there. If accepted, I would live in-house where there were all kinds of exciting extra-curricula activities including a drama club. That was the carrot.

The John Lewis interview turned out to be unpleasantly stressful. We were ushered into a small office where a ruddy-faced retired naval officer with black bushy eyebrows, Captain Somebody-or-other, was seated behind a large desk. There being no chairs provided for visitors, we were forced to remain standing. Although the questions were mostly fired in my direction, it was my father who explained that he was in the clothing business and I was currently working in the linen department of the major store in Ipswich. I was asked if I had set my heart on a career in the retail trade, and I answered, "Yes, sir," probably without a great deal of conviction. The Captain then detailed the life of a John Lewis apprentice with long working hours leading eventually to fine career prospects. The accommodation in the hostel included full bed and board and there were various leisure activities available such as table tennis and snooker.

"I understand," interjected my father, "that you also have facilities for amateur dramatics."

At this, the Captain looked up and eyed me suspiciously. "We find that young people who are interested in *theatricals*," he announced darkly, "tend to be less interested in their work."

With this bombshell, it was agreed that we should go away and decide whether or not to make a formal application, which he would consider in due course.

The meeting at the Royal Festival Hall took place in one of the large public areas and was much jollier. We were greeted by the general manager, Mr Bean, a dapper little man with horn-rimmed glasses. He explained that with no background in the theatre, he had few contacts in this particular field that would be of any use. However, the Festival

Ballet Company was currently in residence and their artistic director had agreed to spare us a few moments. If we did not mind waiting, he would inform him of our arrival.

A short while later, a tall fulsome figure in a light grey suit, pink shirt and blue bow tie bore down upon us. Benn Toff, for such was his name, also sported a pair of rose-tinted spectacles and on one finger of the fleshy hand he proffered, was a gold ring set with one enormous ruby.

Like Mr Bean, Benn Toff admitted that he had little experience with the *straight* theatre but added "I do know a sweet little man called Pembroke Duttson who makes wonderful props for us. He could be a useful contact because he sometimes works for a theatre in the West End." So saying, he produced a piece of paper upon which he had written Mr Duttson's address. "I'm afraid I have to disappear now, as I am due on stage for a lighting rehearsal for tonight's ballet. Do drop Pem a line and mention my name." I thanked him profusely. With a limp wave of his bejeweled hand, he declared, "So lovely to meet you," and bustled off.

I imagined that all my father prejudices and fears about allowing his son to work in the theatre had just been confirmed, but his only comment, typically understated, was "I suppose that's what you call 'a character'."

My letter to Pembroke Duttson received a speedy response. He had spoken to Robert Baty (pronounced 'Bayty'), the Technical Director at the Arts Theatre Club in London's Great Newport Street, who was willing to see me and would be writing or phoning in the near future. The letter contained the following warning:

"If you do manage to get into the Arts, you will be in for a rough time. You will get the push if you do not work hard, but little thanks if you do. The hours will often be long and irregular and your salary will be at subsistence level. The Arts will hold no future for you. You must use the Arts for your own ends, for the Arts will have no compunction in using

you."

I waited impatiently for a letter or phone call but nothing was forthcoming. After only ten days, I wrote again to Mr Duttson asking whether or not I should contact Mr Baty. He replied with two closely typed pages of incredibly good advice, basically warning me that the theatre is not all "glamour" as he suspected I might be thinking. It is a tough business. His letter ended:

"The profession is notoriously insincere, accentuated by there being far too many people wanting employment, and far too few jobs. You are therefore of no importance to Robert Baty. If he forgets you there are twenty others to choose from. It is therefore up to you to chase him relentlessly to show him you are dead keen and he will hopefully grant you an interview for sheer peace and quiet. So get cracking! Ring him at TEMple Bar 7541 and pin him down for an interview."

I have no idea why this incredibly kind man took so much time and effort writing to a green seventeen year old he had never met. From remarks in his letters, he might have seen me as a younger version of himself. All I can say is that he was instrumental in setting me on my career and I sincerely regret never having made the effort to express my gratitude to him in person. Such is the shallowness of youth.

Having first asked permission to use the telephone, as was the rule in our house, I summoned up all my courage and made the phone call. Robert Baty did not seem surprised. He just said, "Drop in for a chat any time you are in London. I am always here."

The following weekend, I took the steam train from Ipswich to London - ten shillings (50p) return fare - and presented myself at the Arts Theatre Club in Great Newport Street, just off Charing Cross Road. I was informed at reception that Mr Baty could be found working in the auditorium and was directed towards some double doors leading into the circle. There, I saw a man standing on a short ladder busy attaching an orange-coloured shade to one of the wall lights. Dressed in sandals, grey trousers and a navy blue sweater, he was average height, quite muscular, with a mop of slightly greying light brown hair, a small but wild moustache sprouting from his upper lip, and a twinkle in the eye.

"Mr Baty?"

"That's me."

"My name is David Collison and I...."

"Ah, it's young Davey. Could you hand me up that screwdriver?"

"Oh..er..yes. Thank you for seeing me. I was hoping there might possibly be...."

"Look. See this lampshade. It is a plastic washing up bowl that I bought this morning and cut in half. The other half is on the light fitting over there. See? Money is tight around here, so one has to be creative. What do you think?"

He seemed wondrously pleased with his efforts and the half bowls were certainly very effective. I stammered my admiration.

"So you want to work in the theatre?"

"Yes, I was hoping that..."

"I'm afraid there's nothing at present, old chap. We have a full crew. But there might be something coming up in the near future. You never know. It is good to meet you though. Would you like to have a look backstage?"

I had never been backstage in a theatre and it was all tremendously exciting and I knew I had to be a part of it. Following a short tour, it was agreed that Mr Baty would telephone me should there be a vacancy.

All too aware of Pem Duttson's warning about the fickleness of theatre people, I did not hold my breath. So the phone call a few weeks later came as a surprise. The telephone did not often ring in our household but when it did, one of the parents would answer. This time it was my father who, having asked the caller to hold, announced that it was that man from the London theatre wanting to speak to me.

"Hello Davey. Good news. One of my ASMs is leaving in a couple of weeks. How would you like to take over?"

I could hardly believe it. "Oh. Yes. Very much. Yes. Thank you".

"We need you to start on Tuesday. Is that alright?"

"Yes. Thank you. Yes"

"Good lad. Make it early afternoon and we can show you the ropes".

"Yes. I will. Thank you."

"Cheerio then".

"Good bye. Thank you."

And he was gone. I did not know that an ASM was an assistant stage manager, or have any clue what this would entail, but so what? I was actually going to be working backstage in the theatre. My excitement at the prospect was speedily brought back down to earth when my father began asking a few practical questions: How much was the salary? Where was I going to live? Could I afford it? Did I realise that I had to give two weeks notice to my present employer? Did I realise that today was Wednesday and I had agreed to be in London the following Tuesday?

I had no answer to any of these questions.

Showing only the slightest glimmer of exasperation, my long-suffering father informed me that I was "a mutt". He then made a telephone call to Robert Baty to discover that my salary would be five pounds a week plus a daily voucher for one shilling and sixpence (7½p) to spend in the theatre snack bar. This turned out to be enough to purchase egg or cheese on toast and a cup of tea or coffee.

There followed a conversation between my father and Rose Fox, a lady who lived in London and worked in the big warehouse of the company he represented. She kindly agreed to provide me with bed and board. I knew Mrs Fox, known to me as Auntie Rose, as I often accompanied my father during the school holidays on his travels that would inevitably include a day at the warehouse.

Finally, he had what must have been a sticky interview with the managing director of Footman and Pretty, the man he had persuaded to give me the job in the first place. I was released from my obligations with nothing further being said.

Getting Started

The Arts Theatre Club

The Arts Theatre Club was known for high quality and often avant-garde productions. Being a 'club' theatre meant that members could see plays that were not subject to the censorship of the Lord Chamberlain to whom all scripts had to be submitted. In the commercial theatre certain topics, such as homosexuality, were completely taboo and any language considered too strong would receive the blue pencil treatment.

Club members, having paid their annual subscription, could purchase theatre tickets at very modest prices. The auditorium only had seating for 350 people, so production budgets were limited. However, such was the theatre's reputation that actors at the top of their profession would agree to appear for the three or four week run of a play for only eight pounds a week when playing, and no payment at all for the two or three weeks of rehearsals. Even the theatre's artistic director had to survive on seven pounds a week.

The author aged 17 arrives in London

I was blissfully ignorant of any of these facts when I presented myself at the theatre that Tuesday afternoon.

"Welcome aboard, Davey," said Bob, grasping me firmly by the hand. (Incidentally, he is the only person ever to have called me 'Davey' and got away with it.) "Have you sorted out somewhere to live?"

"Yes, thank you, Mr Baty".

"Bob. Call me Bob, for goodness sake. We only use Christian names round here. Now, I've an interesting job for you. You will be taking over the panatrope from Lynne. She has already started working for another company but has agreed to come in for our performances until you have learned the ropes. I think you'll find it fun. Meanwhile, why don't you go down on stage and introduce yourself to Mike, our electrician. He is working near the switchboard, cutting colour. See if you can give him a hand."

Already, I was lost. What on earth was a 'panatrope' and how did one take it over? How could you possibly cut 'colour'? And what was a telephone switchboard doing on the stage?

On a platform at the side of the stage above what I later discovered was the prompt corner, I spied a small dark-haired young man clad in white overalls, crouched beside a large contraption bristling with wheels and handles. This, I later discovered, was the "switchboard" that controlled the stage lighting.

I climbed the ladder fixed to the side wall and introduced myself, adding that I had come to help. He seemed less than pleased, but grudgingly showed me how to cut the coloured 'Cinemoid', or 'gels', for the frames that fitted into spotlights. I soon got the hang of it and we worked on in gloomy silence until he declared that we had completed the 'colour call' for the next show.

At the end of the day's rehearsal on stage, I was introduced to the stage management team who were preparing the stage for the evening performance. One of them said, "Could you strike that chair?" I looked blankly at him. Did he really want me to hit a chair? "Its <u>dead</u>", he explained patiently. Well, obviously. I was at a loss. Then, with a sigh, another member of the team grabbed the chair and stowed it off-stage. I was not doing well.

Just before show time, Lynne arrived. Slim, dark haired, in her early twenties, she asked if I was happy to be taking over the panatrope. I assured her that I was looking forward to it very much. Invited to follow her up a ladder on to a small platform on the opposite side to the prompt corner, or O.P. as I would soon be saying, I was confronted with the contraption that was going to change my life. It was a large metal coffin-shaped box with two 78 r.p.m. disc turntables and pick-up arms equipped with groove-locating devices. On a table to one side was a rack with some twenty gramophone records. These were lacquer discs especially cut for the show with two or three different tracks of music and effects on one side of each disc.

Panatropes

The current production was *Saint Joan*, which was halfway through a four week run. I watched in awe as Lynne selected discs, cued them up and, reacting to a cuelight from the stage manager, deftly dropped the pick-up and turned up the volume. Sometimes she had to change a record whilst another was playing and then add a new sound on top of the one that was running. I wondered if I could be capable of such dexterity.

The plan was for me to tackle some of the easier cues at the next performance. So, the following day, I managed to practice for a while when the rehearsal on stage broke for lunch.

That night, for the first time in my life, I operated sound equipment with a live audience. It was under close supervision, of course, and there were no disasters. During the next few performances, I was to take over more and more cues until, on the fifth night, I would be handling the entire show.

The third show came and went with me nervously tackling some slightly trickier sequences. But the next night, Lynne was not in the theatre half an hour before the show as usual and - horror - had still not arrived when it was nearly time for curtain up. Bob Baty said that I had better go up on to the 'pan platform' and get ready to start the show.

Moments before curtain up, when all the actors were assembled on stage, Lynne came clambering breathlessly up the ladder just as the warning cuelight came on for the curtain up music. My relief was short lived. She stood, swaying slightly, peering at the cuelight. Then, waving vaguely at the panatrope, slumped down on to a chair, announcing thickly: "You do it. I'm drunk."

This truly was my baptism of fire. Suddenly, I experienced that sick feeling in the pit of the stomach that was to become so familiar over many years of first nights. I was petrified that I would select the wrong disc and ruin some dramatic moment on stage. Instead of a gentle wind, the sound of cathedral bells would come crashing out, or I would have the front-of-house loudspeakers switched on instead of one of the backstage speakers, or the volume would be up when I dropped the pick-up and the audience would hear a loud 'crack' as the stylus skidded into the groove.

The 'stand-by' cuelight had been on for some seconds. No more time to think. The 'go' light lit up and we were off. I filled the auditorium with sound. Somehow, I got through the show with no major disasters and was congratulated by Lynne, now seriously hung-over, and by the stage manager.

Bob Baty, who knew exactly what had been going on, approached with a broad grin on his face and placed an avuncular arm around my shoulder. I was one of the team.

From that moment on, I was totally involved in and enthralled by life backstage. There is nothing like the feeling of anticipation before a show, being one of the backstage crew standing by at their stations, hearing the buzz of an expectant audience as the cast take up their positions on stage. Then the adrenalin starts to kick in as the stage manager turns on the "stand by" cuelights. A few moments later comes the "go" signal, the curtain rises and we are all off on another journey.

Every night, that journey to the final curtain was a team effort; actors, stage management and technicians all relying on each other to ensure a safe and successful voyage. I could hardly believe my luck being accepted as part of this team. This was where I belonged.

That sense of privilege in being allowed to work in the theatre remained with me throughout my career.

One of the most approachable members of the *Saint Joan* cast with a wicked sense of humour was Peter Wyngarde, later to become famous as Jason King in the television series of the same name. But it was the young man playing the Dauphin who was the big surprise. In the early part of the play, the Dauphin is a hopelessly weak and nervous character who wants nothing to do with war or fighting. In the epilogue, the ghost of Joan appears many years later to the Dauphin, who is now the king. The deep-throated wavering voice of the old man was such a contrast to the effete voice of the young Dauphin that I imagined these to be two different actors. Then, at the end of one performance, I happened to walk by a group of actors who were on stage chatting, and was astonished to hear the wizened old king talking animatedly in the youthful voice of the young Dauphin. It was the same man. His name was Kenneth Williams.

Following the final performance of *Saint Joan* on a Sunday evening (we had two shows every Saturday and Sunday, but no shows on a Monday), the four members of the stage management team, spurred on by Bob Baty, began clearing all the furniture and props and dismantling the scenery. By 2 a.m. we began loading everything into a large removal van. Then it was a five-minute walk to the scenery workshop, a disused Wesleyan chapel in West Street almost opposite the famous Ivy Restaurant. Here we unloaded the van and filled it with the scenery that Ted, the carpenter, had built for the next show.

By about four o'clock in the morning, when everything had been carried into the theatre, Bob announced a fifteen-minute break and we all retired to the snack bar where there was some very welcome tea from the urn and a sandwich.

Then, with his boundless energy and enthusiasm, Bob would rally everyone to begin hanging all the flying pieces of the set and assembling the rest of the scenery. Meanwhile, Mike the electrician had been scuttling up and down ladders removing unwanted lights and adding new ones according to the lighting plot for the next show. It took another five gruelling hours before everything was just about in place.

At 9.00 a.m. the director of the play arrived to start plotting the lighting cues with Mike for the next show. There was no such thing as a Lighting Designer in those days.

Peter Hall

The director for this production was Peter Hall. Still only twenty-three, he had been employed a couple of times previously by the theatre's artistic director, John Fernald. Five months later, he was destined to take up the reins when Fernald left to become Principal of RADA (the Royal Academy of Dramatic Art).

Tall, energetic, with a ready smile, Peter's enthusiasm transmitted itself to all who worked for him. I could not know it then, but he was to have a significant influence on my career.

It was Monday morning and everybody was beginning to move around like zombies, but we still had to be available during the lighting session to move the scenery and props for the different scenes. Meanwhile, the stage manager was noting the cues in the prompt script and Mike was up on the switchboard plotted all the lighting changes.

By mid afternoon the lights were set. The cast would be arriving for a technical rehearsal at 7.00 p.m. so we had a little less than four hours to reset the stage for the beginning of the show, grab something to eat and find somewhere for a short doze.

The technical rehearsal dragged on until there was only just time to catch the last buses or tubes home on the Monday night. We had been in the theatre for thirty-six hours since setting up for the matinee on Sunday. I was exhausted but also exhilarated by what we achieved.

From the theatre to where I was living with Auntie Rose in Turnpike Lane was a journey of some three quarters of an hour. There was only time for a bath and a brief kip before setting off again for the dress rehearsal scheduled for 11.00 a.m.

Following the lunch break, Peter Hall gave notes to the cast and stage management and a few scenes were adjusted and rehearsed. That left time for a quick tidy-up and a chance for something to eat before the opening night performance, which went off without a hitch. Later that night I arrived back at Turnpike Lane completely shattered... but gloriously happy.

The following day, Bob called me into his office to sign a mythical name on a petty cash slip for a mythical late-night taxi home. He explained that his boss, the owner of the Arts Theatre Club, had no idea that we did not all go home in the early hours and this was Bob's ruse to obtain a little extra cash for the stage management. I appended the signature *W.S.Gilbert* and received the princely sum of two shillings and sixpence (12½p) in recompense for working the thirty-four hour shift. However, for that money one could buy a two-course meal in a café, so this unexpected bounty was gratefully received.

The stage management was split into two teams, each comprising a stage manager and usually two assistant stage managers, with the stage director, Bob Baty, in overall charge. (Historical note: A few years later, titles changed and the stage director became the stage manager and the stage manager became the deputy stage manager.)

The senior stage manager, by age and experience, was Anne Jenkins. Not very tall, she had a trim but well-rounded figure with neat black hair cut short. Unusual for the times, she wore spectacles with red or green frames. She was known affectionately by the backstage crew as Mum Jenkins. From my first day at the Arts, she called me 'Junior' and continued using this epithet even years later when I was well established in the theatre.

The only other permanent staff members were Mike the electrician, Ted the carpenter and Lucille Lee the wardrobe mistress. Lucy, as round as she was tall, bustled about during the day, washing and ironing the costumes. She was also there during performances acting as a dresser. A sharp-tongued cockney, she took no nonsense from the stage management or the actors. But she always had a pot of tea on the go and seemed to have a soft spot for me, the baby of the family. In her younger days she had performed on the Halls and her coarse stentorian voice could often be heard echoing down the dressing room corridor as she let rip with he favourite Music Hall songs.

During the three weeks of preparation for a new production, the Team One stage manager would attend rehearsals every day, prompting the actors and marking the moves in the script. The ASMs' task, besides providing tea and coffee for the cast, was to source the furniture and props. With very little budget, this entailed begging local shops and companies to lend as many items as possible, sometimes in return for a programme credit. Only for a specific piece of furniture or an unusual prop was one allowed to go to a theatrical hire company.

Having finished the day's rehearsal and helped to set up for the evening performance, Team One would then become stage hands for that show; shifting scenery, hauling on ropes to fly parts of the set, acting as assistant electricians, and doing whatever else was necessary. If a particular production involved a great deal of scenery and movement of furniture, Bob would engage one or two extra hands just for that show. There were always out of work actors or stage managers only too eager to earn a bit of extra cash.

The stage manager of Team Two who was not rehearsing during the day would be running the current show from the prompt corner with the ASMs overseeing the props, assisting with scene changes and creating the sound effects.

Although the hours of work were incredibly long, being given the opportunity to experience every aspect of working backstage was invaluable. Drama schools did not offer worthwhile technical courses at that time, so where could one learn? In this respect, the Arts Theatre Club was unique. In the commercial theatre, to be an electrician, a stagehand or a flyman one had to belong to the trade union NATKE (National Association of Theatrical and Kine Employees).

Nobody seemed to know the derivation of the word 'panatrope', not even Bishop Sound who manufactured the machines. It was not until many years later when researching my book on the history of theatre sound that I discovered the answer. It goes back to 1927 when Brunswick, an American company, launched the first fully electric record player. They called it the Brunswick Panatrope, possibly because the words 'pan' and 'trope' come from the Greek and mean 'all turning'. Although launched in the USA, I have never found anyone in the American theatre who has ever heard of a panatrope. For some unknown reason the name was only used in the UK.

Not all the sounds were produced from recordings on the panatrope. Nearly every theatre in the country had thunder sheets, wind machines and door-slams in their prop rooms for live sound effects. Doorbells and telephone bells were the real thing, as were gunshots using revolvers with blanks.

Wind Machine

galvanized iron

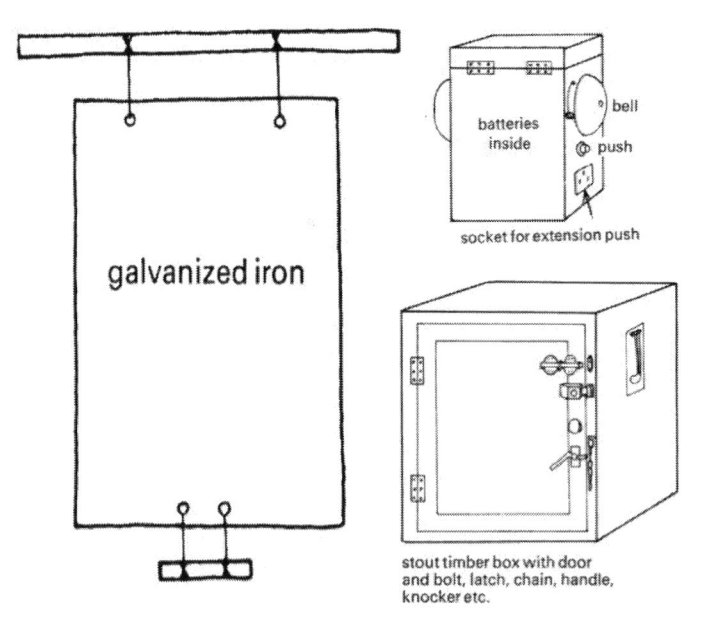

bell
batteries inside
push
socket for extension push

stout timber box with door and bolt, latch, chain, handle, knocker etc.

For one production, I remember standing in the wings hitting a small bell with a six-inch nail to produce a clock chime. These live sounds saved the time and expense of choosing effects from the local sound company's library and having them transferred to lacquer discs. Moreover, the loudspeakers we were using at the time were not exactly hi-fi, so manual effects were often much more realistic.

During the last two weeks of the run of *Saint Joan*, I wondered what backstage tasks I would be given for the new show. Bob had already taken me up to the fly gallery for a lesson in tying knots and to explain the mysteries of the counterweight system (all the pulleys and ropes and carriages filled with weights that allowed heavy pieces of scenery to be "flown" effortlessly from the stage up into the fly tower). He also took me to the top of the fly tower onto the timber grid way above the stage. Here, I was shown how to position a wooden block and pulley, and thread a rope from the fly floor through the pulley to accurately hit a spot on the stage. This looked like fun. So I was a little disappointed when informed that Peter Hall intended to use a lot of sound effects in the forthcoming production and, following my success on *Saint Joan*, I was to return to the panatrope. Bob knew that this director expected perfection and seemed to think I could deliver the goods.

The play was *The Immoralist*, based on a book by André Gide, starring Michael Gough and Yvonne Mitchell. It had homosexual undertones, but by now the penny had dropped and I understood what was going on. You cannot work in the theatre for five months and not learn a thing or two about life.

Rehearsals were fascinating. Peter Hall began by giving the cast a concise description of the piece with details of setting and background. Although he had a clear vision of the play, he encouraged input from the actors. Rehearsing the scenes was interspersed with a great deal of discussion about motivation and movement with new ideas tried out, incorporated or discarded.

Peter Hall
Reproduced with permission by the Royal Shakespeare Company

Peter Hall's obvious enjoyment of the process was infectious. I had never experienced a group of people so involved and excited by their work. This was a far cry from the linen department at Footmans and

Pretty.

During the final week of rehearsals, there was a complete run-through of the play each day, after which Peter gave notes. He would suggest a movement, a gesture, or a stress on a certain word and suddenly the meaning or intention became much clearer. One immediately thought: "Why did nobody else see that?" But, of course, that was his talent.

He also took care to shape the scenes with changes of pace to highlight important points or increase the dramatic effect. Like the chapter in a well-written book, a scene must end on some sort of upbeat or cliffhanger to carry the audience over into the next scene that, in turn, should maintain the energy.

All of this was a revelation and I imagined that this was how all directors worked. In the years to come, I was to discover how few were blessed with Peter Halls's insight and charisma. A remarkable number of renowned directors owed their success to being gifted self-publicists with the ability to talk convincingly about the arts in general and appear knowledgeable about their current projects. However, when faced with the real creative work in the rehearsal room, there was a great deal of indecision and waffle. They got away with it because they were able to engage the best actors whose experience and inventiveness would save the show despite the lack of direction.

The Immoralist was a great success with critics and audiences alike. References in the play to homosexuality were by today's standards incredibly subtle but, of course, it was not allowed to transfer to the West End.

In his autobiography, Peter Hall states that he was asked to direct the play by John Fernald but had considered it pretty banal. He agreed to take it on mainly because he was angered by the prejudice against homosexuals (they were still criminals in the eyes of the law) and indignant that the commercial theatre should be censored in a way that did not apply to publishing, broadcasting or the press. As he said, "I was able to make a statement in a club theatre where members were free to have their morals corrupted - and be burnt to death, for clubs were also outside the fire regulations."

During the following four productions, I was allowed to work as a sceneshifter, propman and, on one occasion as assistant flyman. The few recorded sound effects were handled by the other ASM. The most memorable of these plays, directed by John Fernald, was Pirandello's *The Rules Of The Game* starring Donald Pleasance who, following a very successful career, became internationally renowned as the villain Blofeld in the James Bond film *You Only Live Twice.*

In the play, Pleasance gave a brilliantly sinister performance as a cuckolded husband. The denouement at the end of Act One came when he sauntered casually on stage to confront the pair of lovers with the devastating plan he had cooked up to ruin their happiness. Gasps all round. Curtain.

However, on one memorable performance one of the pair of lovers forgot a large chunk of dialogue and cut to the point where Donald Pleasance was supposed to make his entrance. Unfortunately, he was still in his dressing room way up on the second floor.

In charge of props on this production, I was standing in the wings ready for the scene change and could see the look of panic in the two actors' eyes as neither could think of anything much to say. During the embarrassingly long silence that ensued, from the other side of the stage came the voice of the stage manager anxiously whispering into the microphone for the dressing room loudspeakers, "Mr Pleasance to the stage *immediately* please!" This was shortly followed by the sound of heavy footsteps stumbling down a very long flight of wooden stairs, then a brief pause before the red-faced and wild-eyed actor made his appearance. He managed to blurt out the lines of his final speech between pauses to catch his breath - not quite in the nonchalant manner rehearsed! The curtain came down and he collapsed onto a nearby sofa clutching at his chest.

Around this time, I received a letter from my father complaining that they had not heard from me for many weeks and asking if I was ever going to visit them in Ipswich. My reaction, apart from a feeling of guilt, was that we never had any free time. We were always too busy. In reality, I was so wound up in my new life that I never gave a thought to anything else.

This was not, however, the main reason for the letter. Apparently, he had been contacted by a distraught Auntie Rose. She was concerned about my erratic hours and the fact that I did not seem to eat or sleep enough and the constant worry was beginning to affect her health. Perhaps I should be looking for alternative accommodation.

I asked around and Mike the electrician said there was a room vacant in the house where he was lodging in Putney. So I said thank you and farewell to Auntie Rose and moved in.

The next Peter Hall production, *South*, set at the beginning of the American Civil War was another play with a homosexual theme. The play was full of atmospheric sound to create a feeling of the Deep South. Peter, having discovered that I could time the dropping of the pick-up with precision, began to ask for birdcalls and other effects to appear at exact moments in the text. The actors became used to hearing these natural sounds and often reacted to them as one might in real life. What I was doing was no longer a technical exercise; I began to feel an integral part of the performance. In rehearsals, some performers struggling with their lines would ask if it was necessary to have "all this noise" going on. But more often, it was the opposite reaction. On several occasions when Peter cut a background effect that had been there during rehearsals, an actor paused during the next run-through, feeling that something was not quite right and complained: "Aren't we supposed to have a sound here?"

I treasure the memory of a production meeting between Peter Hall and the set designer Paul Mayo. Paul always produced wonderful designs, ingeniously making the most of the small stage with almost no wing space. Unfortunately, whereas Peter liked to discuss his ideas and involve everyone in the creative process, Paul just liked to be given a brief and then left alone to work his magic. Modest and quietly spoken, he had a wickedly camp sense of humour, not understood or appreciated by everyone, especially our director. On this occasion, Peter was trying, and failing, to get Paul to engage in a proper discussion about the look of the set.

"It is the Deep South, Paul. It has to have a feeling of heat, of oppression."

"Well, it would, wouldn't it?" replied Paul, knowing that this would be an annoying response.

"Yes, but how do we increase the sense of foreboding in this house? The colour is important. There is so much tension between the main character and his wife and the boy. Can we at least talk about the colour?"

"Certainly. I am going to paint it…" he pretended to ponder for a moment, "…Homo Pink. You'll love it."

Peter looked exasperated, but Paul smiled sweetly and took himself off to the workshop. Of course, when the set arrived on stage, painted a warm red with white cornices and ceiling rose for a large glass chandelier and a white balustrade to the veranda seen through enormous French windows, it was a triumph.

Denholm Elliott played the main character in *South* and the cast also included Bessie Love, an aging American actress who had been a star in the silent movies and, during the thirties, she played leads in Hollywood musicals. The play was another great success, with the critics bemoaning the fact that it could not be seen by a wider public.

This was the first production seen by my parents. They said they would like to see a play, and made a special trip to London. I suspect they also wanted to find out what I was up to and why I never seemed to have time to visit them in Ipswich. They were impressed by the performance, declaring it "surprisingly professional". My father asked if the actors were actually paid for turning up every evening, and wondered what they did in the daytime. I had to explain that performing a play eight times a week could be pretty exhausting. They were all professional actors and Denholm Elliott, for instance, had appeared in major films such as *The Sound Barrier* and *The Cruel Sea.* When I mentioned that the play had been banned by the Lord Chamberlain and could not transfer to the West End, they were completely baffled. Any references to homosexuality had gone straight over their heads and had not affected their enjoyment of the play whatsoever.

In May 1955, *The Midnight Family* was the last play John Fernald directed at the Arts Theatre before leaving for RADA. Peter Hall, at the age of twenty-four, was appointed the theatre's artistic director.

The Midnight Family was only a mild success, but it did transfer to a theatre in Cambridge for two weeks after the London run. A panatrope, hired from Bishop Sound in London was transported there on a lorry with the set, costumes and props. This was my first taste of working in a commercial theatre where there was a stage crew to move the scenery and an electrician to plug in the panatrope and run out the cables for the loudspeakers. Not being allowed to touch anything felt very strange. I was glad to return to the Arts Theatre where Peter Hall was rehearsing a mammoth production of Eugene O'Neill's *Mourning Becomes Electra.*

How To Ruin A Performance

Based on the *Oresteia*, a Greek tragedy written by Aeschylus, *Mourning Becomes Electra* is set in 1865 New England. It has three long acts split into fourteen scenes and took a staggering four and a half hours to perform, plus an hour's dinner break in the middle. The critic in the Observer newspaper, who praised the production, commented: "A sort of war-time camaraderie pervaded the audience, as if they were sharing a shelter during an air raid".

One of my main memories was when I fell foul of the leading actress, Mary Ellis. The name did not mean anything to me at the time, but I later discovered why everyone treated her with such awe and respect. She had begun her career singing in opera at the New York Met (once opposite the great Caruso), then went on to star in plays and musicals on Broadway including creating the title role in Rudolph Friml's *Rose Marie*. In 1930 she moved to England to continue a successful career in the West End, starring in the original production of Terrence Rattigan's *The Browning Version* and playing the lead in three of Ivor Novello's musicals at Drury Lane; *Arc de Triomphe, The Dancing Years and Glamorous Nights*. Mary Ellis was a force to be reckoned with.

At the end of the Act Two (before the dinner break) Mary Ellis had her big dramatic moment when her son and daughter confess that they were responsible for their father's murder. With tears and recriminations, the son is ordered to leave the house and she turns to admonish her daughter with savage hatred. Finally, overwrought and exhausted, she walks slowly out of the room. A moment later, there is a gunshot. The daughter, with her back to the audience, gasps and freezes as the curtain is slowly lowered.

Now, it was me, of course, firing the shot. On this particular night I was in position under the stage chatting quietly to the actor playing the brother who had just made his exit.

I had a starting pistol as a back-up in case of emergencies, but I always fired one of the nineteenth century prop pistols used in the show because it made a more convincing sound. It was one of those guns where you had to break the barrel in order to insert a single blank, and I been told by the person hiring it to us that so long as it was set on half-cock, it could not go off. I was later to learn that the expression "Going off half cock" originally referred to a faulty firing mechanism.

The pistol had worked perfectly up until now, but on this particular occasion I closed the barrel and ... '<u>BANG</u>!'. The two of us nearly jumped out of our skins, and then just stood there staring at each other, mouths open, not believing what had happened. The terrible report had rung out right in the middle of Mary Ellis's big final scene. Presumably, the audience was imagining that the son had just committed suicide. Well, they were in for a surprise when he appeared, unscathed, at the beginning of Act Three.

A moment later Bob Baty, who had heard the shot up in his office, came running down the stairs. I thought he would be furious, but he rushed to the first aid box on the wall, grabbed a roll of bandage, and proceeded to wrap it all around my head and neck until just one eye was visible. "There", he said, "She won't be angry when she sees you like that". Grinning like some naughty schoolboy, he beat a hurried retreat from the danger zone.

There was just enough time to remove the bandages before I heard Mary Ellis leave the stage. The cuelight came on for the gun shot and I fired the starting pistol. To get to her dressing room Miss Ellis had to come down some stairs to the under stage area and up the other side. Apprehensively, I waited for the Diva to appear. As soon as she had manoeuvered the skirts of her voluminous Victorian dress down the narrow staircase, she came right up to me and hissed: "You know what you have done, don't you? RUINED THE WHOLE PLAY!"

During the interval, Mary Morris, who played the daughter, sought me out. She was sharing a dressing room with the star and I braced myself for another earful. On the contrary, she took both my hands in hers and said: "Miss Ellis is sorry that she snapped at you but, of course, after playing that scene she was very emotional. I explained that it was an accident and that I had seen you afterwards, ashen faced, looking so worried - and she understood". This very kind woman made me feel a little bit less like an incompetent idiot.

Ronnie Barker And Maggie Smith

A more positive memory of that production was witnessing the first performance on a London stage of a young actor called Ronnie Barker. He had worked with Peter Hall at the Oxford Playhouse and he had now been cast in a very minor role as an inebriated Portuguese fishing captain. He only had a few lines to say but the way he said them, combined with his drunken antics, produced much-needed laughter to lighten a somber evening. Most nights, when he staggered off-stage he received a round of applause.

Five months later, we were to see him again in a Christmas show called *Listen To The Wind* with music by Vivian Ellis, composer of such musicals as *Mr Cinders* and *Bless The Bride*. Ronnie played a gypsy who kidnaps two of the three children in the story. In his one short scene, he sang a not very inspired song entitled "I Do Like Bread And Butter For My Tea", but somehow, once again, he managed to stop the show every night.

As Ronnie Barker only appeared in the first act of *Listen To The Wind*, Peter Hall had also cast him in *Summertime,* a play starring Dirk Bogarde that was running concurrently at the Apollo Theatre. Ronnie Barker just had time to change costumes and make-up and leg it down Shaftesbury Avenue for the third act of *Summertime*. He is probably the only actor to have appeared in two plays in the West End simultaneously.

Across the road from the Arts was a restaurant called The Bacon And Egg that remained open until eleven o'clock or so at night. Most cheap eating places were closed by the time we left the theatre, so occasionally some of the stage management would splash out and have a late supper. One evening, three of us were joined by Ronnie Barker and a very jolly young actress. They had previously worked together in

Oxford and she happened to be giving a cabaret performance in the Arts Theatre's posh members' restaurant. There was a great deal of banter and laughter during the meal, and by the time the manager, who had been joining in the repartee, brought the bill, we were the only people there. None of us had much money and he had to wait while we discussed who was going to pay for what. Then the actress said to the manager: "What happens if we don't have enough money?"

"Simple," he replied, "You do the washing up."

"Right," she said, jumping to her feet, "Come on, boys." And we all marched into the kitchen where she picked up some greasy plates piled beside the sink and started washing them. The manager was helpless with laughter and I seem to recall that he reduced our bill a little for the entertainment value. The young actress was Maggie Smith.

During the run of *Listen To The Wind*, we had Christmas day and Boxing Day off, but in the matinee performance the next day, one of the children, no doubt having overindulged during the festivities, suffered an embarrassing experience. This was during a front-cloth scene in which Miriam Karlin as Miranda the Mermaid was 'fished' out of the sea by the children (in reality, clambered out of the orchestra pit). During the song that ensued, the poor girl knew she was going to be sick and made to leave the stage. However, the front cloth was tight up against the proscenium arch and she could not escape. She was forced to throw up in front of the audience. Meanwhile, Miriam Karlin continued her jolly song, trying to ignore what was going on, as quantities of vomit splattered onto the stage.

In the wings, Bob Baty could be heard calling, "Buckets and mops," and at the end of the scene he ordered a blackout and, with just the lights from the orchestra pit, two of the stage management moved swiftly on to the stage and cleared up the mess. Thirty seconds later, lights up and on with the show.

A Hostile Audience

Before the Christmas musical, the production immediately following *Mourning Becomes Electra* turned out to be a milestone in theatrical history, although nobody was expecting this at the time. One day, during the run of *Electra*, Peter Hall and I happened to be in the loo at the same time. He apologised for the long hours we were all having to work, adding, "but the good news is that the next show is going to be a doddle. With the large cast on *Electra* and all that scenery, I pretty well spent this year's budget, so the next play will have one simple set and only four actors."

I asked what it was about. "That's a really good question," he chuckled, "I expect many people will be asking that before long. Basically, it is an extraordinary dialogue between two tramps. There is virtually no plot and hardly anything happens, but it is a wonderful piece of writing. Goodness knows what the public will think of it. But it will be cheap to put on. That's the main thing." The play was the world premiere in English of Samuel Beckett's *Waiting For Godot*.

Rehearsals were a mystery to us all. The stage manager who was on the book thought that Peter Hall had lost his mind. The cast were equally baffled, and worried that the long pauses in the dialogue would quickly lose the audience's attention. Unexpectedly, the author, Samuel Beckett, turned up one day to watch a rehearsal, at the end of which he told the cast: "Make the pauses longer. Don't be afraid. Boredom is an element of the drama." The cast were not impressed.

My contribution was to play in pieces of music during the action. This included two sequences, one in each act, where the character called Lucky with a rope around his neck was pulled on stage by his master, Pozzo. Every time Lucky moved, a particular piece of music started and then stopped as soon as he came to a halt. It was tricky because I could not see the action from my perch on the side of the stage. To solve this problem, I agreed with the stage manager that every time the cuelight came on, I would start the theme and then cut it when the light went out.

Locating the start of a piece of music quickly and accurately should have been relatively straightforward with a disc revolving at 78 revolutions per minute, but Peter Hall wanted to use a piece by Bella Bartok recorded on something I had not seen before called a Long Playing Record. This "LP" revolved at the incredibly slow speed of thirty three and a third revolutions per minute and, to make matters worse, the grooves were much closer together than on the old 78s. How could one cue anything accurately under these conditions? My solution was to place a white mark on the record label in line with the point in the groove where the music started. Then, when the cuelight came on, drop the pick-up as soon as the white mark was directly facing me. With this method, the music started at some point within half a second, unless the pick-up happened to drop into the previous groove when the music came in a few bars early. Fortunately, this seldom happened. Why on earth nobody thought of dubbing the pieces of music to the traditional 78s I cannot imagine. This must have been the first and last time anyone attempted to spot-cue LPs in a theatrical production.

After the final run-through on the afternoon of the first night, Peter Hall gave a little speech, warning the actors that this was a new experience for the audience and they might possibly make the odd comment, or even walk out. But if this happened, they must not be distracted. They must hold the pauses and play the piece as rehearsed. To say that nerves were on edge before the curtain went up that night would be an understatement.

The premiere of *Waiting For Godot* on the 3rd August 1955, proved more of a disaster than even we had feared. I felt so embarrassed for the actors when, half an hour into the play we began to hear loud yawns and snoring noises. Then came the barracking with people shouting things like "This is rubbish," and "I paid good money for this!" When one of the characters on stage says, "Nothing happens, nobody comes, nobody goes. Its awful," somebody shouted, "Hear hear!" There were a few people, however, who seemed to get it. There was even some laughter, particularly in the second act, and a smattering of applause when the curtain finally dropped.

Next morning, the reviews in the newspapers were universally damning and the audiences for the rest of the week were sparse.

L to R: Peter Bull (Pozzo), Timothy Bateson (Lucky),
Paul Daneman (Valdimir), Peter Woodthorpe (Estragon)
Photograph by Houston Rogers

The owner of the Arts Theatre decided to close the show after the Saturday performance, but Peter persuaded him to hang on for the reviews in the Sunday papers. Thank goodness he did, because Harold Hobson, the respected critic of the Sunday Times, filled an entire page with an explanation of what *Godot* was about, extolling its virtues as an exciting new form of theatre. The influential critic Kenneth Tynan also wrote a reasonably positive revue in the Sunday Observer, but it was because of Harold Hobson that the play was allowed to run into the second week.

The following Sunday, having given it more thought, Hobson produced another long piece about Beckett and the play. Suddenly, it became the talk of the town. Peter Hall was in the news, appearing in newspapers and magazines and was even interviewed on television by a baffled Malcolm Muggeridge. When *Godot* ended its short run at the Arts, it transferred to the Criterion Theatre where it had a long and successful run. This was one play that the Lord Chamberlain had no reason to ban, although he insisted the word "erection" should be removed.

Peter Hall was to direct two more productions of *Godot* over the years, one at the Old Vic in 1997 and, finally, at the Theatre Royal Bath in 2005 on the occasion of the fiftieth anniversary of the original production. I was in the audience on the first night and found it quite an emotional experience. In the interval, I spoke to Peter and he bemoaned the fact that none of the original cast, with the exception of Timothy Bateson who played Lucky, was still alive, and I pointed out that I was the only surviving member of the stage management team. We discussed how different this production was from the original and I asked which of his three productions he was most happy with. "Definitely this one," he replied. "Why is that?" I asked. He smiled, "Because I have *practiced*."

Although I did sometimes work with scenery, lighting and props on other Arts Theatre productions, which is what I really wanted to do, Peter kept asking for me to return to the 'pan platform'. He would say things like: "Sound is an integral part of my next production and I really need someone I can rely on". He was very persuasive and had the knack of making you feel vital to the production. I began to accompany him to Bishops, the sound company around the corner in Monmouth Street, to help select the effects. He would ask my opinion and even appeared to welcome suggestions, which of course, was very flattering for an eighteen year old.

In my book, *Stage Sound*, published in 1976, Peter very kindly wrote the foreword from which this is an extract:

"As a young director, I filled my plays with sound. They not only gave atmosphere at dramatic moments, their sudden absence made silence even more telling. I was fortunate in those early experiments in sound to encounter a technician of genius, David Collison. He could cue a sound to a tenth of a second - by hand on a pick-up. Surrounded by three or four turntables and a mass of records, he built up a soundtrack that was at one with the dialogue. He would have made one of the great Dubbing Mixers (the person who balances all the sound in the final stages of a film) of all time. Fortunately, he stayed in the theatre."

Your Country Needs You

I was enjoying life immensely at the Arts and everything seemed to be going swimmingly until the day I received a brown envelope from the Ministry of Labour and National Service with instructions to present myself at the Medical Board (Room 212), Government Buildings, Bromyard Avenue, Acton. This was a total disaster. With so much going on in my life, I had completely forgotten that every male aged eighteen was obliged to spend two years in the armed forces doing their National Service.

Arriving at the Medical Board, I joined a small crowd of youths lining up for the examination. First, we had to fill in a form with our medical history. I racked my brains to think of every possible ill, from having my tonsils out to mild asthma attacks when staying on a farm at harvest time, to ingrowing toenails. I was the last one to hand in my form before having to strip naked, except for my socks, and join the others who were having various parts of their bodies prodded, poked and tested by a series of doctors in separate cubicles.

When the indignities had been completed, I emerged from the last cubicle to find that all the other young men had disappeared. I was about to follow suit when the doctor who had listened to my chest called me over to join him and a group of his colleagues. "This young man thinks he might have asthma," he announced, "but I am not sure that I could hear anything." Turning to one of the other doctors, he suggested, "See if you can detect a wheeze" The stethoscope was put in place and I was asked to take deep breaths. "No, I can't hear anything," he said. Shaking his head, he addressed a third doctor, "Perhaps you might have better luck." Again I filled my lungs with air and heaved it out, desperately trying to summon up some sort of chesty rattle.

Of course, they were having fun at my expense, but I was too nervous to cotton on. "You don't want to go into the army, do you, old chap?" asked the first doctor. "No," I replied, "I have only just started a job in the theatre and I really don't want to lose it." He regarded me for a moment, then asked his colleagues, "What do you all think?" One of them replied, "Well, I'm not certain, but there might have been just a hint of wheeziness." The first doctor pondered for a while and then declared very seriously, "In that case, I think we have to mark him as Grade Three, don't we?" They all nodded gravely. I had no idea what this meant. "In which case I'm afraid, old chap, that Her Majesty's government will not be accepting you for National Service." It took a moment for this to sink in. With incredible relief, I thanked them *very much* and made my escape before they could change their minds.

Conscription into the armed forces came to an end five years later in 1960.

Leo McKern And Hugh Griffith

The first time I was asked to take charge of the prompt script occurred when my stage manager fell ill during rehearsals of *The Burnt Flowerbed* by Ugo Betti. It was a tense drama and the actors were at the stage of running scenes, but still struggling with their lines. Not being acquainted with the actors or having attended any rehearsals, I was apprehensive as I took my place in the prompt corner. My instructions were to follow the script closely, and to look up if an actor seemed to be struggling with a line. If a prompt was required, they would catch your eye and you must then declaim the next line in a loud clear voice.

This should have been straightforward, but I managed to annoy the cast with a few unwarranted interruptions before realising the problem. By some extraordinary coincidence, not one, but two of the actors had a glass eye. This meant that whenever you looked at either of them, one or other of their eyes was bound to be staring at you. The two gentlemen in question were an ageing actor called Esmé Percy, who had apparently appeared in forty films, and the rumbustious Leo McKern.

In the middle of one intense scene, the action seemed to stop. I looked up. One of Mr McKern's eyes was staring at me. Without hesitation, I sang out the next line. Exasperated, he turned to me and shouted, "That was a PAUSE, boy. It's called ACTING!"

Duly chastened, I did not dare to prompt again unless one of the cast looked my way and said "Yes?" or "Line?"

In the years to come I was to work with Leo McKern on five separate occasions, and even directed him in the recording of a *Son et Lumiere* I produced. He was actually very pleasant. Not frightening at all.

Leo McKern

There was another humiliating occurrence during one of the rehearsals when a message came through from front-of-house that the Broadway star Alfred Drake was in the foyer asking if it would be possible to watch a bit of our rehearsal.

Drake had played leads in the original New York productions of *Oklahoma* and *Kismet*, for which he won a Tony Award, and was very big news at the time in the UK. He was enjoying a major triumph reprising his role in *Kismet* at the Stoll Theatre in London's Kingsway (sadly closed a few years later and demolished in 1958). He had a particular interest in the author Ugo Betti, having adapted one of his plays and taken the lead in a Broadway production.

I passed the request on to Peter Hall who put it, without much enthusiasm, to the cast. They briefly discussed the proposition before deciding that, on the whole, they would rather not have some American actor watch them rehearse. I suspect that most of the cast knew little about this multi-talented actor, writer, singer and director. As for playing the lead in *Kismet*, 'Serious Actors' in this country tended to regard the musical theatre as a bit frivolous.

How do you tell a major celebrity that he is not welcome in your little theatre? My heart was pounding as I approached him and said that the cast were sorry but they were in a critical stage of rehearsal. He looked disappointed and a little surprised, but took it well. He gave a slight shrug, thanked me, and walked out into the street.

The first English translation of Jean Anouilh's *The Waltz of the Toreadors* opened at the Arts in February 1956 with the fiery Welshman Hugh Griffith playing the lead, with Beatrix Lehmann as his wife, and Brenda Bruce his lover; all extremely well-known for their stage and screen work. There were high hopes with this stellar cast that the production would have a further life in the commercial theatre. To this end, the script was sent to the Lord Chamberlain for approval. Several lines or words had to be cut or altered including one anecdote in the play that referred to a soldier in Africa who, having raped a young native girl, had been captured by the tribe. The script went on, "they sent him back to camp, trussed up like a chicken with his bits and pieces between his teeth". There was an objection to the phrase "bits and pieces". This was not to be allowed. The Lord Chamberlain's suggested alternative was "spare parts". This caused the cast much amusement and Hugh Griffith with his rich Welsh voice relished emphasizing the words "SPARE PARTS', making them sound incredibly obscene.

All did not go smoothly in rehearsals. For some reason, Hugh Griffith often seemed irritable with Peter Hall. Perhaps he was nervous about playing such a taxing role where the success or failure of the entire piece lay squarely on his shoulders. He must have also been aware that the recent premiere of the play in Paris had been a resounding flop.

During the public preview, prior to the press night, Hugh Griffith was slurring his words and it was obvious that he had indulged in a bracer or two. Things became worse in the second act. He had to appear, walking up a staircase from below stage carrying his sick wife. We all held our breath, listening to bumping and grunting noises issuing from the depths. The pair eventually appeared, swaying alarmingly, as Hugh

Griffith laboriously negotiated the steep steps. In his arms, his wife, who was supposed to be in a dead faint, was forced to grab the bannisters in order to keep them both from toppling over. Somehow, he managed to get through the rest of the show, although for some reason he felt it necessary to shout most of his lines.

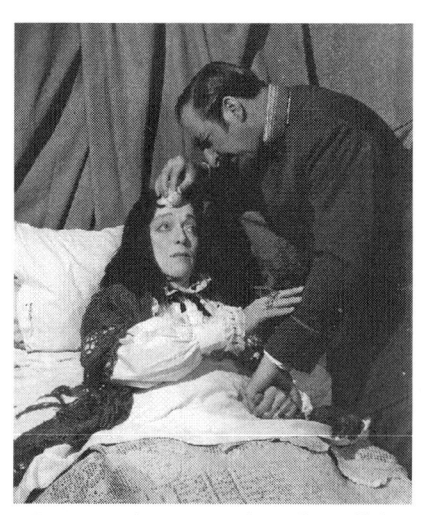

Beatrix Lehmann and Hugh Griffith

The atmosphere backstage was subdued before the opening night. Half an hour before curtain up, raised voices could be heard from Mr Griffith's dressing room. It transpired that Peter Hall was laying it on the line, telling Griffith that last night's performance had been a debacle that had let everyone down. He now needed to put that behind him, get on stage, and give the truly great performance that Peter knew he had in him. Confronting an actor like this, minutes before curtain up on the opening performance was an enormous risk. It could have gone either way. Fortunately, the gamble paid off. Griffith gave a spectacular performance with his pace and energy transmitting itself to the rest of the cast. As the curtain fell, the audience went wild and the critics rushed out of the theatre to telephone in their glowing reviews. The show transferred to the Criterion Theatre where it played for 700 performances.

With two commercial successes under his belt, Peter was receiving offers from West End producers. *Toreadors* became his swansong at the Arts when he accepted an invitation from Donald Albery to direct the play *Gigi* starring Leslie Caron. We bumped into each other in the foyer of the Arts soon after he had started rehearsals and I asked how it was going, adding that I would be coming to a performance, if only to see 'her'. His response was, "You must be like me. I *drool!*". Well, he must have drooled quite a lot, because they were married a few months later.

A Memorable Experience

I never did get to see *Gigi*, but around this time I did have one of my most memorable theatrical experiences. Orson Wells was directing and starring in a production of *Moby Dick Rehearsed* for a brief three-week run at the Duke of York's Theatre. At the start of the play the cast, including Christopher Lee, Patrick McGoohan, Gordon Jackson, Peter Sallis, Kenneth Williams and Joan Plowright, wandered on to the stage, which was completely bare except for a few chairs and a rostrum. Ropes from the grid supported two or three long wooden spars hanging across the stage at slightly crazy angles. There was a large working light suspended quite low in the centre. I also noticed an old wind machine and a metal thunder sheet lurking in the background.

The great man himself, smoking a large cigar, wearing a long overcoat with astrakhan collar and a wide-brimmed fedora hat, strode down the centre aisle of the auditorium. He greeted the cast as he climbed up some steps on to the stage, took off his hat and coat, and announced that he wished to attempt a run-through of the Moby Dick piece they had been rehearsing.

I cannot remember all the details, but the unforgettable climax was the creation of an incredible storm at sea. Orson Wells rehearsed two cast members in making wind and thunder sounds and organized others to set the hanging spars swaying from side to side in opposite directions, while another person had to haul on a rope to set the working light swinging from left to right creating weird shadows. Then, in almost darkness apart from the wild movements of spars and the light, Wells as Captain Ahab sighted the great whale, Moby Dick, and bawled at his crew above the noise of the gale, to launch the boat. This meant dragging the rostrum to the front of the stage and tipping it over into the orchestra pit. Wells then jumped down onto the 'boat' with some of his men and began ranting and screaming at the whale.

The ropes, spars and light swaying crazily in the background with the almost deafening sound created an incredible impression of a ship pitching and tossing in a storm. In the boat, Ahab, brandishing a harpoon, bellowed at the enormous white whale with the evil look in its eye. Then, when the monster that Wells had conjured in our minds was bearing down upon the frail vessel, Ahab, with a terrible cry that echoed through the theatre, lunged forward to hurl the harpoon... BLACKOUT.

The theatre was in total darkness. Silence. The audience was stunned. Seconds later, a door opened at the back of the stage and standing there silhouetted by a light in the corridor behind, was Orson Wells smoking a cigar and wearing the smart overcoat and fedora. He walked casually to the centre of the stage and called for the working lights to be switched on. He then thanked the cast for their efforts, reminding them that rehearsals would continue at ten o'clock the following morning. With that he walked off stage. It was an extraordinarily powerful performance and one I feel privileged to have witnessed.

Promotion

Major changes were now taking place at the Arts. Mike had left to become chief electrician with the Festival Ballet, touring the globe and working directly for the singular Benn Toff. Mum Jenkins was poached by Peter Hall to become his personal assistant. Then, horror of horrors, Bob Baty was enticed away by John Fernald to head up the technical department at RADA.

We were about to mount a musical version of Shakespeare's *The Comedy of Errors* when the remaining stage manager fell ill. Without warning, I was promoted and had the daunting task of stage managing a new musical production. The score was by Julian Slade, composer of *Salad Days*, the longest running musical in history until *My Fair Lady*. It was hoped that *The Comedy of Errors* would become a similar blockbuster.

As a temporary replacement for Bob Baty, the senior stage manager from the Glyndebourne Opera House, June Dandridge, was drafted in. She gave me some very useful tips on how to mark up the prompt script with lighting and sound cues, and pencil in the moves during rehearsals so that if an actor wanted to know, "Did I move upstage on that line?" you could either say "Yes," or explain exactly where the move should happen.

Some of the actors had already been contracted, one of whom was a classically trained mezzo soprano with an extremely powerful voice. This was Patricia Routledge in the very early stages of her career.

I remember being on stage during auditions for some of the other parts and announcing a particularly nervous actor who walked to the footlights, peered out into the darkness of the auditorium and said, "I'm sorry if I am wasting your time. I am not a singer, but I am willing to have a go."

"Yes, all right, carry on," came the bored voice of the director.

It was lucky that they did let him have a go because they were so impressed that he was given not one, but two leading roles, playing both of the twins called Dromio. In the show, when the twins had to appear on stage together, there was a double who always had his back to the audience. The actor playing the two Dromios was Bernard Cribbins.

Although Julian Slade had written some very catchy tunes, the musical was not picked up by a West End producer. However, when it ended its run at the Arts, we spent a week in the BBC Lime Grove studios, restaging it for television. It was to be broadcast live, which was a bit scary for everyone. I was given a box with a push button on the end of a long cable, called a 'cut key'. When pressed, this would cut the studio sound allowing me to prompt the actors without my voice being broadcast. Clutching the script, I stumbled from set to set, dragging the cable with me, endeavouring to follow the TV producer's strict instruction to "Keep behind the bloody cameras". Disappointingly, the actors all remembered their lines.

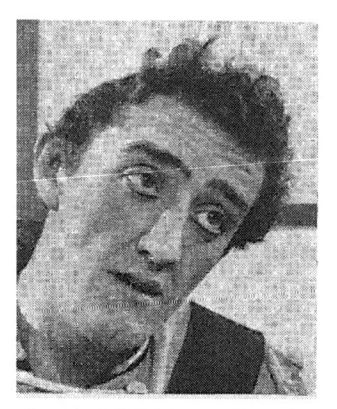

Bernard Cribbins as Dromio
Photograph by Angus McBean

June Dandridge had to return to Glyndebourne for the opera season and a new stage director was appointed. From the very beginning, we did not hit it off. In complete contrast to Bob Baty, he had no backstage technical skills whatsoever and spent most of his time in his office doing 'administration'. During the long change-over of shows, he would only appear on stage from time to time to view the proceedings and complain that it was all taking too long. Great for morale!

Following the Julian Slade musical, there was a play written by and starring Robert Shaw. As I had been absent for a while playing with my cut-key, it was stage managed by another new member of the team.

Although I did not know it at the time, the next play, my eighteenth production in that theatre, was to be the last time I ran the prompt corner at the Arts.

Originally a television production in America starring Lillian Gish, *The Trip To Bountiful* also had a short run on Broadway. A film version was made a few years later for which Geraldine Page won an Oscar.

Our director was to be Alan Schneider, an American, not yet well known, but who went on to direct the Broadway premieres of *Entertaining Mr Sloae, Who's Afraid Of Virginia Woolf?* and several plays by Pinter. I remember him as a small energetic man with big round glasses on a boyishly smiling face.

On the first day of rehearsals, as was usual practice, I marked out the outline of the set on the stage floor with white tape and placed chairs and tables roughly where I thought the director might want them. I also laid out an assortment of cups and saucers and other props that I could see from the script would be required. When Alan arrived, he was amazed. He jumped up onto the stage and gazed around in wonder, like a child in the best toy shop ever. "This is wonderful," he said, "I have never been able to rehearse like this in New York". Seeing my surprise, he explained how furniture and props could only be handled by members of IATSE (International Alliance of Theatrical Stage Employees). "Producers won't pay to have expensive union stagehands hanging about during rehearsals. So we just have some old chairs and tables to play with and then mime everything else until the dress rehearsals. It makes life really frustrating for the actors."

It was fun working with Alan whose directing technique was a little more "method" that I had previously experienced. In one scene where two actresses were having a conversation on a bus, he wanted to generate a feeling of intimacy. I was asked to turn off all the lights on stage and in the auditorium, and we ran the scene several times in total darkness. I have to say that it seemed to work.

Alan took one of the lead actresses aside and asked her to refrain from using a particular mannerism. She replied that she had no idea what he meant. "OK", he said, "So that the rest of the cast don't know what's going on, I'll yell out 'Coca Cola' whenever you do it." Another ploy that had results.

There was a scene where Alan wanted this same actress to hum a tune she had heard on the radio and I was asked to find an up-to-date American recording of something suitable. The man in the specialist gramophone shop in New Row, off St Martin's Lane, produced a record, saying with a grin, "This has just come in. But I don't think it will be quite what you're looking for." He was right. The man singing on the 78 rpm disc was nothing like I had ever heard before. With popular singers of the day like Doris Day, Perry Como and Frank Sinatra, you could always hear the lyrics, but on this recording most of the words were completely unintelligible. My reaction, "I don't believe this. I can't understand what he is singing about." "Neither can I," the man agreed, "but apparently he is becoming quite popular in the States. He's called Elvis Presley."

"Elvis?" I hooted, "Nobody is called Elvis. He's obviously made that up."

Joke over, we got back to serious business. I chose a sensible recording with a decent tune, but asked if I could borrow the 'Elvis' as I thought it would be a laugh to pretend that this was my offering.

Back at the theatre, without comment I played the Presley record to the company causing a great deal of laughter but, to my surprise, Alan Schneider was delighted and wanted to use it in the show. The actress, who was meant to hear it on the radio, objected strongly, "There's no melody. I can't possibly hum to that!" But Alan insisted and Elvis Presley's "Heartbreak Hotel" was played every night in the theatre.

Consequently, I feel justified in claiming that I played a major role in introducing Mr Presley to the British public.

Although the show went well, the whole atmosphere at the Arts had changed. The team spirit had evaporated and the new stage director made his dislike of me obvious. The feeling was mutual.

About To Get The Sack

One morning I was informed that someone was asking to see me in the foyer. It was a great surprise to discover that it was Mum Jenkins. "Good morning, Junior," she said, "How are things backstage at the Arts these days?" "Not that wonderful," I replied gloomily. "So I have heard. And there is a rumour going around that you are not being very cooperative with your new stage director." That was true. I had almost certainly been a pain in the proverbial.

"Have you *met* him?" I asked.

She wrinkled her nose and sniffed. "No, and I have no wish to, thank you. The reason I am here this morning is to give you a warning. I happen to know that your friend is planning to give you the sack."

My heart missed a beat. I knew that the stage director and I had our differences, but it had never occurred to me that I was not indispensible!

Anne patted my hand. "For goodness sake, don't look so worried." She smiled, "I am also the bearer of good news. Peter Hall will soon be starting rehearsals for a new play and he wants you to do the sound. He is just waiting for the producer, Donald Albery, to return from holiday to sort out the details. Then you will get a letter of confirmation."

"That's wonderful," I stammered. "Thank you so much."

"Now, listen to your mother. Take my advice and give in your notice now. Get in first. Rehearsals start in four weeks." With a satisfied grin on her face, she turned to go, saying, "Be of good cheer, Junior, your days in the sinking ship are numbered."

It was with enormous satisfaction that I announced my resignation, casually mentioning that I had been offered an exciting job in the commercial theatre.

The news was received with a mixture of surprise and irritation. My departure meant that I would not be available to stage manage *A Trip to Bountiful* when it transferred to a theatre in Ireland for a two week run. A replacement would have to be found at very short notice. To add insult to injury, the stage director had forfeited the pleasure of being able to inform me at the end of the Irish run that my services were no longer required. Double whammy!

My assistant stage manager was deputed to take my place for the Irish run. As he needed to go over the prompt script to acquaint himself with the cues, he suggested that we should meet at his flat. We had worked together on several shows and become good friends. After rehearsing all day we would often go for a meal together before returning to the theatre for the evening show. He was efficient and had a great sense of humour. So I was expecting a relaxed evening discussing the script, possibly with a cheap bottle of wine, but what occurred was entirely unexpected.

Sitting at a table with the script, I was pointing out a series of difficult lighting and sound cues, when he leaned over to have a closer look. He then placed an arm around my shoulder and began to nuzzle my hair. Used to him larking about, I cried, "Get off, you fool. What if the landlady walks in?"

He then stood up, and looking down at me, declared in a slightly strangled voice, "I am homosexual. Are you?"

Completely taken off guard, all I could say rather stupidly was, "What do you mean?"

"I am very fond of you, David. I need to know. *Are* you?"

"No, I'm afraid not. Sorry," I said with a nervous laugh.

"This is not a laughing matter to me," he replied tersely.

"No. I'm sorry. I'm really sorry."

There was a very long and very awkward pause. Neither of us knew what to say. I was desperate to find an excuse to leave, but did not wish to offend someone I genuinely liked. Eventually, I suggested that we finished going through the script. The atmosphere in the room was, to put it mildly, tense and it seemed a lifetime before we reached the final cues. This seemed the appropriate moment to escape, so I closed the script, wished him well with the show and performed an uncomfortable exit.

Moments later, as I walked along the street, the shock from the events of the past half hour really hit me and I remember gasping out loud, "Oh my God! Oh my God! Oh, my God!"

Later, however, when able to more calmly mull over the recent incident, the thought occurred to me that when another human being takes the trouble to express their feelings for you, perhaps rather than being appalled, one should feel flattered. Moreover, under different circumstances, this could have been a significant moment in my life, possibly leading to my first real sexual experience! On the downside, of course, this is not quite the experience I had in mind.

The Big Time

Into the Commercial Theatre

A contract from Donald Albery arrived ten days later. We were to embark on a four-week tour of the provinces before coming in to the West End, hopefully for a long run. The weekly salary for an assistant stage manager was four pounds fifteen shillings (£4.75) during preliminary rehearsals and nine pounds ten shillings (£9.50) for the last week of rehearsal and run of the play. Riches indeed.

The Gates of Summer by John Whiting was billed as a comedy, although I cannot recall many laughs. The cast included Dorothy Tutin, James Donald, David Kossoff, and Isabel Jeans, all well-known stage and screen actors. Also appearing was Lionel Jeffries, who would later feature in many films before directing such classic movies as *The Water Babies* and *The Railway Children*.

Rehearsals went well and it seemed that I was to be kept busy. Peter Hall went through the script and told me where he wanted sound effects. It was a long list and, for the first time, he trusted me to choose all the effects from the Bishop Sound library and have them transferred to lacquer discs. Some of the sequences were quite complicated and I worked out that we would need to hire four turntables. The cost of the equipment and all the records did not please the producer, Donald Albery. I heard him complain to Peter, "Is it really necessary to have all this racket going on during my play?"

Rehearsals were at the New Theatre (now the Noël Coward Theatre), one of four West End theatres owned by the Albery family. Donald, tall and slim, always moved and spoke rapidly with an air of impatience about him. My first brush with the impresario was somewhat alarming. I was standing beside the panatropes at the side of the stage, waiting for my next cue, when the pass door from the auditorium burst open and a man in a smart grey suit came striding through. Seeing me, he paused and demanded, "And what are you supposed to be doing?" "I'm doing the sound, sir," I replied. "Well, I don't pay you to stand around. Go and do something useful." I was about to explain, but was not given the chance. Waving both arms rapidly in a shooing motion, he said. "Go on. Go on. Off you go!" So I moved swiftly to the back of the stage and round behind the set, where I hid until he had gone. I then returned to my appointed task, praying that he did not return.

Donald Albery

The first date was at the Oxford Playhouse. When we arrived at the theatre Peter Wigzell, our stage manager, greeted the stage doorman by name and shook him warmly by the hand. I was impressed, but as he explained later, "You need to keep in with these chaps. You rely on them for taking messages and it helps if they let you use their telephone". Arriving on stage, amazingly he had the names of the chief electrician, the stage carpenter and several of the crew off pat.

Peter Wigzell was an experienced and personable stage manager with many West End productions under his belt. Not only was he in charge of the show but, as was standard practice in those days, he understudied two of the male leads. Even more surprising was the fact that Bill Parkinson, our company manager, also understudied one of the male characters. Presumably, if Peter had to go on in a performance, Bill would take over the prompt corner. There was only one other understudy, and that was an actress covering Dorothy Tutin and the much older Isabel Jeans for whom, should it come to it, much make-up would be required.

Peter Wigzell was staying with a theatrical landlady renowned as Number One in Oxford. Not only did she provide good breakfasts and evening meals, but when he was working late or through the night during the fit-up and strike of the show, she would actually bring his food into the theatre. The stage doorman had a list of theatrical digs and I chose a Mrs Fuller who charged one pound ten shillings (£1.50) per week. The breakfasts were the "Full English" and when I arrived back after the show, there would be a tasty meal in my room with a flask of tea.

The other member of the stage management team was Ian Albery, son of Donald, who was in the process of learning about theatre, backstage and front-of house, in preparation for the day when he would take over the family business. During the tour, one of my tasks was to introduce him to the mysteries of the panatrope.

The beautiful set designed by Leslie Hurry was lit using the theatre's lighting rig, but we toured some additional spotlights and a portable lighting board. This had twelve large slider dimmers with plugs sockets fixed to a heavy sheet of timber. The board was the responsibility of Ben, an affable enough chap, but perhaps not the brightest spark - as was demonstrated at our first lighting session.
When asked to bring up dimmer number seven, there was a pause, then Peter Hall shouted out from the stalls. "No, you seem to have taken a light out."

Ben yelled back, "That's definitely seven. I just brought that dimmer up.

It should have come on."

"Yes, but something went out. Try bringing up dimmer number five."

Another pause and then Peter's voice again, "Now another light has gone out!"

It had been a long day and our director was beginning to lose his cool. So Bill Parkinson, sitting alongside taking notes (he would be responsible for lighting the show on subsequent tour dates) hurried backstage to see what was going on. A muted discussion with Ben was followed by the sound of something heavy being moved. Then Bill jumped down from the stage into the auditorium, shouting cheerfully, "All sorted. Problem solved. The dimmer board was upside down."

Ian Albery

The reviews in the Oxford press were not enthusiastic but there was plenty of time to rehearse and make improvements. This is what pre-London tours were all about.

The next venue was the Manchester Opera House where, during a long scene without sound effects, I decided to climb to the upper circle to see what the stage looked like from there. The theatre had nearly two thousand seats, but only a quarter of them were occupied for that performance. From the rear of the empty upper circle it was a very steep view down to the stage and it was difficult to hear some of the actors, not helped by only seeing the tops of their heads. That is, with one exception. The actress Isabel Jeans was a performer from the old school of acting. She had first performed in the West End at the age of 15 when cast in a play by the great actor/manager Herbert Beerbohm Tree. Her technique for handling these enormous theatres was to look at the fellow actor she was about to address, then turn her face up and out at the auditorium to deliver her line, at the end of which she would refer back to the actor with a look, a movement or a gesture. It worked perfectly and did not seem at all contrived. You could see her face and hear every line. Isabel Jeans had a long career on stage and in films, including playing Leslie Caron's Aunt Alicia in *Gigi*.

Once again, revues were mixed and it became clear there was tension between Messrs. Albery and Hall. It all came to a head when we moved to the next theatre. Donald Albery had instructed his stage carpenter, who always turned up to organise the fit-ups, to move the whole set a few feet downstage. He had decided, without reference to the director, that the play would be improved if the actors were nearer the audience.

When Peter arrived, he was horrified. What the producer had not taken into account was that the scenery was now so near the vital row of spotlights hanging just behind the proscenium that they could not be adjusted properly to light the actors. It was a disaster.

Peter stormed out to find Albery and one assumes that harsh words were said. When the cast arrived on the Monday morning, they were summoned to the stage. As soon as everyone was assembled, Peter delivered a bombshell by announcing that he could not work with a producer who did not trust his artistic judgement and had therefore reluctantly offered his resignation, which had been accepted. He was apologetic about letting down the actors, but still had enormous faith in the play and was sure that another director, to be appointed shortly, would make it a great success. With that, he wished everyone good luck and departed.

The worried cast had a brief meeting where it was unanimously agreed that for the sake of the show they would all stick together and wait for the new director. A while later, I passed the stage door on my way out of the theatre and overheard one of the leading actors on the telephone saying, "You have to get me out of this mess." Presumably, a plea to his agent. I suspect that this was not the only such phone call.

The Gates of Summer tottered on for two more weeks to conclude the tour and there it ended. The long West End run in the commercial theatre did not materialise. I was out of work.

Resting

By now, I was living in a small attic room above a shop in Monmouth Street. It had a shilling meter to operate the small gas fire that had a ring attached to boil a kettle. The only running water was from a cold tap in a small sink that was hidden in a cupboard. With no bath available, once a week I took a bus trip to the public baths in Victoria.

One evening, there was a tap on my door and I opened it to find the girl who occupied the other attic room. "We haven't met," she began breathlessly, "My name is Frances. Sorry to bother you, but I thought I'd better explain that if you can hear my voice through the wall, I am not talking to myself, I am just trying to learn the lines of a play. I am an actress, you see."

"That's no problem," I replied airily, "I quite understand. I happen to work in the theatre myself."

"Oh, good. I didn't want you to think I was mad or something."

Not many weeks later, she moved out and I was amazed to see her photo in the newspapers and then on displays outside the Wyndhams Theatre. Frances Cuka was being lauded for creating the role of Jo in a new play called *A Taste of Honey*.

My sparse little room in Monmouth Street was cheap, but with no money coming in, I had to find employment. And fast.

Just across the road from my front door was the Bishop Sound recording studio. From my many visits to select sound effects, I knew the Bishop family quite well. There was the founder Jack Bishop, his wife who ran the office, their daughter Mamie in charge of the studio, and her husband Bill Spragg, an electronics engineer. I popped across to see them and they took pity on me, taking me on as a dog's body until such time as I could find another stage management job. None of us expected this temporary job to last for more than a year, but they kept me busy and the work was interesting.

Bishop Sound Limited was founded by Jack Bishop in 1939. It was the first ever company to provide specialist equipment and recordings to the theatre. It was preceded by only four years by Masque Sound Inc., the original company offering a similar service in New York.

Jack's involvement with sound went back to 1927 when he acquired a shop in East London that sold and repaired radios - or 'wirelesses' as they were then known. His real name was Joseph Lipowski, but there was a great deal of anti-Semitism around at the time, so as the shop happened to be called 'Bishops', he changed his own name and became Jack Bishop.

By the early 1950s there were Bishop Sound panatropes in theatres all over the country at a weekly hire price of £4.00 including two loudspeakers. He also had stage manager intercom and dressing room paging systems, known as 'Cuecall', permanently installed in dozens of London and provincial theatres. A great deal of his success was due to his policy of only renting equipment, never selling it. One of my jobs was to help open the envelopes containing the many rental cheques that poured in at the beginning of each month.

Cuecall was not popular with many of the older actors who detested having the show piped to them in their dressing rooms, and were positively affronted by being summoned to the stage by a disembodied voice from the stage manager. Some 'stars' insisted on having personal calls. As late as 1958, the Theatre Royal in Brighton still retained a call-boy. I use the term loosely as he was a diminutive but dapper, middle-aged gentleman who wore tight trousers and sported a very obvious black wig. He would stand near the prompt corner with his list waiting for the stage manager to signal the next call, then scurry off to the dressing rooms to make the announcement.

Although Jack Bishop normally had a gentle and friendly manner, his mercurial temper and dogmatic views often brought him into conflict with people who worked for him, and sometimes his customers.

Years later, Bill Spragg, Jack Bishop's son-in-law, told me of an incident in 1964 concerning a show at the Globe Theatre (renamed the Gielgud in 1994) that relied heavily on sound effects. One morning, the manager of the most important production company in the West End, H M Tennent, rang up to request a reduction in the hire bill on the grounds that the show had been running for some months. Jack was affronted. He considered his prices reasonable and could not see why he should take a cut when the show was making a lot of money. The manager continued to insist and Jack finally said: "All right, if you want a reduction, I will give you one". He slammed down the phone and told Bill Spragg to get out the van. They then proceeded to the theatre and removed all the equipment with total disregard for any consequences to the show that night. That action lost them a lot of business to a rival company, R G Jones, that was gaining a foothold in the West End. Bill eventually managed to broker a peace with Tennents, but Bishop Sound never worked for them exclusively as before.

R G Jones Limited, founded by Ronald Godfrey Jones, had been specialising in supplying PA equipment for dance bands and other events. He became involved in the theatre soon after the end of the Second World War when, in 1945, he attended a show at the King's Theatre in Hammersmith, London. Money being tight, RG had purchased a seat in 'the Gods' (Upper Gallery) from where he had great difficulty hearing the actors. He mulled this over for a few days and then returned to put a proposal to the theatre manager, convincing him that with a microphone and a few loudspeakers he could make the actors voices carry right to the back of the gallery. He installed one of the earliest speech reinforcement systems in this country. Recommendations followed, and soon R G Jones found himself in the theatre business. The company diaries show that equipment was supplied to seven West End theatres during the following year, 1946.

I was privileged to have known and worked with both Jack Bishop and R G Jones, pioneers of recorded sound in the British theatre.

1957

Zuleika

The days of helping to lug the amazingly heavy panatropes with their big valve amplifiers in and out of stage doors for Jack Bishop eventually ended in 1957. I had been "resting" for well over a year.

Once again, Mum Jenkins came to the rescue. She was now working as production assistant to Donald Albery with offices at the New Theatre (now the Noël Coward). She said that they were producing a new musical based on the novel Zuleika Dobson by Max Beerbohm. I was to be engaged as ASM in charge of a great number of props.

The title role in *Zuleika* was a young woman so devastatingly beautiful that everyone fell in love with her. Convincingly portraying this character was the Australian film actress Diane Cilento, who was later to marry Sean Connery. *Zuleika* opened in Manchester and then moved on to Oxford. The show had been running for only a few days in Oxford when we were given the extraordinary news that our star had attempted suicide by slashing her wrists, and was out of the show. The understudy would be taking over. Next bit of news: the director resigned and was replaced by the duo of Peter Powell and the show's choreographer Eleanor Fazan, known to all as Fiz.

Donald Albery held auditions for a replacement Zuleika and cast an unknown with little theatrical experience - best known for advertising 'Little X' corsets - to open the show at the Saville Theatre in London's Shaftesbury Avenue (now a cinema complex).

The musical director was Ron Grainer, later famous for composing the 'Dr Who' theme. His deputy was Charles Mackerras, who went on to become a world-renowned conductor of operas and symphonies. It was noticeable that whenever Mr Mackerras was wielding the baton, the cast perked up and the ensemble singing became much tighter.

Appearing in the chorus were two actresses who also went on to greater things. Patsy Rowlands had a successful career playing comedy parts on stage and in films and television, including nine "Carry On" movies. Patricia Routledge, a natural comedian with a wonderful singing voice, kept us all laughing, but she confessed one day that she was not that keen on comedy and musicals. "No, I'm more interested in playing the 'Heavy Drama'", she said in the Cheshire accent she had in those days, "That's what I intend to do." Ironically, eleven years later she won a Tony Award for playing the lead in the Broadway musical *Darling Buds Of May* and an Olivier Award in 1988 for Best Actress in the musical *Candide*. Subsequently, she became renowned for portraying sitcom characters on television.

Many of the critics liked *Zuleika*, but they were less than kind about Diane Cilento's replacement. The show only ran for four months, during which time I moved out of the rather seedy attic room in Monmouth Street and into a rented flat in York Street, off Baker Street. It was shared with Mike, the electrician from the Arts Theatre days, but I had it to myself for weeks on end when he was touring with the Festival Ballet. For the first time, I had a kitchen and a bathroom with running water. Luxury!

When the writing was on the wall for *Zuleika*, I wrote to Peter Hall. He was to direct Tennessee William's *Cat On A Hot Tin Roof*, a moody play set in the deep South that surely must have a lot of sound effects. His reply dated the 29th August 1957 read, "Nothing would give me greater pleasure than to have you on the panatrope for "CAT". I have told this to Bernard Gordon, Tennent's general manager, and suggest you follow up by writing him a note." Much encouraged, I took his advice, but it was several agonising weeks before I received a reply.

Meanwhile, some sort of income was necessary and I thought it might be possible to get some temporary work as a stagehand. To this end, I visited the offices of NATKE (National Association of Theatrical and Kine Employees) to see if I could join the union. I was told that I could not join unless I was currently employed in a backstage job. When I pointed out that I could not get a backstage job without being in the union, the man behind the desk just shrugged. Catch 22.

I mentioned this ridiculous situation to the stage carpenter at the Saville Theatre, the man in charge of all the backstage staff, who said, "That's no problem. If you want to join the union, I'll get you a ticket." Thus, I became a fully paid up member of NATKE.

Kenneth Williams

As luck would have it, I did not need to use my union card at this point, because a message arrived just days before *Zuleika* closed. Disley Jones, who had created the scenery for *Listen To The Wind* at the Arts, was working on a new project and urgently needed someone he could rely on to change various elements of his complicated set during the show. The two ASMs they already had were also understudies, trained in acting, not in stage management. This was often the case because in order to perform in the West End it was necessary to have an Equity card. One way of getting a card was to get a job in stage management where the Equity contract stated that you would also "perform as necessary". Consequently, most ASMs were budding actors with very little interest or knowledge of technical theatre.

Written by Bamber Gascoigne when still at Cambridge University, the show was a revue with the unusual title of *Share My Lettuce*. It also happened to be the first of many productions produced by Michael Codron.

I joined the company during the final rehearsals at the Lyric Hammersmith. The choreographer/director was Fiz (Eleanor Fazan), following on from *Zuleika*, and the musical director was Anthony Bowles with whom, fifteen years later, I was to work on a groundbreaking musical. Leading the cast, and about to make their names, were Kenneth Williams and Maggie Smith. This was the first time they had worked together and they had a natural empathy. Williams later remarked in an interview. "I love her urchin quality and the fact that she is so physically adroit. She can fold her arms in such a way that they disappear." It was interesting to see how she absorbed and mimicked many of his exaggerated vocal and physical mannerisms, like the way he would purse his lips and twist his head in haughty disapproval. Mannerisms she never seems to have shaken off.

Kenneth was a disarmingly mercurial character. He would come out with the most devastating remarks, appearing to enjoy humiliating the unfortunate recipient while, at the same time, finding some sort of masochistic pleasure in embarrassing himself. During the dress rehearsal of the revue, Kenneth and Maggie were waiting in the wings watching a young member of the cast singing a song while accompanying herself on a lute. This happened to be her first show and she was obviously nervous performing in front of the producer and production team for the first time. At the end of the number, she came offstage and Kenneth Williams casually remarked, "You are not actually going to do that in the show, are you?" Whereupon, the poor girl burst into tears and fled the building.

"Willy! That was a really dreadful thing to say." Maggie rebuked, failing to conceal a smile. Williams turned to her with an expression of complete innocence. "But I was only asking. I mean, it *was* a terrible song, wasn't it?"

Another example of Mr Williams's strange sense of humour occurred much later in the run. For some reason during that particular show I used to keep a packet of Polo mints sitting on the panatrope and the actors often came up and helped themselves. One evening a cast member placed around my neck a garland of Polo mints threaded on a ribbon. This was a jokey thank you for all the mints I had been supplying. During the performance, I continued to wear the garland, attracting various comments from the cast and crew. Kenneth's reaction was to pause and regard me with mock disapproval, announcing tartly, "You really are the original man with the hole, aren't you?" This caused me to smile, but it was not so amusing when he returned later to confide with apparent concern, "I realise why you have to keep sucking those mints. It's because of your bad breath, isn't it?" He wrinkled his nose and pulled back a bit, "You do know you have bad breath, don't you?" With that, he shook his head and left me to my thoughts. I am now perfectly aware that this was a deliberate charade to give him some sort of amusement or satisfaction, but for the star of the show to say something like that to an impressionable twenty year old was most unsettling. I worried about it for some time.

On another occasion, Kenneth took me aside to enquire if I realised that one of the male members of the cast had the hots for me. "I know because I heard him masturbating in the shower and saying your name! You really ought to go and be nice to him." But by this time, I had become immune to Mr Williams's twisted mind, so I showed the right amount of surprise and interest, and thanked him for passing on this interesting piece of information.

The revue opened at the Theatre Royal Brighton in August 1957. During the two-week run, the show was different every night as they tried out new pieces of material and changed the order of the sketches. On several occasions, this caused confusion with the men working on the fly gallery and they dropped in or took out the wrong piece of scenery. There was no intercom from the prompt corner, so each time this happened the stage manager would hiss instructions at me and I had to dash up a very long stone staircase to breathlessly request the head flyman to get his men to drop in or take out whatever was necessary.

There was another hiatus one night at the end of a performance when the stage manager pressed the cuelight button to lower the house curtain and nothing happened. He flashed and flashed the light signal to no avail. Fortunately, the theatre's stage carpenter happened to be standing near the prompt corner and to our surprise, he moved swiftly to a rusty old piece of conduit running up the wall and blew a loud raspberry into the open end where there once had been an electrical socket box. Almost immediately, as if by magic, the curtain came down. The carpenter explained that the flyman sometimes fell asleep while waiting for his cue but, fortunately, the other end of the conduit came out just beside his ear where he was sitting. Who needs modern technology?

Kenneth Williams and Maggie Smith
Theatre Royal Brighton - 1957

The London run at the Comedy Theatre (renamed the Harold Pinter in 2011) was mainly without incident except for one matinee. Following a short morning rehearsal to update one of the sketches, everyone broke for lunch around midday to be back for the 2.30 p.m. performance. One of my jobs was to check that the actors were all in their dressing rooms at 'the half' (35 minutes before curtain up). On this occasion Kenneth

Williams was missing, but I was not overly worried because the whole cast had only recently left the building. At 'the quarter', I knocked on his door again and there was still no answer. This was becoming serious. I hurried to tell the company manager, but he was not in his office. What to do? It was now only fifteen minutes to curtain up. Perhaps the company manager was front of house. He often checked the box office before a show to see how many tickets had been sold. Running round to the foyer, I met him strolling back. Hurrying to his office, he phoned Mr Williams's flat in case he had gone home and forgotten about the show. No reply. He also contacted the producer, Michael Codron, to apprise him of the situation. The clock was ticking and there was no way we could do the show without our star. There was no understudy. I was covered in guilt because I should have reported the situation at the half. Michael Codron arrived, looking worried, and made the decision to cancel the matinee. The company manager appeared in front of the house curtain to announce that Kenneth Williams was indisposed and, sadly, there would be no performance that afternoon. Tickets would be refunded or changed for another day.

Minutes later, Kenneth arrived in a taxi. But too late. It transpired that he had returned to his flat after the rehearsal and had fallen asleep. Woken by the telephone bell, he had rushed from the building, hailed a taxi, and arrived at the theatre in time to witness the audience streaming out into the street.

The poor man was in a terrible state, trying to apologise, but unable to form a coherent sentence. He was taken to his dressing room and persuaded to lie down. Michael Codron made light of the situation by pointing out that the house was less than half full and this was a great opportunity to generate some publicity. These comments failed to lessen the palpitations, and a doctor was sent for to administer a sedative. Fortunately, our star recovered sufficiently in time for the evening performance.

That evening, on the radio and television news there was mention of an actor missing a West End performance and, the following morning, several of the papers covered the story in more depth. During the curtain calls that evening, Maggie Smith stepped forward with a raised hand to stop the applause, and announced to the audience, "You probably have heard that one of our cast members failed to turn up for the matinee yesterday. Well, we have clubbed together to give him a little gift." So saying, she produced a large alarm clock, set the bell ringing, and presented it to Kenneth. The look of surprise on his face was wondrous to behold. More publicity ensued.

When the run at the Comedy Theatre ended, the show transferred to the Garrick for another few months.

Michael Codron the producer and Eleanor Fazan (Fiz)

Who Needs A Lighting Designer?

It was coming up to Christmas and I was soon to be out of work again. There was still no news from Bernard Gordon at H M Tennent about *Cat on a Hot Tin Roof*. There was nothing for it but to present myself at the

NATKE office and wave my union card.

Consulting his files, the man behind the desk said that the Lyric Theatre Hammersmith required an assistant electrician. I pointed out that I had no experience or qualification as an electrician, and asked if there was not something like scene shifting or handling props available. "That's all there is," he stated, closing the file, "If you want a job, get yourself down to Hammersmith at nine o'clock tomorrow morning. Take it, or leave it." I took it.

It turned out that they needed someone to assist the second electrician operate the lighting during the Christmas show, *Puss in Boots.* They had four dimmer boards mounted on a gantry above the prompt corner. Each had twelve wheels with dimmer handles, any one of which could be locked on to a central shaft by turning the handle. Rotating a larger wheel at the end of the shaft drove all the locked-on dimmers up or down depending on the direction of rotation. Between cues, one had to lock on selected handles according to a cue sheet. Specified handles would not be locked on because either those lights were to remain static, or the handles were individually moved to dim lights up or down. It was not too onerous a task.

A 12-way dimmer board - four of which were
linked together at the Lyric Hammersmith.

During the days, one was given menial tasks such as replacing bulbs in the foyer and auditorium, cleaning spotlights or cutting colour gels for the next production, a play called *Arlecchino*. Apparently, there were to be many more lights than usual in this production and the chief, Steve, seemed concerned. Normal practice was for the director to light a show using the standard rig of twelve lanterns hanging on a bar behind the proscenium, plus a few more on the front of the circle, some floodlights for the backcloth and three circuits of footlights. There were also lights on stands to be placed in the wings if necessary. However, this show was not going to be lit by the director. We were to expect a new phenomenon called a Lighting Designer!

This person turned out to be an enthusiastic young man, thin, dark hair and glasses, wearing a brand new camel hair coat, which at that time was a sure sign of affluence and artistic integrity. He bounded in one day to discuss his ideas with Steve. Strutting around the stage clutching a large plan, he indicated where he wanted spotlights to be rigged. The assistant electrician and I were watching from the switchboard platform on the side of the stage. "I've heard about these lighting designers," he confided morosely, "They take longer than necessary to light a show and use far too much equipment. Mark my word, we'll be rigging spotlights all over the place. That will mean using all of our forty-eight dimmer circuits and probably having to hire in another 12-way dimmer unit as well. And another thing I've heard about these lighting designers," he continued, warming to the subject, "is that they insist on asking for dimmers to be half a point up or half a point down, which makes working the switchboard impossible." He lowering his voice, "So what we'll do is move the fader half a point when asked and then creep it back to where it was later. He'll never notice." Much cheered by the thought of this cunning ruse, we retired for coffee.

We might have had a little more respect for this eager young man in the camel hair coat if we had known that within a very few years he would not only be renowned as a lighting designer on both sides of the Atlantic, but revered as an international theatre consultant influencing the design of theatres and concerts halls around the world. His name was Richard Pilbrow, and although we did not become acquainted on that occasion, we were destined to become firm friends and work together for many years.

During the run of *Puss in Boots*, I finally received a curt letter from Bernard Gordon, general manager for H M Tennent, instructing me to attend his office at a given time on a certain day.

The interview did not go well. Mr Gordon began by stating that Peter Hall had mentioned my name as a possible assistant stage manager on *Cat on a Hot Tin Roof*, indicating by his manner his disapproval of directors interfering in the appointment of junior staff. "Rehearsals begin in January. I take it you will be available?" I replied in the affirmative and he placed before me a standard Equity contract for stage management, all filled out with dates and my name, saying, "Just sign at the bottom."

It only needed a quick glance to verify what I feared; there was the dreaded clause with the requirement to understudy or play as directed. Although I desperately wanted the job, I had to explain that I was not an actor and could not possibly understudy. His reaction was almost outrage. His eyebrows shot up and he sat back in his chair regarding me with disbelief. Finally, he spoke, "We *never* employ stage management who do not understudy."

I waited for him to say something else, but he just sat staring at me. Apparently, it was my move but I had no intention of backing down. So following an uncomfortable silence, I mumbled my apologies and made to leave. He let me reach the door before calling me back and, with extremely bad grace, struck out the understudy clause and slapped the contract in front of me once more, indicating the pen on the desk. I appended my signature and was then dismissed with a wave of the hand. I did not make a friend that day, but isn't it great to have influential directors on your side?

Cat On A Hot Tin Roof

Peter Hall wanted an almost movie-like sound track to create the steamy atmosphere of the American south with chirruping crickets, croaking frogs, bird calls, workers singing in the fields, etc. It required four turntables (two panatropes) and a tape machine with a continuous loop of tape recorded with cicadas to be faded in and out as required. This was my very first use of a tape machine in the theatre.

With powerful performances from Leo McKern as Big Daddy and American actress Kim Stanley as Maggie "The Cat", the reviews were positive and we played to full houses. For some reason both Leo and Kim Stanley took against the actor playing Brick, Maggie's husband. Apparently, they were critical of his performance and the poor fellow was sometimes said to be physically sick before having to go on stage and face them. Both Kim and Leo were lovely people, so I never did understand what was going on.

During the limited season at the Comedy Theatre, we were graced one evening with the presence of the 24-year-old and strikingly beautiful Elizabeth Taylor escorted by her then husband, the film producer Mike Todd. She had just had a major success with the film *Giant* opposite Rock Hudson and James Dean and was about to play the lead role of Maggie The Cat with Paul Newman in the movie version of the play. At the end of the show the pair came backstage to meet the cast and Ian Albery had the task of escorting the duo to the dressing rooms. I remember him being scandalized by her low cut gown, saying, "I don't understand why she finds it necessary to reveal in public such an incredible amount of cleavage." For my part, I just stood and gawped.

At the end of the London run, the play was booked by the American actor/producer Sam Wannamaker, for a two-week season at the Shakespeare Theatre in Liverpool where he was currently artistic director. Unsurprisingly, the actor playing Brick did not join us. He was replaced by the understudy.

Now, I have never understood why anyone in their right mind should put themselves through the trauma of walking out in front of hundreds of people every night while trying to remember lines, at the same time as having to rely on fellow actors to know what they are supposed to be saying or doing. Many established actors admit to suffering from stage fright throughout their careers, so why do they do it? Lionel Jeffries once told me that he was physically sick before every first night. I asked him why on earth he became an actor in the first place and he replied, "Believe me, if I was competent to do any other job like, say, being a butcher, I would jump at it." Perhaps that is why, once he had broken into films, he never returned to the stage.

I used to have a recurring nightmare where the star of the show was missing, often this was Kenneth Williams for some reason, and I would be forced to go on in his place, only to discover that I did not know a single word of the script. Well, my worst nightmare nearly became reality one day in Liverpool.

The actress, Bee Duffell, who was playing the major role of Big Mama failed to turn up for the midweek matinee. No understudy, so what to do? It was not a very large audience so the company manager suggested that the performance should be cancelled, but Sam Wannamaker did not agree. He appeared in the prompt corner and stated that one of the stage management should go on with the script and read the part. Looking at me, he said, "You are not doing much. You do it." Mr Wannamaker was a larger than life character and not one to argue with, but I protested that there were a lot of important sound effects and I was kept very busy during the show. This he dismissed with, "Rubbish. Nobody's going to miss a few background noises."

I was beginning to panic. My heart was racing. "I have never been on stage in my life and I'd be totally hopeless at it," I stammered.

"Good God, you can read a script, can't you?"

"I'd really rather not."

Unused to having his decisions challenged, he looked about to explode and I was sure he was going to insist. Then, possibly noticing I was ashen white and almost certainly shaking, he turned to the stage manager in the prompt corner and said, "Alright, it'll have to be you. You have the script. You know the moves. Stand by, and I will make an announcement to the audience." So saying he left.

I nearly passed out with relief. It was now the stage manager's nightmare. Not mine. But the poor man had not been given a chance to explain that he did not know the show well at all. He had only been with us a few days. The original stage manager had other commitments at the end of the London run. This was going to be a fiasco.

There was applause as Sam Wannamaker appeared through the curtain - a bit of unexpected excitement for the audience. When they calmed down, he announced that the actress playing Big Mama was unfortunately unable to appear that afternoon, but – not to worry - the part was going to be read by the stage manager. He went on to sell the idea by explaining that it would be just like a 'real rehearsal' when the stage manager would fill in for a cast member who perhaps was having a costume fitting. "Of course, you are welcome to have your money back," he continued, "but if you stay, you are going to enjoy a unique experience." Such were his persuasive powers, that everybody remained seated.

The cast, waiting behind the curtain, were startled to hear this announcement and not at all happy, but Wannamaker returned to the stage and gave them a short "the show must go on" speech and we all stood by for action. While all this was going on, it had been arranged that the company manager, who was also new to the show, would take over the prompt corner and attempt to give the lighting cues.

Meanwhile, completely oblivious that the curtain had gone up on the matinee without her, Bee Duffel was enjoying a stroll with her dog in a nearby park. On the way back to where she was staying, she was accosted by a member of the stage crew who had been dispatched to see if she was still in her digs.

Horrified, she ran to the theatre, knowing that Big Mama did not make an appearance until a little way into the first act. She managed to get into her costume and down to the stage just in time for her cue to knock on the door and for Leo McKern to say, "That'll be Big Mama. Come in, woman." She made her entrance to the great surprise, and indeed relief, of the cast on stage who were expecting to see a nervous young man clutching a script. What the audience made of it, one can only imagine. Nothing was ever explained.

1958

Peter Sellers And Brouhaha

Following a few weeks filling in as a dayman (stage hand) at the Criterion Theatre, the next stage management job turned up. Peter Hall was about to direct Peter Sellers in what was to be his only appearance in a West End play.

Brouhaha, produced by Toby Rowland, took place in an impoverished Indian state where the Sultan (Sellers) was striving to obtain foreign aid for his starving people. His master plan was to generate a revolution, covertly persuading his people to rise up against him so that the English, French and Russians would take pity and send food and money. Unfortunately, his starving people did not understand and did not join in. It was left to the Sultan to fabricate an uprising and, with the help of the American ambassador they conducted acts of terrorism such as blowing up the British Embassy.

The American was played by Jules Munshin, famous as one of the trio of sailors with Frank Sinatra and Gene Kelly in the film *On The Town*. The English ambassador was Lionel Jeffries, the Russian ambassador Leo McKern and the 'Wali', adviser to the Sultan, was John Wood.

Sellers was an instinctive actor, not happy, or perhaps not capable of rehearsing a scene and then reproducing it many times in performance. His first reading of a piece of dialogue was often his best, which was probably why he was more at home on the film set. One day during rehearsals, the author brought in a new piece of script. It was a short monologue where the Sultan talked about his love for his people and, although he had tried his best, he had failed them and the future was bleak. Peter had a quick look at the words and then performed it with tears streaming down his face, at the end of which, totally distraught, he dropped the script and walked away to the other end of the rehearsal room. Nobody spoke. We were all stunned. One or two of the cast were actually crying. Peter Hall went up and put a consoling arm around his shoulder and there followed a muttered conversation. Eventually, they returned to the group and, despite several actors congratulating him and saying how moved they had been, Sellers was adamant that he would not perform that piece again. It was one of the most heart-rending examples of acting I have ever experienced and only a handful of people were there to witness it.

The play opened at the Theatre Royal, Brighton where, on most days, there were rehearsals to make changes and improvements. On one of these occasions, we nearly lost our director for good when a new prop arrived. This was a guillotine with an incredibly heavy metal blade that, when released, dropped to the base with a terrifying metallic clang. In the play, this was all part of the Sultan's plan to demonstrate to the world that revolutionaries were now having to be executed, and the Wali, played by John Wood, had to place his head on the block. The guillotine was provided with a metal peg to be placed in one of the wooden guides that held the blade so that, when the time came, it would look as though the blade had got stuck two thirds of the way down.

Even though the company manager demonstrated it crashing safely to a halt on the safety pin several times, not surprisingly, John Wood was most reluctant to place his head beneath this massive blade. Peter Hall, wishing to get on with the rehearsal, said, "It's perfectly safe. The blade cannot drop down when the pin is in place. Look, I will put my head on the block if you like." The company manager, who had some concerns about this fearsome device, suggested, "Let's just test it one more time." The heavy blade was lifted to the top, released, and came crashing down. It hit the metal pin, split the wood holding it, the blade came out of the guides and dropped exactly where Peter's head would have been, striking the stage floor with a sickening thud.

Nobody spoke for a while. Then John Wood whispered, "Oh, my God!" and Peter Hall added, "I suggest we all break for lunch."

The scenery company came up with a replacement guillotine that had a lighter blade. It did not drop with such a dramatic metal crash but, on the plus side, it was not lethal.

Following another morning rehearsal, the stage management team were having a drink in the pub when we saw Peter Sellers walking by in the street. One of us remarked, "He seems to be on his own. Do you think we should ask him to join us?" The company manager ran out after him and Sellers appeared genuinely pleased and almost grateful to be asked. There followed an entertaining half hour in the bar, before he insisted on buying us lunch in a local Indian restaurant.

Although Sellers was a leading movie actor (he was currently making his second feature film) and a star of the country's most popular radio programme, "The Goon Show", he treated everyone - cast and crew - as equals. This was not only remarkable but it was extremely good for company morale. Later, I worked on a couple of musicals with another member of the "The Goon Show" who had the same quality of being "one of the boys" - Harry Secombe.

Lionel Jeffries was another equally friendly member of the cast who surprised us one Sunday when he and his wife invited the five members of the stage management for an evening meal in the flat they were renting in Brighton. It is most unusual for leading actors to befriend the backstage team in this way; but there was no sense of "us and them" with Lionel. "We're all in this together," he said, "and I'd just a soon chat to you lot as a load of actors any day."

Later, during the run of *Brouhaha* in London, Lionel was filming *Bhowani Junction*. He played a British officer in India whose big scene was the attempted rape of the star of the movie. One evening he came up to me, looking extremely pleased with himself, "You won't believe what I have been doing today on the film set," he said with glee, "I've had to spend the whole day rolling around in the sand wrestling with Ava Gardner, that's what! The whole day! Gooah! Life doesn't get better than that!"

One morning, the stage doorman handed me a large envelope that had arrived in the post. Who on earth would be writing to me in Brighton? Very few people even knew I was there. The surprise was to discover a 21st birthday card in the shape of a key, sent from my parents. I had completely forgotten that I had just come of age. I managed to get the entire cast to sign that key and it is one my most treasured possessions.

Photograph by Allan Warren

On one side of the stage at the Theatre Royal, Brighton, was a bar called "The Single Gulp" in which many of the cast and friends congregated after a performance. On one such occasion, I was enjoying a glass with a group of actors including Peter Sellers and Leo McKern when a young member of the cast joined us and began pontificating about the play in a most pretentious way; he suggested scenes that could be improved, changes that could be made to the script, and described what he thought were the true intentions of the author. All the while, Leo McKern kept murmuring, "Yes," and "Possibly," and "You could be right", in a tone that everyone except for the speaker realised was completely insincere. Then, to my amazement, he casually removed his glass eye and gently placed it in the glass of whiskey the man was holding. At first, he did not notice. Then, because of the expressions on all of our faces, he glanced down and did the most wonderful double-take at seeing an eye bobbing about in his glass. This and the general laughter put an end to his flow. Leo bought him another whisky.

On another night, we were joined by the American actor, Charles Laughton, who had come to see the show. Apparently, he had originally been asked to play the Sultan, but had told the producer that the part was unplayable. He did not know how he could convincingly portray an Indian who had been educated at a posh English school. As second choice, Peter Hall had offered the part to Sellers after seeing him as the pompous and stammering Trade Union official in the film "I'm Alright, Jack". And, of course, juggling with accents was exactly what Sellers relished.

The play generated a lot of interest and one never knew who was going to turn up in that bar. For example, the American comedian George Burns with his wife Gracie Allen wandered in with Peter Sellers one evening. Well into his eighties, Burns was smoking a cigar as he always did on stage. I cannot remember what was said, but I know there was a good deal of laughter. Burns went on performing until he was ninety nine, just missing his ambition to appear in Las Vegas on his hundredth birthday, but only because he had a fall at his home and was unwell.

Brouhaha transferred to London's Aldwych Theatre where it played for a few months, during which time there were a number of memorable incidents.

At the end of Act One when the British Embassy was blown up, there was an extremely loud explosion from a pyrotechnic suspended in a metal tank (known as a 'bomb tank') backstage. This deafening noise was augmented by recorded explosions and the sound of falling masonry. Simultaneously, part of the set on stage collapsed, followed by an assortment of bricks, plaster, sheets of paper and a dead cat falling from above. After a long pause, once the audience laughter had died down, Peter Sellers, crouching at the front of the stage with fellow actor Jules Munshin, would ask anxiously "Do you think we have gone a trifle too far?" - Curtain.

On one unforgettable night, the laughter died down during the pause following the explosion, and before Peter could say his line, it started again. Baffled, he looked round to see what was causing the amusement. Completely oblivious of the fact that the curtain had not yet come down, an elderly propman carrying a large basket was wandering about the stage studiously collecting the bricks, the plaster, the pieces of paper and the dead cat. By the time he had finished the task and wandered off-stage, Peter Sellers was lying on his back, legs in the air, helpless with laughter. He made several attempts to say his final line, but eventually gave up. With tears running down his cheeks, he waved frantically at the prompt corner for the stage manager to bring down the curtain.

When the company manager asked the propman what on earth he thought he was doing, walking on stage while the curtain was up and the actors were still performing, he totally denied all knowledge of the incident, insisting "That wasn't me, sir. No, that wasn't me." This, despite the fact that he had been seen by several hundred people.

On another night, I noticed someone standing at the rear of the stage, right beside the bomb tank, just before it was due to explode. This was odd because everyone knew to keep well clear. Unfortunately, there was a deputy fireman in that night. He had arrived on stage to lower the fire curtain in the interval - a law in all British theatres to prove that the fire curtain was operational. Theatre firemen are often elderly people who have retired from the fire service, and this one was no exception. Needing to rest his legs while waiting for the end of the act, he made himself comfortable - on the bomb tank. The thought flashed through my mind that I really ought to make a dash for it and save him from a possible heart attack, but then I would miss my cue. No time. The 'GO' cuelight came on, I went into action on the panatrope as the stage manager pressed a switch and the bomb exploded with a deafening boom. Some time later that evening, I passed the poor fellow shuffling along the dressing room corridor. He was shaking his head and muttering, "They nearly got me. They nearly got me."

At the end of the play, Peter Sellers and I performed a kind of sonic duet. Peter stood in the middle of the stage excitedly shouting directions into the auditorium at an imaginary flotilla of ships arriving from England, Russia and America bringing the food and aid to his country. The ships were all trying to enter the harbour at the same time. Each instruction was followed by a sound effect of, say, a warning siren before two ships collided, men shouting, a ship going aground, another one sinking with bubbling noises, etc. During half a page of script, there were twenty or more sound cues using four turntables and a collection of records.

A little while into the run at the Aldwych, the sonic duet became more of a sonic duel when Peter decided to have a little fun at my expense. The sequence began as usual with sounds for the arrival of the American ship and I hurriedly cued up my records for the British ship - a siren playing the first few bars of "Rule Britannia" - when he called out "And now here come the Russians!" He then turned to look into the wings and, vastly amused at the spectacle of discs flying in all directions, cried gleefully, "Aha, that caught you!".

These script changes tended to happen quite often thereafter and I arranged to have a disc with a melee of men shouting and ship' sirens standing by to fill in as I hurriedly rearranged the turntables.

Many of these noises were standard library effects, and Peter Hall left me to source them from the relatively new company, Stagesound. He also asked me to organise the sound system and I made sure that we had more and better loudspeakers than was usual for a play. A few eyebrows were raised as this was normally the province of the company manager who, working on behalf of the producer, was expected to negotiate the cheapest deal for the minimum amount of equipment.

Apart from the library effects, we also needed a number of weird comical sounds, so I bought a second-hand tape recorder and proceeded to experiment. With little knowledge of recording, except for a few tips I had picked up from the sessions at Bishop Sound, I managed to create a selection of crazy effects that amused the director and went into the show.

To cover the scene links, Peter Hall wanted some well-known tunes played in a mock Indian style. These we recorded one night in Peter's flat. Both Peter Hall and John Wood were musicians, so Peter played the piano and harpsichord while John accompanied him on the penny whistle and recorder. My job was to operate the tape machine and provide the percussion section consisting of tambourine, small drum, and a variety of boxes and vases that sounded interesting when hit. Great fun was had by all.

During the run of *Brouhaha*, I told a few stage management friends what I had been up to and they asked me to sort out some effects and playback equipment on their productions. The libraries were limited, so if nothing really fitted the bill I would try to record it myself. It was all a bit hit and miss, but the directors seemed pleased with the results, and as I attended some of the rehearsals to make sure that everybody was happy, I found myself being referred to as "the sound expert".

One evening, I was discussing this new turn of events with Peter Sellers and, always keen on the latest gadgets, he asked if I knew about a variable-speed tape recorder that had just come on to the market. "It's called a Reflectograph. You really should get one," he enthused, "varying the speed would be incredibly useful for creating effects. Slowing things down and speeding them up. It would be great." I agreed absolutely, but explained that this was something completely out of my price range. Until I made my fortune, I had to get by with my one second-hand tape machine.

The following evening, he called me into his dressing room and gleefully revealed a spanking new Reflectograph. He kept it there for a few days and we had fun experimenting with the speed control. One recording was of him singing as I slowed down the machine so that his voice rose to an incredibly high pitch when played back, at which point he called for his nurse to adjust his "Tenors' Friend Truss"! Then, after suitable adjusting noises, he completed the song as I quickly wound the machine back to normal speed. Having exhausted the possibilities of the machine and had a lot of laughs, he said that he would like me to have it. Completely taken off guard, I protested, but he insisted, "What am I going to do with the thing? I've had my fun and I'd much rather you got some use out of it; otherwise it will only sit at home in a cupboard."

I accepted this extraordinarily generous offer with gratitude. He then asked if I had a Garrard transcription turntable for playing discs, adding, "They are the best, you know. All the recording studios use them." I was aware of that, but explained that I was managing with my portable gramophone.

When I knocked on his dressing room door the next evening to check that he was there for the half, he called me in and excitedly revealed an expensive Garrard transcription turntable. "Look," he said, "I found this at home. It has hardly been used because I have just installed a whole new hi-fi system. So, here you are. It's yours. I don't need it."

I was not the only person to be a recipient of his generosity. During a break in rehearsals when we were in Brighton, he noticed the youngest member of the cast, a lad of fourteen, strumming away on a guitar. They got talking about music and the next day, he brought in his own superb guitar and they had jam sessions during the lunch break and on a couple of other occasions when nothing much was going on. At the end of the run in Brighton, the astonished young actor was presented with Peter's guitar on the grounds that it was only gathering dust at home and he would rather it was being used and giving pleasure.

During the London run, Peter was contracted to star in the film *The Mouse That Roared*, playing three different characters. It was a demanding schedule and he had to be on set early every morning. At the end of each performance of *Brouhaha* during this period, he would take off his makeup, change into his pyjamas and, clutching the next day's shooting script, climb into a private ambulance he had hired and snuggle into bed. He was then transported to Pinewood where he remained tucked up until it was time for his make-up call in the morning.

One evening I asked Peter how the filming was going and he said, "Why don't you come along and see for yourself? I spend most of the day sitting in my dressing room, bored out of my mind. Filming is mostly hanging around waiting to be called."

So the following afternoon, I turned up at Pinewood Studios where he was, indeed, sitting alone in his dressing room. He apologised that I was unlikely to see any action. "They have just set up some new scenery and the crew are now working on the lighting. They won't be ready for ages. But come along and have a look at the set anyway." This turned out to be a recreation of the entrance to a New York subway. They had copied everything in minute detail from a large photo of the real thing, even down to small cracks and marks on the walls of the subway and the number of leaves on the trees in the painted background. Peter explained that he had already been filmed in New York with the other actors emerging from the real subway, and now they were going to cut to the studio set for the close-ups. The care and expense involved in building this set seemed extraordinary for just a few moments of dialogue.

Peter was, of course, notorious for his weekly radio appearances in the incredibly popular *Goon Show* and he arranged a ticket for me to see one of the recordings that took take place in the Camden Theatre. Written by Spike Milligan and also starring Harry Secombe, their zany humour influenced many later writers and comedians, not least the cast of *Monty Python* and even *The Beatles*.

At the front of the stage were three microphones, behind which stood the trio clutching their scripts. A fourth microphone was provided for the imposing figure of straight man announcer, Bob Greenslade. There was a small booth at one side of the stage where the very important sound effects man created a stream of extraordinary noises using an assortment of unlikely objects.

Behind the performers were the musicians. The show was in three parts with musical interludes provided by the Ray Ellington Quartet, the harmonica player Max Geldray and a full orchestra conducted by Wally Stott. The orchestra also played the opening and closing music, plus short themes during the show to denote changes of scene. No expense was spared in those days.

The listeners at home would be unaware that many of the laughs came when one or other of the trio, Peter Sellers in particular, broke into uncontrollable giggles and the others had to fill in with ad libs or funny noises. I remember one line when Sellers had to refer to "The poor Count" a few times and on the final occasion mischievously mispronounced "Count" so that it sounded extremely rude. This set them all into hysterics, hardly managing to recover by the time the laughter in the auditorium had died down. The enjoyment of all concerned on stage transmitted itself to the audience and everybody had a wonderful time.

Some months after *Brouhaha* finally closed, I happened to be walking along Panton Street when I saw a familiar brown Rolls Royce draw up. Stepping out of the car, Peter Sellers's face lit up and he beckoned me over. I wondered what he was doing there. "My office is here." he explained, "Come in and have some coffee." In the outer office, I was amused by a large framed cartoon hanging on one wall with the *Goon Show* character Bluebottle depicted as a young lad with big eyes, a large head and spindly legs sticking out of his baggy shorts. He was towing a small box on wheels containing a bomb with smoking fuse. The caption was a catchphrase from the show, *"Did you call me, my Capitaine?"*

There was a boardroom with leather chairs set around a large polished table and on the far wall there hung an imposing portrait photograph of Peter Sellers in smart evening dress. The brass plate in the gilt frame announced: "The Chairman". It was only when looking more closely that one noticed the bow tie was very slightly askew, one side of the shirt collar was bent over and the smile on his lips was distinctly down in one corner.

Soon Sellers had to leave for an appointment and when we walked back into the street, his parting words before he drove off were, "Do keep in touch, won't you?" But how do you "keep in touch" with someone who was already a well-known film actor and was about to become a Hollywood star in such films as *Dr. Strangelove* and the *Pink Panther*?

I have never understood why he was so kind to a young chap who really had nothing to contribute to his busy life.

1959

The Pigalle

With my new equipment, I was better able to create sounds for the smattering of requests received. Always surprised and flattered to be asked, the fees I charged for my services were ludicrously modest. I loved the creative process and somehow it did not seem right to be paid to enjoy myself. It was only a kind of hobby and in order to live I needed to find proper employment. A friend mentioned that they were looking for stagehands at the Pigalle Theatre Restaurant in Piccadilly. This was ideal - an evening job that would leave me free for my recording activities during the day.

There were two shows every night featuring an orchestra, singers, dancers, showgirls and a profusion of feathers and sequins. Considering one had to be there at 7.30 p.m. to set up for the 8.15 show and not leave until gone midnight after the 10.45 performance, the salary of £7.00 a week was not overly generous. There were four of us shifting the small pieces of scenery and opening and closing various sets of curtains. I ended up operating the sound equipment, of course. There was also an electrician in charge of the lighting and we all answered to the stage manager, John Moss. He and I were to become great friends and years later he was able to put some interesting work my way.

During performances of these revues, the small wing space would often become overcrowded as the scantily-clad girls congregated to make their entrances, or came whirling offstage at the end of a number. For me, the proximity of so much young female flesh was a novel, and not altogether unpleasant experience.

The shows changed every few months and the five while I was there including an all black company, a Japanese company and a visiting dance troupe from Spain. I fell in love with one dancer in every company, but was far too insecure to do anything about it. My excuse, which did have some credence, was that I hardly had enough money to spend eleven pence (4½p) on a pint of lager in the interval, let alone ask anyone out for a meal - or even a coffee.

Then, to my surprise and confusion, the most attractive girl in one of the companies became quite chatty. In one of our conversations she mentioned that one of her brothers rode horses and she arranged for me to spend an afternoon recording walking, trotting and galloping hooves. All of which did little to further the relationship, but I obtained some marvellous additions to my ever-growing sound effects library.

We managed to meet on a few occasions during the following weeks, but when the show ended she went abroad to work. We continued to communicate by letter and on one of her brief visits home, our friendship developed into something more. Admittedly, all this did take a few years, but one doesn't like to appear pushy.

This unsatisfactory on/off situation continued for another eighteen months or so until by the time she finally returned to the UK, I had become involved in another relationship.

At a first night party when everybody was fairly well oiled, I was approached by a most attractive lady. I knew she was married and this was taboo, but I was smitten and the encounter led to a clandestine affair that lasted several years. I was not proud of this arrangement, but I was extremely grateful.

Going back to my days at the Pigalle, the owner Al Burnett, who was related to the West End producer and theatre owner Bernard Delfont, announced a season of famous recording artistes, each playing for two weeks. From America, there was Patti Page, Eydie Gormé with husband Steve Lawrence, Betty Hutton, Peggy Lee, Tony Bennett and Sammy Davis Junior. From the UK we had Alma Cogan and Shirley Bassey. The

American performers were particularly appreciated as, unlike the English, at the end of their engagements they gave the backstage staff generous tips. Mostly this was five pounds, which was almost equal to a week's wages.

I became a life-long fan of Peggy Lee. For an hour and a half, she would just stand there, close to the microphone, and sing her songs with that soft silky sexy voice. In between the numbers she chatted quietly to the audience in a rambling sort of way, as though they were all friends who had just dropped by. For her entire set, apart from applause at the end of each number and laughter at her occasional jokes, they all sat there, completely rapt. It was a lesson in how to mesmerize an audience.

Tony Bennett was the most approachable of all the stars, relaxed and happy to chat with us minions as though we were friends and equals. On one occasions, he came off at the end of his set before returning for an encore, and asked us what we thought about his performance, "The audience seemed more appreciative last night. I'm not sure I'm performing as well. What do you think?" Amazingly, for a man of his eminence and talent, he genuinely seemed to want our opinion. Naturally, all his performances were impeccable.

The major revelation, however, was Sammy Davis Junior. It was his first time in the UK, combining the Pigalle engagement with a performance at the Palladium in the annual Royal Variety Show. On his first day at the Pigalle, we waited for his arrival while the band was rehearsing under the control of his own piano-playing musical director. All the Americans brought two or three musicians, always including the essential drummer. Suddenly, our star, who had been rehearsing all day at the Palladium, arrived... and it was like a whirlwind had hit the place. He marched through the restaurant, jumped up on to the stage, said "Hi, fellers" to the musicians, grabbed the microphone, yelled, "Hit it!" to his musical director and the band struck up. He then performed two numbers straight off with incredible power and energy, as though his life depended on it. The restaurant staff laying up the tables, normally a pretty blasé bunch, all stopped in their tracks, rivetted. When the second song finally came to a crashing end, we and the restaurant staff spontaneously burst into applause. Even the band joined in. Davis just said, "Thanks fellers. See you later," and disappeared to his dressing room.

During the next three weeks, I watched every single performance from the wings. He never repeated exactly the same routine. Some nights he would break off in the middle of a number and join the band to play the drums or give a trumpet solo. On two or three occasions he did a whole comedy routine with a xylophone, which he played brilliantly. We were treated to unbelievable tap dancing routines. His impersonations of actors and singers were spot on; somehow he even managed to look like them. One night, without announcing who he was about to mimic, he turned upstage, somehow reshaped his face and posture, turned back to the audience and, without saying anything, received a round of applause. Even though he was a short, skinny black man with a broken hooked nose and one glass eye, the crowd immediately recognized Marlon Brando.

Sammy Davis Jnr.

Sammy Davis's appearance at the Pigalle attracted full houses that most nights included celebrities and show business personalities. Quite a few people wished to visit the star at the end of the shows and one of our tasks was to vet whoever tried to come up the steps from the auditorium and through a set of doors that led backstage. Lionel Blair always had free access because he was appearing with Sammy Davis in the Royal Variety Show, but absolutely nobody else was to be allowed to the star's dressing room without his express permission.

We took it in turns to act as bouncers, which was sometimes quite embarrassing. Imagine the door opening and you are suddenly faced with the smiling face of Nat King Cole, elegantly dressed in black tie and tuxedo, and you have to ask him to wait in the wings while you scurry off to see if he will be granted an audience. Or a tall and immediately recognisable Boris Karloff, surprising handsome for the man renowned for portraying the original Frankenstein's monster on screen, who politely enquires if he might pay his respects to Mr Davis. Then there was the occasion when I was confronted by Edmundo Ross, a popular bandleader with a regular weekly radio programme on the BBC. I explained to Mr Davis who he was and that Mr Ross wished to invite him to the nearby nightclub in Regent Street that he owned, but the offer was declined. I had the unpleasant task of conveying our star's apologies, which he had not actually given.

Possibly the most embarrassing encounter was with a tall good-looking Englishman asking to see his friend Sammy. I had no idea who he was and had to ask his name. "Tell him it's Peter Lawford," Of course! He was one of the infamous Rat Pack with Frank Sinatra and Dean Martin. But we had strict instructions. I still had to go and ask if he was allowed through. Mr Lawford was extremely courteous and patient as, indeed, were all of these eminent gentlemen.

One night, I was on the opposite side of the stage when a woman was escorted backstage by the Pigalle's owner, Al Burnett. With little or no make-up, she wore dark glasses, flat shoes and a long navy blue raincoat covering her dress, obviously not wishing to be recognised. My colleagues and I, plus some members of the orchestra playing on stage, only caught a glimpse as she passed by, but we were all immediately transfixed. I cannot explain it, but she exuded some kind of aura and you simply had to stand and ogle. The stunning mystery woman was Sophia Loren.

There was only one unpleasant incident and that was when a thickset man with a cockney accent, probably the worse for drink, demanded to be let through. I was politely trying to explain that this would not be possible, when our electrician took it into his head to come to my assistance. He informed the man in no uncertain terms that members of the public were not allowed backstage and he should return to his seat in the auditorium. Whereupon, the intruder rounded on him, shouting, "Who the hell are you telling me what I can and can't do?" Before the electrician, who was a lot smaller than the man, could answer, he received a vicious punch in the face that sent him crashing through the doors to the auditorium where he stumbled and fell. To my relief, the man then marched off into the auditorium, ignoring his victim lying on the floor.

What we did not know until some time later was the drama that followed. A diner sitting at a table near the stage stood up and grabbed the man by the arm, saying, "What do you think you are doing, hitting that little fellow?" The reply was "If you want to make something of it, come outside." The diner happened to be a wrestler by trade and although the villain was obviously a tough customer, he accepted the challenge. On the way out into the street, the villain muttered, "This is going to be with tools. Are you tooled up?" The wrestler, angry and not understanding the question, just said, "All I know is you're in for it, mate".

When they emerged from the entrance into Piccadilly, the villain produced a gun and fired it point blank at the wrestler who felt a thud in his chest, but could not believe he had been shot, until he felt blood oozing through his shirt. He looked up to see his would-be assassin legging it towards Piccadilly Circus. Beginning to panic, the wounded man staggered over to a parked taxi and said, "Take me to Charing Cross Hospital, quick?" "Sorry, mate," said the driver, who put up his window and drove off. Managing to hail another cab, he was taken to the hospital where he was told that if the bullet had gone a fraction to the left or to the right, he would have been dead. It was an incredibly lucky escape.

Somehow or other they managed to arrest our villain and I was summoned to appear at Bow Street Magistrates' Court for the indictment. This was when I met the wrestler and he told me what had happened that night. In the courtroom I was asked if I could identify the accused. Pointing him out, I said, "Yes, that's him," and was then told I could go. I thought that was the end of the matter until, months later, an official looking document arrived in the post stating:

"You are bound by a recognizance in the sum of forty pounds, to appear at the next Court of Assize to be held for the jurisdiction of THE CENTRAL CRIMINAL COURT, at Justice Hall in the Old Bailey on the 6th day of December, at ten o'clock in the forenoon and there to *prosecute and give evidence* on the trial of JOHN JAMES BUGGY."

The day came. The long walk in hushed silence through the courtroom at the Old Bailey to take my place at the witness stand and swear to tell the truth, whole truth and nothing but the truth, was intimidating and surreal.

To say I was nervous when the council for the defence began his cross-examination would be an understatement. I was expecting some searching questions, but was totally unprepared for what happened.

He began by asking if I recognised any person in the courtroom who looked like the man I now knew to be John Buggy. I pointed him out.

"When you entered the court at Bow Street," he continued, "somebody spoke to you, didn't they?"

"I'm sorry, I'm not sure what you mean."

He turned to the jury with raised eyebrows and gave a look, indicating that he was dealing with a complete idiot.

"If you cannot understand a simple question, let me put it to you again. When you walked into the court at Bow Street, a policeman spoke to you, didn't he?"

This was several months in the past and, thinking back, I replied, "I believe someone told me where to go."

"And that someone also pointed out the accused to you, didn't they?"

"No."

"So you are saying that all those weeks after the incident that occurred at the Pigalle, you were able to identify the accused?"

"Yes."

"It is true, isn't it, that there is a dim blue light over the door where you claim to have spoken to the accused? And now you are saying that you are able to recognise this person who you only saw for a fleeting moment under a dim blue light."

This statement took me completely off guard because he was totally bending the facts. There was indeed a dim blue light over the door to the dressing rooms for the cast to find their way during the show in a blackout. But this was at the back of the stage, whereas the incident took place near the doors to the auditorium where we were brilliantly lit because the band was playing on stage bathed in several thousand watts of theatre lighting. I must have looked dumfounded and while I tried to summon up some sort of reply, he turned to the jury with a sigh, declaring, "No more questions."

That was it. I was not allowed to speak. However, I imagined that the prosecuting council for the Crown must be aware that all this was nonsense and I waited for him to spring to his feet and make mincemeat out of these ridiculous assertions. But nothing happened. The man remained seated and the judge said, "Thank you. You are dismissed."

Presumably, unlike the defence, the prosecution had failed to do their homework or surely they would not have allowed a key witness, able to identify the accused, to be so ridiculed.

In conversation with the wrestler while waiting at the Bow Street court, he had been extremely angry. It was only by chance that he had not died, and he was determined that the man would pay for it. Surprisingly, a few months later, when he was called to the stand at the Old Bailey trial, he found himself unable to recognize his attacker. A detective working on the case, another witness at the Old Bailey, explained while we were waiting to be called that this was not unusual. The victim had either been paid off, or threatened, or both.

Because he had not been identified, the trial ended with Buggy being found not guilty of attempted murder. He got away with a short sentence for the possession of a firearm and two fake passports found in his flat. My detective friend remarked stoically. "That's alright. We've nabbed him before and we'll nab him again. We know that, he knows that. It's just a game."

A year or so later, there was an article in a newspaper stating that the body of a known criminal, John James Buggy, had been found washed up on a beach.

While Sammy Davis was at the Pigalle, I had another brush with the underworld. This followed an event one evening when his limousine drew up in Piccadilly and he was greeted by a small crowd of National Front supporters, jeering and waving banners proclaiming such slogans as "Blacks Go Home!" and "Blacks Out!" He was surprised and disappointed to receive such a demonstration in this country but he was, of course, used to worse instances of racism back home. For example, when he was starring in the Rat Pack show at the Sands Hotel in Las Vegas, he was not allowed to stay there with his colleagues.

Chatting to his valet, Murphie, a gentle and friendly soul, he related how, back home, he liked to drive to the beach on his day off and sit in the car just looking at the sea. "Don't you like to go on the beach?" I asked innocently. He gave me a look as if to say, "You must be kidding!" Then added, in case I was still being dumb, "We're not welcome."

The National Front demonstration was in the newspapers the following morning, and that evening a waiter came backstage to say that there was someone on the kitchen telephone who was demanding to speak to Sammy Davis and would not take no for an answer. I agreed to talk to the caller and, picking up the receiver, apologised that Mr Davis was unable to come to the telephone at present, adding, "But I could take a message if you would like." The voice that answered was a kind of throaty growl with an East End accent. "If I said the name Jack Spot, would you know who I'm talking about?"

"Yes, I have certainly heard of him," I replied nervously.

Jack "Spot" Comer happened to be a notorious East End gang leader, often mentioned in the press. A man not to be trifled with.

The gruff voice continued: "Well, Mr Spot is not at all happy at the way Mr Davis, a visitor to our shores, has been treated. He is very unhappy about that demonstration. Very unhappy. Do you understand? So, tell Mr Davis that Mr Spot is offering to have some lads standing by every night outside the Pigalle. So if anything like that happens again, our lads will deal with it. You get me? Pass that on."

"Yes, I certainly will."

"With regards from Mr Spot."

"Right."

"And ring me back and tell me what he says."

He gave me a telephone number and I went off to give Sammy Davis the good news. He was amused when informed exactly who was offering this service. However, he asked me to decline with thanks. He did, after all, have his own bodyguard, Big John Hopkins, a scary black gentleman who was twice the size of his boss. I also happened to know that Hopkins carried a gun.

Chatting in the wings one evening, Big John said that he had just ordered some tailor-made shirts from an outfitters in Princes Arcade, just round the corner from the Pigalle. "I was going for light brown, and I asked the man to add a monogram on the pockets - my initials - in a darker colour. *'Certainly, sir,'* the man said. Then he produced this brown silk thread, saying, *'Might I suggest nigger brown?'*" Big John grinned broadly. "Nigger Brown! Can you believe that? I didn't know whether to thank him or shoot him. You English!"

Michael Elliott

While all this was happening during the evenings, by day I was creating sound effects for a few minor shows, all with tight budgets. Quite often, if a deadline had to be met, this entailed carried on through the night after finishing at the Pigalle. If you want to continue working for a director, you can never say, "Sorry, it's not ready."

One of these shows was a revue at the Lyric Theatre, Hammersmith called *One to Another* where once again I was working for director Eleanor Fazan (Fiz). For one of the sketches I had to go to the rehearsal room and record the three stars of the show. I remember being somewhat overawed when faced with Beryl Reid, Patrick Wymark and Sheila Hancock.

Not long after that experience, out of the blue, came the big break that was to change everything.

Two young directors, Caspar Wrede and Michael Elliott formed The 59 Theatre Company to produce a series of plays at the Lyric Theatre, Hammersmith. The stage manager, with whom I had worked at the Arts Theatre, put my name forward and I found myself contracted to organize the sound for what turned out to be a notably successful season for all concerned.

The scene changes for one of the plays, *Danton's Death*, were in view of the audience, during which the lighting designer lit the stage with a ghostly negative effect. Michael asked me what I would suggest for an appropriate sound to cover these changes. It was unusual for a director to ask my opinion and I ventured that something played on a harpsichord might be appropriate - 18th century France and all that. He seemed less than convinced. "I am not sure about music. Shouldn't it be a less definite sound?" Thinking on my feet, I replied, "Yes, but what I had in mind was more of a nebulous sort of non-music. Chords and things." Even to my ears, this sounded pretty lame but Michael offered to put it to George Hall, his composer. George was all for having a go, but he had a very limited budget and was concerned about the cost of hiring a recording studio and a suitable instrument, particularly if the idea did not work. Fortunately, I had an answer, "Peter Hall has a harpsichord and I am sure he would allow us to use it if I asked."

The look of astonishment on their faces was totally unexpected. I was not trying to impress. It just struck me as a good idea. But casually mentioning that I could ask a favour of Peter Hall, the country's leading director, now in charge of the Royal Shakespeare Memorial Theatre, did earn me a few brownie points.

A few days later, we presented ourselves at Peter Hall's house and the door was opened by Leslie Caron. With a coy smile, she said, "Do come on in. Peter said I should take you up to the bedroom." All completely star-struck, we could only grin and mumble our thanks as we were led up the stairs into Mr and Mrs Hall's boudoir where sat the harpsichord. I set up my recorder and George began to create some atmospheric chords, arpeggios and riffs that, when played in the theatre, beautifully complemented the lighting effect for the scene changes.

In the ceiling of the Lyric's auditorium, there was a dome with a circular opening at its centre. When I discovered one could gain access, I decided it would be a wonderful place for a loudspeaker. It gave an ethereal sound to the harpsichord effect as there was no apparent source. It seemed to be coming from everywhere.

I used the same loudspeaker for a wind effect in Ibsen's *Brand,* directed by Michael Elliott, in which I also had to create an avalanche. The crucial element for this was provided by a device called an 'electronic thunder sheet'. This was a square of wire mesh held taut in a large wooden frame with the mesh connected to the innards of a gramophone pick-up. When the mesh was touched it created a rumbling sound from an enormous bass loudspeaker. When it was hit, there was a fearsome explosion. The avalanche sequence started with a low sinister rumble, gradually increasing in volume and intensity by adding more speed and pressure until both hands were drumming on the mesh leading up to the final crescendo. This was augmented with recordings of landslides and fallings rocks. The actor portraying Brand had to shout as the avalanche approached, but because the thunder sheet could be played like an instrument, the volume and intensity could be varied between the lines so that he could be heard. The actor in question was Patrick McGoohan, already incredibly famous for producing and starring in the cult television series, *The Prisoner*. The following year he was to follow this by playing the spy John Drake in *Danger Man*.

That season at the Lyric Hammersmith turned out to be significant in several ways. The plays received critical acclaim and there were even enthusiastic comments about the sound (never mentioned in those days) and of the innovative lighting. Michael Elliot and Caspar Wrede made their names, and ten years later were able to build the Royal Exchange Theatre in Manchester for their 69 Theatre Company.

Although Michael began rehearsals, as did Peter Hall, with a crystal clear vision of the arc of the play, he always encouraged the actors to discover their characters and make their contributions. Because he was so articulate, incisive and confident in his work, I viewed him with a great deal of awe. Years later we laughed about this when he admitted, to my utter amazement, that he had been slightly in awe of me! "I had never worked with a Sound Man before," he said, "and didn't know quite what to expect."

Michael Elliott

Michael Elliott went on to create more wonderful work, but he died tragically young at the age of fifty-three. While waiting for a kidney transplant, he had apparently been given a bad batch of blood for his dialysis machine and had to be rushed into hospital. When I paid him a visit he was very cheerful, so it was a terrible shock when a short while later we heard that he had died. Michael was the father of the very talented Marianne Elliott who became associate director of the National Theatre in 2002 and has since won many awards for directing plays and musicals in the West End and on Broadway. She definitely inherited the genes.

Richard Pilbrow

The lighting designer who received so much recognition for his work in that season at Hammersmith was the man I had spied from the wings when acting as assistant electrician in this very same theatre two years before. I now had the opportunity to get to know Richard Pilbrow and we seemed to hit it off from the start.

The idea of having a lighting designer was relatively new to the theatre. There was a man called Joe Davis who was permanently employed by H M Tennent to light their many productions, and there was Michael Northen, a designer who occasionally lit shows but could not have made a living at it. Richard Pilbrow was the first truly commercial lighting designer in the country.

At the age of 24, some eighteen months or so before the 59 Theatre Company season, Richard had formed his company, Theatre Projects Limited.

Richard Pilbrow

He was already making a name for himself in the West End, so I wondered why the word 'lighting' did not appear in the company name. He explained, "This is because my vision for the future is to encompass all aspects of theatre - lighting, sound, design, equipment, costumes, production, you name it. Hence Theatre Projects. In fact," he continued as an idea struck him, "how would you like to become the Theatre Projects sound department? I am sure we could make a space for you in our office."

Within days, I had moved my recording equipment from my one-room flat to the third floor of an old building in Whitcomb Street, just off Trafalgar Square. The Theatre Projects office consisted of three tiny rooms accessed by a rickety wooden staircase winding past open doors where tailors could be seen toiling away at their sewing machines and steam irons.

I was introduced to the other members of Richard's team: his wife Viki who ran the office and his assistant, Bryan Kendall. There had been no proper discussion about rent or exactly how the arrangement was going to work. I had no money and neither did Theatre Projects. The company was only able to keep afloat by renting out some second-hand lighting equipment, supplemented by Richard's design fees, which were pretty derisory in those days. The truth is that neither Richard nor I was particularly interested in money, a fact that was to become both the strength and weakness of Theatre Projects in the future.

A limited company, Theatre Projects Sound, was formed with Richard on the board and me as managing director. I seem to remember that I had a 90% shareholding because I owned all the equipment, such as it was. It was all pretty meaningless as none of us had any money and it would be years before there was sufficient income to pay me a salary. Theatre Projects Lighting Limited, entirely owned by Richard, was also created at that time. These two companies were the beginnings of what was to become the Theatre Projects Group

With this new arrangement, I was hoping that we might become successful in our chosen careers and perhaps one day make a reasonable living. But Richard's sights were set far higher. During the coming months, it became increasingly apparent that he was totally committed to his dream of building an empire and improving technical standards in the British theatre. And that was just for starters!

1960

Struggling To Make A Living

Having joined Theatre Projects, I continued working at the Pigalle while providing recordings for a few shows. The most prestigious of these was *The Wrong Side of the Park*, a new play written by John Mortimer, directed by Peter Hall and starring Margaret Leighton, Robert Stephens, Wendy Craig and Richard Johnson. I think I received a mention in the programme down amongst the credits for scenery construction, suppliers of lighting equipment, wig makers, and all the 'freebies' negotiated by the management such as 'Wardrobe care by LUX' and "Cigarettes by Abdulla". I tended to forget about publicity and on most shows, the programmes were already being printed by the time I thought about requesting a mention.

Back in 1958 the blockbuster musical *My Fair Lady* had opened at the Theatre Royal Drury Lane, and Stagesound became the first company in this country to produce a tape deck especially designed for stage use. It did not take long for theatre producers to see the financial benefit of this new technology. Instead of hiring panatropes with the cost and complication of having discs specially cut, all the sound effects could now be recorded in sequence on one piece of tape. Even better, there was no need to pay someone with the skill to operate a panatrope. Any fool could press the start button on a tape deck.

This might have been good for the producers, but the inflexibility of a pre-recorded tape was artistically inhibiting. With a collection of discs and a number of turntables, the director could experiment with different combinations of sounds during rehearsals, but when tape came along the director was expected to choose his music and effects and specify the running order in the antiseptic atmosphere of a recording studio. Inevitably, when the tape was played in the lively acoustic of a theatre, it sounded completely different and more often than not, the timings were out. The impatient reaction of many directors under fraught rehearsal conditions was simply to shout, "Cut it".

Paradoxically, the increasing use of the tape machine with all its problems actually did me a favour. Most directors begrudged the time spent choosing sound effects from the limited libraries available and were frustrated by the inability to make changes during rehearsals. So here was I, offering to relieve them of these problems and create what he or she had in mind - hopefully something better. They were delighted to have someone on their team to organise the recordings and playback equipment.

I would turn up at the final stages of rehearsal with my editing block, non-magnetic brass scissors and razor blade to make adjustments as required to the tape or tapes I had recorded. If a different sound or mix of sounds was required, I would dash back to the studio, create a new recording and return to the theatre to splice it in.

For many years, I was the only person supplying this service, which is not surprising as it made no commercial sense whatsoever. I did not actually charge a fee for all those hours hanging about during rehearsals. No producer would have paid me, even if I had dared to ask. On the other hand, I was meeting and being allowed to work with a succession of famous directors and actors in theatres around the West End, playing a small part in the creation of many exciting pieces of drama. What fun! What a privilege!

Meanwhile, the lighting department of Theatre Projects was expanding and Richard moved the company from the tiny office above the tailors in Whitcomb Street to one of the quaint little bow-fronted Queen Anne houses in Goodwins Court, just off St Martin's Lane. Within months, he had taken on two other buildings in that little court. I was given a space amongst the drawing boards in the lighting designers' office.

1961

Suddenly In Demand

It was in 1961 that things began to take off. Peter Hall asked me to organise the sound for five productions at the Aldwych Theatre, the first season for the Royal Shakespeare Company's London base. These were *Ondine* starring Leslie Caron, *The Duchess of Malfi, The Devils of Loudun, Becket* and *The Cherry Orchard*.

The London general manager of the RSC was not happy about my involvement. The theatre owned two tape recorders, very forward thinking at that time, and the stage management was quite capable of ordering whatever effects the director specified from a standard library. It was then a matter of simply playing them back during the show. What was the problem?

Consequently, negotiating a fee was difficult and I ended up working for many days on each production for a pittance.

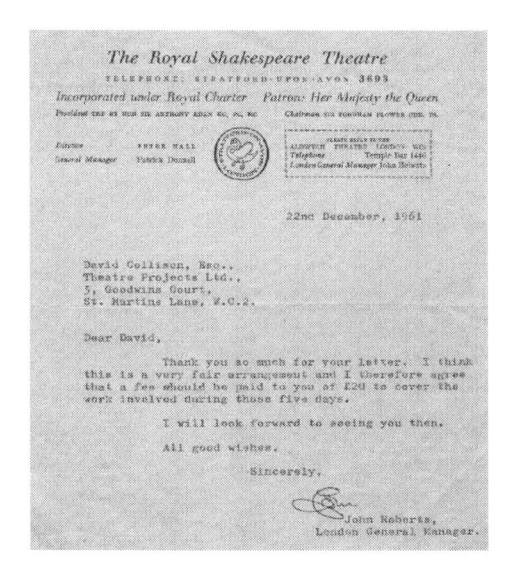

The letter from the General Manager regarding *The Cherry Orchard,* specified a fee of £20 that was supposed to cover my time in the studio recording the effects - and there were many - plus attending rehearsals over a period of five days. Small wonder I had to continue with the evening job. On the other hand, being asked to make a not insignificant contribution to these productions for the Royal Shakespeare Company was an exciting prospect.

Similar fees were negotiated for providing effects for the next three productions. I was never cut out to be a businessman.

Actors in the company that year included Dame Peggy Ashcroft, Sir John Gielgud, Christopher Plummer, Eric Porter, Ian Richardson, Siân Phillips, Gwen Ffrancon-Davies, Roy Dotrice, Peter Jeffrey, Dorothy Tutin, Judi Dench and Ian Holm.

Playing a small part and understudying in *Becket* was a young actress who was friendly with the girl ASM operating the sound equipment. I happened to come upon them the day after this understudy had taken over the role of a leading actress at very short notice. I now squirm with embarrassment as I recall saying, "I saw you on stage last night," adding encouragingly in a tone that almost certainly suggested surprise, "I thought you were very good." The understudy, who I hope took my comment the right way, was Diana Rigg. In my defense, everyone likes praise, especially actors, and she did have the good grace to thank me very graciously.

For *Ondine*, Peter Hall asked if was possible to give the voices of Leslie Caron and the other Ondines (water sprites) an other-worldly feel. I experimented with four microphones placed strategically on the stage with the sound coming from a loudspeaker located backstage way up on the fly gallery. It was an interesting effect, but needed something extra, so I used what was called tape-delay to create an echo. The voices from the microphones were recorded onto a tape machine and played back simultaneously with the time delay between the record head and the playback head producing an echo.

By accident, this echo device was switched on during the rehearsal for another Shakespeare play when a live fanfare was being played. The enlivening of the sound was so good that 'switch on echo mikes' became a standard feature on the sound plot for all on-stage music for years to come and a duplicate system was set up at the theatre in Stratford-upon-Avon.

Leslie Caron as Ondine
Keystone Press/Alamy Stock Photo

In the final dramatic scene of Chekhov's *The Cherry Orchard*, the family, having lost their estate through being in debt, are preparing to leave when they hear the sound of their beloved cherry orchard being chopped down. During the technical rehearsal of this tense scene when Judi Dench and Ian Holm had some lines to deliver, I was surprised to see them in fits of giggles. Somehow, despite this unprofessional behaviour, John Gielgud was managing to maintain his wonderful performance as the father, nervously pacing about upstage and occasionally interrupting with the odd line. I was sure that either he or the renowned French director, Michel Saint-Denis, would soon lose patience. Of course, the rehearsal was mainly for the benefit of lighting and sound, but there was only one more day before the opening night.

Surprisingly, nothing was said and after the rehearsal I asked the stage manager what on earth had been going on. She said that everyone backstage had also been in fits because while Gielgud was pacing about, between his scripted interjections, he was quietly reciting Bea Lilly limericks. Bea Lilly was a comedienne, sometimes called "the funniest woman in the world", who was famed for her absurd songs and sketches. I had been fooled by the technique of an extraordinary actor.

In that same year, Michael Elliott was a guest director at Stratford-upon-Avon for a production of *As You Like,* and he requested that Richard Pilbrow and I should be on the team. It was a tremendous success, both with the public and the critics. The 24-year old Vanessa Redgrave made her name with rave reviews for her portrayal of Rosalind opposite Patrick Allen's Orlando. Richard designed some wonderful lighting for the woodland setting and I installed loudspeakers around the auditorium to create a deep-in-the-woods atmosphere with birdsong. Although this might seem mundane now, at the time people were most surprised to be surrounded by tweeting birds. One critic wrote, "If you do not agree that the production and particularly the performance of Vanessa Redgrave is unmissable - you can always sit back and enjoy the birdsong." The birdsong in question was a dawn chorus recorded around four o'clock one morning in Chorley Wood.

The BBC televised the production in 1963 and I actually received a credit along with the composer and lighting designer.

As a complete contrast to all this high art, there was *The Pub Show* at the Comedy Theatre in London. Directed by Fiz (Eleanor Fazan), the stage was decked out as the interior of a pub in which the audience could witness a disparate collection of performers, including an eighty year old veteran of the music halls, a knife-throwing act and a young comedian just down from Liverpool by the name of Jimmy Tarbuck. The music hall star was Ida Barr, a large lady who had been six foot tall in her day, but was now slightly bent and walking with the aid of a stick. However, when the chairman introduced her, she dropped her stick and strode on to the stage. And when the chairman adjusted the stand microphone that all the acts were using, she brushed it aside, saying, "Take it away. I don't need that thing." This became evident when the piano struck up with "Down at the Old Bull and Bush" and she let forth with an incredibly rich deep voice that filled the auditorium and could probably be heard in the foyer. After treating us to a medley of songs including "If You Were the Only Girl in the World" and "Oh You Beautiful Doll" to which the crowd joined in, she ended with "You Are my Honey Honeysuckle, I am the Bee" which she claimed had been written especially for her.

Arriving for one of the rehearsals, I entered through the door at the back of the stage and immediately recognised a voice I had so often heard on the radio when I was growing up. Mrs Shufflewick kept the nation, and my grandmother, laughing during and after the war years with material that was amazingly risqué for the day. The character of Mrs Shufflewick was a slightly tipsy cockney charlady who frequented her local, "The Cock and Comfort" about which she would complain, "A lot of comfort, but not much of anything else."

Well, I could not wait to actually see the lady in the flesh after all these years and hurried to have a peek from the wings. I was gobsmacked! Standing in front of the microphone was a dapper, dark haired, slightly balding little gentleman dressed in a smart pin-striped suit. Mrs Shufflewick was actually a man – whose real name I later discovered was Rex Jameson. He was always billed as Mrs Shufflewick and never appeared to the public as himself, so he must have fooled a lot of us during a more innocent era.

For four years or so up until now, I had relied on the Pigalle for a meagre existence. When it was necessary to attend an evening rehearsal or spend a few days at Stratford-Upon-Avon, even that income dropped because I had to pay for a friend to fill in at the Pigalle.

This arrangement worked until one night this friend created a major cock-up during the big production number at the end of the show. It involved a sequence with three microphones dropping down from the ceiling, one at the back of the stage, one centre, and the third at the front. On this particular night, as the band struck up with the intro and the lead vocalist, resplendent in feathers and sequins, took her place at the back of the stage, my understudy dropped down the centre microphone instead of the one at the rear. At the end of the first chorus during which the audience had not heard the singer's voice at all, she moved towards the microphone in the centre of the stage only to see it disappearing into the ceiling while the one at the front of the stage dropped down. This farce concluded when the poor girl moved to the front of the stage for the final chorus just as that microphone rose out of sight and the one at the back was lowered.

This must have been uproarious for the audience but the stage manager, John Moss, received an earful from the embarrassed performer and insisted that I should take no more days off. Fortunately, the necessity did not arise. Circumstances changed and I was finally able to hand in my notice and say farewell to the Pigalle.

1962

Lionel Bart And Blitz!

Once again, it was Mum Jenkins who came to the rescue. I was summoned to her office in the New Theatre, where she was now working as Donald Albery's production assistant. Miss Jenkins had become a force to be reckoned with in the West End and I had been surprised to learn on the grapevine that many actors and their agents found her incredibly intimidating. I knew that she could speak her mind and was a tough negotiator, but she had always treated me with great kindness and humour.

"Now, Junior," she announced, "We have a nice job for you. Donald is producing a new musical by Lionel Bart set in London during the Blitz, and we want you to create all the noises."

This show about the German bombing raids on the city had been much talked about and I could hardly believe my luck. Airplanes, bombs, explosions, guns, building falling down, fire engines... a soundman's dream!

During the next couple of weeks we agreed a fee to produce all the recordings and, as it was going to be a complicated sound track, the production would also pay for me to operate the equipment. The weekly salary was £14.00. This was twice the amount I was earning at the Pigalle.

Richard Pilbrow was engaged as lighting designer so, once again, we would be working as a team.

On behalf of the management, I arranged for Stagesound to provide all the equipment. They were now the leading sound company in the West

End and over the past two years I had recommended them on a number of occasions. The owner, Bill Walton, always seemed appreciative, but it must have rankled that he was losing out on supplying the effects from his extensive library because I was recording my own. And now I was to be working for a leading impresario on a major new musical written by the creator of the current West End blockbuster *Oliver!*. One morning I received a phone call. Bill Walton began by congratulating me on winning the contract. He then took the wind right out of my sails by offering me a permanent job at Stagesound. I would be based in his plush new studio premises in Covent Garden with access to his library and all his state-of-the-art equipment. "You will be doing exactly what you are doing now," he continued, "but with all our facilities at your disposal. Give it some thought and call me back. The salary would be twenty pounds a week."

Twenty pounds a week! Twenty pounds a week!

I discussed it with Richard Pilbrow and he agreed it was an extremely tempting offer. He would be sorry to see me leave Theatre Projects, but it was a decision I would have to make for myself.

Richard had become extremely successful as a lighting designer. His services were so much in demand that he was taking on assistants and training them to become designers in their own right. For the rapidly expanding hire business, he had recently acquired a building in Neal's Yard, just off Monmouth Street, to use as a store. Theatre Projects was now seen as a major player in the rental business.

In contrast, I was still a one-man band with my three tape recorders and gram deck now set up in a corner of the smart new lighting design office in Goodwins Court. Being practical, there was no way I could envisage acquiring the type of investment required to build a recording studio, let alone compete with Stagesound's thousands of pounds-worth of rental equipment. Facts that Bill Walton had taken pains to point out.

So, should I accept a permanent job with a good salary, or base my future on this one show that might fail and disappear within weeks, hoping that something might turn up afterwards? Within Theatre Projects, I was in charge of my own destiny, whatever that might be, and I cherished this independence. The decision I made was finally down to pride and a stubborn refusal to admit defeat. I picked up the telephone and politely declined the offer.

Before he left the Arts Theatre, Bob Baty had asked me to keep him informed about what I was up to, and this seemed a good moment to visit RADA and tell him about the exciting new show. When I arrived, he was talking to a young man in his office and I was introduced to his stage manager, Antony Horder - a chance meeting that was to have significant repercussions for both of us. They broke off their discussion to hear my news and I told them as much as I knew about *Blitz!* and how it promised to be a spectacular event.

Bob expressed pleasure that his erstwhile employee, Anne Jenkins, was doing so well and had been putting work my way. Meanwhile, his stage manager, who I came to know as Tony, must have been intrigued by my description of the forthcoming musical because he contacted Mum Jenkins and asked for a job. The next time we met, he was a member of the *Blitz!* stage management team.

Lionel Bart not only wrote the music and lyrics for *Blitz!*, but with Fiz (Eleanor Fazan) as associate director, he was also directing the most expensive musical ever produced in the West End. Short, dark, energetic, with a cheeky smile and a gentle East London accent, this charismatic genius totally captivated the cast. Sometimes, to make a point, he would sing part of a song while demonstrating how he wished the character to perform some piece of business. Unfortunately, his performances were usually more electrifying than the actor or actress in question ever managed. Some of us thought that so much money had been budgeted on the spectacular scenery that the management had skimped on the casting. With a couple of big star names, perhaps the show would have had a much longer run, as it certainly deserved.

At the end of one of the rehearsals, Lionel Bart took me aside and suggested going back to his house to hear a demo tape of the show, adding that we could then discuss the sound track. Moments later, I was sinking into the upholstery of his outrageously ostentatious car being whisked through the streets of London.

Lionel was reputedly earning £16 a minute, day and night, from his shows and his vast portfolio of pop songs, and one of the ways he spent this cash was by collecting luxury limousines. "This particular set of wheels," he explained, "is a Facel Vega. Made by the French. This is the latest model. Just bought it."

When I remarked that heads were turning in the street as we passed, he replied dismissively, "Yeah, well, the French claim it's the fastest and coolest four-seater sports coupé in the world. But I'm not that impressed. In fact, I'm thinking of ditching it."

Lionel Bart

At the house, I listened on headphones to a studio recording of all the songs performed by Lionel and a group of his musical friends. At one point, he caught me grinning and demanded to know what I found so amusing. "It's the song called The Day After Tomorrow", I explained, "It is so like the ones Vera Lynn actually sang in the war, I can't believe you've just written it." Obviously pleased, he said, "That is going to be one of your most important sound cues. It happens in the scene where the people are sheltering from the bombing in the underground station. Somebody turns on their radio and we hear the song, then everyone joins in and gradually the orchestra takes over. Vera's agreed to record it for me."

For another radio sequence, I visited the BBC Sound Archives for recordings of Winston Churchill's famous "Fight them on the beaches" speech and the British traitor known as "Lord Haw-Haw" broadcasting pro-German propaganda. We also needed a recognizable BBC announcer reading something that was not in the archives. Fortunately, one of the wartime announcers was available (1962 being only seventeen years after the war ended) and Frank Philips came into the recording studio I used to hire. Although he only had four or five lines to record, he insisted on going through his broadcasting ritual of taking off his jacket, removing his watch, removing his cufflinks and rolling up his shirtsleeves. When he began the recording by announcing: "Here is the news and this is Frank Phillips reading it," it immediately gave me goose bumps. Frank Phillips was the first BBC newsreader to announce his name at the start of a bulletin, a practice soon taken up by all his colleagues. I was transported right back to the war years, hearing that unmistakable voice on the radio when I was only six or seven years old.

At the end of the recording that lasted all of 25 seconds - no second take required - he rolled down his shirtsleeves, replaced his watch and his cufflinks, donned his jacket and presented me with the script, saying, "This is for you. The S.A.B." Seeing my blank expression, he explained, "Script as Broadcast". With that, he said "Good Day" and took his leave.

The BBC was helpful in supplying some genuine recordings of the Blitz, as was Bishop Sound. When London was being bombed every night by the German Luftwaffe, Jack Bishop installed a disc recorder in the basement of the Comedy theatre, wired to a microphone on the roof, and often stayed up all night recording the air raids. These incredible recordings were added to the library of sound effects he was compiling. By now, I had spent four years recording sound effects for my own library, which eventually grew to more than two thousand items.

One vital effect was an air raid siren played loudly in the auditorium at the start of the show. This was a problem because all the wartime recordings were unusable because of the poor quality and surface noise from the discs. However, my father who had served as a fireman during the war, pointed out that identical sirens were now being used in fire stations to call the men to "action stations". He contacted someone he knew in the Ipswich Fire Brigade and they agreed to set their siren going for me.

On the day, I set up my microphone in the courtyard near where the siren was mounted on the roof of the building. At a signal, they turned it on and it was so incredibly loud that the meter needle on the tape machine shot up and almost wound around the end stop. Another take was called for and it was suggested that within the building it was less ear-splitting, but still very clear. So I positioned myself alongside the fire engines - or "fire appliances" as they were more correctly called. The men had previously been warned that the siren was going to be switched on for a recording and to pay no attention. No one thought to tell them that we were doing a second take, and this was ruined when firemen appeared sliding down the greasy pole from the room above shouting "Is this it?"

Apologies all round and everyone was informed that we were doing one more recording. This time a success.

During the war, to signal an impending air raid attack the siren was made to wail up and down, a chilling sound that still produces goose bumps to anyone who is old enough to remember. Known as the "Alert", the sound was produced by letting the siren build in volume and pitch until running full out, then turning it off to run down and then on again repeatedly to produce that iconic wail. For the "All Clear" the siren was left running constantly.

It was the Alert that was required for the start of the show, but I was not allowed to record this. The wailing siren was officially prohibited on the grounds that it might alarm the local populace into believing that the Luftwaffe was once again on its way. So the effect had to be created in the studio. Today with computers and digital recording, that would be simple. Back then it was a complicated process.

I had the sound of the siren winding up, running at full pitch and dying down at the end. So I recorded part of the rise and part of the fall and spliced them together. The result was then copied several times and all joined together. Finally, the full wind up and wind down were recorded and edited on to the beginning and end. It sounds easy, but to achieve seamless transitions took hours of trial and error. My siren was used at the start of the cast album and might be the only clean close-up recording of a World War Two Alert in existence.

The set designer for *Blitz!* was Sean Kenny, another character who was to have an important influence on my career. A stocky Irishman with a boyish grin and a twinkle in the eye, with his soft Irish brogue and quiet sense of humour, he oozed charm. During the time I knew him, he had a succession of glamorous girlfriends and was married for a time to model and actress Judy Huxtable who later became the wife of Peter Cook.

His influence on theatre staging was enormous. At a time when most designers were striving to create naturalistic settings, he tended to avoid canvas flats and backdrops. Starting with a bare stage, often with the back wall in full view, he would introduce stark structures that provided an impression of 'place' and allowed the actors to work three-dimensionally. Adding movement to these structures allowed the action to flow seamlessly without having to wait for scene changes. This concept was demonstrated in his innovative design for *Lock Up Your Daughters* in 1959 at the Mermaid Theatre and then in his revolutionary setting for *Oliver!*.

Blitz! opened for a trial run at the Regal Cinema Edmonton. Built in 1934 when it was the fashion to have spectacular live shows between the films, it had a stage large enough to accommodate Sean's complicated scenery.

Sean Kenny
Photograph by Lewis Morley
National Science & Media Museum/Science & Society Picture Library

We had been shown a model of the elaborate design, but it hardly prepared us for the scale and complexity of the real thing. This gargantuan production introduced groundbreaking technology, never before seen in a theatre. On a bare stage, were four three-storey 'buildings' made of steel measuring about 24 feet (7.5m) high x 5 foot (1.5m) x 10 foot (3m). Each of these juggernauts, weighing more than two tons, was on castors and could move in any direction under the control of a "driver" sitting in a small camouflaged cabin. At the same time, the drivers were able to revolve the entire structures around them. With four different fascias on each, a realistic three-dimensional street scene could fluidly change into another.

As if this were not complicated enough, there was a bridge spanning the entire width of the stage, supported by two steel towers containing staircases for the actors. Not only could the bridge rise from floor level to 30 foot (9m) up, but when raised above the height of the moving buildings, the entire structure could track from the back of the stage to the front.

Scene from *Blitz!* showing two of the four mobile "buildings"
Photograph by George Walker

Everything had to be accurately controlled because a number of scenes required pieces of scenery hanging from the grid above the stage to be lowered into place. With a cast of forty actors moving amongst all this free-ranging machinery, plus several large items of scenery flying in and out, there was enormous potential for disaster.

It required two stage managers working in unison to keep everything under control by giving instructions on the first radio cueing system to be used in a theatre. Transistor radios, fairly new on the market, were purchased from the English company, Perdio, and adapted to receive a single frequency. These were distributed to the entire stage management team and the flymen.

One of the stage managers gave lighting, follow-spot and special effects cues from the prompt corner, while the other, located high up on the non-working side of the fly gallery, controlled the movement of the massive bridge and directed the drivers of the mobile buildings. From this high vantage point, he could see when everything was in place and it was safe to instruct the flymen to drop in the big pieces of scenery.

Stage manager cueing by radio from above the stage at the Adelphi
Photograph by George Walker

Inevitably, there were occasions when things went wrong. The heavy mobile buildings would get stuck if one of the castors came up against the tiniest object dropped on the stage. It was not unusual to see a man wearing what appeared to be a deaf-aid, walk along the street and give one of the houses a hefty push. Everyone - cast, crew and stage management - was in full view of the audience, but they were all wearing appropriate clothing so it did not matter. It was just people walking about the streets.

The production manager coordinating all these technical innovations was Donald Albery's son, Ian. Working long days and sleepless nights, it was largely due to him that everything came together and finally worked.

Although the creation of the sound track was a vital part of the production, in those days theatre sound was regarded as being just a technical exercise. Consequently, I received only a small mention in the programme below the credits for the stage management reading: "Sound supervised by David Collison (Theatre Projects Limited)". As lighting designer, Richard Pilbrow's name appeared on the main page of the programme along with the rest of the creative team: Lionel Bart, Fiz, Sean Kenny, the musical director and the costume designer. After the show had opened in Edmonton, my contribution seemed to have been noticed (how could it not have been?) and as the souvenir brochures had yet to be printed, I was promoted to the main page with a credit reading: "Sound effects by David Collison". That was a surprising but very welcome breakthrough.

Rehearsals to improve the show did not go entirely smoothly during the run in Edmonton. One night there was an almighty row between Lionel and Donald Albery over changes Donald was demanding and Lionel was refusing to instigate.

The following morning Lionel arrived at the theatre to find that he was barred from the building. Later that day, the production team was summoned and Donald gave us the startling news that Lionel was no longer involved with the production. If he was seen lurking around the theatre, Donald was to be informed immediately. Lionel was popular with the team and I cannot imagine that any of us would have complied with this request.

This fiasco left co-director Fiz in a very difficult position, having to continue working to Donald's instructions with a bemused and dispirited cast. Every day's rehearsal was followed by a clandestine phone call to discuss progress with a distraught Lionel.

She pleaded with Donald to reinstate him. *Blitz!* was Lionel's baby and she was convinced that the show needed his input. Moreover, if the news got out of Lionel's sacking, bad publicity would inevitably follow. By the time the show was being set up at the Adelphi in the West End, there had been some kind of rapprochement and Lionel was back.

Lionel Bart, Sean Kenny and Ian Albery
Photograph by George Walker

To play back all the effects in the theatre, I had three tape machines and a special mixing desk constructed to my specification (another innovation) so that I could send sound to any combination of fourteen loudspeakers. For example, in the first scene where people were using an underground railway station as an air raid shelter, I was able to simulate a train passing through the station starting on one side of the stage and quickly adding speakers in the orchestra pit - very loud - as it went through the station, disappearing on a speaker stage the other side of the stage. Synchronized with a flickering lighting effect, this was very convincing, although it was unpopular with some members of the orchestra.

For the spectacular air raid sequences, Richard Pilbrow and I collaborated on plotting when and where there should be flashes and explosions, and the sound of falling buildings followed by the crackle of fire combined with smoke and projected flame effects. We were left to our own devices and it was all most satisfying.

I requested that the sound control should be positioned in the auditorium at the Adelphi as it was vital for me to see and hear what I was doing during the show. This was unheard of in those days and Donald Albery refused to contemplate what he termed a preposterous idea. But when it was pointed out that there was absolutely no space available backstage, he reluctantly agreed to allot me a small area at the side of the upper circle.

Officially, I had nothing to do with the microphone system to amplify the voices of the actors, apart from asking Stagesound to install one of their standard systems. This simply consisted of five big black microphones positioned along the front edge of the stage and large column loudspeakers mounted either side of the proscenium - two for the stalls and the other two vaguely directed at the dress and upper circles. To control the microphones, a mixing panel was placed in the prompt corner so that the stage manager could turn the master control up for the songs and down for the dialogue, as was at that time normal procedure for any musical.

Aware that the company who produced those big black microphones had recently brought out a much smaller version, I requested that these should be installed. However, when Donald Albery saw them he instructed me to have them removed. "How do you expect to get a decent sound out of silly little things like that? Take them away." I tried to explain that these were more sensitive and had been designed specifically for stage use, but he would not even agree to hear them in a rehearsal. A big fat microphone would obviously produce a better sound than a little stick less than half the size. They were to be replaced immediately.

This was one of my earliest experiences of everybody thinking they are sound experts.

Previews began in May 1962. At every performance there was some kind of technical hitch, but the only time the show actually ground to a halt was on the Royal Gala preview before the official press night. This was during the spectacular finale to Act One when we created a full-scale air raid on London. It began with distant air raid sirens followed by a nearby siren as the sound of far off anti-aircraft guns and the drone of German bombers grew louder, culminating in all hell being let loose: whistling bombs and explosions from all sides of the stage, falling masonry, burning buildings, fire engine bells, and airplanes zooming low overhead through the auditorium. At its peak, my sound effects managed to top a 30-piece orchestra playing flat out. Meanwhile on stage, bright flashes of light synchronized with explosions and flames projected onto the buildings. Firemen ran out their hoses and erected ladders to rescue people from high windows, ambulance workers carried people on stretchers, others ran through the streets in panic. Smoke gradually filled the stage, created by two stage managers walking around with smoke guns - unnoticed in the melee. The climax came when the buildings gradually parted - a magnificent sight in the smoke and flames - to reveal an enormous projection of the famous image of St. Paul's Cathedral wreathed in smoke as all London burned. Almost immediately, the projection screen was gently flown out - but the image of St. Paul's remained, ghost-like, projected on to the smoke, gradually dissipating.

Air Raid on London.
To the left, firemen with hoses standing on the descending bridge spanning the stage. In the centre is one of the mobile structures. To the right at the back is the projection of St. Paul's.

For the Royal Gala performance before the official first night, it was decided to add more smoke because the projection had not been satisfactory the night before. Unfortunately, it got out of hand. There was so much smoke that the actors disappeared entirely from view, then it rolled forwards into the auditorium, filling the orchestra pit so that all one could see was the conductor standing waist high in smoke. The musicians could no longer see him, so the music petered out. The audience began to laugh. Although we could not see them, the cast on stage continued to shout and rescue people from buildings, and I continued to drop bombs and have ambulances arrive and planes roar overhead. But still the dense fog surged onwards, filling the entire stalls and rising to the first balcony level where the Princess Royal and her party were sitting. Fortunately, someone backstage had the presence of mind to open the emergency skylight in the roof of the fly tower and the rising heat quickly drew the smoke back on to the stage. As it dissipated, the actors (by now becoming hoarse) came into view and were applauded wildly by the audience. Then, as the smoke cleared from the pit, the orchestra struck up and the show continued.

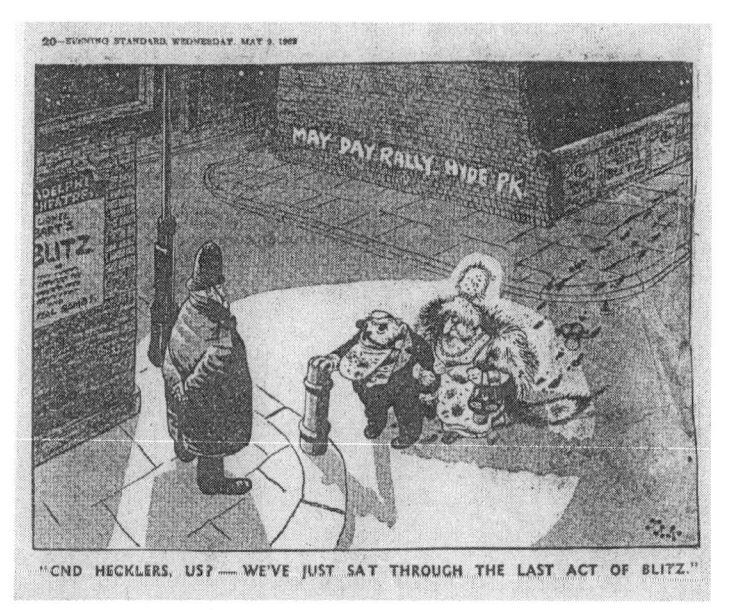

Cartoon by JAK in the Evening Standard making fun of two events in 1962: the Campaign for Nuclear Disarmament and the excess of smoke in *Blitz!*

The following night was the premiere and because there had been teething problems with the new lighting switchboard, Richard Pilbrow was sitting behind me at the sound control with an intercom just in case any dimmers failed to respond and improvisation became necessary. When we reached the big air raid sequence with all the scenery moving through the smoke and the flames and the projection of St.Paul's, everything came together perfectly for the first time. Richard became so excited that he began thumping me on the back and shouting above the tremendous din: *"Isn't this exciting? Isn't this what theatre is all about?"* My reply was: *"Get off, I am trying to do a job here!"* but I knew that this was probably the most heart-stopping evening I would ever spend in the theatre.

We got through the premiere without a single hitch. The audience was swept away by the spectacle and the applause was tumultuous.

One of the final scenes in *Blitz!* contained yet another sensational scenic effect. During a wedding that takes place in a pub, a nearby landmine goes off with an enormous explosion. Ceilings and walls crash to the ground and when the dust settles, the wedding party has to be rescued from the rubble.

For the explosion we used a particularly loud pyrotechnic in a 'bomb tank' placed at the back of the stage near the large scene dock doors. On the other side of these doors, in the street, there was a notice warning passers-by that there would be a loud explosion at approximately 10.00 p.m. each night and 5.00 p.m. Wednesdays and Saturdays. One summer evening, a member of the stage management was out there having a cigarette break, keeping track of the show via the earpiece connected to the receiver on his belt, when along came a member of the public wearing a similar earpiece. *"Wonderful things these, aren't they?* the man proclaimed in a loud voice, indicating a big old fashioned deaf aid pack clipped to the front of his jacket, *"I expect you have come along here like me... to hear the bang!"*

One of my favourite incidents during the run was when Tony Horder, the man I had met in Bob Baty's office, dramatically demonstrated great presence of mind in a crisis. There was a scene in which the juvenile lead emerged from a pub and went into a drunken song and dance routine. On this occasion, as he spun round, the bottle he was holding came into contact with part of the steel set and shattered. With the stage covered in pieces of glass, it was inevitable that the small castors on one or more of the massive mobile 'buildings' would become jammed - and there was a big scene change coming up! With great presence of mind, Tony dashed to the prop room, grabbed a broom and purloined an old trilby hat from one of the cast. The next thing I saw from my vantage point at the side of the upper circle, was an old street cleaner - a 'deaf' old street cleaner - calmly working around this drunk who was singing and dancing for some reason, occasionally giving him a disapproving look, as he brushed away the offending glass. The audience totally accepted that this was part of the action. That is what I call stage management.

One of the things you should never do is be late for a show. Another thing you should never do is be responsible for a complicated sound plot and have no understudy. I was guilty of both crimes almost causing a major disaster.

Having worked late recording sound effects for another production, I arrived back at my room in London's Bayswater in the early hours of the morning. For some reason, perhaps I did not set it properly, my alarm did not go off. I was roused by my landlady knocking on the door, saying that she had received a phone call from some gentleman who seemed to think that I should be in some theatre or other.

I glanced at the clock and was horrified to see that it was five past two and there was a matinee performance starting at 2.30. In panic, I leapt out of the bed, threw on some clothes and dashed out into the street to find a taxi. I made the decision not to telephone the company manager as this would have wasted several vital minutes. Consequently, nobody knew that I was on my way. I begged the driver to get me to the theatre as fast as he could; but he seemed to stop for every pedestrian and slow down at every traffic light. Whilst sympathizing with my predicament and appreciating the urgency of the situation, he was not prepared to do anything that might jeopardize his licence.

The journey was interminable. By curtain up time we were only half way there and in the thick of London traffic. It was nearly a quarter to three when we arrived at the stage door. I raced up the four flights of stairs to the stage management office where the three tapes were kept - but the door was locked. I could hear on the dressing room loudspeakers that they must have delayed the show for at least ten minutes, but it was now well under way. I had missed the air raid siren and some airplane and bomb effects that started the show and they were about to arrive at the point where one of the group of people in an air raid shelter turns on a radio to hear a news bulletin. Praying that someone had taken the tapes to the control position, I ran all the way down to the stage door, then up several flights of a back staircase to the very top of the building where a passageway ran across the roof of the auditorium to more stairs leading down to the side of the upper circle.

By the time I arrived, hardly able to breathe, I found Tony Horder, groping around in the dark desperately trying to find the mains switch. At that moment we were about to miss the first of two important radio cues. The actor turned the switch and when nothing happened he complained that there must be something wrong with the set. With great presence of mind, one of the other actors pretended to read from a newspaper, brilliantly paraphrasing what should have come from the tape. The next radio cue was only moments away. This is the most important one that began with Vera Lynn singing "The Day After Tomorrow" which was gradually taken up by the cast until, after the first verse and chorus, the orchestra joined in. How were they going to get out of that one?

The system was now switched on, but there were only seconds to spare. I grabbed one of the tapes, slapped it on the machine, threaded it with fumbling fingers and fast forwarded to what I hoped was the right cue, just as one of the actors said: *"Murphy, try your wireless again and see if it is working now."* With my heart in my mouth, I pushed the button, half expecting to hear an explosion or a fire engine. The gods were with me. Never have I been so pleased or grateful to hear the voice of Vera Lynn, or anyone else for that matter. Somehow, I managed to pull myself together and get through the rest of the show without incident. Subsequently, the company manager suggested, quite forcibly, that one of the stage management should learn how to operate the show.

At the time, *Blitz!* was the most expensive West End musical ever produced. It ran for 568 performances. Vera Lynn attended the first night and took a bow from the Royal Box. Noël Coward, who was also there, was reported to have commented that it was "twice as loud and seemed twice as long as the real thing." There might have been a touch of jealousy here, because his musical *Sail Away* at the Savoy Theatre was not doing particularly well.

Blitz! was my last show working with Fiz, but in 2016 I made contact with her via her agent when I discovered a book she had written about her life in the theatre. I sent an email saying how much I had enjoyed her story, reminding her who I was in case she could not remember after some fifty-four years. She replied with a chatty email beginning with, "Of course I remember you. You were the young man who was always there in the background and we never had to worry about the sound." I have to admit that I found that rather touching.

Tony Horder

I became friendly with Tony Horder during *Blitz!* Sturdily built and with a deep mellifluous voice, he had impeccable manners and was always eager to please. He was also extremely well read. Although he was usually all graciousness and affability, he was known on occasions to lose his temper – usually through the stupidity of others – and shout, curse, bang doors or slap table tops in a most spectacular fashion. Seconds later, with a broad grin, he would return to his customary self and all would be calm and loveliness. I was never able to display this kind of emotion despite his advice that it was much better to have a short outburst and get it out of your system, rather than bottle everything up.

During the run of *Blitz!* I acquired a second-hand Vespa motor scooter and sometimes gave Tony a ride back to his flat after the show. On one such occasion, early in December 1962, we were faced with a thick choking smog. London suffered from air pollution, but this was a peasouper to end all peasoupers. It was so dense that one could see less than three feet ahead. The only was we could proceed was by following the line of the kerb.

Crawling our way along the Strand we reached Trafalgar Square, where policemen with flaming torches were doing their best to direct the traffic. We located what we thought was The Mall and continued with caution, occasionally having to break hard when, just a few feet ahead, the rear lights of a stationary car suddenly loomed up. This meant feeling our way around the obstacle to once again locate the kerb. After what seemed an eternity, another policeman standing in the middle of the road brandishing a flaming torch, informed us that we had reached the Victoria Memorial in front of Buckingham Palace. The actual monument was entirely invisible and we lost contact with the kerb while negotiating the roundabout to head into Constitution Hill. Soon the kerb came into view again and we resumed the journey with more confidence. Unfortunately, we had completely missed the turning into Constitution Hill and were travelling back up The Mall, a fact that did not become apparent for some while.

Finally we made it home, having ridden through the most severe smog ever experienced in London. It continued for five days. As a result, various Clean Air Acts were introduced and Londoners were given financial incentives to replace coal fires with alternatives such as gas. It turned out to be the last serious London smog.

The large basement in the Neal's Yard lighting store was vacant and I was talking to Tony Horder one day about my plans to move my recording activity there. Being handy with hammer and nails, he offered to help construct a recording studio. During the space of a few weeks, almost single-handed, he built a sound-proof studio and recording booth. We paid for the materials of course, but no money changed hands for his efforts. He did it out of the kindness of his heart and an interest in what I was trying to achieve.

I was now living off my salary from *Blitz!* Any extra income from creating sound effects was invested in sorely needed recording equipment. The fees I was charging were still pitiful because as far as theatre producers were concerned, they could get Stagesound to install the equipment and supply the sound effects, so why would they pay for a third party to become involved? I had to rely upon directors recognizing that I could provide something a little extra for their production.

Noticing how I was sometimes struggling on my own with installing equipment, usually hired from Stagesound, into theatres where I was engaged to provide effects, I was very grateful when Tony offered to assist when he had the time. Once again, no money changed hands but we enjoyed each others company and appreciated the opportunity to work in a number of West End theatres, mingling with some of the leading directors and actors of the day.

As things became busier, Tony began to assist with the recordings. Even when the run of *Blitz!* finally came to an end and he had become technical stage manager at the Central School of Speech and Drama, he would often help out during the evenings or even skive off during the day if there was an emergency.

Final Season Of The Old Vic Company

1962 was a milestone year. I had worked on my first big musical, and now became involved in the final season of the renowned Old Vic Theatre Company. The Old Vic was about to become the temporary home of the newly formed National Theatre Company while waiting for their complex to be built on the South Bank of the Thames. Michael Elliott was the artistic director for the season and I was asked to create the sound for *Measure for Measure, Peer Gynt, The Alchemist* and *Othello* for which I would receive a fee of £75 per show.

During an early production meeting, I was surprised when Michael Elliot took me aside and stated that he regarded sound just as important in a production as lighting or scene design and he thought it only right and proper that I should received an equal credit in the programme and on the poster. As far as I can discover, this was the first time in a major London theatre or, indeed, on Broadway that sound was so acknowledged. A precedent was set and, from that time on, I was able to negotiate a poster credit either as "Sound by..." or, "Sound Design by..." on most productions.

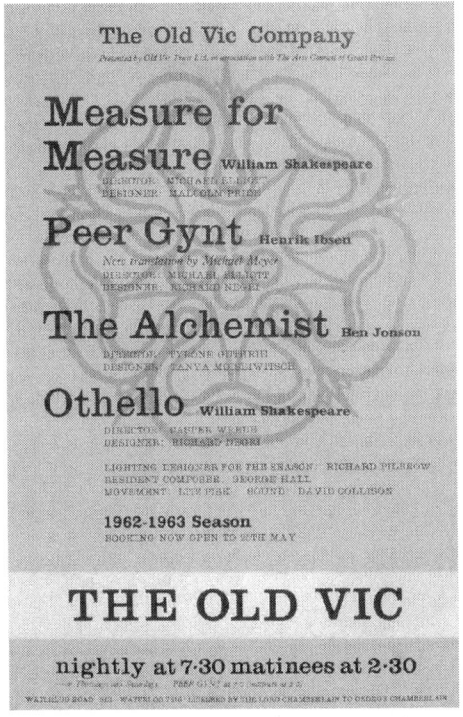

The first equal billing for theatre sound, 1962

The two Shakespeare plays were full of all the usual music and effects, and *Peer Gynt* seemed to have non-stop noises from beginning to end. Because of the many complicated sound sequences I had two major concerns; firstly, the only space available was in a little corner right at the back of the stage for the two tape machines, secondly, the company manager had engaged the wife of the chief electrician to operate them. I was assured that, although she knew nothing about sound, she did have stage management experience and "was very bright". Fortunately, she turned out to be brilliant. However, it demonstrated that, although directors were now accepting the importance of sound effects, there was no awareness that the person making them happen every night might benefit from actually hearing what they were doing. The process was still looked upon as a technical exercise, a matter of just pressing a few buttons.

Once *Peer Gynt* was running and *The Alchemist* was in rehearsal, I waited for the director, Sir Tyrone Guthrie, to specify his requirements but nothing was requested. Eventually, I informed him that £75 had been allotted to his budget for my services and, after a little thought, he suggested that one scene could possibly be enhanced by the inclusion of an ancient clanking lavatory flushing effect. So I provided him with a choice of several flushes and he selected the one that sounded the most rickety.

When we came to the run-throughs, I kept receiving notes to reduce the volume a little. Eventually, when I pointed out that it could hardly be heard at all, he agreed saying, *"Ah yes, but you and I know it is there"*. That must have been the most expensive unheard flushing lavatory in the business.

Being on hand for last minute adjustments, provided the ideal excuse to watch this legendary director at work. During the rehearsal period there was the usual exploration of character and motivation between cast and director, but two days before the first public preview he decreed that the play was now set and all discussion had to stop. During the next run-through he would stop from time to time to ask individual actors to move a pace to the left or take half a pace up-stage, or when making an entrance, to pause between the chair and the table. With these minor adjustments, no actor was being masked (obscured from the audience by another actor) or upstaged (where another actor takes the audience's focus). In addition to that, the audience was now being presented with a series of the most wonderful stage pictures. I know that many modern actors would object to having their movements constricted in this way, but perhaps from time to time, we all need reminding that a show is being performed for the benefit of the audience, not the actors.

The final performance of the 1962-63 season was also the final performance of the renowned Old Vic Company. Following the curtain calls, the cast was joined on stage by the entire backstage crew, stage management and all of us in the production team. Then Michael Elliott invited Dame Sybil Thorndyke to say a few words. Now in her eighties, Dame Sybil had joined the Old Vic Company during the 1914-1918 War, becoming one of the greatest actresses of her day. In 1924 she wowed the West End audiences playing Saint Joan in the play especially written for her by George Bernard Shaw.

In her speech, she recalled how Lilian Baylis had taken over The Old Vic in 1914 and was the first person to present all of Shakespeare's plays. Then in 1929, she established The Old Vic Company with John Gielgud as her leading actor. Subsequently, many illustrious stars began or enhanced their careers at the Vic, including Laurence Olivier, Ralph Richardson, Michael Redgrave, Donald Wolfit, Alec Guiness, Edith Evans, Richard Burton, Maggie Smith, and Judi Dench, all of whom became knights or dames. Judi Dench made her professional debut straight out of drama school playing Juliet.

Dame Sybil concluded by insisting that this should not be seen as a sad occasion. "It is, indeed, the end of an important era of our theatrical history," she said. "but it is also the beginning of something new and exciting, our very own National Theatre under the capable hands of young Larry there, sitting in the front of the stalls." She meant Sir Laurence Olivier, of course. "So this should be a celebration."

1963

The Wars Of The Roses

Peter Hall did not direct any new productions at the RSC in 1962, but I continued working for him during the three ensuing years. It began with a not very encouraging phone call from the General Manager at Stratford saying, "Peter has asked me to contact you about working on our forthcoming productions of *The Wars of the Roses*. Personally, I think that our in-house staff are quite capable of handling this, but Peter has been under a great strain recently and has not been at all well, so we are doing everything we can to keep him happy." Well, it is nice to feel appreciated.

However, after this unwelcoming start, a collaboration with resident composer, Guy Woolfenden to produce some spectacular audio sequences, turned out to be one of my most enjoyable and creative periods.

The Wars of the Roses was a trilogy compiled by John Barton based on Shakespeare's *Henry VI parts 1, 2 and 3* plus *Richard III*. It was a tremendous success, and the following year were added *Richard II*, the two *Henry IV* plays, *Henry V* and *Edward IV*, thus covering more than 100 years of English history.

There are many major battle scenes, and these are always difficult to create convincingly with a limited number of actors, so by the time we were working on *Henry V*, it was decided to evoke the Battle of Harfleur entirely with sound.

It started with the stage fading to blackness as thundering hoofbeats from the back of the stage build to a crescendo. Suddenly, from the rear of the auditorium comes a flight of arrows, immediately followed by the agonising screams of men and horses on stage. Then, filling the entire theatre, the ferocious impact of two great armies meeting head on with the clash of arms, fearsome shouts, horses, bugles, arrows and all hell let loose. The arrows become a grating metallic sound as the general battle turns into a screeching high-pitched whine. When the entire audience has their teeth truly set on edge, the metallic horror sound in the auditorium fades into the uproar of a realistic battle on stage as the lights come up and the focus is brought back to the live action. The whole sequence lasted only a matter of minutes, but it was much more effective than watching a few actors rushing about the stage, shouting and clashing swords in a vain attempt to portray two vast armies.

The Wars of the Roses received universal praise from the media. Writing for the *Daily Mail*, Bernard Levin called it "a monumental production. One of the mightiest stage projects of our time, a production to remember all our lives."

As a complete contrast, produced at the Aldwych Theatre was a satirical comedy by Henry Livings called *Eh?* It starred David Warner with Donald Sinden and Janet Suzman, all of whom had been in *The Wars of the Roses*. The setting was a boiler room in a factory with the enormous boiler being one of the main characters, humming, roaring, hiccupping, glugging and hissing throughout the play. Sadly, I have lost the recording I made of Peter Hall and Henry Livings vocalising the kind of sounds they wished me to create. *Eh?* was later made into a film with Janet Suzman's role played by Cilla Black. I supplied a tape of all the effects, but the film-dubbing editor chose to use only a few of them and the result was far less impressive than the stage version.

Half A Sixpence

1963 was turning out to be ludicrously hectic. Whilst heavily occupied with those major productions at Stratford, there were the daily requests for sound effects from various amateur and repertory companies up and down the country. On top of which, Theatre Projects had been engaged as lighting and sound consultants for the National Theatre Company at the Old Vic, for which I was trying to design a new sound system. Then panic set in when the director Peter Coe asked me to provide the effects for *Half a Sixpence*, a new musical, starring Tommy Steele.

Since the end of *Blitz!* I had to rely on Theatre Projects Sound for an income. Creating noises for people had become more than a full-time job, and although Tony Horder did his best to help whenever he could, it was obvious that I was not coping. So I offered him a derisory salary to join the company - although this was a tad more than I was paying myself. Not really expecting him to leave a safe job at the Central School of Speech and Drama for the general mayhem at Theatre Projects, I was greatly relieved when he accepted. We went on to work together, with never a cross word, for more than fourteen years.

After a couple of meetings with Peter Coe who, as the director of *Oliver!*, was an important person to keep in with, I arranged for Stagesound to install the equipment for *Half a Sixpence* and was then able to leave the creation of the sound effects in the capable hands of my new colleague.

Harry Secombe And Pickwick

It was around this time when we were busying about in the studio that I received a phone call that was to change my life. I recognised the familiar Irish brogue of Sean Kenny. He sounded worried.

"David, I'm glad I caught you. We have a serious problem. I'm in Manchester working on this new musical called *Pickwick* with Harry Secombe - and nobody can hear a word. You have to get up here right away."

"I'm sorry, Sean" I replied, genuinely surprised at this request, "but I don't know how I can help. I'm up to my eyes in work at the moment and, as you know, I create sound effects. I don't know anything about miking shows."

"Yes, but it's all *sound,* isn't it? Anyhow, you have to come because I have told the producer Bernard Delfont that you are the greatest audio expert in the country and he is expecting you here tomorrow morning."

I began to feel a rising sense of panic. "Oh, great. Thanks!"

"Let me put it this way, whatever you do it has to be better than the mess we are in at present. It is a big set and the microphones along the front of the stage are not picking up the voices. But it's a good show," he added brightly, "You'll enjoy it. And when we can actually hear it, everybody else will enjoy it too. We'll see you tomorrow, eh?"

I dropped everything and rushed round to Stagesound to hire one of every type of microphone they had in stock, including a 36-inch (90cm) rifle and even a microphone set in a parabolic reflector (only useful, I was to discover, for recording high-pitched bird sounds). My plan was to sneak into the theatre during the morning rehearsal, evaluate the problems and, during the lunch-break, spend some quiet time trying out the various microphones.

When I slipped into the back of the stalls, an orchestral rehearsal was in progress. The entire cast was on stage and a group of people clustered around the lighting designer's desk in the auditorium. Unfortunately, Sean Kenny looked round and saw me lurking in the darkness.

"Ah, David, you got here. Great. Come and meet Mr Delfont."

I shook hands with the famous producer who escorted me to the stage and stopped the rehearsal. He introduced me to Harry Secombe, who exclaimed, "Thank God you are here. Sean has told us that you are a genius, and that's exactly what we need at the moment, a genius. The rehearsal is yours. What would you like us to do?"

The entire cast, orchestra and production team seemed to be holding their breath, waiting for the saviour to pronounce. To admit that I had not the foggiest idea would probably be less than a shrewd move. To gain time, I proposed that the rehearsal should continue so that I could study the extent of the problem.

Although on a more modest scale than *Blitz!*, Sean had once again designed a set with motorized structures, or trucks, The performers, Harry Secombe in particular, were often expected to sing on the upper levels, some 8-foot (2.4m) high, sometimes with the trucks moving during a song.

There were no wireless microphones available in those days, so to supplement the microphones at the front of the stage, they had hung a whole lot more overhead. When the orchestra struck up, my heart sank. I had never heard anything so awful. With all these microphones, a hard reflective stage floor and no curtains to soak up the sound, all you could hear of Harry Secombe's tenor voice was a thin strangulated sound like a bad PA system in a railway station with added echo.

Logic told me that all those microphones hanging over the stage must be turned off and some way had to be found of getting a single microphone near the singer. That night, I worked out with the help of the stage manager where each truck would be whenever someone was singing on the upper levels. The stage crew then rigged several bars above the stage for me to hang directional microphones. The cable to each microphone ran through a pulley so that they could be raised and lowered from off-stage. Thus, when someone was about to sing, the relevant microphone was lowered. I persuaded the director, Peter Coe, that if a truck had to move during a song, it would only happen during an orchestral section so that when it came to rest, another microphone could be lowered in place before singing resumed. The microphones were painted black, and as the space above the set was also black, they went almost unnoticed. Crude, but hopefully effective.

Stagesound sent up a larger mixing unit to handle the five dropping microphones and the five foot-mikes. When everything was rigged, there was a special rehearsal to test the new system. There was a lot riding on this, as the following day was to be the world premiere. My pulse was racing as the rehearsal began with Harry Secombe singing high up on one of the trucks that moved to another position during the song. Wonder of wonders, we could hear him. Unbelievable relief. It worked... although nobody seemed quite as surprised as I was. They were pleased, yes, but what else would they expect from the greatest audio expert in the country?

In order to achieve a seamless transition from one microphone to another, I wanted the person operating the sound to be located in the auditorium so that they could hear what they were doing. This idea did not go down well, as it would mean employing an extra person. However, I finally won the argument and the equipment was installed in a box out front with a curtain to screen the operator from the audience. I stayed in Manchester for a few days until the management had employed an additional ASM to take over the controls.

Harry Secombe as Pickwick

At the end of the run in Manchester, *Pickwick* transferred to the Saville Theatre in London where it ran for twenty months. It was the first West

End musical to have a multi-microphone rig with a control position in the auditorium and a dedicated sound operator.

After the show opened in London, Harry Secombe became worried that the sound system might fail during a performance and he would have no way of knowing. To allay his fears, a couple of lights were installed either side of the proscenium backstage connected to a sound-to-light controller as used in discos to flash lights to music. By this means, Harry could see that the sound system was working - the brighter the lights, the louder the sound.

Apart from the daily commitments in the studio, we had hardly recovered from all the productions at Stratford-upon-Avon, plus working on *Half a Sixpence* and *Pickwick,* when Sean Kenny called again. This time sounding more relaxed.

"Hello David. How would you like to spend Christmas in Las Vegas?"

I was momentarily speechless, which was obviously Sean's intention because he gave a little chuckle and continued without waiting for a response.

"The owner of the Dunes hotel in Vegas saw *Blitz!* and he wants me to design something spectacular for a new revue he is planning in his supper theatre. He also wants me to bring along the man who made all the noises. So there you are. Should be a nice little job for you."

At a subsequent meeting with Sean, it appeared that I was to create the sound effects for a number of major set pieces, including a scene based on James Bond, a Space adventure and a recreation of the French Revolution. As the cast, apart from two vocalists and a few speciality acts, consisted of boy dancers and a bevy of scantily clad females, just how they were going to achieve all this was going to be interesting. The brief was very vague, so Tony and I set about concocting a large selection of weird noises that would hopefully cover most eventualities.

We had two months or so before I was due to leave for Las Vegas. Meanwhile, there were major projects to be dealt with in London.

A Funny Thing Happened On The Way To The Forum

The musical *A Funny Thing Happened on the Way to the Forum* was enjoying a successful run on Broadway when Tony Walton, who had designed the sets and costumes, suggested to producer Hal Prince that the show could be equally successful in the West End. Tony Walton had been a friend of Richard Pilbrow since school days and suggested that Theatre Projects could be the London production office. Tony introduced Richard to Hal Prince and the three of them set up a company within Theatre Projects called Forum Ventures.

The "Funny Thing.." team outside the Goodwins Court office; Richard Pilbrow, Larry Gelbert (book) Tony Walton, Burt Shevelove (book), Stephen Sondheim (music and lyrics).

A Funny Thing was to be the first of several Forum Ventures productions in the West End of Broadway musicals produced and/or directed by Hal Prince. They managed to assemble an extraordinarily stellar cast headed by Frankie Howerd, including Jon Pertwee, Kenneth Connor, the music hall comedian known as 'Monsewer' Eddie Grey, and a wonderful old actor, particularly renowned for appearing in Ben Travers farces, Robertson (Bunny) Hare. My job entailed organising a sound system to amplify the actors' voices; five microphones along the front of the stage controlled by a little mixer in the prompt corner.

On the first night, I was standing on the side of the stage when the show was about to begin. Frankie Howerd was waiting to make his entrance and perform the opening number, "Comedy Tonight", during which he introduced all the other members of the cast. As the overture was coming to an end, he suddenly cried out in panic, "I can't go on." The stage manager, who was about to cue the curtain to rise, looked round, startled.

"It's no use," he continued, his voice rising, "I can't go on."

An actor playing the minor role of a Roman soldier who was also waiting in the wings, said, "You <u>have</u> to go on, otherwise there is no show!"

"I'm sorry," Howerd replied now visibly shaking, "I can't do it."

"Think," pleaded the actor, "you'll be letting down the whole cast."

By now the overture had ended and the stage manager made the decision to cue Curtain Up. There was a pause. The star made no move to make his entrance. The actor hissed, "Some of us really need this job. We're relying on you."

Then giving him a firm but gentle shove said, "You'll be great!."

And Frankie Howerd walked out into the spotlights to enthusiastic applause from a delighted audience. The success of the show gave a great boost to Frankie Howerd's career, leading to a long running television series, *Up Pompeii* and appearances in two *Carry On* films.

Stephen Sondheim wrote the music and lyrics of *A Funny Thing,* and there is an anecdote I like to think of as "Sunday in the Park with Sondheim". After lunch at the Pilbrows' house one Sunday, I accompanied Stephen and Viki Pilbrow for a walk on Hampstead Heath to exercise her bassett hound. During the walk, I mentioned that seeing *West Side Story* some twelve years before had been one of my greatest theatrical experiences, and I suggested that it might be time for a revival.

"No. We've done that. It's completely out of date now, and the songs are not that good anyway."

I could not believe he was so dismissive of such a masterpiece and protested, "There are wonderful numbers in that show."

"For instance?"

"Well, 'Maria' for one."

He chuckled, "Oh, you mean the cigarette song."

"The cigarette song?"

"That's how we referred to it, because during all the previews in New York when that number started, the whole production team went out for a cigarette break."

Twenty-one years later, I recalled that conversation when Richard Pilbrow presented a revival of *West Side Story* at Her Majesty's, the same theatre that had seen the original London premiere.

Tactfully changing the subject as we walked, Viki asked Stephen if he was working on anything new.

"Well, I'm thinking about a crazy idea for a story set in an old tumbledown theatre that's about to be demolished. A group of ageing actors who used to be stars in their day are having a reunion and reminiscing about the shows and their relationships. Perhaps we see the ghostly figures of showgirls drifting about the stage. Then at the end of the show we have the big theatrical moment when, with a great roar, a bulldozer comes crashing through the back wall of the stage. Curtain! What do you think?"

Nine years later, when I happened to be in New York, the Hal Prince office gave me a ticket for the show he had described, which of course was *Follies*. Before curtain up, I spied Hal's sound designer, Jack Mann who I had come to know. He was in the auditorium at the sound control. As the overture was about to begin there was no time to talk, so I suggested meeting up in the interval.

"There's no interval in this turkey," he drawled, "If you let the audience out, they won't come back."

During an interminably long and tedious evening, I came to appreciate his sentiments. The show started reasonably well with the audience recognising the American actors playing the elderly stars and applauding enthusiastically as each one made their entrance. I was less impressed as the only one I had even heard of was a film star from the 1940s and 1950s, Yvonne de Carlo.

As the show progressed, we all sank into a kind of coma of boredom. Eventually, as the piece drew to a close, I perked up in anticipation of the great *coup de theatre* when the bulldozer would come crashing through the back wall... But it did not happen! The actors left the stage and the curtain came down.

According to Variety, the American entertainment weekly, the production was a financial failure losing $792,000 - an enormous loss today, but even more so back then. Although Hal Prince was both the producer and co-director with Michael Bennett, he did not personally lose money because he never risked investing in his own productions. He preferred to rely on the income from managing the shows, plus any personal fees and royalties for the many successes he directed. Bizarrely, *Follies* won a raft of Tony Awards for direction, choreography, scenic design, costume design, lighting and original score.

The successful version of *Follies* that opened in London in 1987 had four new Sondheim songs and an extensively reworked book. It also had an intermission. But still no bulldozer!

The National Theatre Company

Back in 1963, work was continuing apace on the major lighting and sound re-fit at the Old Vic for the National Theatre Company's inaugural season. The budget for lighting was substantial and Richard Pilbrow took the opportunity to specify a new lighting control board and install what in those days was an enormous quantity of spotlights to cope with the number of plays that would be running in repertoire. The money allotted for a new sound system, on the other hand, was a mere £2,000.

The limitations of what could be achieved with this paltry sum were very much in my mind when Sir Laurence Olivier explained how he envisaged the ghostly voice of Hamlet's father moving rapidly around the stage from speaker to speaker; but when the artistic director of the newly created National Theatre Company, who also happened to be the most revered actor on the British stage, puts his hand on your arm and says, "Do you think you could do that for me?" what can one say, except that it is not feasible with the standard equipment available, but there is a way...

I described how I was able to move sound from speaker to speaker with the mixing console created for *Blitz!* To my surprise, he immediately grasped the principle. And when I suggested that in order to properly control the sound I really needed an operating position within the auditorium, his comment was "No question, dear boy. Of course you need to hear what you are doing. Go and talk to my General Manager and tell him to arrange it."

Lord Olivier
Photograph by Allan Warren

Encouraged by his enthusiasm, I mentioned that providing everything we wanted within the meagre budget might be a problem. But at the mention of money, his eyes clouded over. "Talk to my General Manager. He deals with all that sort of thing".

The meeting with the General Manager did not go well. He was not prepared to lose any seats in the auditorium and the budget, about which I had never been consulted, would definitely not be increased. Fortunately, I had a card up my sleeve. I was able to quote Sir Laurence saying that he thought it "essential".

Consequently, I was grudgingly allotted just three seats to one side at the rear of the stalls, partially obscured by a pillar. The seats were removed and to hide the equipment, some money was found from somewhere to construct a wall with a large opening window around this area.

This incredibly constricted space became the first sound control room ever installed in a British theatre. I managed to cram in a very slim control desk and three tape machines mounted in a vertical rack. This was installed by Stagesound at a total cost of £1,758. There was very little left in the budget for the loudspeakers needed on stage for the sound effects, so I bought some good quality loudspeaker units and commissioned a carpenter to construct the cabinets. Not exactly hi-fi, but superior to the loudspeakers found in most theatres.

The author in the tiny control room at the Old Vic 1963

Having created a control room away from the stage, the need for a permanent sound operator was evident and a young lady who had a background in stage management was employed to fill this post. As the sound for *Hamlet* was quite complicated, I was at the controls for the opening, handing it over after a week or so. I did not get paid for turning up every night but I needed to ensure a smooth hand-over. Besides, I enjoyed being hands-on in the theatre once again.

The first night was not without incident. A piece in the Guardian newspaper read: *The director, Laurence Olivier, had chosen to direct Hamlet uncut. His weighty production warranted a weighty set designed by Sean Kenny: a monolithic staircase that left the Daily Sketch's critic "trying hard not to be grossly hysterical", such was his joy regarding this "blinding piece of revolving poetic engineering". On opening night the trapdoor tomb jammed, and stagehands had to rush on to squirt it with oil.*

What the press did not realise was that out of sight, under the stage, the Production Manager George Rowbottom was striving to free the trap mechanism when he touched a wire and received an electrical shock that flung him backwards and knocked him unconscious. An ambulance was called and he was carted off to Charing Cross Hospital. Some time later, when he was just about able to sit up in bed and drink a cup of tea, the doctor advised him to spend the rest of the night in hospital and then take it easy for the next day or two. "You're joking", said George. "I have to get back for the grave scene in Act Five to make sure the trap is now working." And he was off.

George need not have worried because during the interval, the stage crew got the trap working properly. But he was ultimately responsible and, as with most theatre people, he had an insane belief in that old adage "The Show Must Go On."

During a subsequent performance there was another hiatus, compounded by the fact that the new intercom system was not yet working. This meant that the stage manger, Neville Thompson, who was running the show from a control room at the back of the circle could not communicate with the technicians on stage or, of course, me. He was having to rely entirely on giving cuelight signals.

He gave the GO signals at the start of the show, which was my cue to begin a crowd effect followed by a cock crow and then a clock striking. It was all supposed to be taking place in the semi-gloom as dawn breaks. I was about to carry on with the next effect, when it dawned on me that the sounds did not seem as loud as usual; moreover, nobody was speaking on stage. I was not able to see the actors at this point because they were standing on a high rostrum, obscured to my view at the rear of the stalls by the balcony overhang. It was then that I noticed the houselights creep up a just glimmer to reveal that the house curtain was still closed! Obviously Neville had sneaked the houselights up to check that the curtain was indeed still down. I gently faded out the sound, set back the tapes and waited for a cue to start the whole sequence again. But nothing happened. After what seemed a lifetime, I decided to run up to the control rooms at the back of the circle to get an update from Neville. I met him tearing down the stairs into the foyer on his way out of the theatre and round the building to the stage door in order to get backstage and discover what the hell was going on.

The puzzled audience was left in the dark for some while before some lights appeared on the house curtain and to everyone's surprise, Laurence Olivier made an appearance. Emerging from an entrance in the proscenium downstage of the curtain, to a burst of delighted applause, he made his way to centre stage. After apologizing for the unforeseen delay, he explained that, unlike the old house curtain that was suspended from a counterweighted bar and hauled up and down manually, with the advance of technology all this muscle and sweat was no longer necessary. The brand new curtain, controlled by an electric motor, could rise and fall at the push of a button. Unfortunately, the motor had seized! Much laughter. It was going to take some minutes before the backstage crew could rig ropes from the grid to attach to the curtain and pull it up. *Manually.* More laughter. So he suggested that everyone should retire to the bars where they would be informed as soon as the performance was able to proceed. Exit knight to more applause.

Installing any form of motorized equipment in the theatre without any form of manual back-up was not just an oversight, it is a cardinal sin. The production normally ran for a tedious three and a bit hours, but on this night it did not end until 11.30 p.m. and many people left before the end to catch their trains – or maybe because they had suffered enough.

The first performance of the National Theatre Company at the Old Vic was on the 22nd October 1963, and they were to perform there for thirteen years before the National Theatre building on the South Bank of the Thames was finally opened by the Queen in 1976.

At the end of a crazy year, with the National Theatre Company having been launched, it was time to start packing my bags for Las Vegas and to transfer my thoughts from the Bard to 'Tits and Feathers'. Sublime to the ridiculous or what!

New York

As it turned out, I was to stop off in New York on the way. Following the success of *A Funny Thing Happened On The Way To The Forum*, Hal Prince had produced and directed the musical *She Loves Me*, now running on Broadway. Hal had asked Richard Pilbrow to co-produce it in London, and he and his wife Viki, who ran the Forum Ventures production office, had flown out for a meeting. I was scheduled to leave for the West Coast a few days later, and Richard suggested that I reschedule and meet them in New York. This would give me the opportunity to see *She Loves Me* and talk to the veteran American soundman, Jack Mann, who worked on all Hal's musicals. This would be extremely useful, as I would be attempting to reproduce the Broadway sound in London using British equipment.

I was in the office when Richard was on the phone to his assistant from Hal Prince's office in New York. Suddenly he broke off when he heard a scream. "Hold on a minute," he said, "there's something going on."

There was a short pause then, "Oh My God, Hal's secretary has just heard on the radio that the President has been shot!"

By pure chance, we in the Theatre Projects office were possibly the first members of the British public to learn of President Kennedy's assassination.

With all that had been going on, I had overlooked the fact that a visa was required to enter the United States. This would be the first time I had been to America, or indeed ever flown in an airplane. So, on the Saturday before I was due to fly out on the following Monday, I presented myself at the American Embassy. The timing could not have been worse. This was the day after the death of President Kennedy had been announced.

On the steps up to the Embassy with flags flying at half-mast, an armed guard barred my way and demanded to know my business. I explained that I had a flight booked to New York and needed a visa. "Don't you understand that the entire American nation is in mourning?" he said. "You need to respect our feelings. I suggest you change your flight." Feeling terrible, I apologised profusely and explained that everyone in Britain was equally shocked and horrified, but I had a flight booked and a business appointment and would be terrible grateful if someone could help. Reluctantly, and with an air of distaste, he permitted me to enter the building where I was interviewed in hushed tones by a sombre official and issued the visa. I came away feeling a complete heel.

I arrived in New York in time to see *She Loves Me*. The audience response was muted and afterwards, over dinner in a restaurant, Hal remarked that he had cancelled the Friday and Saturday performances and probably should have cancelled this one. The cast felt uncomfortable performing a light-hearted musical so soon after the tragedy.

He and Richard and Viki went on to discuss whether or not the show would work in London. They were beginning to have doubts after this evening's poor reaction. Then, suddenly remembering that I had just seen the show for the first time, Richard turned to me. "You've never seen the show before. What did you think?" "Well, I understand that the audience were naturally a bit subdued, but it is one of the best evenings I have ever had in the theatre. I thought it was just wonderful."

Hal, who was deeply depressed, seemed to notice my presence for the first time. "Are you serious?"

"Absolutely. It was funny. It was moving. Wonderful songs. I absolutely loved it."

Everyone seemed surprised, but it changed the tone of the conversation and they began discussing possible dates and casting for the London production.

Las Vegas

The following morning, I was on my way to the gambling centre of America, clutching a bag full of tape recordings.

Las Vegas is now the largest city in Nevada with more than 640,000 inhabitants, but in November 1963 as we came in to land on a dark winter evening, it appeared a small blob of bright sparkling lights plonked down in the middle of a vast desert. What has become a bustling international airport was then just a single runway with the terminal building little more than a hut.

Emerging from the terminal, I was confronted by what looked like a cowboy. Tall, brown boots, blue jeans, check shirt and stetson, he was leaning lazily against the side of a bus. As I approached he enquired: "You figurin' on going downtown?" "No thank you," I replied merrily, "I am walking." This response caused him to raise an eyebrow and peer at me suspiciously through narrowed eyes, almost as though I had just announced that I was off to shoot my old granny.

It was unexpectedly hot as I trudged across the sandy scrub lugging my heavy holdall towards the hotel. The building in the shape of a mosque was outlined in red neon with "The Dunes" in brightly lit letters. Beneath this was an enormous backlit sign for "Casino de Paris", the not very original title for the show, with flashing images of girls in sequins and feathers. Shades of the Pigalle, I thought. The sign was so big that I had actually it seen from the air, shining like a beacon in the darkness. Now, as I came within a hundred yards or so, I realised that it was just that - a sign. There was no building there at all. Nothing. It was just a colossal frame standing alone in the desert.

Somewhat embarrassed, I retraced my steps. The cowboy was still leaning against the bus, regarding my approach with mild curiosity. "Do you go to The Dunes hotel?" I enquired, now somewhat sweaty and out of breath. "That's way down the other end of The Strip," he drawled, "Ten minutes. Climb in." The Strip, now part of a thriving metropolis was then just a road stretching out into the desert from the small town centre. Spaced out along this highway were the famous gambling hotels; the Stardust, the Flamingo, the Tropicana, the Sands and, of course, the Dunes. But first, we travelled through the downtown casino area where I was overwhelmed by the dazzling lights. Most of the buildings were completely covered in glittering coloured neon tubes upon which there was enormous lettering either fashioned in more neon or as back-lit panels proclaiming the names of the various establishments. At street level, above the glass doors, they all had canopies blazing with more neon and strings of moving lights, each casino competing with the next for brightness and garishness. It was all so wonderfully tasteless that it was somehow magnificent.

Arriving at the Dunes, the cowboy driver drawled. "Ok, feller, this where you get out." I thanked him and headed for the hotel reception desk. I was directed to the theatre where I found Sean Kenny on stage with a team of men manhandling some massive steel structure that was to become part of the set.

My story of mistaking a sign for the hotel amused Sean beyond all reason. Unable to control his giggling, he insisted that we should go at once and tell the owner of the hotel, Major Riddle. I had imagined that Major Riddle must be a military gentleman, probably some kind of war hero. But no, Major just happened to be his Christian name.

On our way to his office, we encountered Riddle's personal assistant and Sean took great delight in regaling her with my story. Not only was she amused, but she appeared to be overjoyed to hear of my humiliation. "That's really great!" she said, "This is something that might cheer him up at last. The old boy is in a deep depression at the moment. Yesterday was meant to be the grand opening of our new golf course. It has taken months for the acres of turf to be flown in from Los Angeles and laid in the desert with miles of underground pipes for the watering system and, finally when all seemed ready for him to cut the ribbon, wouldn't you know it, the fountains didn't work. Disaster! On top of this disappointment, tonight he went down to the airport to see the biggest free-standing sign in the world switched on for the first time; and wouldn't you know it, some of the neon tubes failed to light up. He is now sitting in his office, in a complete grump. Let's go brighten his day."

Major Riddle was a large man in his mid fifties who, having inherited a fortune from his father's interstate trucking business, had invested in Texas oil wells and gambling clubs. Riddle became a major shareholder in the failing Dunes hotel and turned it into a mammoth success. There were rumours of connections with the Mafia, but that was par for the course with Las Vegas casino owners at the time.

We were conducted into the great man's office where I received a limp handshake and a gloomy welcome. "Mr Collison has an interesting story that you are really going to like," piped up the PA. "Go on, David. Tell Major Riddle what you just told us." So, once again with Sean grinning from ear to ear, I related my embarrassing episode. Riddle noticeably began to perk up as the tale unfolded, at the end of which his press secretary was summoned. When the man arrived, I was forced to go over the whole thing again while he took notes. Two days later, I was shown a copy of the local Los Angeles Times, also sold in Las Vegas, where in the top left hand corner of the front page it stated:

" *The new Dunes sign down at the airport is the largest illuminated electric sign in the world. It covers 5,000 square feet, is 80 feet tall and 60 feet wide. The 'D' in Dunes is 18 feet high! Last Thursday night, a British gentleman named David Collison arrived at the airport, saw the big new Dunes sign and said, "By Jove, the Dunes Hotel is much closer than I thought. I won't need a taxicab." He then picked up his bags and started walking towards the sign.*"

In these gambling hotels you always have to pass through the casino in order to get to the restaurant, the bar, the theatre, or the bedrooms. Presumably someone was pointing me out because during the next few days, when walking through the casino I was accosted by complete strangers with broad grins on their faces who came up and said things like: "Hey, enjoy your trip?" or "Seen any big signs lately?"

There are many ways the casinos have of encouraging you to spend money in the slot machines, and one of these is by giving change in the restaurant in coins. On one occasion when I had a pocket full of quarters, I unloaded a quantity into a machine - they had satisfyingly tactile handles in those days, not sterile push-buttons - and four cherries appeared in the window, although not all in line. Whenever there was a win, this was signalled by a bell ringing, a light flashing on top of the machine and the sound of coins flooding out into the metal tray. Lights and bells going off throughout the casino with its hundred of fruit machines all added to the excitement, of course, and the sense that one really could get that unattainable jackpot.

In my case, nothing happened, no satisfactory tinkle of coins, but I thought that four of the same kind in a window should have produced something. So I wandered off to find one of the security men who constantly patrol the aisles. This one was a dead ringer for the shambling overweight sheriff one often sees in Westerns, even down to the chunky wooden gun handle protruding from the holster hanging from his leather belt. When I enquired about my four cherries, he looked down at me with concern, "You shouldn't have left the machine. Come on, take me to it quick."

When we arrived, and discovered that no outlaw had claimed my fruit, he growled, "Wipe the smile off, feller." I thought this completely uncalled for in the circumstances. I was not even aware that I was smiling. When I gave him an affronted look he repeated, "Wipe the smile off the machine." I was confused. "Put a coin in *the machine*," he said, losing patience, "Wipe off that smile." The penny dropped. Or rather, the quarter did when I slipped it into the slot and pulled the handle. I was then given a ticket and told to take it to the cashier where I was presented with a very large cardboard cup brim full of quarters. Back to square one. What does one do with that much change? Simple. It took just a few minutes to feed it all back into the coffers of my employer.

The theatre at the Dunes had a brand new sound system in a luxurious control room with a budget that would have provided equipment for half a dozen West End musicals. The engineer in charge of all this expensive gear pointed out the two tape machines installed for my sound effects, the like of which I had only seen in professional recording studios. I was intrigued to see that he had a number of wireless microphones. I had not seen one before and it would be some ten years before they were being used successfully in the UK. These were like normal hand-microphones but with a transmitter built into the handle. Two of the female singers wore only sparkly bras and G-strings with feathered head-dresses and I wondered what they were going to do with the microphones during the big dance routines. Facetiously, I suggested sticking them in their wigs. To my surprise, he said that I had got it in one. Special wigs were being built for exactly that purpose.

I was introduced to the gentleman from Los Angeles responsible for designing the audio system. He called himself a Sound Consultant. A bit pretentious, I thought, not knowing that I was destined to become one myself in the near future. He talked grandly about the special loudspeakers and the novel reverberation system he had designed especially for this theatre. When somebody asked what other projects he was working on, he replied, "We have some exciting new ideas coming out of our laboratory. Right now we are working on a tooth-microphone. Fits right there at the back of the tooth." This announcement engendered raised eyebrows and expressions of admiration around the table. "Of course," he went on, "we are having a little trouble with saliva right now." Not quite comprehending, I asked him if it was really possible to fit a radio transmitter into the mouth. The answer was: "No, we have a little wire coming out from the corner of the mouth, but we're working on it." There followed an awkward silence until someone chirped up with a comment about how the rehearsals were going, successfully changing the subject.

A few days later, the audio engineer offered to show me the unique echo system the Los Angeles expert had, at great expense, designed for the show. There had been much talk about a large sound proof chamber built to a specific shape and size with reflective walls containing loudspeakers placed at carefully calculated angles, and - above all - a revolving microphone! As it was such a unique concept, he had the only key to the room and the designer had insisted - on pain of death - that he should never show it to anybody. As a fellow soundman, however, he was prepared to trust me because he thought I might learn something - which was certainly the case. The door was opened to reveal a small square room with a standard loudspeaker placed against one wall and, from a hook in the centre of the ceiling, a microphone hanging by a piece of string. That was it!

Meanwhile, they were having problems with the scenery and it was obviously not going to be ready for the scheduled opening. Once again, Sean Kenny had designed something extraordinary. Similar to the moving "houses" in *Blitz!*, there were two structures in the shape of curved staircases, the tops of which abutted the higher levels of two tall towers. Driven by stagehands, the staircases and towers could wander freely around the stage to form different shapes.

But the central feature was a far more complex creation. It took the form of an enormous circular platform with a second identical platform some eight feet above, supported on slim pillars. Tucked between these surfaces were two more large discs. This massive structure was capable of gliding silently from the back to the front of the enormous stage and as it moved, the two internal discs could swing out sideways on steel arms. There was also a smaller disc at the front that could rise from ground level, transporting performers to and from the upper level.

All this was operated from a little booth way up at the back of the stage where the technician could look down on the action. Mounted on a console was a scale model of what Sean had named the "Octuramic Stage". The operator could position the arms and the discs to where he wanted them to end up. Upon pressing a button, the great machine below would come to life and move to replicate the layout set on the model. Push buttons controlled the raising and lowering of the small disc at the front and also trundled the entire monster to any position from the back to the front of the stage.

It was the first time a theatre had scenery controlled by a computer. Inevitably, there were many teething problems. Sean had brought out from England the engineer who had worked on *Blitz!* who was familiar with standard electric motors. The mysteries of robotics and computers were way beyond his experience. For some days we had odd bits of the contraption working and it would lumber up and down stage and then judder to a halt. The arms would swing out but not stop at the required positions. Rehearsals with the set were abandoned when the cast refused to perform on this unpredictable piece of machinery.

The engineer had been struggling for some weeks without success to get everything working and the opening date was nearly upon us. The pressure became too great. One morning, he appeared on stage and with a look of innocent amazement on his face announced that someone had been into his hotel suite and stolen all the drawings. They had completely disappeared. Without the drawings, he could do nothing.

Sean immediately arranged for the boffin who had actually designed the system to be flown out from England to rescue the situation. Within a few days, everything was working perfectly. Rehearsals continued, but the date for the grand opening had to be postponed until after Christmas.

Christmas day in Las Vegas was the weirdest experience. As nothing was happening in the theatre that day, Sean's assistant Bob Bahl suggested that we should wander over to the Show Bar to see their production of *Cinderella*. This was a short show lasting about 45 minutes that was repeated at regular intervals throughout the day.

We sat at the bar sipping "stingers", a cocktail that we had recently discovered and rather taken to. It consisted of brandy with a dash of white Crème de Menthe served on the rocks. As the performance took place immediately behind the bar, we were virtually seated in the front row. At 10 a.m. the music started and the curtains opened to reveal a sizeable stage with scenery depicting Cinderella's home. Later, the stage would revolve to bring into view the palace scene.

To say that this was the traditional story of Cinderella was stretching it a little. For the Las Vegas audience they had put a new spin on the fairy tale. Basically, it went like this: instead of losing a shoe at the ball, Cinderella accidentally drops her bra. The King is an old letch who lusts after Cinderella, while she fancies the Prince who is not interested, being outrageously gay. I cannot quite remember how the ugly sisters fitted into the plot as several stingers were consumed during the performance, but there was a great deal of business with the lecherous old King removing and replacing sparkly brassieres.

What I do remember was a sensuous dance routine between the Prince and Cinderella who was an exquisitely beautiful dark haired girl with a fantastic figure. For some nefarious reason, during this dance she was naked except for a small G-string and he was just wearing ballet tights. There was a moment when he took her by the waist, lifted her high above his head, and then very gently brought her down with her breasts rubbing against his chest. At this point, I asked Bob if he thought the boy playing the Prince really was gay. "Oh my God," he replied, his eyes popping out on stalks, "To do that several times a day, he would *have* to be!"

These free shows in the big hotels were extraordinary. On another occasion, Bob and I visited The Sands hotel and on the stage behind the bar there was a band playing. After we had been sitting at a table chatting away for a while, Bob suddenly remarked, "Hey, that trumpeter leading the band. I don't believe it. That's Harry James!" One of America's leading trumpet players, Harry James and his orchestra were incredibly famous, appearing in several films and making hit records. He was also renowned for being married to film star Betty Grable.

After a while, the band stopped playing and the stage revolved to reveal another orchestra, this time with a singer who looked vaguely familiar, but as soon as I heard his distinctive voice, it was my turn to exclaim, "My God, that's Billy Eckstein!" Here was a major recording artist with many hit singles and albums to his name, singing in a bar with nobody paying much attention. Unbelievable! The big casino hotels paid so much money that the stars swallowed their pride and took the cash. Meanwhile, if you could get a ticket for the main dinner theatre in the Sands, the headline act was *The Rat Pack* (Frank Sinatra, Sammy David Junior and Dean Martin).

Rehearsals resumed on the 26th. By then all the technical problems had been ironed out and a few days later an amazed audience was treated to an extraordinary experience with a spectacular finale.

During the course of the show, the "Octuramic stage" never opened up fully or moved completely downstage, but in the finale it glided menacingly towards the audience, only coming to a halt at the very front of the stage as all the arms opened and the two biggest discs, carrying exotically dressed showgirls, swung slowly out over the heads of the front few rows. It is always a good idea to give the punters a fright at the end of a show.

"Vast, opulent, beyond the imagination of Ziegfeld," ran a review in a Las Vegas magazine, *"CASINO DE PARIS is the quintessential use of theatre as physical stimulation and the reduction of thought to zero. On a fantastical apparatus called the "Octuramic" stage, created by the noted Irish designer Sean Kenny, long lines of bare-breasted girls pose endlessly in costumes a Pharoah's wife would have envied. Muscular Hungarian male acrobats cavort, a troupe of ten agile gymnast-dancers contort at breakneck speed, and the blond veteran French chanteuse, Line Renaud, croons. Periodically, the theatre explodes with sound and*

sights that would make Belasco retreat to a monastery. A discussion with the man behind it all, hotel owner Major Riddle, is like a conference with J. Paul Getty. "I have just spent $47,000 on replacing some costume jewelry and $69,000 for a load of feathers. The costumes have been flown in from Milan. It is more expensive, but it is good workmanship." The production has cost well in excess of $5 million, equal to the ten most expensive musicals in Broadway history. But in a city of money it makes sense; it makes more than sense, it makes more money."

The Control Console

Model of the set

Major Riddle and Sean Kenny

Grand Finale

1964

Shakespeare's Birthday

1964 was the 400th anniversary of Shakespeare's birth, and to celebrate the event there was a major exhibition in Stratford-upon-Avon. It took place in a temporary building on the banks of the Avon opposite the Shakespeare Memorial Theatre and was the brainchild of Richard Buckle who had devised several successful exhibitions. Art lover, biographer and ballet critic, always meticulously, if somewhat flamboyantly, dressed, and with an air about him of being well-nourished, he engaged Richard Pilbrow and me to create the major feature in the exhibition. This was an automated light and sound production in a third scale model of the Globe Theatre, to be viewed by the audience from what would have been the rear of the auditorium. Richard arranged for the walls of the model theatre to be painted gauze so that they would look solid when front-lit, but disappear when light was flooded on to the wrap-around sky cloth behind.

In a series of scenes, the voices of all the Knights and Dames of the British theatre were heard speaking their favourite purple passages, to which I added music and sound effects.

The audio programme was on a standard quarter inch tape that also had pulses to activate a big switching unit. This was pre-wired so that each time the switch stepped to the next cue, different combinations of lighting dimmers would fade up or fade down and loudspeakers hidden within the theatre set could be selected.

For the time, it was a sophisticated piece of kit, but it required a great deal of pre-planning and hours on site to set and test the various lighting states. Richard's assistant, Robert Ornbo, rigged a remote control that allowed him to quickly step through the sequences to work on a particular scene without having to run the half hour tape from the beginning. This device took the form of a push-button mounted in an old tobacco tin connected by a long piece of wire to the control room. It worked beautifully and eventually the lighting states were all successfully programmed.

Just before the Royal Gala Opening by His Royal Highness the Duke of Edinburgh, we decided to run the show one more time for luck. To our horror, the tape played but it refused to activate the switching unit. The engineer from the company that supplied the equipment, dived in with his screwdriver - but too late! We were told to stand by because the Duke's helicopter had just landed outside the building. The only thing for it was for Robert to use his remote control to activate the cues manually.

Moments later, the Duke was escorted into the theatre by a group of officials and introduced to Richard Pibrow. I started the tape and crossed my fingers. The Duke seemed to enjoy the show and, being interested in technology, asked how it all worked. Richard explained about the tape, the pulses, the switches, and the pre-set dimmers. The Duke was impressed. "So the whole thing is automated?" Richard nervously assured him that it was, praying that His Highness did not lean forward to peer over the four-foot high barrier against which they were standing. If he had done so, he would have witnessed Robert Ornbo lying on his back amongst the cables and lighting equipment, clutching a tobacco tin and sheaf of papers with scribbled lighting and sound cues.

Typically, the system worked perfectly for the remaining six month run of the exhibition. In a review of the event, one newspaper rather wickedly wrote, "It was conceived by Richard Buckle, who must be the country's leading exhibitionist!"

She Loves Me

And then there was the very great pleasure of working on the wonderful musical *She Loves Me*. With music by Jerry Bock and lyrics by Sheldon Harnick whose next venture was *Fiddler on the Roof,* it was a Forum Ventures production directed by Hal Prince. The cast included Anne Rogers, Gary Raymond, Peter Sallis and Rita Moreno.

It opened on the 29th April 1964, only six days after the opening of the Shakespeare exhibition. Consequently, there was a great deal of rushing up and down the M40 for a number of weeks.

The premiere received a tumultuous reception. Excited by what looked like a major success, a few of us gathered to celebrate in the central London flat rented by fellow director of Forum Ventures, Tony Walton. Apart from Tony, there were Richard, his wife Viki, and Julie Andrews who was married to Tony at the time. Originally, it had been hoped that Julie would take the lead in the show, but having recently completed filming *Mary Poppins*, she was now involved in shooting *The Sound Of Music*. She had won an Oscar for her performance in *Mary Poppins* and husband Tony had also received an Oscar for his costume designs.

In true Broadway style, a group of us decided to stay up late to get the reviews as soon as the papers came out. At about four in the morning, Richard and I set off for Fleet Street, which was still the home of all the major English newspapers. We went from building to building buying copies straight off the press. Rushing back to the flat, we excitedly riffled through the pages to discover that most of the reviews were, at best, luke warm. Following the standing ovation and repeated curtain calls, this came as a complete surprise, causing serious concern about the future of the show.

I have never understood why many theatre critics feel it necessary to denigrate shows that have a good story incorporating gentle humour, a touch of romance and a happy ending. They seem to feel this kind of entertainment unworthy of serious consideration, presumably not being intellectually challenging. This first came to my attention three years before when I saw a wonderful show starring Ronnie Barker called *The Fantasticks*. It was a simple, charming musical, full of invention and whimsical humour. I loved it. The London critics were totally dismissive and it closed after only 44 performances. In contrast, the Off-Broadway production ran for 17,162 performances! So somebody got it wrong.

Because of the critics, *She Loves Me,* which remains one of my favourite musicals, only had a six-month run. There was a London revival in 1994 and, once again, the critics damned it with faint praise and it did not last very long. After the show closed, it won a raft of Olivier Awards for Best Musical Revival, Best Actor, Best Actress, Best Supporting Role and Best Director. Ironically, it also won the Critics Circle Award for Best Musical!

Sammy Davis Junior Again

One afternoon later that year, Richard Pilbrow called from America. He was devising some complicated scene projection for *Golden Boy*, a new musical starring Sammy Davis Junior. The show was running in Philadelphia prior to opening on Broadway. Apparently the sound was terrible and the English director, Peter Coe, who had been responsible for *Pickwick,* was requesting that I should fly out immediately.

Bearing in mind I had only got away with the sound reinforcement on *Pickwick* by the skin of my teeth and on *She Loves Me* I was just recreating the Broadway design, I did not feel qualified to tell an American soundman how to do his job. But before I had time to think of a good reason to reject the offer, Richard informed me that the producer had arranged a first class flight for the following morning to New York, where I would be met by a chauffeur and driven to Philadelphia.

There followed a few hours of panic as I extricated myself from various commitments, packed my bags and travelled to the airport. I had never flown first class before - or since come to think of it - and the charming BOAC staff (this was prior to British Airways) felt it their duty to distribute as much free alcohol as possible. There were aperitifs before lunch, white wine with the fish, red wine with the meat, brandy with the coffee and the delightfully unexpected, "Of course, sir will take champagne with his fruit?" So although the captain announced that we were cruising at 27,000 feet, some of us were flying a great deal higher.

When the plane arrived I was poured down the gangway and, once through customs, gathered up by a gentleman in a blue blazer and peaked cap and whisked away in an enormous black limousine. This was the life!

Upon arrival at the theatre, the show was about to begin. The producer, Hillard Elkins explained that there was a new man at the sound control that night. "I fired the previous one," he continued.

"Why, what happened?"

"I think the man was deaf. We had this terrible humming noise from the loudspeakers during the rehearsal, and this idiot sitting in his box at the side of the auditorium claimed he couldn't hear it. We held up the rehearsal while he tinkered around at the back of his equipment. Everyone waiting. Then he cried out 'Is that any better?' 'No,' I shouted back, 'everybody in the theatre can hear the damn noise. What's the matter with your ears?' So he tinkered about a bit more and suddenly the hum disappeared. 'Is that any better?' he shouted. 'Yes. Thank you. Now we can get on with the rehearsal.'"

"So why did you fire him?"

"I'll tell you why I fired the creep. When the rehearsal continued, the actors were inaudible. Couldn't hear a word. So I went and put my ear to one of the loudspeakers and it was dead. Nothing. Sure there was no hum. He had switched the whole cockamamie system off!"

As I later discovered, Hillard Elkins completely lost his rag and banished the technician from the building, having failed to consider there would be no one available to control the microphones that night. It was not possible to get a replacement until the following day. So, nothing daunted, and knowing absolutely nothing about sound equipment, he announced that he would do it himself. It was at this point that director Peter Coe, in despair, requested my presence.

Mr Elkins suggested that after seeing the show, I should attend a production meeting in his hotel suite and make my report. There being no seats available, I had to stand at the back of the stalls. It was hot, I had a cracking headache, and the change of pressure when the airplane came into land had caused both my ears to block up. No matter how hard I tried to un-pop the drums, I was unable to restore them to manufacturer's specification. By the time the show ended, I was jet-lagged, badly hung-over and deaf. It was also 6 o'clock in the morning in the real world. The last thing I felt like doing was to attend a production meeting and give an account of myself.

Production meetings in England are usually low-key affairs with the producer and members of the creative team, so I was not prepared for the extraordinary scene awaiting me in Mr Elkins' sumptuous hotel suite. It was like walking into a Hollywood B movie. On one side of an enormous room, the composer Charles Strouse was seated at a piano going through the score with the musical director; in a corner, Peter Coe was sitting with his secretary reviewing his notes on the performance; on the other side of the room, flash bulbs were going off as Sammy Davis, reclining on a leather sofa with a large bourbon and coke, was being interviewed by several members of the press; and in the centre of the all this confusion was Hillard Elkins, clad in powder blue pyjamas, stretched out face-down on a medical couch having his back professionally massaged while talking on the telephone, drinking whisky and giving instructions to two secretaries seated on either side. He broke off when he saw me.

"Hi, David. What did you think of the sound? Not good, eh?"

Because of the general hubbub in the room, but mostly because of my hearing problem, I had to ask him to repeat the question. Not a good start. It was true that the amplification of the show was abysmal, but not wishing to cast any slight on the new soundman, who had only operated the show twice, I replied, "It is not the best sound I have ever heard."

"You ain't kidding! But can you fix it?"

"I am sure that improvements can be made." I assured him.

A look of concern crossed his face. This was not what he wanted to hear. He was used to hearing confident, upbeat Broadway bullshit with brash promises of impending miracles. There was a distinct pause, presumably while he considered the not inconsiderable cost of transporting this incompetent loon all the way from England. Then his face broke into a broad grin.

"Oh, I get it." he chuckled, "It's that famous British understatement!"

I shrugged my shoulders and assumed what I hoped was a confident smile.

Hillard Elkins promised that I could have any new items of equipment I needed. "Say what you want and I'll get it flown out from New York tomorrow." But all I wanted at this point was to have the stage to myself the next morning with the new sound technician in order to quietly go through the system. This was agreed and I was told to be in the theatre at ten o'clock.

What I did not appreciate was the American union situation and the fact that the soundman was one of the electrical staff. Apparently, my request to have the sound system turned on constituted a call for the entire electrical crew. It was remarkably off-putting, not to say intimidating, to wander about checking the microphones and listening to the loudspeakers while being stared at by a group of grim-faced men, presumably wondering why this foreigner – who was not in the union - had been allowed into their theatre. Heaven knows what this two-hour session was costing.

I decided that there were two main problems: inadequate coverage of the auditorium by the main loudspeakers and the fact that there were no written instructions for mixing the show. The soundman was basically winging it.

Some additional loudspeakers were shipped in the following day and I created a cue sheet by writing down which microphones should be on at any given point in the show and at what levels. All very basic stuff, but it created a better overall balance between voices and musicians and the lyrics could now be heard. After the performance that night, Mr Elkins expressed himself pleased. I had got away with it.

In conversation with Sammy Davis on my last day in Philadelphia, I explained that I had to leave for the UK the following morning as I was due to start work on a new Lionel Bart musical, *Maggie May*. He knew Lionel and asked if he could possibly record a message. This was no problem as back in the hotel room I had my trusty portable tape recorder I took everywhere in case there were sound effects to be collected. This was a big green EMI machine as used by the BBC using ¼ inch tape on 5 inch reels. We agreed to make the recording that evening in a local bar where many of the cast congregated after the show.

Come show time, when I took the tape machine into the theatre, the soundman asked if he could borrow the microphone to compare it with his American microphones. Of course, I agreed. But at the end of the performance when I made my way to the sound control to say goodbye and thank you, he had gone - and so had my microphone.

This was embarrassing, and when Sammy Davis and his entourage arrived at the bar, I had to pluck up courage to explain why I could not record his message to Lionel. Here I should point out that our star was something of an Anglophile. He was fascinated by English accents and often assumed a posh upper class voice or slipped into Cockney. I remember one of the first things he did when visiting London to appear at the Pigalle, was to order a smart three-piece suit from a Saville Row tailor and purchase a bowler hat. This explains his reaction when I approached him in the bar and confessed, "I'm very sorry, but I can't do the recording because someone pinched me bloody mike."

His reaction to the announcement was unexpected. He regarded me for a moment with a mixture of surprise and delight before repeating in a pretty good imitation of my own voice, "Pinched me bloody mike!" Then, with a hoot of laughter, he repeated "Pinched me bloody mike. I love it!" and reaching up, took my head in both his hands and kissed me roundly on the forehead. Before I had regained my composure, he continued, "Don't worry. I have a tape recorder at my hotel. Drop by in the morning before you go to the airport and we can do it then."

So ended my time in Philadelphia. I had no further connection with the show because, as things often turn out in the rough and tumble of a pre-Broadway tour, the director Peter Coe was replaced before the next date and, quite sensibly, a sound company from New York was brought in. *Golden Boy* ran for 568 performances on Broadway and Sammy Davis repeated his role for a limited run in a production at the London Palladium in 1968.

Maggie May

Because of the success of the sound on *Pickwick,* I was approached by Maurice Fournier to work on a new musical titled *Maggie May*. Maurice was the production manager for all of Bernard Delfont's productions and he was one of the great characters in West End theatre.

Set in Liverpool's docklands, the show starred Rachel Roberts and Kenneth Haigh. The book was by Alun Owen with music and lyrics by Lionel Bart. Sean Kenny was designing the scenery, so I was amongst friends. Moreover, this time I was promised a credit for sound design, although disappointingly none of the production team was featured on the poster. Still, a proper credit in the programme was not to be sniffed at.

The cast of *Maggie May* also included Barry Humphries. I had briefly come across Mr Humphries three years previously when he was playing Mr Sowerberry the undertaker in *Oliver!* The stage manager of that show had asked if I could record an Australian member of the cast who wanted to send a message back home. I still had my recording equipment in a corner of the lighting design office in Goodwins Court at that time, and when a tall young man with dank black hair hanging down below his ears arrived, I persuaded the two designers working at their drawing boards to take a coffee break. The recording did not take long and a fee of £10.00 was agreed. I did not possess a really good microphone, so I hired one when necessary. The cost of the microphone plus a small reel of tape in a smartly labelled box amounted to some £6.00. So there was little profit to cover my time. The recording along with an invoice was delivered to the stage door. Barry Humphries still owes me £10.00.

Maggie May opened in Manchester for a two week run. During this time the cast were called in most days to rehearse changes and improvements. At the end of one morning's rehearsal, the lighting designer and I were standing in the middle of the stalls beside the production desk with the director Ted Kotcheff. He was discussing some new piece of business with Rachel Roberts, which for some reason was bothering her. She tended to worry a lot and was constantly seeking reassurance.

Suddenly, I felt a presence behind me. Turning round, I found myself gazing into the familiar face of Professor Higgins. It was Rex Harrison wearing the same pork pie hat he wore on stage in *My Fair Lady* and later on in the film. At the time, he was married to our star and had just arrived in Manchester to see the show.

Completely engrossed with her problems, Rachel Roberts continued to discuss her concerns with the director until Mr Harrison, losing patience, interjected: "Do stop wittering on about your boring little musical. I am sure these gentlemen need a break. We are going to the pub. Now!" With that he shepherded us all out of the theatre and into the nearby hostelry.

Such was his presence that, although the bar was crowded and people were waiting to be served, he held up his hand and immediately attracted the attention of the barman. "Have you champagne?" he enquired, and when assured that they had, turned to us and asked, "Is everyone happy with black velvets?" "Yes. Absolutely," we answered, although I, for one, was not at all sure what this was. "Then I would be most grateful," he continued to the barman, "if you would kindly mix us five black velvets."

The very pleasant drink turned out to be equal measures of Guinness and champagne. And as the champagne bottle was still half full, we were all forced to enjoy a second round. The rehearsal that afternoon went swimmingly.

The only other time I saw Rex Harrison was back in 1958 when he was playing Professor Higgins at Drury Lane. The producers of *My Fair Lady*, H M Tennent, had several shows running in the West End including *Cat on a Hot Tin Roof* where I was employed as ASM. Tennents decided to set aside a number of tickets for the Royal Gala Preview and raffle them to the cast and stage management of all their other productions. Incredibly, I won four seats in the front row of the Royal Circle.

Tickets were like gold dust and my parents could hardly believe it when I invited them to attend this event and bring a friend.

The show had been running on Broadway for two years before Rex Harrison, Julie Andrews, Stanley Holloway and Robert Coote came to London to reprise their roles. The Broadway version continued with another cast for a further four and half years.

In those days, recordings of Broadway musicals were not allowed to be sold or played on the radio until the show opened in this country, so for most people the songs from this American blockbuster came as a glorious surprise. I had, however, been fortunate enough to attend a party some months before where the host had been to America and smuggled back a cast recording. We all sat round and listened to the LP from start to finish in rapt silence, marvelling at how the American authors, Lerner and Loewe, had created a score and lyrics that sounded so incredibly British.

Some years later, I worked with the stage manager of *My Fair Lady*, Robert Stanton, and he told me that I had witnessed one of Rex Harrison's best two performances of the entire run. The first was that Royal gala in front of the Queen. The other followed an almighty row with Stanley Holloway, a stage actor of the old school who was playing Eliza Doolittle's father. He had accused the star of unprofessional behaviour. Apparently, Rex Harrison would arrive at the theatre dressed in his Professor Higgins costume only minutes before curtain up, stroll on stage, give a 'relaxed' performance, then immediately following the curtain calls, head for the stage door where his car was waiting. The rest of the cast, as is the unbreakable rule, would be in their dressing rooms and checked by the stage management thirty minutes before "Beginners" was due to be called. The poor actor understudying Professor Higgins had to stand by every night in case the star did not make it on time.

Infuriated at being criticised by another member of the cast and told that he was giving the audience less than a hundred per cent, Rex Harrison stormed on to stage the following evening and gave a stunning performance.

Back to *Maggie May* in Manchester, there was a misunderstanding with Bernard Delfont about the new "shotgun" microphones I was experimenting with. These were placed along the front of the stage and were supposed to pick up the voices of the actors at a greater distance than conventional microphones. The main drawback was their size and shape. Projecting from the base, there was a tube about a foot (30cm) long pointing up at the stage. Maurice Fournier thought them a complete eyesore, remarking that these black objects sticking up in the air, "look like a row of donkeys' dicks."

Following the technical rehearsal before the opening, Bernard Delfont was concerned that Rachel Roberts could not be heard performing a particular number when she was high up on one of Sean Kenny's platforms. Maurice turned to me and said, "Can you position one of your donkeys' dicks up there?" "No problem," I replied.

Now Bernard Delfont, although an astute and very successful producer, was not known for his sense of humour or appreciation of irony. At the end of the rehearsal, when Miss Roberts brought up her concern about not being heard during the song we had been discussing, Delfont placed a reassuring hand on her arm and declared, "Don't worry. It's all in hand and will be sorted by tomorrow. This gentleman is going to erect one of his donkey's dicks for you." As the star, uncharacteristically bereft of speech, raised her eyebrows in astonishment, Maurice grinned broadly and gave me an enormous wink.

During the second week of the Manchester run, Sean Kenny's design assistant revealed with some amusement that there had been a bit of a boozy session in Sean's suite at the Midland Hotel the previous night. At some point the conversation turned to religion - never a good idea - and Sean decided to illustrate his feelings on the subject. Producing his big black felt pen, he sketched a row of little men and women along the lower part of one of the walls. He then drew a bearded figure at the top of the wall sitting on a cloud. To this figure he appended a large penis. Finally, he drew dotted lines from the penis right down the wall. "That," he declared, "is God pissing on all the people! That's what I think of religion." At the time he was hugely amused by his piece of artwork, but it was a different story when he woke up sober the following morning.

The next two days saw him sneaking in and out of the hotel, determined to avoid an encounter with the manager. On the third morning, he emerged furtively from the lift to find the manager standing in the middle of the foyer waiting for him. "Ah, Mr Kenny, good morning. I would be grateful if you could spare me a moment. I wanted to have a word with you about the... the mural... in your suite. You must understand that while the hotel does not wish to destroy a work of art by a famous artist such as yourself, the subject of the mural might not be appreciated by some of our guests. Therefore, I am proposing that we preserve your creation by covering it with a layer of plain wallpaper. I hope this might be agreeable to you."

"Sure," said Sean, mightily relieved.

"Although I am afraid," the manager continued ingratiatingly, "we do have to request a contribution towards the cost."

Sean, highly amused, regaled us with this story saying that he had informed the manager that he was more than happy to pay for all the costs.

The main thing I remember about the London opening of *Maggie May* in September 1964 was an incident towards the end of the show when a vital piece of scenery got stuck and we all thought that the final scene was heading for a serious train crash.

The set was typical Kenny with moving metal structures giving a feeling of ships and cranes and docks. The incident occurred when the cast, all singing lustily, had to walk up a staircase within one of these trucks as another one moved alongside. A small metal bridge was then supposed to hinge down to form a link for the actors to process across and down the stairs within the second truck. On this particular night the bridge juddered a bit but did not fall.

There was only a minute or two to go before the leading member of the cast would reach the top of the stairs and find nowhere to go. Apparently, Lady Delfont sitting in the stalls, grabbed her husband's hand and hissed, "Look. The bridge is stuck!" Delfont remained completely unruffled saying, "Don't worry. Maurice will think of something."

At that moment, Maurice Fournier sauntered onto the stage and began to work his way up the staircase in the second truck. He had thrown off his jacket and tie, grabbed a hat and a coloured neckerchief from a startled actor and now looked, for all the world, like a dockworker going about his business. Reaching the top platform, he casually untangled the wire that was holding up the bridge and lowered it by hand just in time to stand back and watch the cast pass by, all singing merrily, totally oblivious of how near they had been to a disaster. The episode was reminiscent of that moment in *Blitz!* when Tony Horder 'saved the day' by appearing as a road sweeper.

Maurice told me later that he had been summoned to Lord Delfont's office the following day, and after being congratulated on his quick thinking regarding the bridge episode, Delfont said, "I appreciate all your hard work getting this show up and running and you deserve a couple of weeks off. You've earned it. There's an envelope on the table for you. Take your wife abroad somewhere nice. Come and see me when you get back." To Maurice's surprise, the envelope contained a generous wad of cash.

The show ran for 501 performances at the Adelphi theatre and won the Novello Award for outstanding score and the Critics' Poll as best new British musical. Rachel Roberts was only contracted for the first six months. She was then replaced by Georgia Brown, who had been the leading lady in *Oliver!*. Apparently, Lionel Bart had originally written *Maggie May* with her in mind.

During that year, we created the sound for two RSC productions at the Aldwych Theatre. The first was *Hamlet* featuring a wonderfully compelling performance by David Warner. In his autobiography, Peter Hall stated his belief that this performance defined the play for a decade.

Sir Peter Hall
Photograph by James Hamilton

After that, we were involved in a Christmas show, *The Thwarting of Baron Bolligrew*, an extraordinary piece by Robert Bolt largely concerned with knights of old venturing out to fight dragons of assorted sizes and colours, each with its own particular sound, of course. Sadly for me, this amusing piece was the last time I worked on a show with Peter Hall. We continued to record music for the RSC and supply sound effects, but the RSC now had its own sound department.

1965

Becoming A Guru

The economy of the UK had recovered during the twenty years or so since the end of the Second World War, and a wave of civic and university theatres was being planned and built across Great Britain. Many of these were designed by architects with no experience or particular interest in the theatre. Consequently, there were too many examples of bad audience sightlines, no way of getting scenery onto the stage, inadequate wing space, actors' dressing rooms without mirrors, lighting or daylight, and woefully inadequate technical facilities.

A few architects aware of Richard Pilbrow's reputation sought his advice on where to put the lights and, with his practical experience and general knowledge of theatre, he was soon advising on all aspects of theatre design. I was brought in to specify the sound and communication systems and thus became known as a Sound Consultant.

Four years earlier, Richard had co-founded the ABTT (Association of British Theatre Technicians), an organisation whose purpose was to produce guidelines for the building of new theatres and generally raise technical standards. I had been co-opted onto the sound committee and we had issued a number of publications.

Now, to my horror, the chairman proposed that the committee should give a lecture to an invited audience with each of us speaking on our particular subject. Appearing in front of an audience was my worst nightmare.

Following serious dissertations on the use of microphones, types of loudspeakers, standardisation of wiring and connectors, and the future use of wireless microphones, by way of relief I was to end the session with a demonstration of my dexterity cueing discs with four turntables. Also, because people seemed terribly worried about these new-fangled tape machines, I was to show how easy it was to cope if a join in the tape came apart in the middle of a performance. I cannot recall this ever happening in a show, but for some reason this was a genuine concern at the time.

Somehow, I survived the ordeal and a year or two later when the chairman resigned, I was elected to replace him. We continued issuing pamphlets and many of our recommendations, including my design for the layout of a stage manager control desk, are still broadly followed more than half a century later. I also wrote articles in The Stage newspaper and other theatre publications about the desirability of having sound control rooms in new theatres and why operating sound should be recognised as a specific job. Many people thought this was all codswallop, but the message was gradually being accepted.

The Horrors Of Twang!

Not only did I try to avoid speaking in public, but I also had to steel myself to make phone calls to directors and producers in order to tout for work. Fortunately, this was not often necessary as they usually contacted us first. A typical example was the unexpected phone call from Maurice Fournier inviting me to work on yet another Lionel Bart musical, the third in as many years. He explained that this was a spoof on the Robin Hood story to be directed by the legendary Joan Littlewood. Lionel had previously worked with her at the Theatre Royal Stratford East composing the music and lyrics for various productions including *Fings Ain't What They Used To Be*. It was to star Barbara Windsor as Maid Marion and James Booth as Robin Hood, both of whom had worked at Stratford East. The show also featured Ronnie Corbett as Will Scarlett. This all sounded like great fun.

The musical was entitled *Twang!* and we were to create the sound effects, the most important of which was the really juicey 'twang' of an arrow to start the show. *Twang!* was to have a two-week try-out in Manchester where they had their own system for amplifying the voices, but I was to specify the sound system when it came to the West End.

My memory of Joan Littlewood is of a slightly unkempt dumpy figure in a dark skirt and thick stockings, with short straggly dark hair at all times partially covered by a black or navy-blue cap. During the weeks of rehearsals in London, I tried in vain to get her to discuss the effects, but she kept putting me off, saying that it was "too soon to worry about that".

Disturbing rumours were issuing from the rehearsal room. One of the cast described what happened on the first day of rehearsal when they were all expecting a read-through, the usual start of the rehearsal process. Miss Littlewood asked, "Have you all got your scripts?" They all answered in the affirmative.

"Right," she continued, "hold them in your right hands and when I say 'go', I want you to throw them backwards over your heads on to the floor. Ready? Go!"

This they all dutifully did. After all, she was the director.

"That," she declared, "is the last time we shall look at those."

Joan Littlewood's reputation was founded upon her ensemble work with a group of actors in the slightly seedy Theatre Royal Stratford East on the outskirts of London. Productions were based upon an idea with weeks of experimenting and improvising until Miss Littlewood decided that they had created a satisfactory piece of theatre. It was all extremely low budget. The actors worked for barely subsistence wages, some of them actually having to live in the dressing rooms. So if a production failed, the financial loss was not significant.

Although it was all a bit hit and miss, once in a while the talent she had gathered around her would come up with the goods. The musicals *Fings Ain't Wot They Used T'Be* and *Oh, What a Lovely War* were picked up by West End producers and later made into films. The Theatre Royal Stratford, and presumably Miss Littlewood herself as the director, would have done extremely well out of these. There was a story going round, possibly apocryphal, that during the rehearsals for one of these West End transfers, while pleading for more funding for the arts and bemoaning the fact that her poor gifted actors were forced to exist on breadcrumbs, she was staying at the Savoy Hotel.

Incredibly, she was now approaching *Twang!* as if it was one of her theatrical experiments rather than a major West End musical with an enormous budget. Perhaps that was the only way she knew how to work. But it was the script, combined with the name of Lionel Bart, that had persuaded Delfont to mount the production and it was why the theatrical 'angels' had agreed to invest their money. Disaster loomed!

Towards the end of the rehearsal period I telephoned Maurice Fournier to explain how I had failed to receive any information whatsoever from the director. "Therefore," I continued," I have made up a tape with what I deem to be all the relevant effects and will send it up with our sound operator. As I am not involved in the microphone system, there seems little point in paying me to go to Manchester just to hang around." Maurice's reply was, "Oh, no. You don't get away with it that easily. I want you up there in Manchester. You are going to suffer with the rest of us."

I can hardly describe the chaos of the technical rehearsal in Manchester when the cast was faced with the scenery for the first time. They did not know their lines and nobody seemed to have a clue where or when they were entering or exiting. It was as though they were just starting to rehearse the piece rather than it being two days before the opening night. Miss Littlewood showed no sense of urgency, holding long discussions with members of the cast before running little scenes, then changing her mind, going back and running things again. Oliver Messel's beautiful sets seemed to come to her as a complete surprise. At one point, she decided that an actor would look good standing on a rostrum, so she simply used a piece of staging from another scene. She continued, on a whim, to take other items, including complete backcloths, from one set and mix them with items from another with total disregard for the visual mayhem she was creating.

All this resulted in even more confusion for the actors and the backstage staff. The poor lighting designer had no idea what he was supposed to be lighting from one moment to the next. So much time was wasted that we never had a proper run-through of the whole show before the opening night. Everyone involved was going to have to wing it.

I had given up worrying about my contribution. I had the important opening effect of the twang of a bowstring behind the audience with the swish of an arrow across the auditorium to be heard at the end of the overture. After that, I made my own selection of noises and the sound operator played them in when seemed appropriate.

At one point during the first public performance I went out front, but could not bear to watch the cast struggling against such impossible odds, missing their lines and floundering about the stage. The appalled audience failed to laugh at the feeble jokes and could hardly bring themselves to applaud at the end of musical numbers. It was all too embarrassing. I retired to the bar.

In the interval I went backstage and was standing near the prompt corner when a wild-eyed Lionel Bart crashed through the pass door from the auditorium. He spied me, grabbed me by the jacket lapels and hauled me into a nearby prop room. Still holding my lapels, he screamed into my face, "What the hell do you think you are doing? The audience cannot hear a word of my songs. You've completely ruined the show! What are you going to do about it? The sound system is a disgrace!"

As soon as he paused for breath, I replied as calmly as I could, "Yes, I agree with you. The sound system is not good." He opened his mouth but was for a moment lost for words, so I quickly continued, "I'm afraid it's entirely out of my hands. The management decided to use the theatre's own sound installation. I have only been asked to provide the sound effects in Manchester, but I will be designing a system for London."

He released his grip on my jacket and apologised. "I'm sorry, Dave. I didn't realise. Is there anything we can do?" All I could suggest was that the musical director was asked to keep the orchestra in check during the songs.

The reviews in the local press next morning were disastrous and a totally dispirited cast spent the day rehearsing in a vain attempt to rescue what the Americans would call a "turkey". Sound effects were the least of their problems, so I was surprised when at the end of that night's performance, the company manager said that Joan Littlewood had requested a meeting on stage at ten o'clock the following morning to discuss the effects before a full company call at eleven.

At this memorable meeting, Miss Littlewood was solely concerned with the off-stage sound of horses arriving at a gallop. She refused to listen to the recorded examples I had painstakingly put together, insisting that the effect should be "live". Members of the stage management were instructed to collect pieces of chain and bits of wood. She then had them prancing around the back of the set, jingling the chain, knocking the bits of wood together, and making occasional snorting noises. When the long-suffering company manager pointed out the futility of this exercise because the stage management would be busy elsewhere during the performance, she brushed this detail aside and spent the next half hour directing them into the art of feeling what it was like to be a horse. None of the other sound effects called for in the show were discussed before the cast began to congregate on stage. This completely pointless charade confirmed my growing conviction that our director was completely off her rocker.

I noticed that the producer Bernard Delfont and the entire production team had also arrived and were lurking in the stalls as Joan Littlewood gathered the actors about her. She then made a very brief speech informing the dumfounded assembly that it was impossible to work for "these commercial managements who were only interested in making money." And because they stifled any form of artistic creation, this is was why she had resigned. With that, she thanked the cast for their hard work and left the stage, never to be seen again.

Bernard Delfont then stepped forward and told the stunned cast that he was arranging for a new director and scriptwriter and that an improved and fantastic show would definitely open in London.

I did not have such faith that this disaster could be turned into a success. I envisaged having to install a big sound system in a London theatre only to take it out again a few weeks later. The rental charge for such a short period would nowhere near cover the costs. I was yet to be contracted for the London production so I informed an unhappy Maurice Fournier that we would not be available. It is always a risk letting down an important client but as it turned out, I need not have worried.

The new director, Burt Shevelove who was co-writer with Larry Gelbart of *A Funny Thing Happened on the Way to the Forum* did his best during the following days, but Delfont finally decided that the show was not good enough to bring in to the West End.

I had escaped from the horrors of *Twang!* but by an extraordinary twist of fate, Richard Pilbrow became involved. Burt Shevelove asked him to take over the production. Having travelled to Manchester and seen the show, Richard did his very best to persuade Lionel Bart that the show was so bad it should close. Lionel did not agree. Such was his faith in the musical that when Delfont and his investors pulled out, he signed over the rights to all his past and future works including *Oliver!* to United Artists who then agreed to back the show.

United Artists was not in the business of producing stage shows, so mainly because Burt Shevelove was a friend, Richard agreed to help by providing a general management service - anonymously.

It was later reported that this deal cost Lionel £100m in lost royalties from his musicals and catalogue of pop songs but, of course, it made a fortune for United Artists.

The show opened at the Shaftesbury Theatre to universally awful reviews and closed after five weeks. Lionel Bart declared himself bankrupt.

Tragically, this whole sorry enterprise had the effect of stifling his incredible talent. Reduced to living in a seedy flat in Acton, overcome by depression, he turned to alcohol and substance abuse that lasted for some twenty years before he managed to get himself straight.

Sir Donald Wolfit

During the rest of 1965 we remained busy creating sound effects for West End shows and for repertory companies and amateur groups around the country. Many of our customers still required 78 r.p.m. lacquer discs, which were cut for us by a specialist studio.

One of the West End productions was *Dear Wormwood*, a play written by James Forsythe based on the novel *The Screwtape Letters* by C.S. Lewis. It was particularly notable for featuring the last of the great actor-managers, Sir Donald Wolfit, in his final appearance on the London stage.

Throughout his long career, Wolfit was both acclaimed as one of the greatest actors on the British stage, and simply dismissed as a terrible ham. Kenneth Tynan, when a critic on The Observer newspaper wrote, *"There has never been an actor of greater gusto than Donald Wolfit. He has dynamism, energy, bulk and stature, and he joins these together with a sheer relish for resonant words, which splits small theatres as wine glasses."*

The playwright Ronald Harwood worked with him for several years, becoming a good friend. In his biography of Wolfit he wrote: "I have never encountered anyone with Wolfit's size of personality, or anyone more unashamedly individual. I remember well the awe in which I first held him, the terror I experienced in his presence, both on and off the stage." Later, Ronald Harwood was to write *The Dresser*, a play based upon his experiences with the great man.

My colleague Tony Horder created all the sound effects for *Dear Wormwood* and was directly involved with the production. He recalls an extraordinary incident early in rehearsals concerning the leading lady, American actress Yolande Donlan. One morning Wolfit marched into the rehearsal room and stunned everyone by addressing Yolande in a loud voice, "Ida and I were discussing you in bed last night and we came to the conclusion that you are evil!"

After that outburst, never explained, in all the scenes they played together, they never made eye contact. Yolande would say her lines looking steadfastly into the distance over his shoulder.

During the out of town opening in Brighton, one scene turned out to be a wonderful cock-up. Wolfit, whose character was the devil, was sitting on the edge of the stage anchored by a long tail that disappeared into the orchestra pit. There was the sound of a convoy of lorries from offstage which the audience had been informed were laden with inflammable materials. Wolfit was supposed to take a flaming arrow, conveniently placed for him in the orchestra pit, and fire it towards the lorries. There would then be a dramatic lighting effect of flames from where the convoy was supposed to be, followed by a loud explosion.

Unfortunately, in spite of pleading and threatening, Tony never persuaded the director to have a straight run-through of this particular scene. Consequently, he was not able to accurately time the lorry effect and explosion that were on the same tape.

On the first performance, when the moment came, Wolfit reached down into the orchestra pit, produced the arrow, but the flame mechanism did not work. Nevertheless, he fitted the arrow to his bow and made as if to fire. Unfortunately, the arrow fell off the bow and disappeared back down into the pit. Despite what everyone had seen, Wolfit claimed loudly to have succeeded in setting fire to the lorries. This, despite the fact that the stage manager had not cued the offstage fire effect At this point, the girl operating the tape deck realised that there was too much lorry noise and she needed to get to the explosion. Panicking, she stopped the tape so that the convoy sound ended abruptly, ran on to the explosion, turned up the volume, played the cue - far too loud, practically bursting the loudspeaker - panicked again, grabbed the volume, turned it down - too far - completely cutting off the explosion in its prime. Silence!

Tony, witnessing this carnage from the back of the circle, set off at a pace towards the auditorium box where the sound equipment and the distraught sound operator were located. But the moment he left the circle, the funny side of this fiasco suddenly hit him and he sat down on the stairs and began to laugh. Seconds later, a concerned lighting designer emerged from the auditorium and not knowing how long Tony had been sitting there, announced the shocking news: "They missed a sound cue!" This set Tony off again and, between fits of giggles, he explained to his concerned colleague exactly what had happened - or rather had not happened. By the time he finished the sorry tale, both of them had tears rolling down their cheeks. The play, according to Tony, never again achieved that level of entertainment.

Around this time, Richard Pilbrow set up a trust to run a stage management course at LAMDA (London Academy of Music and

Dramatic Art).   The teaching of technical theatre in the major drama schools was, at best, patchy. His idea was that the student should be in contact with people who were actually working in the theatre, rather than professional teachers who might, or might not, have had much practical experience. Robert Stanton, the veteran stage and company manager of many West End shows including *My Fair Lady,* was persuaded to run the course.

Along with some of the Theatre Projects lighting designers (there was a growing team of creative talent in-house), I was persuaded, against my better judgement, to give a series of lectures and demonstrations on every aspect of sound to an audience of eager 18 - 20 year olds, all thirsty for knowledge. Although still only 28, I had a growing reputation as a sound designer and, not unreasonably, everyone assumed that I must be some kind of electronics genius; whereas, any skill I might possess, apart from being blessed with a pretty good ear, was in knowing how to use the equipment. To me, this was like being an excellent driver without fully understanding the working of the engine. People often asked me if I could sort out a problem with their hi-fi system or explain the working of some piece of electronics and when I said that I had no idea, they imagined that I must be joking.

Presenting myself in front of a group of students was a frightening prospect. Inevitably, within the group there would be lurking a dangerous nerd, determined to catch me out. What if some Smart Alec asked for a detailed explanation of "impedance" or required a description of "Ohms Law"? I discussed this dilemma with my friend Tony Horder and he suggested that we should work as a double act. Between us, we could bamboozle them. If one of us was talking on a particular subject and a student interjected with a difficult question, the other would chip in and say something like, "That's very interesting. I'm not sure we want to go into that now, but it does remind me that we have not talked about...." and then go on to some other subject.

Tony was very convincing and I *think* we got away with it. After two years of lecturing, we had confidence enough in this technique that one or other of us was able to give a solo performance.

1966

On the Level

Two musicals came our way in 1966. The first was called *On The Level*, directed by the wonderful Wendy Toye and starring Leslie Phillips. With a score composed by Ron Grainer, the story centred around the GCE (General Certificate of Education) 'O' and 'A' levels. The production called for a number of electronic musical effects and Ron Grainer turned to the BBC Radiophonic Workshop and Delia Derbyshire, who had created the electronic arrangement of his theme music for *Doctor Who*.

The tape arrived for a rehearsal in the theatre, but there were several hold-ups when I had to get out my razor blade and editing block. Perhaps a music cue was in the wrong place and had to be cut out and spliced into another part of the tape, or a cue had to be edited because it was too long. Soon, discarded sections of tape were littering the floor. Wendy Toye decided that one of the sections I had edited was too short. Could I reinstate it? Unfortunately not. I would have to go back to Delia and request a copy.

The following morning, I phoned Delia and explained that we needed a copy of one of the items from the master tape. Her reply was:

"But you have the master tape. I gave it to you."

"What?"

Delia was not a theatre person, nor had she even worked in a commercial recording studio, or she would never have let a master tape out of her hands. Clients always went away with a copy. It must have taken many hours, if not days, working with Ron Grainer to produce all these extraordinary sounds. Fortunately, we were able to recreate the missing item by painfully identifying similar musical phrases in different parts of the tape and piecing them together.

On The Level played at the Saville Theatre for 136 performances.

The only other musical show that year, *Ad-Lib*, featured the world-famous harmonica virtuoso, Larry Adler, and singer Libby Morris. When Mr Adler came into our studio, I remember asking if he had ever recorded a duet with another harmonica player. His modest reply was, "Not possible. There's no-one good enough." Of course, he had played alongside people like Duke Ellington, Benny Goodman and George Gershwin, and pieces had been specially composed for him by Malcolm Arnold, Arthur Benjamin and Vaughan Williams; so he probably was in a class of his own.

He always carried a harmonica in the top pocket of his jacket and, given the slightest excuse, would produce it and play a few bars. I took it for granted that he would have a favourite very special valuable harmonica. But apparently not. There is no equivalent of the Stradivarius. When a reed fails in the instrument, it is useless. The German company Hohner simply kept sending him replacements.

Madame Tussauds

During the 1960s, a new managing director at Madame Tussauds was determined to upgrade the presentation of waxwork figures by providing theatrical elements to the static displays. Up until then, there had been little attempt at any form of atmospheric lighting. The figures just stood there silently in the blandly lit galleries. That is, with one exception; an elderly uniformed attendant was standing halfway up the main staircase who many people, including me, thought was real until they were up close - a nice touch - only every few minutes, rather alarmingly, the eyes would move. It was amusing to witness visitors, convinced that this was a dummy, suddenly gasp or cry out. I was told that it was a model of a former member of staff, a difficult gentleman generally unpopular with his colleagues. Upon his retirement some wag had decided that he should continue to haunt the building and he was thus immortalised in wax.

The swivelling eyes of our curmudgeonly friend was the one small attempt at automation since Madame Tussaud opened her exhibition in Baker Street in 1835. This was to change over the next few years.

Enticed away from his job as technical director for the English National Opera Company, James Sargant became the production manager at Tussauds. Apart from improving the lighting and the general look of the exhibition, major innovations were planned in the form of animated settings for different groups of waxwork figures. To create these, James brought in theatre scene designers and Theatre Projects was engaged to provide atmospheric lighting, sound and music.

The first of these events was based on The Battle of Trafalgar. In a separate section of the building, the public would walk through a faithful reconstruction of the lower gun deck of HMS Victory. In this, we recreated what it might have been like at the height of the battle with four full-size cannon and sculpted figures of men in action. Below, in the Orlop deck, surgeons were attending to the wounded around the famous scene of Admiral Nelson on his deathbed.

Determined to make the sounds as realistic and authentic as possible, an approach was made to HMS Victory, a major tourist attraction in the Naval Dockyard at Portsmouth. This produced an enthusiastic response from the Captain, Lieutenant Commander Dick Whittington. When we asked for details of the correct gun orders for the period, he offered to assemble a gun crew of naval ratings and re-enact the whole sequence on board the actual ship. We were able to record the rumbling of the wheels on the deck as the massive cannon was "run out" and heavy thumps and crashes as the cannon was moved when the gun captain ordered the men to "take aim" and "train right" or "train left", accomplished by shoving wooden poles under the sides of the carriage and hoicking the entire leviathan one way or the other.

Lieutenant Commander Whittington could not actually fire a gun on board the ship, but he put in a request for the Royal Navy Gunnery School to fire one of Victory's cannon on the quayside beside the ship. Once persuaded, they entered into the enterprise with gusto, to the extent of providing a drummer to "Beat to Quarters" before carrying out the correct loading, aiming and firing procedure. There was a bugler to sound "Cease Fire" after the explosion, and they had even gone to the trouble of fabricating papier-mâché cannon balls.

The gun was fired several times, ostensibly for our benefit although it was obvious that the naval personnel were thoroughly enjoying this unique opportunity, probably the last, to see one of Victory's guns in action. Although only a one-eighth charge was used, the noise was deafening even in the open air. Heaven knows what it would have been like in the cramped condition of a gun deck during a full broadside.

Firing one of the cannons beside HMS Victory for the recording

We now had the recording of Lieutenant Commander Whittington shouting out the orders with his crew responding, but the tableau had four guns. We needed a lot more voices, but with no budget to engage professional actors, we invited twenty or so male employees of Theatre Projects to the studio one evening and plied them with quantities of cheap red wine. When everyone was sufficiently inebriated, I circulated with a hand microphone and gave each person a word or a phrase to yell at the top of his voice. I then exhorted every individual to scream or cry out as though they had been hit by a musket ball or lost a limb by a piece of flying timber. They all entered into the exercise with gusto, and much uncalled-for laughter, but after several hours of work with a tape splicing block and razor blade - the result sounded incredibly convincing.

For the tableau at Madame Tussauds, we created a four-minute battle sequence that ended with a bugle call and cries of "Cease fire" followed by a few quiet moments with just the sound of the sea and timbers creaking. It then all started again with the drum beating to quarters, a cacophony of voices as the gun captains along the deck yelled "Run out the gun", continuing with the loading and aiming sequences until the first gun was fired, followed by another, then another, then another. We had learned that they never fired all the guns at the same time because the amount of metal ejected from the barrels in a broadside - equal to the weight of a London double-decker bus - would have tipped the ship over.

Richard Pilbrow's dramatic lighting effects included bright flashes of light and even smoke belching from the barrels when the cannons roared. Through the portholes, the horizon could be seen swaying to give the impression of a ship at sea, and to add to the atmosphere, a specialist company produced the smell of tar and cordite.

As this was before the days of multi-track recording, all the sounds heard from an array of loudspeakers hidden within the tableau were played from a bank of domestic tape decks. These were synchronized with the lighting by a control system invented by some geniuses we discovered working out of a couple of rooms in a house in Greenwich. This two-year old company, Electrosonic, later grew into an international organisation creating some of the world's most prestigious audio-visual installations. Multi-media technology was pretty new at the time and *The Battle of Trafalgar - As It Happened* (the official title) was the first exhibition to use lighting, sound, smoke and smell. It remained a popular attraction for twenty-four years.

"The Battle of Trafalgar - As it Happened" Madame Tussauds 1966
Section of the lower gun deck of HMS Victory

The First Lord of the Admiralty, no less, made a speech and cut the ribbon at the glittering launch party. It was well attended by the media whose reports were universally glowing.

I was button-holed by a man from BBC radio who asked if he could visit our studio to discuss how the complicated sound track was put together. He arrived early one afternoon with his portable tape machine and began by asking how we fabricated the ship's creaking timbers, I explained that it was a creaky chair played back at half speed, just as a squeaking door at half speed sounded like ropes stretching under tension. He stopped the recording and asked if I could play him the actual effects so that he could record them. This stop-start process continued with several other sounds. One of the more complicated montages was of an enemy cannon ball crashing through the side of the ship. This began with a sharp crack and splintering of wood recorded in the studio (again slowed down), then the sound of a crate filled with heavy weights being dragged rapidly along a concrete floor, followed by a series of crashes and thumps. The final composite effect, lasting about three seconds, gave the impression of a heavy lump of metal bursting through the wooden side of the ship and crashing along the deck. Adding a few shouts and screams completed the picture.

After some two hours of recording, he declared that there was sufficient material for a good spot in the BBC News Roundup programme. I offered to splice together all the sections of dialogue and noises we had recorded, but he said that there was no time for that. He had to get back to Broadcasting House. It was now four o'clock and the programme started at five. "But surely the piece is not going out tonight!" I was appalled at the thought. "Absolutely. I will start editing in the taxi and finish it when I get to the studio. Don't worry. This is normal pressure for me. Tune in and, hopefully, there will be no mistakes. Must dash." He must have had thirty or forty edits to complete, but *"How they made the sound of the Battle of Trafalgar"* was broadcast to the nation at around five thirty that evening.

Trafalgar inspired Richard Pilbrow to come up with a concept for a musical. It would depict the romantic love story of Nelson and Emma Hamilton set against the drama and spectacle of great sea battles.

Richard put the idea to Jerry Boch and Sheldon Harnick knowing their talent for evoking different periods and cultures, as exemplified by *Fiorello, She Loves Me,* and their current Broadway success *Fiddler on the Roof*. He could hardly believe it when they both agreed to come on board. The playwright, John Arden, also agreed to join the team and everybody got to work.

Jerry Boch spent some weeks in London researching music of the period and before long he had written a number of songs to Sheldon's lyrics. John Arden was working away on the script at his home in Ireland, so to give him a flavour of what they were doing, a recording was suggested. Richard had a piano in his house, so I turned up with my tape recorder. Jerry played and sang eleven songs and they were amazing; memorable tunes and clever lyrics with an unmistakable ring of eighteenth century England. This, I thought, was something special.

Then, partly because of the Vietnam War that was raging at the time, the whole project began to fall apart. The very left-wing John Arden became increasingly anti-American and although Jerry and Sheldon were against the war, even to the extent of joining in the Washington protests at weekends, the atmosphere between the English and American collaborators deteriorated until they agreed to part company. After all their work, what I imagined was going to be a great musical was not going to happen.

John Arden continued to write a play about what he now called "the warmonger Nelson" in which our naval hero was portrayed as a complete buffoon. Called *A Hero Rises Up*, it was produced at the Roundhouse in London. Out of interest, I attended a performance. It was one of my worst evenings in the theatre and I am glad to say it had a very short run.

1967

Heroes Live

Following the success of *The Battle of Trafalgar - As It Happened*, we embarked upon a new project for Madame Tussauds called *Heroes Live*. This was a celebration of some of our living heroes, each with their own settings, lighting and sound. Initially included were people like Frank Sinatra, Cassius Clay (Mohammed Ali), Richard Burton and Elizabeth Taylor, El Cordobes (the famous bull-fighter), Rudolph Nureyev and television personality Malcolm Muggeridge.

There was a bathroom scene where, with the screeching violins from the film *Psycho,* the shower curtain gradually opened to reveal the portly figure of Alfred Hitchcock.

The very young model Twiggy was seen in a photographic studio with her image in various poses projected on to a large screen. The designer of *Heroes Live* suggested that the tableau should include a short movie film of Twiggy out in the street, but the idea was quashed when her hairdresser boyfriend Nigel Davies, now her manager and calling himself Justin de Villeneuve, stepped in and started talking money. There was nothing in the budget for this and the designer said how disappointed he was because he had also wanted to include Justin in the film. Suddenly, "Twigs" became available.

A few years later, there was another brush with the famous model and her manager when she came to our studio to record a song from *The Boyfriend.* Ken Russell was about to direct the film version of the musical and wanted to see if Twiggy could sing before casting her in the lead. She had not sung professionally before and had difficulty maintaining the high soprano cut-glass voice required for the part. She kept veering off-key and collapsing into giggles. People peering at her from behind the glass were off-putting, so we had to switch off the lights in the control booth and work in the dark. Eventually, a sufficient number of stop-start takes were recorded of "I Could Be Happy With You" to piece together the best bits. To our surprise, she did get the starring role in the film. From this shaky start in our studio, she later went on to appear on stage in musicals and concerts, and recorded a number of albums.

The intention with *Heroes Live* was to keep it up to date. For example, when Russia invaded Czechoslovakia in 1968 and arrested the Communist leader Alexandre Dubcek, within days a tableau with Dubcek was installed. A few months later, to celebrate the first manned moon landing, we had the figures of Neil Armstrong and Buzz Aldrin standing beside the lunar module.

Another hero added to the exhibition was Robert F. Kennedy, brother of the late John F. Kennedy and hotly tipped to be the next president. His figure was standing behind a cluster of microphones on a podium with a projection of waving flags and cheering crowds. Early one morning, James Sargant telephoned me at home to say that he had just heard on the news that Kennedy had been shot shortly after winning the presidential primaries in Los Angeles and was in a critical condition in hospital.

It was not clear whether Kennedy was going to survive or not but it was obviously inappropriate to have the tableau continue with his voice and the video projection of cheering crowds. I drove to Madame Tussauds as speedily as possible and we turned off the projector and the sound. James suggested that our lighting designer and I should be at the exhibition before opening time the next day to make further adjustments.

As part of the *Heroes Live* ethos of being up to date, there was a teleprinter in the exhibition constantly typing out world news from the international news agency Reuters. It so happened that at around nine o'clock the following morning we were standing beside this machine discussing what we should do with the lighting and sound, when it suddenly burst into life and typed out the message: **"Senator Robert Francis Kennedy died at 1:44 a.m. Pacific Daylight Time this morning - June 6, 1968."**

For a moment, we just stood there stunned, not knowing what to say; but something had to be done quickly before the public arrived. It was not possible to remove the tableau as waxwork figures are extremely heavy and with the scenery and all the electronic paraphernalia, it would take the staff at least two hours. All we could do in the time available was reduce the lighting to a single static spotlight. Meanwhile, James disappeared to return a few minutes later with a black wreath that Madame Tussauds always had standing by for this kind of eventuality. The wreath was placed in front of the tableau.

On a much lighter note, in another part of Madame Tussauds was an area called "Swinging London" featuring figures from the world of fashion and pop music. Every few weeks I had to update the background music with the latest chart hits. One of the great perks I was able to enjoy was the addition of all these great discs to my personal record collection.

During the years we worked for Madame Tussauds, which included an exhibition on The Battle of Britain, I was asked to provide some atmospheric sound for the famous Chamber of Horrors. I decided that this should be spooky music and I asked Guy Woolfenden from the Royal Shakespeare Company to compose something suitable. The Chamber of Horrors was a large dimly lit gallery peopled mostly by murderers from days gone by, right up to the last miscreant to be hanged the UK. These characters were the "horrors" that gave the chamber its name.

There is a story that, as a publicity stunt, a financial reward was offered to anyone who had the nerve to spend the night alone in the chamber.

Whether or not this is a myth I do not know, but if true, I would certainly be in the running for the prize. The sound control equipment was positioned in a pit below the scaffold where some poor soul with a rope around his neck was waiting for the drop. I had to spend some hours sorting out the tapes and adjusting the volume levels for the loudspeakers distributed around the gallery, and this work had to be carried out at night when the exhibition was closed. I was totally on my own apart from a night watchman in some distant part of the building. All the main lights were switched off and I was working in this large space with just a single 100 watt bulb hanging on a hook beneath the scaffold. Being surrounded by all those villains, standing and staring in the shadows was unnerving. Occasionally, out of the corner of my eye, I was convinced that one or other would occasionally shift their weight from one leg to the other.

Fiddler On The Roof

Although my sound company remained in Neals Yard along with the Theatre Projects lighting hire department, Richard Pilbrow now took on the lease of a large four-story building in Long Acre and moved the offices from the cute little houses in Goodwins Court. We all thought he was mad. The office staff moved in and although they spread themselves out, it was still half empty. But Richard had big plans, and within a year, the place was bursting at the seams.

One of the first projects to take place in the new office was another co-production with Hal Prince. *Fiddler On The Roof* was a big hit on Broadway and was to prove an equally major success in this country.

Originally directed and choreographed by Jerome Robbins, the show was rehearsed in London by his assistant. It all went very well and the first public previews were received with enthusiasm. I had arranged to hire a standard sound system with just the five microphones along the front of the stage, and nobody complained they could not hear! Producers and cast were smugly confident that they were on to a winner. Then Mr Robbins flew in.

As the first act came to a close, Robbins turned to Richard Pilbrow and said grimly, "Richard, full company, orchestra, dress rehearsal, ten o'clock tomorrow."

The actors were dumfounded. With the fantastic audience reaction every night, they were expecting congratulations and perhaps a few notes; not a call for a full rehearsal.

The following day, Robbins went through the entire show, constantly stopping to challenge the actors to explain what they thought they were doing or saying at that particular moment.

"Why are you waving your arms in the air?" he asked one member of the chorus.

"Because on the third bar, we all raise our arms…"

"Nonsense, boy! You're worshipping your God. This is not choreography! It's because you cannot avoid raising your arms to worship Him".

When he was working with the three daughters who were sweeping the floor during the song "Matchmaker", he barked at them, "What are you doing with those brooms?" Puzzled, they answered that they were carrying out the movements they had been given.

"Wrong answer. You are supposed to be sweeping the floor. Put some energy into it"

He then made them sweep the stage properly, pointing out bits of dust they had missed, before returning to the number. The difference was fantastic. His final note to the cast was, "If you don't believe in what you are saying or doing, you might as well leave the stage. Truth! Truth!

Truth!"

That night, an exhausted but inspired company gave a totally transformed performance. The music, the words, the moves were the same but the whole show had an extra spark. From the lead actors through to the lowliest members of the chorus, everyone gave 10% more. After the opening night, without exception, the press raved about the show.

One of my other memories of Jerome Robbins was at a lunch with Richard Pilbrow and his wife Viki. Robbins, insisting on paying for the meal, produced a leather wallet that opened to reveal a string of ten or twelve different credit cards. I think that Richard did own an American Express card because of his visits to the States, but it would be many years before they were in general use in Britain.

Casting the leading role in *Fiddler* is an unusual story. When they were searching for the right person to play the part, Richard Pilbrow was told of an Israeli film featuring an old actor who might be of interest. A copy of the film was obtained and everyone was impressed with this grey-haired man's strong voice and powerful presence on the screen. The actor's agent was contacted and the elderly performer was invited to travel from his home in Israel to London during the week they were holding auditions at the Theatre Royal Drury Lane.

Richard was sitting in the stalls with his wife Viki and the authors, Jerry Boch and Sheldon Harnick, seeing a number of possible actors when a strapping young man with black hair was ushered into the auditorium and introduced to them as Chaim (pronounced 'Hyam') Topol. This was not what they had expected. Even worse, the young man seemed to have little grasp of the English language.

Richard's immediate reaction was that they had just wasted a lot of money paying for an expensive airfare from Tel Aviv. But the man had taken the trouble to travel all this way, so they asked him to go on stage and sing something. He chose to perform the opening number from *Fiddler*, "Tradition" and it would be an understatement to say that he knocked their socks off. At the conclusion of this rendition, they all rushed up to the stage to congratulate him. Was he willing to take a rapid course in English? Would he like to play the part in London? Would he like to come to lunch?

As Topol was completely unknown outside Israel, Richard decided to keep it that way and gamble on him being a surprise sensation on the first night. There was to be no advance publicity. He also had the idea of dropping the name Chaim, and just letting him be known as Topol.

Some weeks later, when rehearsals were about to begin, Richard and Viki held a party at their house with Topol as the honoured guest. When I first saw him, I could not comprehend how this charming rather shy man who smiled a lot but still had trouble speaking English, could possibly have the dynamic stage presence Richard talked about. That was, until I attended the first run-through in the theatre. Whenever he was on stage, you could not take your eyes off him. Few actors have this magnetism. When the show opened, Topol was hailed as a major new star bursting onto the West End stage.

Sadly, becoming a major star in the West End went to his head. As his 12-month contract was coming to an end, he announced that he would stay on longer, but only if his salary was doubled and Richard guaranteed that the show would close as soon as he departed. This was, of course, unacceptable, so Topol said he would leave at the end of the year, warning Richard that, without him, the show would fold.

Nothing could be further from the case. *Fiddler* ran for nearly five years first with Alfie Bass as Tevye, later replaced by a wonderful Dutch actor named Lex Goudsmit who had played the part in Amsterdam. It was the show that was the real star.

Four Tevyes: Lex Goudsmit, Topol, Alfie Bass and George Little the understudy who also successfully played the part.

The scenery was by Boris Aronson who was nominated for a Tony Award for *Fiddler* and later won awards for *Cabaret, Zorba, Company* and *Follies*. Son of a Rabbi, he was born in Kiev, not far from Anatevka, the village where *Fiddler* was set. Boris based his designs on paintings by Chagall, who also happened to be born in Kiev.

Robert Ornbo, senior lighting designer with Theatre Projects, had a story about Boris Aronson when they were working on a show in Boston. During a fraught dress rehearsal there were some problems with the set and the head of the scenery construction team, a young man working on his first big show, was being given a hard time by the producer. They broke for lunch and as Boris and Robert walked out of the stage door, they came upon the young man looking disconsolate. Taking him by the arm, Boris spoke in the thick Russian Jewish accent he had never lost during more than forty years living in America, "Listen, I gotta tell you some advice about the American musical. There are just two rules you have to know. The first rule is that there is always going to be a wictim. They gotta have someone to blame when things go wrong. It could be the leading man, it could be the scenery man, it could be the lighting man. They will always find a wictim. That is the first rule. Now the second rule... and this is very important. The second rule is: *Never be the wictim."*

When working on subsequent shows with Robert, we would often conjecture who was going to be the 'victim'. One of us might say: "I got it on Friday, you were in trouble yesterday. Who is going to be the wictim today?" "How about Wigs!" "That's it! Wigs. It has to be their turn to be the wictim."

Harry Secombe As D'Artagnan

Although a few producers were beginning to see the advantage of having someone on the team responsible for making sure the actors could be heard, budgets remained extremely tight. There was a reluctance to spend money on something the audience could not see. Although one was employed to produce "a really good sound", when the budget for the necessary equipment was presented, inevitably there would be demands to reduce the price. If I had only thought of it, I might have taken the same line as Broadway Sound Designer Otts Munderloh who, years later, explained his response to demands for reducing rental costs. He would reply, "O.K. So exactly which part of the show do you not need to hear?"

In 1967 after *Fiddler* opened, I worked on two more musicals. The first was *Sweet Charity*, staged and choreographed by Bob Fosse, starred the sexy Juliette Prowse, she of the incredibly long legs. It was a charming show that ran for 476 performances at the Prince of Wales Theatre.

The other musical was *The Four Musketeers*. Produced at the Theatre Royal Drury Lane, it was not a great show but it did run for fourteen months, largely due to the huge popularity of Harry Secombe, the star. Loosely based on story by Alexandre Dumas, it was directed by Peter Coe with scenery by Sean Kenny. The vast steel multi-level set filled one of the largest stages in the West End with moving platforms and motorised staircases that seemed to have little to do with 17th century France. It was not one of Sean's most successful creations.

The cast seemed to spend the whole performance climbing up and down from one level to another. During the long technical rehearsal before the show opened, there were constant stops to sort out problems. They would then have to go back and replay the scenes. There were rumblings of discontent, but nobody felt they had a right to voice a complaint because the star remained in good humour throughout, cracking jokes and keeping everyone amused, despite having nine major numbers to sing.

At one point, when the rehearsal was paused and he had to clamber back up a long staircase for the third time to start a song, he paused breathlessly half way up and announced to Peter Coe sitting in the auditorium, "You don't need a tenor for this part. You should have cast a mountain goat!"

The Four Musketeers, Harry Secombe at the front in a white shirt.
Permission by the Bennet-Muir Musical Theatre Archive Trust

There was one exciting incident during rehearsals; it was apparently sparked off when one of the actresses, an attractive girl with a fiery temper, had a row off-stage, accusing one of the actors of trifling with her affections. Peter Coe was sitting in the stalls calmly giving directions, "Harry, it would be good if you could..." when a blood-curdling shriek was heard off-stage, followed by the actor in question running across the stage, leaping over the orchestra pit and haring up the aisle, hotly pursued by the actress brandishing a large knife and screaming that she was going to kill him. Everyone on stage froze. Peter paused as they shot past him and crashed through the doors at the rear of the auditorium. Then, without a flicker, he continued, "...if you could move down stage on that line. Let's try it again, shall we?" Peter was amazingly laid back. Even during the most stressful moments, I never saw him lose his temper or hardly even raise his voice.

After curtain down on the first night, I was standing backstage talking to Sean Kenny when Lionel Blair happened to pass by. Presumably he had been in the audience and was on his way to see Harry. Noticing Sean, he stopped and, unusually for him, seemed at a loss for words. The done thing, of course, was to offer gushing praise and congratulations, but as the reviews of the show were to confirm, Sean's set design really was a bummer. Quickly recovering himself, Lionel's face lit up and with a beaming smile he came out with the wonderfully nebulous line, "What can I say, Sean, you have done it again!"

Later in the run, performing eight shows a week took a toll on Secombe's voice and it was agreed that he should mime to two of the most demanding numbers using the vocal tracks from the cast album. Being the clown that he was, after a couple of nights he could not resist playing for laughs. He pretended to have forgotten there was another verse and stopped miming. Then when the voice carried on, look horrified and hurriedly tried to catch up with the lyric. It went down so well that on subsequent performances he introduced a variety of antics, such as blowing his nose or gargling with a glass of water while apparently singing the song. The audience loved it.

By this time, I had become quite friendly with Sean and his small team of designers, often visiting them in the Soho office just a few minutes walk from our studio. The trick was to arrive around midday because more often than not one was invited to lunch. Sean employed a chef named Josh who came in every day to serve mid morning coffee and then prepare a lunch for the staff. This included senior designer Michael Knight assisted by Bob Bahl and George Djurkovic, plus a young lady graphic artist.

With his gift of the blarney, Sean was extremely good at selling himself to prospective clients. Given a brief, he would produce a large artist's sketchpad and with flourishes of his felt-tip pen come up with all kinds of outlandish ideas, often involving new and untried technology. When queried about the expense, he assured them that with careful design this would not be a problem. Such was his charm that many producers were persuaded.

Having sold a concept to the client, he would have to confess to his design team what he had let them in for. It was then up to his long-suffering design assistant, Michael Knight, to create something workable from Sean's wild sketches. Sometimes this meant simplifying or making radical changes to the original concept but, nothing daunted, Sean would go back to the client and convince them that he had come up with something far superior.

Expo 67 Montreal

On one occasion when I dropped into Sean's office, he was working on a project for the Canadian government. By now, he was undoubtedly the most celebrated theatre designer in the UK and they had asked him to create a major event for their forthcoming international exposition in Montreal, EXPO 67. He had come up with what he called "The Gyratron". This, he explained, began as a ride into outer space where visitors would glide past strange planets, asteroids and space vehicles as they spiralled to a dizzying height within a vast blacked out building to emerge high up above the Saint Lawrence river. They would then travel towards the mouth of another building to plunge down into what turned out to be the inside of a volcano at the bottom of which they would be threatened by a fearsome metallic crab-like monster before landing back on terra firma.

"That looks fantastic," I said.

"Yes, and I'm hoping it will be even more fantastic when you add all your wonderful sound effects," he replied with a grin.

"Are you serious?"

"Absolutely. You are officially on board. And I haven't finished yet. The Canadians also want a design for a "Faith Pavilion", which is meant to be a contemplative space encompassing the various religions of the Western World. I can't think what sort of sound that requires, but I am sure you will think of something."

"I don't know what to say. Thank you."

"Don't thank me yet, because I haven't told you about the other one. I'm working on a big project for the British government. We're going to devise the main event in the British Pavilion. This is going to involve a lot of programmed lighting and projection, and it will need a complete sound track." Seeing my gobsmacked expression he laughed. "How's your diary for the next few months?

For the British Pavilion, Sean had devised an extraordinary concept entitled "The Shaping of Britain" wherein visitors entered a kind of cavern and stepped on to a moving platform revolving around a central control room. Images of Britain's history starting with early caveman and ending up with modern technology were projected on to a series of different rock formations. For the sound track, I turned once again to Guy Woolfenden and persuaded him to compose four musical sounds evoking different eras on the journey through the centuries. He came up with four tracks that, when combined, produced a triumphant musical finale. This brilliant piece of writing was supplemented with a variety of evocative sounds that I ensured were in the right key.

For the Faith Pavilion, I simply recorded prayers being intoned by ministers of various religions and mixed them into a gently overlapping voice montage. It was surprisingly moving.

Sean had contacted a Swiss cable car company to quote for the Gyratron ride system. Clear plastic gondolas would glide silently up and around the enormous space building, out into the open and then down into the volcano. Unfortunately, the Canadian government department in charge of the budget failed to place the order before the final date specified by the Swiss company. With time running out, the panic solution was to resort to a Canadian company specialising in bucket conveyors for coal mines. Instead of the futuristic plastic capsules suspended on wires, they came up with clunky metal trucks with four-abreast seats and safety bars to imprison the punters. Travelling on steel rails, propelled by a continuous cable connecting the cars, the noise of the mechanism and the wheels on the tracks was horrendous. By no stretch of imagination did it give the feeling of travelling through space and, of course, the series of ethereal sounds I had carefully created could hardly be heard. The volcano was not such a problem as I had several very large loudspeakers eclipsing the noise of the trucks with deep rumblings, hisses and explosions in a most satisfying way.

My first trip to Canada was to attend a planning meeting held by local government officials some months before construction began. All the main designers and contractors were in attendance, sitting round the largest boardroom table I had ever seen. I was seated at the opposite end to the chairman and had some difficulty hearing what he was saying. This was because the change of air pressure during the flight had once again caused my Eustachian tubes to block. I did my best to follow the proceedings, but it was like listening to voices through wads of cotton wool. At one point, somebody asked the chairman a question - totally inaudible to me - but I did manage to catch the chairman's response when he turned his gaze on me and announced: "I think that is something for our sound expert from England, Mr Collison." All eyes turned my way, but all I could do was stammer, "I'm sorry. I'm afraid I didn't hear the question." Embarrassing or what?

Initial testing of the sound system took place during the winter, some months before the EXPO opened, and I have never experienced such cold. With the wind chill effect, the temperature was hovering around minus 30° centigrade. The control equipment for the Gyratron was up in the tunnel where the trucks emerged to cross the bridge into the volcano. The only way to reach this platform at a dizzying height above the Saint Lawrence river was by climbing up a series of vertical ladders lashed to the tubular structure that supported the building. This was a trip I really did not wish to make.

Despite wearing thick gloves, one's fingers soon became numb, which made gripping the wet and icy rungs of the ladders a hazardous business. Half way up, I began to wonder, "Are these few stupid sound effects really worth dying for?" and "Did these crazy Canadians not have any Health and Safety rules?" Obviously not. "And come to think of it, Tony Horder helped to make these recordings. Why wasn't he out here suffering?"

THE GYRATRON
The bucket seats can be seen crossing the bridge into the volcano.

I made that vertiginous ascent twice, each time finding the return journey down to the frozen ground equally, if not more, scary. It is amazing what one will do for one's art!

Shortly before the opening that Spring, the engineers had the bucket system running and I was allowed to take a ride so as to get close to my various noises and take notes for adjusting sound levels. My particular bucket had trundled three quarters of the way up when the whole system clanked to a halt. I waited for it to restart, but nothing happened. Then Sean appeared on the floor way below and shouted, "There's a bit of a problem."

"I can see that," I yelled back, "How long before they fix it?"

"They hope to have it working by tomorrow morning." He was grinning broadly and seemed to find my predicament incredibly amusing. "Don't worry," he continued, "rescue is at hand."

A short while later, a tall muscular man wearing brown overalls, a safety helmet and builder's boots appeared with an enormous coil of rope over one shoulder and began to walk gingerly up the narrow rails supporting the trucks. There was nothing to hold onto between each truck, a distance of some 12 feet (3m), so it was like an uphill tightrope walk on slippery steel. Every time he reached a truck, and there must have been at least twenty of them before he reached me, he had to hoist himself up and clamber over the high back.

Eventually, he climbed into my truck and announced, "I hope you are good at heights, because I am going to drop you down on a rope. OK?"

"OK" I replied, endeavouring to sound nonchalant.

He then let the rope down to a colleague waiting below, who attached a larger coil of rope to be hauled up, one end of which was thrown over a handy girder. The other end was tied to itself so as to form a loop.

"Put this over your head and sit in the loop," he instructed, "and I will push you out of the truck and lower you to the ground."

We must have been at least 70 feet (21m) up and the prospect of hanging from a rope, with my life literally in the hands of this stranger was, shall we say, interesting. A little crowd of workers had gathered to watch the fun, giving a little cheer when I was pushed out into space and applauding good-humouredly when I landed, unscathed apart from seriously chafed thighs from the rope cradle.

Everything was up and working when Expo 67 opened to the public. During the summer there was a special British Day Parade for which we were to provide the sound track. This was a kind of pageant, inevitably featuring a Morris Mini painted as a Union Jack, a London black taxi and, of course, a red Groupmaster double-decker bus. Written and hosted by the writer and satirist John Wells, it turned out to be a great success. Because of my recurring problem with flights affecting my hearing, Tony Horder handled this one and, of course, had a most enjoyable experience in sunny Montreal. Huh!

Consultants To The New National Theatre Building

In 1966, Laurence Olivier asked Richard Pilbrow to join the National Theatre Building Committee and it soon become apparent that he was the only member with any knowledge of technical theatre. Now, a year later, Richard was appointed Theatre Consultant for stage planning, lighting, sound and stage equipment.

To cope with this and several other projects in process, it was evident that a separate company was needed and Theatre Projects Consultants Limited was formed. Richard persuaded an old friend, Richard Brett, a senior planning and installation engineer at the BBC, to head up the new company.

For me, it was ironic that having met a "Sound Consultant" in Las Vegas and been singularly unimpressed, I now found that I was one. Although I had no technical training whatsoever, I knew what was required in a theatre from a practical point of view, and an engineer within the company who was qualified to do so translated my specifications into electronic gobbledygook.

When Denys Lasdun, the architect, presented Laurence Olivier with his final set of plans for one of the two main theatres, and although the plans were meant for Olivier's eyes only, he passed them on to Richard for comment. It so happened that Richard and Viki were about to take a short break on the Isle of Coll off the west coast of Scotland. Not for the first time, I was delighted to be included in the trip to the cottage they had renovated over a number of years.

Once installed on Coll, with great excitement Richard unrolled the drawings of the proposed theatre, but was immediately concerned about the size of the auditorium. Rolling up the drawing, he said, "Come on. We'll mark this out, full size, on the beach, so we can really get the feel of it."

There is a beautiful sandy bay near the cottage and moments later, using a tape measure, we were laying out large stones and scribing lines in the sand to create the outline of the Olivier Theatre.

"I hope no helicopter flies over with a camera," Richard declared. "These plans are top secret. I gave my word to Sir Laurence that nobody would see them."

Fortunately, the chances of a spy plane flying over the Inner Hebrides was pretty remote and before long the tide would wash away the evidence.

Our layout completed, we scrambled up the rocks at the side of the bay and from this vantage point viewed our work. It looked enormous. In fact, with only 1,100 seats it had a larger footprint than the Theatre Royal Drury Lane with 2,400 seats. However, it was now far too late to suggest any radical changes to the structure. Back in London, concrete was already being poured.

The planning and design stage before and during the building of the National Theatre lasted another nine years before The Royal Opening by the Queen in 1976. We introduced a number technical innovations, and there are many stories that Richard has included in his semi-autobiographical book "A Theatre Project" and in the more recent "A Sense of Theatre".

One of my main memories of this time is a rather frightening session with the Building Committee regarding our proposed budget for sound equipment. It has to be remembered that in those days British theatres did not have sound control rooms, did not employ sound technicians, and mixing desks were a thing of the future. So they were horrified when I produced plans for spacious control rooms in the two main theatres featuring large and expensive mixing consoles.

The consoles cost so much because microprocessors were not yet available, so they had to be wired entirely by hand. It was really only recording studios and broadcasting organisations that could afford them. One incensed committee member demanded:

"Why on earth do we need a studio quality mixer with hundreds of knobs in order to play a baby crying effect?"

Another blurted out, "This is the National Theatre. We will not be putting on MUSICALS!"

A third committee member challenged with, "Can you name a single theatre in this country with a control room in the auditorium and all this extraordinary equipment?"

I could not, but I had brought along a number of photos of German theatres that all had large control rooms with mixing consoles. I finally won the argument by suggesting that the flagship theatre of Great Britain should surely not be equipped to a lesser standard than a provincial theatre in Germany.

During the 1970s, as consultants on a number of new theatres around the country we always specified sound control rooms, but this had an unforeseen effect on our studio business. We were supplying sound effects to many provincial theatres, but as the ever-increasing number of new ones were equipped with tape machines, they were able to record their own sounds. We kind of shot ourselves in the foot.

I may have won the argument for control rooms at the National, but my proposal for a recording studio within the complex did not receive approval. I argued that the sound department - for there would have to be one - would need a soundproof space to record voices and special effects. Moreover, as the use of recorded music was banned by the

Musician's Union, if music was needed for a production, it would be possible to have musicians playing live in the studio and pipe it through to the stage via the control room. This was all deemed fanciful nonsense and vetoed unanimously.

At a subsequent meeting with the architect, he was persuaded to include about half the space requested as an unfinished storage area, possibly to be converted into a studio at a future date. It was to be 1999 before the sound department was given a budget to turn this storeroom into a studio. Twenty-seven years after the theatre had opened, the empty cableways to the theatre control rooms we had specified all that time ago came into their own.

A couple of years after Richard Pilbrow was appointed consultant to the National Theatre, Peter Hall, at that time still running the Royal Shakespeare Company, asked him to advise on their new London home to be built in the Barbican Centre. So, apart from several other projects around the UK, Theatre Projects became consultants for the two major subsidised drama theatres in the country.

The reputation of Theatre Projects Consultants Limited rapidly became world-wide. At the time of writing, it is thriving and has advised on more than 1,500 theatres, concert halls and arts centres in eighty different countries.

1968

Judi Dench and Cabaret

The only new musical for us in 1968 was *Cabaret*, directed by producer Hal Prince, starring the wonderful Judi Dench. This was another co-production with Theatre Projects of a Broadway hit.

Richard Pilbrow had known Judi Dench from drama school days and thought that she would be ideal for the part of Sally Bowles. Contrary to the popular perception of Sally as a glamorous star exemplified by Liza Minnelli in the film, the Sally Bowles of Isherwood's original novel was a struggling singer/actress who came from a small town in Yorkshire. So too did Judi.

Richard recalls Judi arriving at the audition for Hal Prince a bundle of nerves. "I just can't sing!" she protested. But she did, wonderfully, and Hal was enchanted. "This," he declared, "will be the real Sally Bowles."

The cast included Peter Sallis who, of course, became renowned as Norman Clegg in the long-running television series *Last of the Summer Wine*, and also voiced Wallace in several Wallace and Gromit animation films. In *Cabaret*, as Herr Schultz, Sallis played opposite the charismatic Russian-born Lila Kedrova who had recently won an Oscar for Best Supporting Actress in the film *Zorba the Greek*. Herr Schultz was an elderly Jewish fruit shop owner who falls in love with Kedrova's character. Never failing to bring a lump to the throat was a scene where Schultz tries to persuade the Fraulein to marry him. She finally agrees during a beautifully touching duet entitled "Married", a song that regularly stopped the show. But they are in Germany during the rise of the Nazi party and following their engagement party, the Fräulein is convinced by others that marrying a Jew would not be wise. The joyous duet and much of their poignant story is omitted from the sugarcoated

Hollywood movie.

Judi Dench visited the Pilbrows' house in Hampstead on a number of occasions, where I was also a regular visitor. She confided one day to Viki and me that the actor Michael Williams had recently asked her to marry him.

"He flew all the way out to Australia where I was touring with the RSC,' she added, "How romantic is that? Of course, I said yes. What do you think?"

Viki was effusive with her congratulations but my reaction that made her laugh was, "Great for him, but jolly rotten for the rest of us."

There was an impressive game she used to play in order to discover people's character and traits. This involved imagining a forest and deciding whether there was a path or not, then describing your reactions when coming across a cup, finding a key, seeing some water, and finally arriving at a wall. You had to give details of the objects and what you would do with them. For example, a cup could be anything from a chipped mug to a silver chalice. Her summing up of my secret self was frighteningly accurate. Viki's imaginings were wildly different from mine, but Judi also summed her up to a T.

Obviously, she knew quite a bit about us already, so we decided to test her with people she had not met. Three people wrote down their very different stories and the next time we met, Judi pronounced. Her readings were uncannily true to the individuals, even down to gender. Studying one of them, she started by saying, "This is female." Then after a pause, "But it could be male." Another pause. "No, I think this is definitely a gay chap." And she was right. When we expressed our amazement at her talents, with a throaty chuckle she replied, "Well, I am a witch, you know."

Cabaret was very well received and seemed set for a long run, but after eight or nine months business suddenly began to decline. The weekly box office receipts were hovering just above the 'break' figure. This is the income agreed in the contract between the producers and the theatre owners. Should the it fall below the break figure, then either side could give two weeks notice to close the show. However, receipts were falling faster than seemed normal and there was a suspicion that something was not quite right at the box office. Could this be the old trick used by theatre owners - in this case, Emile Littler - to nudge ticket sales down in order to take back control of the theatre? This turned out to be the case when it was discovered that ticket sales were being heavily discounted and phone calls to the box office were not being answered. These tactics eventually led to the show's closure. The theatre was offered to another producer for a show that presumably Emile Littler was convinced would run longer than *Cabaret*.

The show he brought in was a musical called *Two Cities*. Despite the lead, Edward Woodward, winning the Evening Standard Award for Best Musical Performance, *Two Cities* received a critical drubbing and only managed to stagger on for 44 performances. Everyone involved with *Cabaret* naturally felt heartbroken for Mr Littler.

There was the possibility that year of becoming involved in another musical. Tony Horder took a call one morning from a gentleman wanting to hire a quantity of hand microphones for a new musical opening at the Shaftesbury Theatre. We were not in the hire business at the time and to purchase that number of microphones would be a large investment for us, but worth it if the show were to run for a few months. However, Tony had heard on the grapevine that the producers had failed to lodge two weeks salary for the cast and stage management as required by the Society of West End Theatre Managers. Moreover, the show apparently featured rock music (horror!) and was all about American hippies (even worse!). Tony declined the offer, and I agreed that it was far too dodgy a proposition to contemplate. The show, of course, turned out to be the mega-successful *Hair*. In subsequent years, I was sound designer for two West End revivals of *Hair* - both most enjoyable experiences.

Forty Years On

We continued providing sound effects for many drama productions, but Alan Bennett's first play in the West End, *Forty Years On,* was particularly memorable. It was set in a public school where an end of term play was being put on for the parents; i.e. the audience. The play is about the loss of innocence and the loss of a generation of young men following the end of the Great War in 1918. Sir John Gielgud played the headmaster. Paul Eddington and Alan Bennett were also in the cast. It had a successful run at the Apollo Theatre (still called the Apollo Theatre at the time of writing!)

The Ruling Class

Peter O'Toole starred in the premiere of another play, *The Ruling Class* by Peter Barnes for which we created the sound effects. It was a black comedy revolving around the attempts to cure the 14th Earl of Gurney (O'Toole) of insanity. At one point he develops the delusion that he is Jesus Christ, explaining that when he prays to Jesus, he finds that he is talking to himself. Ergo, he must be Jesus. It played at the Piccadilly Theatre. O'Toole acquired the film rights and starred in the 1972 film version.

It is a tradition in the theatre to send colleagues and friends good luck (or break-a-leg) cards on the first night of a show. In the good old days before emails were invented, the only way of ensuring a message would arrive on the same day was to send a telegram. This entailed visiting the post office and filling in a form. The message was then telegraphed to the post office nearest the recipient. The printout in the form of a paper strip was stuck on a telegram form and immediately delivered by hand, usually by a boy in a smart uniform riding a bicycle. Tony and I always looked forward to receiving the cheery messages we sent to each other and to our sound operators. We liked to make them jokey if possible and there was one I particularly remember sending Tony. He was working on a new play opening out of town that required the actors' voices occasionally to be heard with an echo. The available reverberation machines were pretty basic and Tony was having a great deal of trouble achieving the effect required by the director, who happened to be the actor Nigel Patrick. So my first-night telegram simply said, "Good luck - luck - luck - luck - luck - luck."

I only discovered later that this had greatly amused Tony and Claire Laver the sound operator, but they were convinced that I had shot my bolt. Surely, I could not come up with anything to equal it for the London premiere. Apparently, they were not disappointed. The telegram just read, "Ditto - ditto - ditto - ditto - ditto - ditto"

Claire and Tony during a performance.

1969

Ginger Rogers in Mame

By and large, producers of musicals were coming to accept that it was necessary for the mixing desks to be located in the auditorium - so long as they were located in a side box or tucked away in a far corner. As the equipment became more complicated, I was able to insist on providing our own people to control the equipment, and with four musicals currently running in the West End, we had gathered together a small team of talented knob twiddlers.

Up until now, I had mainly been specifying the equipment from the company Stagesound, for which they gave us a small discount. Sadly, the founder of Stagesound died and a 'businessman' who knew nothing about theatre was now running the company. Focused on profits, he alienated his customers by raising rental prices and when he cancelled our discount arrangement, we made the decision to purchase our own equipment and rent it to the next big musical. And the next musical was definitely a biggie.

Mame starring Ginger Rogers opened at the Theatre Royal Drury Lane and ran for more than a year. It was produced by Harold Fielding who had previously employed us on *Sweet Charity*. The last of the great showman impresarios, Harold invited the national press to welcome his star stepping off the liner at Southampton docks. They then all boarded a train called "The Mame Express" for London. On the journey, Miss Rogers gave interviews while champagne was served and a selection of Fred Astaire and Ginger Rogers films were shown. At the theatre, two dressing rooms set aside for the star had been completely refurbished and decorated with wallpaper to her choice; a fact that was widely leaked to the media.

Harold was a small man with a sparkle in his eye and an obvious delight in all aspects of putting on a show. He spent money to provide the audience with a lavish experience, but only after negotiating hard with his suppliers.

An example of Harold's sense of showmanship was when he stopped the dress rehearsal at the point where Miss Rogers first entered. He turned to the director and choreographer saying, "No, no. I can't have Miss Rogers just walking on from the side of the stage like that. She is a star and I want a star's entrance. Please reset the scene so that she appears upstage centre, pauses as the entire company turns to greet her, before she proceeds down towards the audience. It will stop the show." And it did.

Ginger Rogers arriving at Southampton
PictureLux/The Hollywood Archive/Alamy Photo Stock

Mame ran for fourteen months during which time Juliet Prowse covered for Miss Rogers when she took a two-week break.

Before *Mame* opened we had become involved in a revue at the Palace Theatre. Staged by Lionel Blair, *Danny La Rue at the Palace* was scheduled for a limited run and we were able to leave our equipment there for the next musical, *Phil The Fluter*. Starring Stanley Baxter, Evelyn Laye and Mark Winter, this one ran for only 123 performances. Both shows were handled by my colleague Tony, as much more of my time was being taken up as a theatre consultant working on an ever-growing list of new theatre buildings.

1970

Who Do We Have In The Studio Today?

We now employed a secretary/receptionist, who had to be aware when making studio bookings that one or other of us - sometimes both - might be attending rehearsals or installing equipment in a theatre. We worked six days a week - often seven - with many evenings spent at rehearsals or performances.

In those days and in all weather, jacket and tie were worn at all times, even when hauling heavy pieces of equipment from the van and setting them up in a theatre. One had to look presentable because the next moment one might be meeting a director or producer to discuss a production, or dashing back to the studio for a recording session.

In the recording studio, every day was an adventure. We would consult the diary to see what we were supposed to be doing and who was booked in. Tony and I recorded many illustrious voices in our little wooden studio, but during the past few months a new studio was being built in our Neal's Yard basement.

For the opening of this more sophisticated recording complex at the beginning of 1970, we employed a 'proper' sound engineer. This was Michael Moor.

Michael's background was in music recording and he introduced us to a different kind of client. Pop music was really big business during the seventies and record companies were constantly on the lookout for the next big sensation. They would book small studios like ours for unknown bands or singers to make demo recordings. Once in a while, they would discover another Tom Jones or a group to possibly rival The Beatles. Music publishers also hoped to arouse the interest of established artists by recording new songs with professional 'soundalikes'. We would hear the voices of Cliff Richard, Shirley Bassey or Englebert Humperdinck emanating from the studio. But nobody got excited. It was not the real thing.

With Michael's clients and our theatrical customers, there was an eclectic mix of people visiting our basement. The singer Labbi Siffre or the folk-jazz band Pentangle might be followed by Christopher Plummer or Janet Suzman making a voice recording for the Royal Shakespeare Company. Sometimes our more venerable thespians were surprised by having to negotiate their way into the studio through a group of cheery long-haired youths manhandling electric guitars and drum kits.

There was an alarming occasion when Tony and I arrived one morning for a studio recording session with Laurence Olivier and Michael Horden for the National Theatre, to find the whole place reeking of a smell reminiscent of a dentist's surgery. Michael, who had just finished an all-night session with a rock group, explained that his clients had been snorting cocaine. In an attempt to dispel this noxious odour, all the doors were propped open and the three of us plus our secretary/receptionist rushed around flapping towels and tea trays. This activity was suddenly brought to a halt when one of us noticed that the distinguished guests had appeared at the top of the stairs to our basement. Hoping they had not noticed our weird behaviour, we pretended to be tidying up.

Another one of the many all-night sessions was with an unknown group with the extraordinary name of Tyrannosaurus Rex, later to be modified to T. Rex. They did not have drugs - they probably could not afford them in those days - but they did arrive with two crates of Newcastle Brown Ale.

One evening, Bill Oddie, famous at the time for the TV series "The Goodies", came in to try out a few numbers. Because there was not enough room in the studio for the musicians plus a large group of singers, Michael placed the backing chorus outside in the foyer. This high open space turned out to have a suitably lively acoustic. Bill Oddie's rock version of the hymn "All thing bright and beautiful" sounded wonderful and was later re-recorded in a big studio and released by Decca. Mike's version had an exciting Phil Spector-type wall of sound that the Decca version failed to achieve.

Lionel Blair was a regular visitor. We compiled tapes of recorded music for fashion shows for which he was director and choreographer. On one occasion he overran his allotted time and was surprised when the next client, also compiling a tape for a fashion show, walked in. It was his sister Joyce.

Sean Kenny booked a session one evening, saying that he was bringing along the director of a play for which he was designing the sets. This director just happened to be Sean Connery. At the pinnacle of fame playing the suave and ruthless agent, James Bond, I suppose I anticipated a decisive and even intimidating presence. On the contrary, he turned out to be a charming, quietly spoken man with a faintly worried air about him. More of an uncle figure than a superhero. It was probably the first piece of theatre he had directed and he was far from clear about what he wanted. The more choices I gave him, the more difficult it became. And it was not helped by the presence of his young son Jason who, when not complaining of boredom, was holding up proceedings by fiddling with bits of equipment. Mr Connery would remark vaguely, "Don't do that, Jason," which had no effect whatsoever. It was disappointing to discover that 007 was not able to control a small boy.

That recording session was the last time I worked with Sean Kenny. He died from a heart attack in 1973 when he was only forty-three.

A surprising entry in the diary one day was the name Edward G Robinson. He had been booked in to record a voice-over for a special auction at Sothebys. Once again, this great film star, renowned for playing tough New York gangsters in the 1930s and 1940s, turned out to be a pleasant, softly spoken gentleman who collected art. He sported a grey goatee beard, was elegantly dressed in a three-piece suit, wore a bow tie and carried a silver-topped malacca cane. He was unrecognisable until, of course, he spoke.

Other notables who descended the stairs into our basement in Neals Yard included Nigel Patrick, Leslie Phillips, John Le Mesurier, Michael Bentine who laughed uproariously at his own jokes, and Ravi Shankar recording sitar music for a play set in India. It was known that he had recently been teaching George Harrison to play the sitar and I asked if this member of The Beatles had mastered the instrument. Shrugging his shoulders, Ravi Shankar replied with a smile, "He's trying".

The ninety-something year old Dame Ninette de Valois, founder of the Royal Ballet and the Royal Ballet School, was due to arrive for a recording. We were all worried about how she would negotiate the long staircase into the basement. This formidable nonagenarian had no problem with stairs, but when she sat down and prepared to read her script, she discovered that she had forgotten her glasses. What to do? Tony had a bright idea. In the lighting store above us, there were hundreds of theatre spotlights, all with lenses. One of these was borrowed and the dame was able to read her script peering through a chunky 10cm spotlight lens.

One of the most recognisable voices we ever recorded was that of Bob Danvers-Walker. His rich, distinctive tones became familiar to cinemagoers as the commentator for the twice-weekly British Pathé newsreels, a job he held continuously from 1940 to 1970. The upbeat, patriotic, "stiff upper lip" style he adopted is often parodied today when television programmes or films want to suggest 1940s and 1950s news coverage. He told us that the newsreels were recorded direct to the edited film, so the commentaries had to be completed in one take. There was no opportunity for stopping or editing which meant that he had to read the script while, at the same time, keeping an eye on the pictures. Occasionally during the war, a bomb would explode nearby during the recording and although this could be heard on the soundtrack, you just had to keep going.

Being asked to record the voice of a Dalek for a stage production of *The Curse of the Daleks* was a challenge. We had no idea how to create that strange electronic sound. Fortunately, one of our contacts put us in touch with Dave Stripp, an electronics genius who was involved in creating the BBC's Radiophonic Workshop in 1958. He supplied us with what he called a "wobbulator", the device that produced the iconic metallic gargling effect.

A cast member of the theatre show came to the studio and we endeavoured to make him sound like an authentic Dalek, but failed miserably. Eventually, the director decided there was nothing for it but to book Peter Hawkins, the actor who had originated the voice. When Peter arrived, he explained where we had been going wrong. Dalek speech is all about intensity and pitch. The voice has to be kept flat with no inflections, but it becomes more rapid and higher pitched when they are excited. This he demonstrated without the help of the electronic device and it became clear that 95% of the sound we all recognised was down to him. The "wobbulator" (or ring modulator) was merely an additional effect. When we came to do the actual recording he would sometimes stop and refuse to say a particular line, insisting, "I'm sorry, a Dalek would just never say that." He was right, of course, and the line would be changed. Everyone went away at the end of the session, extremely happy with the result.

There was a similar refusal to accept the script when the man who was the voice of another television programme, *The Magic Roundabout*, came in to record a piece for another stage version. Eric Thompson used to watch the original children's television programme created in France - without listening to the sound - and then write and narrate a completely new version in English. This very successful series was transmitted from October 1965 until January 1977. In the studio, when Eric was presented with the text of what the author had written for the stage show, he was very unhappy. Following a discussion with the director, it was agreed that he would paraphrase the narrative in his own individual style. It took him a few minutes to read the story and make a few notes, then he spoke the whole thing, off the cuff in one take. Very impressive.

Mark Wilkinson and Guy Woolfenden, musical directors for the National Theatre and Royal Shakespeare Companies respectively became regular visitors. That is until an unfortunate contretemps involving the Musician's Union. Recorded background music for drama productions in the British theatre was outlawed in the 1950s by the Musicians Union. They decreed that any music in a live performance must be played live by a minimum of six musicians. As this ridiculous rule was not technically or financially viable, mood music for plays became a thing of the past. However, the National Theatre and the Royal Shakespeare Theatre had special arrangements with the union to use recorded music because they both employed permanent groups of musicians on their staff. But even this came to an end some time during the 1970s, and it happened in our studio. We were recording some pieces for the Royal Shakespeare Theatre for which Guy Woolfenden had engaged some session musicians. Overhearing a chance remark, one of these musicians discovered that an actor was going to sing to the recording, live on stage. On the grounds that, according to union rules, a singer had to be present when recording a backing-track, they all stopped playing. Guy phoned the union, but they upheld the complaint. We never recorded music for a theatrical production again. The union had, of course, shot themselves in the foot, because work dried up for all the session musicians used for these recordings.

Broadway also suffered from mad rules; for example, if any instrument was played on stage, the production was deemed to be a musical, and the minimum complement of union musicians had to be employed. Apparently, this ruling came as a shock to the famous comedian, Victor Borge, whose one-man show in the 1960s consisted of telling jokes and playing the piano. Outraged at having to pay a number of expensive musicians for doing nothing, he was determined to stop them checking in at the theatre at the start of the show and then going off to earn fees elsewhere. To ensure they stayed to the very end of the show, he made each one of them take a bow at the curtain call. After completing his final number, he would take a bow and walk off. The applause continued with the audience expecting his return. Instead, a completely unknown gentleman wearing a DJ would walk to the centre of the stage, solemnly take a bow, and walk off again. The audience was mystified, but when another man appeared followed by another, and then another, they joined in with the joke - although probably unaware of the reason behind it. So successful was this ending to the show that when he came to London, where the theatres did not have this rule, he recreated the event by using the stage staff. When I saw the show at the Palace Theatre, by the time five or six unknown gentlemen wearing an assortment of overalls, woolen cardigans, tweed jackets and caps had solemnly plodded to the centre of the stage and taken a bow, we were all rolling in the aisles. Finally, the great man himself emerged and we all rose to our feet as he took the final bow.

The Library

The sound effects library, now run by Tony Horder, had more than two thousand catalogued items, and we continued to supply sound effects on disc or tape to repertory and amateur companies up and down the country. Requests would come in for all manner of weird noises, which we would somehow manage to fabricate. I think that we were only stumped on one occasion when a director seriously asked for a five-minute tape of "almost recorded silence".

With every show, our sound effects library was growing. If we did not have a suitable effect, we would go out and record it; but there were a few splendid effects in our library that were not actually authentic. In particular, Leo McKern recorded for us an extremely deep and throaty dog bark, and there was the machinegun fire we had fabricated with a kind of early synthesiser constructed for us by Dave Stripp, our friend from the BBC Radiophonic Workshop. We also had a very good cockcrow recorded by the then famous animal impersonator, Percy Edwards. Without saying anything, we would offer these sounds to directors along with recordings of the real things. Inevitably they would chose the fake effect because it was "the most realistic". We never let on!

Tony and me in our suits and ties creating sound effects.
Photo for a Christmas card.

One of our stranger requests was to provide a night-time jungle track for the nocturnal mammal house at London Zoo, where the lighting was so arranged that it was light at night and dark during the day so that the animals would be active for the visitors. When Tony and I arrived at the zoo in our van, the man at the gate asked our business. I explained, "We've come to install sound equipment in the nocturnal mammal house." We were then treated to my favourite ever traffic directions. Indicating an alley lined with cages, he said, "Well you can't miss it. Go straight down there and turn right at the vulture."

For a play called *Two Stars for Comfort* starring Trevor Howard in 1962, Richard Pilbrow specified a visual rain effect using a perforated water pipe suspended horizontally above and behind a window of the set. Below the window was a long canvas trough with a runaway at one end. The idea was to sidelight the falling drops of water so that the audience would actually see real rain. Unfortunately, it was hardly discernible through the gauze (scrim) that covered the window and even when a character entered through the door at the back of the set, there was no time to register it because the door was quickly closed as one would in the pouring rain. Despite this disappointment, the director, Michael Elliott agreed to retain the effect because the shower of water hitting the canvas sounded superb. Later, we tried to record it for our library, but the result was totally unconvincing when reproduced electronically.

Acting the part of a barman in that show was the actor Esmond Knight. When serving in the navy during World War Two, he lost an eye and the other was badly damaged. His disability did not, however, deter him from continuing his acting career. In *Two Stars For Comfort* he had to deal with a multitude of props, locating glasses and bottles, pouring drinks and moving around the stage to serve them at tables.

Before all the other actors arrived for the first rehearsal on stage, I noticed him moving around behind the bar and then walking carefully to the tables, feeling them, and retracing his steps. He was memorising the layout and the number of paces to each location. Later, at one point during the first rehearsal on stage, he had a problem when trying to clear a quantity of glasses and bottles from the tables. A couple of glasses ended up on the floor. Concerned, director Michael Elliott suggested changing the business so that one of the other actors returned everything to the bar. Esmond would not hear of it. So long as everyone remembered to place their glasses and bottles in exactly the same positions every time, he would learn where they were and it would not be a problem. Incredibly, in performance he was able to bustle around, say his lines and handle the props without faltering. No one would guess that he had a severe visual impairment.

The only person who might have had problems with the props was Trevor Howard who was not always entirely sober.

Incidentally, I was amused to learn that Mr Howard had a clause in his contract stating that he would not appear on any days when a Test match was being played at Lord's cricket ground. The power of a star!

Tommy Steele

In April 1970 we were somewhat stretched. Tony was running the studio with me helping out on occasions between specifying systems for new theatres. And somehow we had to fit in three new musicals.

With surely the shortest titles for any musical, *'Erb* was a London transfer by Theatre Projects of a production from the 69 Theatre Company in Manchester. With music and lyrics by Trevor Peacock, who also played the main part, this was a story of young love set to a background of early Victorian railway trade unionism. Directed by Braham Murray, it was not a big success. It ran for 38 performances at the Strand Theatre (renamed the Novello in 2005).

Harold Fielding had a new show called *Meet Me in London* to be produced at the Adelphi (memories of *Blitz!).* Harold explained that before he could issue me with a contract, his star, Tommy Steele, wanted to meet me. In other words vet me. I suggested that the meeting should take place at Her Majesty's Theatre where *Fiddler* was still running.

We met in the auditorium and I was treated to a lecture on how to install a sound system. "We are going to need six loudspeakers on the proscenium and foot-microphones along the front of the stage."

"Just like we have here," I suggested.

"Yes, and a tape machine and a hand mike on a stand."

"We can cope with that."

"And," he went on, "the loudspeakers must cover the whole auditorium. I want good sound everywhere."

"Like we have here," I suggested.

There was a pause while I was subjected to a beady look. Then, he grinned. "Well, I suppose you know what you are doing." With that, it appeared that I had passed muster and got the job.

The first half of the show was in the form of a revue with The Young Generation dancers, comedians Hope and Keen, and the singer Clodagh Rogers. The second act was all Tommy Steele. Rehearsals were sometimes fraught with members of the cast and production team receiving what seemed to be unnecessarily acid comments from the star. One poor chap found himself in hot water for forgetting to set a prop. He was called on stage - "Come out here. No, right out here. Come on. Right to the centre so we can all see you." - to receive a dressing down in front of the entire cast and production team. As the humiliation continued, from the mixing control at the side of the upper circle, I slowly faded down Mr Steele's microphone until he yelled, "Put that microphone back up!"

Following the final preview, there was a major drama when it was decided the show was running too long. Various items had to be trimmed for the first night, and when Miss Rogers was told that one of her numbers had to be cut, she walked out. At the eleventh hour she was replaced by Susan Maughan, who was a delight.

All went well, so after the opening we left the sound operator to get on with it, until one morning there was a panic call from Harold Fielding. During a dance sequence in the previous night's show when Tommy Steele was miming to his recorded voice, the brand new tape machine had decided to slow down. Unaware that they were hearing a recording, the audience was amazed when Tommy began to sing out of key, and even more surprised when the voice ran down like an old wind-up gramophone. This was entirely due to a technical defect and by no means the fault of the man in charge. Nevertheless, Harold insisted, "You have to come in tonight. My star refuses to perform with that man at the controls. And, believe me, he will look through the curtain and check before going on."

There was nothing for it. We replaced the tape recorder and I agreed to take control that evening. We went into the performance with me at the mixing desk and the sound operator sitting out of sight on the floor behind the balcony front, clutching the cue sheet and hissing instructions. Fortunately, there were no hiccoughs, but to expect someone to take over a complex sound show without rehearsal, demonstrates a certain ignorance of what is involved. Mr Fielding informed his "Star" that the tape recorder had been replaced and the following evening, to my relief, the sound operator was allowed to continue.

While all this was going on, the run of *Mame* had come to an end and we were setting up for another show at Drury Lane. Tony Horder took the lead in this one, and it turned out to be one of his worst nightmares. He is prone to remark with a certain amount of bitterness how before that production he had quite a lot more hair.

Carol Channing Disaster

The problem was trying to use a wireless microphone when the technology was not yet up to it. In the UK, theatres were only allowed to use a very narrow band of frequencies. This meant avoiding the use of more than two microphones at a time, as they tended to interact and make horrible hissing sounds.

Frustratingly, they often worked perfectly during rehearsals, but then on the opening night they would start spluttering and crackling and losing signal. It was all incredibly nerve-racking. Perhaps the actor's first-night nerves produced some kind of electricity that affected the radio waves, or maybe it was just an excess of moisture from their sweat glands. Who knows?

In America they had been using radiomikes with reasonable success for some years. This was because the frequency bands were not so restricted. The downside was that other users also had access to these frequencies and at any moment a hotel paging system or a radio taxi might break in. For example, when Gwen Verdon was playing the lead in the original Broadway production of *Sweet Charity*, she was surprised one night when, mid song, her voice cut out and was replaced by a man saying: *"Calling Doctor Klein. Calling Doctor Klein"*.

The reverse situation occurred in London when Ethel Merman insisted on using her American microphone, quite illegally, for a cabaret performance at the Talk of the Town. Unfortunately, she was operating within the same frequency band as the London Metropolitan Police, who were totally baffled when issuing from their car radios came a brassy American voice singing, *"You don't need analysing. It is not so surprising that you feel very strange but nice..."* Apparently, it took them some days to track down the source of the problem, by which time she had completed her engagement.

Returning to Tony's nightmare, this particular fiasco concerned Carol

Channing, a major Broadway star who, during an illustrious career, created the lead roles in *Gentlemen prefer Blondes* and *Hello Dolly*. She was bringing to Drury Lane her show entitled *Carol Channing With Her 10 Stout-Hearted Men* in which she performed with ten male dancers and a large orchestra.

Carol Channing
Photograph by Allan Warren

Many of her numbers were choreographed, so she had to wear a wireless microphone. Unfortunately, during some very stressful public previews the signal kept breaking up. Different frequencies were tried and aerials were repositioned until, at last, the system seemed to be stable.

The opening night went without too many clicks and crackles and everybody began to relax a bit. Then, during a performance a few nights later, the star's voice was completely eclipsed every ten minutes or so by a brief but extremely loud buzzing noise. Eventually, she stopped in mid routine and told the audience that she was going off-stage to change her microphone. There was a spare unit standing by tuned to a different frequency. The transmitter pack was on a belt under her dress, so she had to remove her costume to complete the change, which took several agonising minutes. The Ten Stout-Hearted Men waited patiently, as did the audience, until she reappeared - to loud applause - and the show resumed. All went well for a while and then "BUZZ". A few minutes later there was another buzz and the ghastly noise kept reappearing at regular intervals.

Totally frustrated, she stopped the show again and announced, "I don't need this fucking thing." and demanded that it should be switched off. More wild applause from the audience. She continued, and although the sound operator brought the foot-mikes up to feedback point…. against the large orchestra nobody could hear a word.

In the interval, many people complained and had their money refunded. Meanwhile, every electrical device in the building was switched off, including the stagehands' television set and even the neon signs outside the theatre. All to no avail. The show was completed with the orchestra playing softly.

Tony discovered the cause of this debacle through a chance remark from an acquaintance who happened to be in the audience that night. She had noticed, parked in the street just behind the theatre, a Mass Radiography Unit giving people free chest X-Rays. She wondered if the radio interference had occurred every time the machine was activated for a new client. This was obviously the case because, for the remainder of the run, there was no X-Ray unit and no buzzes.

Many years later, the sound designer on Starlight Express had an even worse nightmare. The entire cast, all performing on roller skates, had wireless microphones. Technology had moved on and theoretically they could now be relied upon. However, half way through the show all but six of the microphones became unusable because of a continuous loud buzzing sound. They discovered, too late, that the interference was coming from a BBC outside broadcast van. It was parked outside the theatre, preparing for live interviews with the celebrity audience at the end of the show. They were using a very powerful transmitter within the same frequency band to relay the interviews back to the studio. It was perfectly obvious to the audience that some of the microphones were not working and when one of the characters sang a verse from a song that began: *"When the power goes dead..."*, they burst into sympathetic laughter and applause.

The Great Waltz

It was to be three shows in a row at Drury Lane for the Theatre Projects Sound company. Following Carol Channing, *The Great Waltz* produced by Harold Fielding opened in July and ran for 600 performances. This was a lavish musical loosely based on the real-life rivalry between Johann Strauss Senior and his son.

Richard Pilbrow had just returned from lighting the musical *Zorba* on Broadway and he related how the soundman, Jack Mann (of whom more later) had experimented with small microphones on very low stands pointing *at the floor!* This seemed nonsense. Logic dictated that the microphones along the front of the stage should be as high as possible and pointing up at the actors. The height of the microphones was often the subject of tedious arguments with producers and directors. *"Surely it would make no difference if you dropped them a few inches".* Well, of course it would. The microphones would be further away from the actors' mouths.

However, Richard insisted that *Zorba* sounded great, so we decided to carry out a test. Some of the microphones were installed on stands pointing up in the traditional way, and others were on lower stands pointing down at the floor. I was amazed. There was no question. Against all reason, it worked.

The explanation was that a microphone up in the air receives the direct sound from an actor plus, a few milliseconds later, the voice reflected from the floor. So if the microphone is near the floor, the microphone receives the direct and reflected voice almost at the same time. A much cleaner sound. So we used them like that for *The Great Waltz* and never went back to our bad old ways.

To make the microphones even less obtrusive, we commissioned some foam rubber mounts for a particular microphone that had its head on a swivel allowing it to point downwards. As these rubber mounts were long and thin and grey, someone remarked that they looked like mice. The name stuck.

For once, the theatre was ahead of the audio industry. It was to be ten years before the American company Crown introduced a small microphone mounted on a metal plate especially designed to sit on a flat surface and collect direct and reflected sound waves coherently.

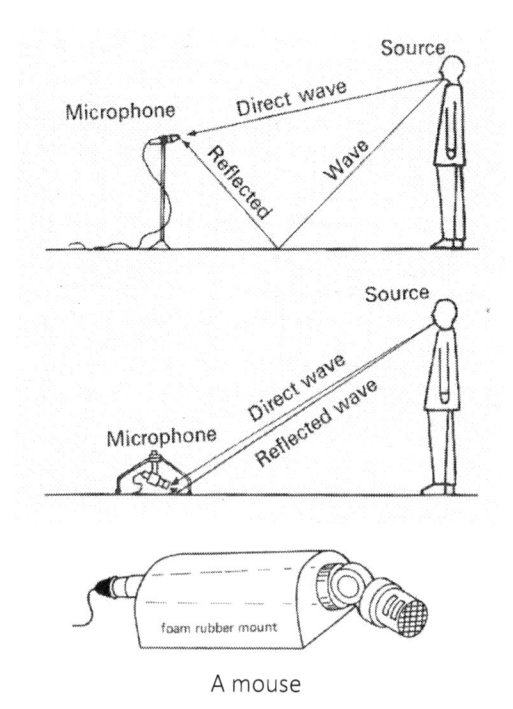

A mouse

We were amused by an incident during the first orchestral rehearsal with the cast on stage. This is when the sound department has an opportunity to assess the problems and make adjustments. It is usually a two-hour session, but this includes the time taken for the musicians to get their instruments into the pit and sort themselves out.

There was a large orchestra and the string section was taking a frustratingly long time to make themselves comfortable within the cramped space. Valuable rehearsal time was being wasted and Harold Fielding, losing patience, shouted at the musical director to get a move on.

"There's no room for us to bow," complained the lead violinist as they continued to shuffle around chairs and stands, arguing amongst themselves.

More minutes passed and then Harold marched down the stalls and announced to the musicians, "Right. There is obviously not enough room down there. Somebody should have worked out that the pit is not big enough for everyone. So this is what we will do. We will cut two of the violins and I will have the score re-orchestrated accordingly."

I have never seen musicians move so quickly. Suddenly the entire string section was magically seated and ready to play.

Jaques Brel

Leaving the theatre after the first night of *The Great Waltz*, we bumped into a beaming Harold Fielding, pleased that it had gone so well. He thanked us, adding "It's been hard work, but it was all worth it. We can now all go home, take a break and recover." That might have been true for him, but we were heading straight to the Duchess Theatre to oversee the rigging of some microphones for a show with a technical run-through the following day.

It was the custom for first night audiences to dress formerly, at least in the stalls and dress circle, with the men sporting dinner jackets and black ties. As every member of the production team would be similarly dressed, this is how we arrived at the Duchess Theatre where the fit-up was in progress. Our purpose was to oversee the hanging of two ropes from the grid so that we could attach a short bar (length of light aluminium tube) from which we intended to hang three microphones. These were to amplify the musicians performing on a rostrum to the rear of the stage.

The show was the charming Off-Broadway hit *Jacques Brel is Alive and Well and Living in Paris* in which the two male and two female performers sang Jacques Brel songs, translated into English, backed by a group of four musicians with musical director Colin Sell.

The show had just closed in New York after a run of more than four years, and the original cast, including co-creator Mort Shuman, was embarking on a busman's holiday in order to see a bit of Europe. A short tour had been arranged beginning at the Duchess Theatre for a season of just forty-one performances.

Tony was working on the sound for this one, and he had previously discussed the rigging of the ropes and bar with the stage carpenter (the man in charge of the backstage crew) and we expected it to take not more than twenty minutes. But when Tony explained to the head flyman what was required, the man flatly refused, saying that he was too busy.

"So what are you suggesting?" Tony demanded. "We must have these microphones rigged for the dress rehearsal. Are we supposed to go up in the grid and do it ourselves?"

As we were not members of the staff or, for all he knew, members of the union, this would be unthinkable in any normal situation. So when the unpleasant man growled, "Help yourselves", turned on his heels and left us standing there, we were dumbstruck. Presumably, he imagined that these two young men in their smart tuxedos would never wish, or even have the knowledge, to undertake such a task. But the job had to be done.

We headed towards a vertical ladder attached to the side wall of the stage and clambered all the way up to the fly gallery. This we found to be in a disgustingly filthy state. The previous two shows in that theatre had standing sets and it was obvious that nobody had ventured into the flies for years. No wonder the so-called flyman was not keen to go up there.

Several large coils of rope were hanging from the fly rail, two of which we selected. We then climbed up another vertical ladder to the grid some fifty feet (15m) above the stage, each of us with one of the heavy coils of rope slung over a shoulder. No Health and Safety rules in those days.

We had removed our pristine dinner jackets, preferring to soil the white dress shirts underneath with the greasy hemp. Struggling to the top of the ladder, we crawled on to the wooden slats of the grid that were covered with a good half-inch layer of dust and grime. The next happy half hour was spent groveling around in the dirt, made even more uncomfortable by the considerable heat rising from the brightly lit stage.

Fortunately, we had both been trained by the same mentor, Bob Baty, so pulley blocks were soon located and fixed into place. Ropes were threaded through the blocks down to the stage with the other ends dropping back to the fly gallery via the permanent pulleys installed at the side of the grid. Returning to the stage we hung our piece of aluminium tube from the two dangling ropes, fixed the microphones and cables, and climbed back up to the fly gallery to pull everything up to the required height.

It was gone one o'clock in the morning when two perspiring and grubby young men reported to the flyman that the operation had been successfully completed. He showed little interest. Tony, being less reticent than I, made an acid comment on the appalling state of the fly gallery. The man merely gave him a disparaging look, sniffed, and wandered off to continue whatever he had been doing.

This episode reminded me of why I had chosen a career in the theatre: it was for the art, the glamour, the easy life.

Kiss Me Kate

There came an unusual request from Peter Coe, director of *Pickwick, Golden Boy, Half a Sixpence* and *The Four Musketeers,* to install some microphones at the London Coliseum for a limited revival by the Sadler's Wells Opera Company of *Kiss Me Kate*. The cast and the management of the Coliseum were aghast at the very idea of microphones in an opera house, but Peter was very persuasive. He pointed out that this was the largest auditorium in the West End and, not being actors, the opera singers would benefit from "a little assistance, but only in the dialogue scenes of course."

The microphones had to be low down and screened from the audience and there must be no loudspeakers in evidence. However, Peter had noticed some unobtrusive speakers built into the auditorium walls, probably from the days when the theatre had been used for musicals. We cleared the dust, wired them up and found them to be working.

During the dress rehearsal with the orchestra, the microphones were switched on for the dialogue scenes at a discrete level that would not be noticed by an audience, and it certainly helped. During the second act Peter wondered what it would be like if we forgot to turn them off for the musical numbers. So, for the next song we left the faders up. Peter wandered around the auditorium and then approached our control position, "I rather like it," he whispered with a mischievous smile. "We'll be in trouble if anyone finds out, but let's leave it like that, shall we?" We were sworn to secrecy and no one ever knew.

1971

A Rival On The Scene

It had been seven years since the musical *Pickwick* and twelve years since I began recording sound effects for shows, and there was still no other person in the West End calling themselves a Sound Designer. But now a rival came on the scene. A musical produced by the 69 Theatre Company in Manchester was brought to the West End by the Theatre Projects production company. Along with the show came the 69 Theatre Company's Sound Designer, Ian Gibson.

Catch My Soul, based on *Othello*, was directed by Jack Good who also covered himself in black make-up to play the lead. Others in the cast, most of whom came from the pop music world rather than the theatre, included P.P. Arnold and P.J. Proby. I had nothing to do with the production, but I do recall that the Theatre Projects production assistant, Pamela Hay, had a strange encounter with one of the performers. She was standing on the side of the stage at the end of a performance when he passed by and casually confided, "I got travelling feet and that's the truth". Pamela was puzzled. "I can't help it," he explained over his shoulder as he continued on to the dressing rooms, "I just got travelling feet." The meaning of this curious remark only became clear the following day when he did not turn up for the show and was never seen again.

Catch My Soul might have been one London musical without my name attached, but *The Great Waltz* was still running and in July we were working for the National Theatre Company on their production of *Tyger*, described in the programme as "A Celebration of William Blake". Unfortunately, it was not very good and did not have a long run. The National Theatre building still had five years before completion, so this musical was staged at the New Theatre in St Martin's Lane.

Two years later the New Theatre was renamed the Albery Theatre as a tribute to Sir Bronson Albery, a successful director whose step-father, Sir Charles Wyndham, owned the Wyndham, New and Criterion theatres. Following the death of Sir Charles, Bronson assumed joint control of the theatres with Wynham's son. Having worked in his theatres, I know that Sir Bronson was much admired and respected by those who worked for him.

In 2006, there was another name change. The Albery Theatre became the Noël Coward. It is true that Coward's first play was produced there, but why do people keep changing the names of London theatres without regard for their history?

Paris With Peter Brook

A phone call one morning from Richard Pilbrow in Paris heralded a curious episode. "You need to get on a plane today and come to Paris. We have a meeting with the great director Peter Brook at midnight to discuss a major project taking place in a desert."

Richard was lighting the French production of *Oh! Calcutta!* having stepped in at the last moment for an American lighting designer friend who had to rush back to the States. Richard had split up with his wife, Viki, the previous year and was now living with Molly Friedel, an American lighting designer who had been his assistant on a Broadway musical. She was now working with him on *Oh! Calcutta!*.

When I arrived, they told me how there had been a misunderstanding about the hotel booked for them by the French impresario. After the first day's rehearsal, Richard could not recall the name of the hotel, but thought he remembered the street. So he instructed the taxi driver to take them to a hotel in La Rue des Beaux-Arts. They were dropped off at L'Hôtel, which just happened to be the most expensive 5-star luxury establishment in Paris. The receptionist had no record of the booking, but was pleased to offer them a suite. It was, of course, the wrong hotel. The next day when Richard thanked the impresario for her generosity in arranging such lavish accommodation, she was so amused at the confusion that she agreed to let them stay on.

Richard had asked if the manager of L'Hôtel could book me into a cheaper hotel in the vicinity for the night, but was told that something could be arranged within the hotel at a budget price. When told that my room was on the top floor, Richard observed, "They're probably putting you in the servant's quarters. Never mind. When you are settled into your attic, come and join us for a drink in our suite on the second floor."

A smartly dressed member of staff escorted me to a small, but magnificent lift with a chandelier and walls covered in rich brocade. Arriving at the top floor, we walked a few paces on thick carpet to a door, which he unlocked and indicated that I should enter. Inside, there was a short corridor with three more doors. I hesitated. "Which room?" I asked.

"All of them," came the reply, "You are in the Mistinguett Suite, decorated in honour of our famous actress and singer". Opening each door with a flourish, he continued, "This is your bathroom, this is your sitting room, and here is your bedroom". Then, having opened the curtains leading on to a balcony with a wonderful view of Paris, he withdrew, saying with a broad grin on his face, "Enjoy your evening."

The suite was full of period furniture and genuine works of art adorned the walls. The bed was enormous and on a bedside table sat a leather-bound book that, when opened, revealed controls for a television set concealed in an ornate cabinet. In the sitting room there were plush armchairs, a writing desk, and a silver tray with an array of fine drinking glasses sitting on a small sideboard containing a fridge filled with an assortment of alcoholic beverages. The bathroom, of course, came with fluffy white bathrobes, slippers and a wonderful range of smellies.

Descending to the second floor in the exquisitely camp lift, I knocked on

Richard and Molly's door. "Come in," he enthused, "and see how the other half lives. What do you think?"

"To be honest," I replied, giving the place a quick look, "compared with mine, it is a bit pokey."

Before too many drinks were consumed, we had to set off for the meeting with the celebrated theatre director Peter Brook. This took place in an old warehouse in the Paris suburbs where we found him reclining on a pile of cushions in a large candle-lit space amid a circle of actors all tapping long sticks on the floor and humming, "Ooooom". After a while, he noticed us and dismissed his acolytes.

Peter explained that the project in the desert was for the Shah of Iran who later that year, would be celebrating his country's 2,500th anniversary in the ruins of the ancient capital Persepolis. Six hundred guests, including sixty members of various royal families and heads of state would be arriving for a feast in a specially constructed tent-like banqueting hall. The catering was to be by Maxim's of Paris who would be flying in 18 tons of food.

Peter Brook's involvement was to provide an exciting theatrical experience. In collaboration with the poet Ted Hughes, he was creating an experimental piece of theatre based on the myth of Prometheus. It was to be written in a completely new language called **Orghast**, which was also the title of the event.

He was full of ideas for the use of atmospheric lighting and sound, which he said was crucial, but there seemed to be one major problem. This vast remote area of desert was completely devoid of any technical facilities. Lights and loudspeakers, it was pointed out, require electricity to make them work, but he was not interested in such practical details. This was up to us to sort out. So we left, promising to come up with a workable scheme.

Knowing that the Philips office in Paris had installed a *Son et Lumiere* within the ruins of Persepolis, Richard had a meeting with them to discuss the supply of power and equipment. Back in London, he and I spent many hours working on a lighting and sound plot covering three miles of these amazing ruins. It was an enormous budget, but the Shah of Iran would be footing the bill. The scheme was sent to Mr Brook but there was no response. Richard badgered his secretary several times as time was running out to get everything in place. Finally, she came back with the message, "Mr Brook does not want all this equipment. He is an artist."

"If Mr Brook imagines something," Richard responded, "he has a text and some actors to deliver it. If I imagine lighting but there are no lights, nothing very much occurs. It will all be rather dark."

He could have gone on to mention that I could create all the wonderful noises he had asked for, but without a sound system... well, you get the drift.

Ignoring Richard's remark, the secretary came back with a puzzling request, "But Mr Brook does want you to come to Persepolis during the two months of rehearsal." When the subject of fees was mentioned, she replied that this would not be acceptable as there was no budget for a lighting designer!

Orghast went ahead without us.

Later, we discovered from newspaper accounts that the invited celebrities never did witness this theatrical event. To have six hundred members of royal families and heads of state, some of whom were quite elderly, wandering around the ruins of this vast city was presumably seen as impractical; a detail that had concerned us from the very beginning. The guests had to be content with a sumptuous banquet in a fantastic setting.

Orghast, it turned out, was advertised as part of the anniversary celebrations and was performed on several nights for the benefit of tourists, university professors, international journalists and middle-class Iranians. According to reports, for each performance an audience of 70 to 100 were driven on a bumpy road for about an hour from Shiraz, and then had to climb on foot up a steep gravel path to where the performance took place overlooking the ruins. The show began with a "faint spotlight" (a torch?) revealing an actor on a ledge 70 feet above the audience, bare chested, arms outstretched and chained to a rock, where he remained for the rest of the evening. Poor chap. From then on, the actors were only seen either by the light of the moon, with flaming torches or from the glow of fires. The performance then moved - with its audience - a couple of miles across the desert to end at dawn as the sun rose above the mountains. Apparently, at one point there was a battle scene with actors carrying torches, which must have been interesting.

Peter Brook is quoted as saying, "The essence of theatre is magic, and *Orghast* will bring the audience to alternate modes of consciousness, either beyond themselves or below themselves."

I am sure it was lovely.

Returning for a moment to my experience at L'Hôtel, when it was time to check out, I was extremely concerned about the bill. I only had a few francs and I did not possess a credit card. Richard and Molly signed their bill and then the young and very suave manager turned to me. "Ah yes, Mr Collison. I trust you enjoyed your suite?"

"Yes, it was wonderful."

"I thought you might," he said, smiling broadly as he handed me the bill. Incredibly, it amounted to less than today's equivalent of £30.00. I was mightily relieved, he was clearly amused, and everybody was happy.

There is a corollary to this story that concerns Charlie Watts, the drummer of the Rolling Stones. I met him through some friends who knew the owner of an antique shop in Sussex where, one weekend, Charlie walked in and started looking around. The owner, wary of this long haired young man wearing T-shirt and jeans (not his normal clientele), kept a beady eye on him, and when Charlie asked if he could purchase an expensive grandfather clock, he was informed in no uncertain terms that cheques would not be accepted.

"No problem," said Charlie, producing a large wad of cash from his back pocket.

After that, Charlie became a regular customer of the antique emporium. Subsequently, I was included on a couple of occasions when my friends invited Charlie and his wife Shirley to dinner. They were a charming couple with a gently sly sense of humour and we got on well.

On one of these evenings Charlie related how, as he had recently been working hard, he thought they deserved a treat. "So I took Shirley to Paris for the weekend and we stayed in the most expensive hotel I could find. Why not, it's only money? It was called L'Hôtel."

"Oh, yes," I remarked casually, "I stayed there, in the Mistinguett Suite actually. Very pleasant."

This put a halt to the conversation and, of course, I had to explain.

Charlie's laid-back personality was completely at odds with a rock and roll life-style. On the contrary, he seemed to enjoy simple pleasures; like the time he decided to hold a small medieval party. One sunny evening a select twenty or so of us turned up at his house in period costume. The party was set in a candle-lit barn with rushes on the floor and a trestle table groaning with sides of meat, fish, savory tarts, bread, cheese and candied fruit - no potatoes as they had yet to be discovered. This was all eaten with sharp knives. No forks allowed. To drink, there were flagons of wine and mead. The extensive lawn outside was lit with flambeaux and just glimpsed through the trees beyond was a full-size unicorn. Shirley, being a sculptress, had created this splendid creature for the event.

Everybody enjoyed it so much that Charlie and Shirley decided to stage another party the following summer with many more guests, including all of the Rolling Stones and their current partners. But somehow it lacked the magic of the original. Not everybody entered into the spirit of the thing and at one point during the evening someone decided they had to have a cigarette. A small party set off in a car to find a pub. Apparently, all conversation ceased in the bar as two members of the Rolling Stones and two attractive young women dressed in medieval garb strode in, purchased cigarettes and matches, and departed again.

In their splendid house, Shirley had a collection of period dolls displayed in a small turret room. She took me to see them one day but as soon as we entered the room she left me there, saying that she had something to do and would be back in a few minutes. I found these small effigies ranged upon shelves around the room, all staring at me with those blank eyes, somewhat disquieting. After a while, Shirley returned and asked what I thought of her family.

"Interesting, but a bit spooky."

"Is there one in particular that upsets you?" She immediately asked.

I pointed at a doll with dark eyes and a kind of malevolent expression.

"Yes," she cried, "That's the evil one!"

She went on to explain how she liked to leave people in the room to see their reactions, adding with delight, "Sometimes they can't take it and have to escape."

Shirley also had horses and loved to ride. Remarking on a splendid open carriage standing on the lawn, I enquired of Charlie if he ever hitched up a horse and went for a drive. "No, I leave the horses to Shirley."

"So why do you have it?"

"Well, it's nice to look at. And I sometimes like to sit in it with a cup of a coffee."

That seemed fair enough to me.

Charlie Watts

There were two other incidents that amused me. One was discovering a mutual enthusiasm for Fred Astaire films and the other was when the Stones were recording a new album while living in France for tax reasons. Charlie had to travel some distance to and from his rented chateau to the studio, so he was flown there every day in an open two-seater bi-plane. Becoming bored with these flights, he sent an urgent message to our mutual friends for some books featuring Biggles, a fictional pilot who had adventures during the First World War. Charlie also requested a long white silk scarf to wear on the flights. I love the image of Charlie in seated his cockpit behind the pilot, engrossed in the daring escapades of Biggles, clad in leather helmet and goggles with the white scarf fluttering in the slipstream.

Working With Dolphins

Providing lighting and sound for a theatrical enterprise starring dolphins is not an everyday experience. The London Dolphinarium opened at 65 Oxford Street. It had a tank that was 46ft (14m) long x 16ft (5m) wide and 10ft (3m) deep with the audience sitting in tiers at one end. There was a small off-stage holding tank where the performers waited for their cues to make an appearance.

Even though the dolphins were allowed free range of the main pool between performances, the space was too restricted for these large creatures to get proper exercise. Every few days one of them had to be craned out of the water on a kind of canvas stretcher and transported in a van to recuperate in a decent sized pool elsewhere.

The show, loosely based on the story of Robinson Crusoe, began with a mighty storm. During the thunder and lightning we created, gauze curtains in front of the audience opened to reveal an exhausted Crusoe in the water clinging to a wooden spar. Fortunately, a passing dolphin notices that he is in trouble, grabs hold of his shirt and tows him to the safety of an island. This was the best bit. It was all down hill after that.

A live commentator acted as a storyteller and filled in whenever one of the dolphins remembered that this was all complete rubbish and decided it could not be arsed.

Basically, the whole concept was a terrible idea. Acting out a drama in a swimming pool with intelligent dolphins, who sometimes had ideas to improve the script, had severe limitations. More importantly, the whole exercise was cruel and demeaning to the poor mammals who we all agreed were a good deal more intelligent than the management.

When working poolside, it could be unsettling to catch a dolphin staring at you. One just knew that behind those bright unblinking eyes there was a considerable intellect. This was demonstrated one evening when all the technical equipment was being set up and a couple of dolphins were swimming around in the main pool, seemingly interested in what we were doing. One of the crew was up a ladder threading a load of bobbins (runners with curtain hooks) on to the curtain track when he fumbled and dropped several into the pool. Cursing, he came down from the ladder and stood gazing hopelessly into the water. Without the missing bobbins, there was no way he could hang the curtains that were needed for the dress rehearsal the following morning.

Sizing up the situation, one of the dolphins dived down, collected a bobbin and brought it up to the poolside. The astonished man, took the bobbin from the creature's mouth, whereupon it dived down again to retrieve a second one, and so on until all the bobbins had been rescued. Meanwhile, the rest of the crew downed tools and we all just stood there open-mouthed. Having completed the task, this incredible creature remained looking at us for a moment, then uttered a series of high-pitched chirping sound as though saying, "Mission completed," and swam off.

The London Dolphinarium tottered on for two years, doing pretty poor business. The stars of the show were then hopefully transported to a more suitable and a less stressful life.

The Consultancy Company

During the previous two years, I had become increasingly occupied with the consultancy company, designing permanent sound and stage management systems for new theatres. 1971 saw the opening of the Birmingham Repertory Theatre, the Sheffield Crucible and the Wyvern in Swindon.

As technical consultants we were responsible for lighting, sound and stage machinery, but because of Richard's reputation as a Man of the Theatre, the company had now become involved in theatre planning as well. This included specifying the size and shape of the stage and the auditorium, plus all the backstage facilities (dressing rooms, workshops, offices, etc.), with recommendations for the front-of-house areas. As our reputation grew, these details were often agreed with the client even before an architect was appointed.

During the next few years, apart from the on-going design work for the National and the Barbican, we saw the opening of the Derby Playhouse, the Sherman Cardiff, the Mercury Colchester, the Theatre Royal Nottingham, Theatre Y Werin Aberystwyth, the Royal Exchange Manchester, the rebuilding of the Lyric Hammersmith, and theatres for the University of Warwick and Christ's Hospital in Horsham.

More commissions kept piling in, not only in this country but from around the world including the United States, Canada, Mexico, Hong Kong, Iceland and Iran. The consultancy company was a thriving hub of activity leading to offices being opened in New York, Los Angeles, and Tehran.

1972

Company

1972 was a landmark year with an involvement in eight musicals. Sound design was accepted at last and most producers gave us poster credits without us having to negotiate. More significant was discovering a technique to produce a much better sound. This revelation came about during preparations for Stephen Sondheim's groundbreaking musical, *Company*.

Produced by Hal Prince with choreography by Michael Bennett, *Company* opened on Broadway in 1970. At the end of its run, the show transferred to Her Majesty's Theatre as another co-production with Theatre Projects. It was the first American musical ever to be airlifted across the Atlantic in its entirety - cast, sets, costumes, *et al*. Only the lighting and sound equipment were British.

The American cast was scheduled to arrive only three days before the first public preview at Her Majesty's theatre. This posed problems for the technical team as there would too little time to get to know the show and sort out any problems. So with the senior Theatre Projects lighting designer Robert Ornbo who had lit *Company* on Broadway, and Tommy Elliot our production manager, I flew to America on a fact-finding mission. The show had closed in New York, so we caught up with it on tour in Philadelphia.

The first time I saw *Company*, I really did not get it. It was lacking the jolly tunes I was used to and the subject matter about failing relationships was unusual, to say the least. Upon second viewing, however, I was completely won over and became totally involved in the intricate score and wonderfully acerbic lyrics.

A meeting was set up with veteran soundman Jack Mann who worked on all Hal Prince's shows. He had not been invited to oversee the London production, so I was apprehensive about his reaction to some foreigner asking for details of his design. I need not have worried. Jack was a charming man who was to become a dear friend. Most generously, he went out of his way to explain the rigging and running of this complicated show and, most importantly, introduced me to a loudspeaker that was an essential part of the 'Jack Mann sound'. I had never experienced such a natural reproduction of the human voice.

"But," said Jack, "It is no good having brilliant tools if you don't know how to use them."

Up until now, we had been placing loudspeakers on the proscenium wherever seemed convenient and pointing them in the general direction of the audience. Obviously, the nearer you were to the loudspeakers, the louder the sound. That was inevitable. But no longer. Jack explained how he could achieve a remarkably even coverage of the entire auditorium by directing the maximum output of these very directional loudspeakers to the back of the house.

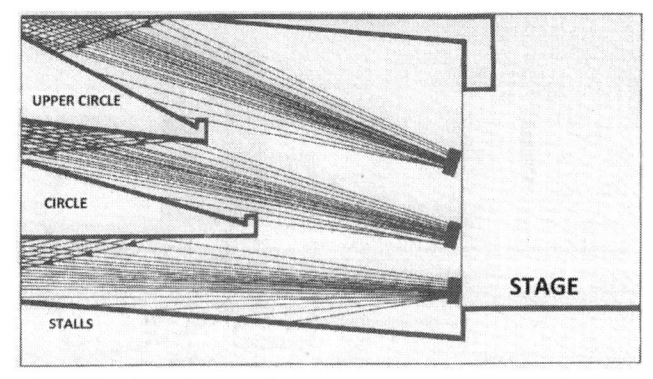

Directional loudspeakers with maximum sound to rear of auditorium

They were more than three times the price of what everybody was using in the UK, but there was no question - we had to have them, and it was arranged that eight would be flown over with the scenery.

In a discussion with Stephen Sondheim, he stressed the importance of hearing the lyrics, despite the complexity of some of the vocal arrangements. Today, of course, this should not be difficult with every member of the cast wearing personal radios, but back then we had to rely on microphones positioned around the set.

Stephen also explained about an off-stage chorus requiring microphones, as their voices were integral to the orchestrations. He always referred to these four singers as "The Unseen Singing Minority". Stephen also requested microphones for three instruments, explaining, "When we get into rehearsals, I might ask you to give a slight lift to, say, the flute for a few bars, or I might say that this number is all about the clarinet." Orchestras were never amplified in those days, so this was the very beginning of studio recording techniques coming into the theatre.

This musical would require a sensitive control of all the microphones and I recently heard of a company using printed circuits to produce affordable mixing desks. With slider faders and tone controls on each channel, this was far more sophisticated than the little twiddly-knob mixers we had all been using up until now. So *Company* became the first West End musical to have a professional sound console. And in order to enhance the sound of the "Unseen Singing Minority" I decided to introduce a touch of echo. Thus, this was also the first show to have a studio quality reverberation unit.

The American cast arrived in London and we went straight into three days of technical rehearsals and run-throughs. On the final day, I was astonished to see Jack Mann and his wife, Jean, walking down the stalls towards our control position in one of the side boxes. He explained that they were on a trip to Europe and thought they would just pop in to see how things were going. Later, I discovered that Hal Prince was so concerned about the tricky amplification for his show that he had paid for Jack and his wife to come over.

After sitting through that evening's run-through, Jack only had two comments: one, that the stall speakers needed lifting a few inches so that the entire cabinet could be seen by every person seated in the back row; and two, that if we increased the size of the cables to the loudspeakers, it would improve the bass response.

After the first public preview the following night, he said in his typically laid back manner, "Well, it's pretty good and I am sure you will get it right by the opening."

"Come on, Jack," said his wife Jean, "You just told me that it sounded sweet as a nut." They both laughed and his parting words were, "You're doing OK."

During the tedious technical rehearsal, there was one of those moments that find their way into theatre folklore. It was gone midnight and yet another hold-up because some lights had to be fixed. Everyone was flagging, and Elaine Stritch, who had been stopped in mid number for the umpteenth time, suddenly barked out in her wonderful gravelly voice: "Will someone tell me who the hell you have to sleep with to get out of this mess?" Immediately, from the darkness of the auditorium the voice of Stephen Sondheim shouted back: "The same person you slept with to get into it!"

Richard Pilbrow tells a wonderful story about how Elaine Stritch insisted that she could not come to England without her pet dog. When it was pointed out that the animal would have to go into quarantine for six months she was finally persuaded to come alone. When Richard and Molly met her at the airport, she burst through the doors of the customs hall wearing a long fur coat and carrying a large handbag. "Get me out of here," she screeched, marching towards the exit. They rushed after her and piled into Richard's car, "Elaine, where's your luggage?" he asked.

"Just get me out of here," she shouted, "I've left my damned luggage." So saying, she opened her large bag and, like a jack-in-the-box, out sprang a long-haired dachshund. There was a policeman standing about ten yards away and Richard had visions of Elaine being arrested, sent to jail, and the show not opening.

"Molly," he said, "you have to drive Elaine to the Connaught Hotel and I'll try to rescue the luggage."

Molly, who was also a new arrival in England and had never driven on the left hand side of the road, asked nervously, "Which way is London?"

It took Richard more than an hour to persuade the Customs and Excise officials that his very famous, but quite mad, star had rushed off leaving her luggage before he was allowed to take custody of the fifteen suitcases.

Elaine Stritch
Photograph by Martha Swope - New York Public Library

Back in London, Elaine had smuggled the dog into her hotel room, but apart from dogs not being allowed in the hotel, there was the problem of someone discovering that the animal had been brought into the country illegally.

Richard hatched a plan. He and Molly would look after the dog for a few days and then he would announce that the cast of *Company* had clubbed together to buy a dog "to cheer her up, being so far away from her beloved pooch." So a likely looking dachshund was purchased and presented to her on stage - an excellent photo opportunity for the press and great publicity for the show. Later, the dogs were swapped and the understudy was sold on to another caring person.

Company opened on the 18th January 1972 at Her Majesty's and ran for 344 performances.

Although Stephen Sondheim had expressed himself happy, right up until the opening I continued to worry about the audibility of his lyrics, so I was particularly chuffed when one reviewer stated, "It is wonderful what they can do with wireless microphones these days."

The reviews were not universally enthusiastic, with a couple of major critics failing to appreciate the book's subject matter and revolutionary score. In future years those same critics would be writing about *Company* as "Sondheim's fabulous ground-breaking musical."

During the run of the show, Richard Pilbrow invited me into his office one day and astonished me with an extraordinary proposition.

"I had dinner last night with one of the actresses in the show. You know, the tall one with the dark hair."

"Yes, of course, the zany lady."

"We had a great time. Lovely girl."

"That's nice," I replied, non-committedly while thinking, "Lovely yes, but mad as a brush!"

"Well, it seems that she is keen to move to this country, make a career here, but of course, being American, she would never get a work permit. I suggested that she needed some nice British man to marry. We discussed the possibilities for a while and then I said, 'Hold on, I might know just the chap'. So what do your think?"

"What do you mean, what do I think?"

"Well, you of course. You are single and unattached and she really is a very nice person. You could do worse." I realised he was not joking. He continued, "What have you got to lose? You can always get a divorce after a year or so if it doesn't work out. You could at least meet her."

I was dumfounded. "No. No thank you."

"Can I tell her you are thinking about it?"

"Richard, this is really something I don't want to get involved with."

"Fair enough," he said and moved on to discuss other matters.

Because of the investment in equipment, the hire charge for *Company* was many times more than any other musical to date. I imagined that this would be a one-off. I was wrong. Producers seemed to appreciate the improved sound quality and it set a new standard. Surprisingly, it would be another ten years before Broadway started using professional mixing consoles. The first one was installed in 1982 for *Cats*, and even that was flown over from England.

Stitched Up

Earlier in the year, Harold Fielding made contact again to say that *The Great Waltz* was ending its run at Drury Lane but, exciting news, he was going to replace it with a lavish new musical, *Gone with the Wind*. Could I come up with a scheme and a budget as usual? He had purchased the equipment for *The Great Waltz* but it did not have a proper mixing desk, so I just needed to add the price for this plus the cost of installing a number of loudspeakers around the auditorium for a special surround-sound effect.

I never had a formal contract with Harold. It was always a gentleman's agreement with, perhaps, a personal letter to say 'go ahead'. This time, however, my trust was misplaced. I knew what pleasure he gained from screwing a few pounds here and there from his suppliers as he would often gleefully relate these little victories, but I never thought it would happen to me. Having received the details of the recommended equipment along with the costs, he showed this to the sound operator on *The Great Waltz* and asked him if he could order everything on the list and have it installed. We only heard about this second-hand and, of course, when I tried to contact Harold by telephone, he was not available.

As it turned out, Harold did not make a saving at all. In fact, it cost him. My fee in those days for designing a show was still a paltry £100 or so and I only marked up the equipment by 10-15%. This is why we never became rich! Anyhow, it turned out that the sound operator did not know how to correctly wire up the surround-sound speakers and they were still not working properly on the day of the first public preview. Even Harold did not have the gall to ask for our advice, so he paid through the nose for a technician from another company to drop everything and rescue the situation. I had always enjoyed working for Harold Fielding and it was sad to end like this.

Not to worry, because Peter Coe got in touch and we were soon at work on a new musical he was directing. *Tom Brown's Schooldays* starring Roy Dotrice opened in May at the Cambridge Theatre. It did not catch on, and only ran for ten weeks.

As my friend Tony used to say, "One door closes - another door falls off its hinges."

Jesus Christ Superstar

In July, Neville Thompson, who I had last worked with at the Old Vic on the dreaded *Hamlet*, paid us a visit. He was now the company manager of a new and much-heralded musical called *Jesus Christ Superstar*. He began by enquiring, "Are you busy at the moment?" This was an intriguing question because his show had only three weeks to go before the first preview, so all the technical facilities must have been organised at least a month before this.

I replied that we were not exactly sitting around, but why did he ask? He replied that the producer and the authors were extremely concerned about the sound, because of the problems experienced on previous productions. I was not aware of the history, so he filled me in, beginning with the world premiere in New York nine months back.

The first mistake was when producer Robert Stigwood decided that a rock opera needed someone from the world of rock concerts to handle the sound, not a theatre person. It proved to be a disaster and, at the eleventh hour, he was replaced by Abe Jacob, whose previous experience was mainly handling big concert sound for such artists as Jimi Hendrix and the Mamas and Papas. They were already into previews when Abe arrived and he had to work incredibly fast to rescue a desperate situation. The wireless microphones they were using were not working properly, so he decided to go with wired hand-mikes. One of the difficulties they then had was trying to avoid a large cast becoming completely entangled in cables.

The production received mixed reviews and subsequent productions in Germany and Australia were equally problematic. It was not until a concert version in Paris that Andrew Lloyd-Webber and Tim Rice experienced the kind of sound they were seeking. Static microphones could be used as the cast were not attempting to act or move about the stage.

With the West End premier looming, the two engineers from the French recording studio who had organized and mixed the concert were engaged to handle the London production.

"And here," Neville said, "we get to the crux of the matter. During the past weeks they failed to respond to my repeated requests for their technical requirements and they failed to attend a meeting I set up at the theatre. They did not show up again for a meeting I rescheduled for yesterday. I am now beginning to tear my hair out."

"Are you suggesting," I ventured warily, "that with just three weeks to go that I should take this on?"

"Well, sort of."

"Sort of?"

"As you can imagine, everybody is incredibly concerned. Robert Stigwood is aware that Ian Gibson was the sound designer on the only other British rock musical, *Catch My Soul,* and he has instructed me to see if you and Ian Gibson would work together on this project."

This was not what I was expecting, but I fully understood the reasoning. Abandoned by the French team and with time running out, this was a desperate situation. Nobody had ever staged a rock musical in this country requiring the amplification of a large pit orchestra, augmented by a rock group on stage and a large cast of singers. *Catch My Soul* was tiny compared with *Superstar*, but Ian Gibson had actually worked on a rock musical; I had not.

My immediate reaction was, "Even if it was possible to put a system together in the time, which is doubtful, that idea would never work. Somebody has to be in charge. It would be like two people trying to paint the same picture. Sorry, Neville, but I have to say no."

To tell the truth, it was a relief to have this get-out. The project was far too scary, so good luck to Ian if he was willing to take it on. Apart from that, we were already working on a musical, *Trelawny,* which was due to open the week before *Superstar.* It was impossible.

Neville sounded disappointed, "I understand what you are saying. I will report back to Mr Stigwood."

A couple of hours later, the phone rang. "We've had a meeting. They want you to do it. If you say yes, it gets me out of a big hole." He was almost begging.

I gulped. "Can I come back to you tomorrow? I have to make some phone calls to see if we can possibly put everything together in time."

The first thing I did was to ask the owner of the company that supplied the 12-channel mixing desk for *Company* if he could produce a massively larger one for delivery at the Palace Theatre in less than three weeks. There was a very long pause. Then he said, "Wow! This will need thinking about. We've never built anything this big - and in three weeks! I need to sit in a darkened room for a while." A few hours later, he called back to say that they were on. Only seven months after introducing the first mixing console to the West End, the second one was going to handle 80 microphones.

Not knowing of any British loudspeakers with sufficient power or performance to handle a large orchestra with electric instruments, I was aware that many big Broadway shows used a company called Altec. I contacted the British agents who promised to have eight "Voice of the Theatre" loudspeakers flown over. A call to AKG confirmed that they were more than happy to provide the range of microphones required.

We could never have handled such a large project without the expertise and willingness of two men. Roger Straker who was in charge of all the hire equipment we had been accumulating, and Sam Wise, an electronics genius who had just joined the company as a studio maintenance engineer. As the only person in Theatre Projects with any detailed knowledge of electronics, one of his first jobs was to assist Roger with the installation for *Jesus Christ Superstar*. American by birth, his full imposing name was Samuel Paul Wise IV. He had a young son whose name was Samuel Paul... well, you can work it out for yourself.

Somehow, by working ridiculously long hours, all the wiring was installed, including a massive multi-core cable running from the stage to the control position at the rear of the dress circle. The enormous mixing desk did not arrive until the day before the first sound rehearsal with the cast and musicians. Miraculously, the first time everything was plugged in, it all worked!

As his forte was recording musicians, I persuaded Michael Moor to leave our studio for a day to oversee the orchestra sound. I remained in charge of the other half of the console devoted to the vocal microphones. The first hour was spent with each section of the orchestra - strings, woodwind, brass, percussion, guitars, synthesiser, etc. - playing individually while tone controls were adjusted. Then Michael set a balance with the entire ensemble.

This idea of amplifying a theatre orchestra was totally new to everyone and I had a surreal exchange with one of the musicians. The microphones for the violins were fixed to metal bars spanning the pit above the musicians and, during the break, I asked the leader if any of the microphones were in the way of their bowing. "No, they are fine," he said. Then rather surprisingly added: "But they won't be there for the actual performances, will they." I still cannot imagine what he thought we had been doing all morning.

Having done a wonderful job creating a natural orchestral sound, Michael returned to the studio never to be seen in the Palace Theatre again. I invited him to see a show, but the very idea appalled him.

"The thought of sitting at a mixing desk during a live performance is completely horrifying," he said. "I couldn't even bear to be in the audience. Anything could go wrong at any minute - and in front of all those people! I don't know how you do it. In the studio we can stop, sort things out and do another take."

Even if it had been technically possible at that time to use wireless microphones, Tim Rice and Andrew Lloyd-Webber wished to reproduce a quality of sound similar to the concert version in Paris. Consequently, every member of the cast had access to a handheld microphone.

In order to minimize the risk of all the cables becoming entangled, the set for the London production was specifically designed to contain the action. There was a relatively small central stage with microphones available at the entrances for the principles. Behind this, there was a high platform connected to steep ramps running down either side of the main stage. More microphones were located there for the chorus who often appeared up there as a crowd commenting on the action below.

The orchestra filled the pit, so the rock group was located within the set; the electric guitars and drum kit on one side of the stage and the electric keyboards on the other. Even so, there was no room for the large percussion section (tympani, tubular bells, gongs, etc.), so this had to be accommodated on a separate platform at the rear of the stage.

I was pleased when the musical director, Anthony Bowles, insisted that the audience for *Superstar* should not be subjected to what he described as *"an aural assault course"*. It had always been my plan to save the power in the system for those moments when the action and the score actually warranted it. For example, when Jesus was singing the heart-rending "Gethsemane" at the finale to Act One, the orchestration ranged from piano and voice with hardly any amplification, swelling to a thrillingly loud sound when the thirty-piece orchestra and rock group all joined in. The effect was spine-tingling. It is this kind of dynamic range that makes a truly exciting aural experience.

If everything is loud from the outset, there is nowhere to go. It becomes boring.

Jesus Christ Superstar at the Palace Theatre, London, August 1972. Keyboards at the bottom of the ramp to the left. Guitars and drums on the right. Percussion can just be glimpsed upstage on the right.

On the prestigious opening night, nerves were jangling. Rehearsal time had been limited and Michael Moor was right. Anything could go wrong. My colleague, Roger Norwood, known as 'Big Rodge' because of his height, brought up the faders for the start of the overture and wonderful music filled the theatre. I was standing by to bring up the fader when Paul Nicholas, playing Jesus walked on stage and raised his microphone. My finger on the fader was getting very sweaty. I knew I was touching the right fader, but I kept checking my cue-sheet just to make sure. As he made his entrance, Paul had to pick up the microphone with red tape on the handle. Not the blue, not the green, not the yellow, not the white. What if he picked up the wrong one? His hand would be covering the tape, so there was no way I could know. It went through my mind as the overture was drawing to an end that if no sound came out when he started to sing, I could quickly bring up all the other principal's microphones. He must be holding one of them. On the other hand, he might have the correct microphone, but the connector could have come loose. By now, my hand was so slippery with sweat that I had to quickly rub it on my trousers. Then, there he was. Jesus walked down to the front of the stage, raised his hand with the microphone, I brought up the fader…. and his voice gloriously filled the auditorium. I had never heard anything so wonderful and seldom felt such relief.

Me at the vocal end of the *Superstar* console
with 70s style long hair and beard. My 'Jesus' look.

From then on everything went perfectly, despite a little competition from the Salvation Army band that could sometimes just be heard playing very loudly outside the front of the theatre. They were part of a group of protesters that had gathered in the street before the audience arrived, waving banners with slogans like: "Jesus is not Superstar". Before the show, everyone entering the stage door also had to run the gauntlet of a small crowd thrusting anti-superstar leaflets at us.
Aware of this hostility by these religious groups, there was a moment of concern when, at the end of Act One, I noticed a Bishop wearing dog collar and purple vest making a beeline for our control position at the

rear of the circle. Not knowing how he might be reacting to what many deemed a musical blasphemy, my colleague and I decided to run for it. Unfortunately, we were completely hemmed in by the crush heading for the bar, so all we could do was to sit tight and wait. When His Grace finally arrived, he placed one hand firmly on my shoulder and, with the other, made a sweeping gesture at the console. "You boys," he said, pausing for effect, "are doing a fine job." With that, he continued on his way towards the bar - and we felt blessed.

The production was received by the critics with enthusiasm. One wrote, *"Jesus Christ Superstar* exploded onto the musical scene - stunning audiences and changing the face of musical theatre forever." Another even mentioned the sound, commenting, "You can actually hear lyrics that are worthwhile over the pounding orchestration." *Superstar* ran for eight years, becoming the world's longest-running musical at that time.

Considering the amount of angst and hullabaloo there had been about the sound, one might have expected some kind of acknowledgement from the authors, but we only saw Andrew Lloyd-Webber once. This was during a rehearsal when he found his way up from the stalls to see what we were up to. "That looks complicated," he said, indicating the console, "What does it all do?" We gave him a short demonstration of how we could adjust the volume and tonal quality of individual voices and instruments, and he seemed impressed. "Jolly good," he said, nodding and smiling, and that was the last we saw of him.

The only meeting with Tim Rice was in the theatre bar during an interval in one of the previews. I was with company manager Neville Thomson when we bumped into him in the crush. "Can I introduce David Collison?" said Neville. Tim looked nonplussed. Neville explained, "David is in charge of the sound."

"Oh," said Tim, "you must be the French chap."

The average cost of a sound installation up to that point was around

£1,400. The exception was *Company* that had come in at £5,500, an increase of nearly 400%. *Superstar* had what seemed a colossal budget of £20,000. Six years later, however, American sound designer Abe Jacob was to spend £60,000 on the London production of *Evita*.

Superstar premiered on the 9th August 1972 at the Palace Theatre, just six days after *Trelawny* opened at the Prince of Wales. This meant attending the technical rehearsal and previews of *Trelawny* while organising the installation of the biggest sound system ever installed for a musical. I really needed to be at the Palace Theatre, but both the producer who was paying for my services and the director expected to see me busying about at the Prince of Wales. So Tony and I resorted to a subterfuge employed successfully on a previous occasion when the opening of two shows clashed. This was to ensure that both of us were seen by the producer and director at the curtain up of a preview, then after a while I would slip away. Tony would continue checking the sound and making notes as we always did. If asked my whereabouts, he would say that I was probably wandering around the upper circle or gallery. Producers and directors never go up there. At some point during the second act I would return to be filled in on any problems. Thus, at the inevitable production meetings after each performance, I was able to answer questions. Should some incident be mentioned of which I was not aware, Tony would quickly butt in with, "We discussed this problem, didn't we? It will be fixed for the next show." "Oh yes," I would agree, "It's all in hand."

Starring Gemma Craven, *Trelawney* played at the Prince of Wales for 177 performances.

I continued to be in charge of the vocal microphones on *Superstar* for a number of weeks before reluctantly handing it over. Sitting at the controls for two hours every night listening to this large orchestra playing such an exciting score was a glorious experience. Nevertheless, in September I had to make preparations for three more musicals due to open the following month - within fifteen days of each other!

John Schlesinger

The first of the three was another Theatre Projects production, *I and Albert*. Directed by John Schlesinger, it had Polly James playing the young Queen Victoria. The music was by Charles Strouse with lyrics by Lee Adams, the duo who were responsible for such shows as *Bye Bye Birdie*, *Golden Boy* and, later, the smash hit *Annie*.

Integral to the plot, was a complicated recorded sequence requiring three tape machines in which a procession with the Royal coach was heard approaching from behind the audience, then through the auditorium to the stage. At the same time, there were cheering crowds and a band playing. There was no computer memory available in those days of course, so all the controls had to be operated manually at each performance. John Schlesinger spent a long time sitting beside me at the controls as we tried to achieve exactly what he had in mind. We ran the sequence several times after which he would suggest different timings and alterations to the order or volume of events. After a number of attempts, he cried, "That's it! Print that one. Oh, you can't, can you? Damn it! I don't remember what we did, do you?" Fortunately I did. "That," he said, "is why I like making films."

After one rehearsal when the cast had gone home, John Schlesinger and I had a note session that happened to take place in Polly James's dressing room. When we had finished, Schlesinger picked up Polly's wig and put it on his head. Regarding himself in the mirror, he said, "I should be playing this part. I would be very good." Then he quoted a few lines from the script using a convincingly imperious female voice. What made us laugh was the realisation that, with his profile and the wig, he did look astonishingly like Queen Victoria.

I and Albert was an intimate story that worked really well in the confined space of a rehearsal room but, on stage, the actors were overwhelmed by an enormous set with a background of projected images. Opening at the Piccadilly Theatre on the 6th November, it had lukewarm reviews and only ran for 120 performances.

John Schlesinger
Photograph by Michael Childers

Lauren Bacall

The previews for *I and Albert* had overlapped with rehearsals for the London premiere of another Strouse and Adams musical, *Applause*. It opened at Her Majesty's Theatre only ten days later. With a book by Betty Comden & Adolph Green, this one starred the indomitable American star Lauren Bacall.

Six weeks earlier, Maurice Fournier had warned me that Miss Bacall would only agree to do the show if we could provide a suitable wireless microphone. She had a number of dance routines for which she wore a close fitting top with a skimpy skirt over tights. The only place to hide the battery pack incorporating the transmitter was strapped to a leg immediately beneath her left buttock. The British battery packs were quite a bit larger than the American versions. What could we do about it?

I was able to report that the London-based radiomike company were willing to manufacture a special pack, a little fatter than standard, but with one end of the casing nicely rounded to fit snuggly beneath the buttock in question.

This news was relayed across the Atlantic but Miss Bacall was still concerned, so Bernard Delfont arranged for her to fly over to test it for herself. We had only employed radiomikes on two previous shows, one of those being the fiasco with Carol Channing. I was therefore - shall we say? - tense when the day arrived and I was introduced to the great movie star. She had brought with her an entourage of four gentlemen that included the two American producers.

Company was still running, so the meeting took place on stage at Her Majesty's. The battery pack that all the fuss was about was produced and Miss Bacall hitched up her skirt and strapped it on while I clipped the microphone to the front of her dress. The entourage then descended into the auditorium to have a listen. As she began talking, one of the American producers complained that the sound system was not switched on. Fortuitously, at that very moment, she happened to turn her back on us and walk upstage. To the gentleman's surprise, there was no lessening in sound level or clarity. Thus, thanks to Jack Mann's wonderful loudspeakers, the demonstration was deemed a success. We got the job.

One of the problems with being able to produce such a naturalistic sound was that after sorting out the audibility problems during the early rehearsals, everybody forgets about you. Then, when the producer comes to see a dress rehearsal, he wonders why he is paying for all this expensive equipment. Occasionally, when it seemed necessary to justify my existence, I employed the ruse of closing the master faders in the middle of a technical rehearsal. When the voices suddenly disappeared behind the orchestra, all eyes would turn to the mixing desk. "Sorry, just a little technical problem." I would gaily call out. Then, push the faders up again.

During the run of *Applause*, the wireless system turned out to be reliable. The only real drama was on the first night. The first half went well, but when I caught up with the sound operator towards the end of the interval, he said that he thought - but was not sure - that the radiomike had begun to break up towards the end of the act. On such an important performance we could not take risks, so I grabbed the spare transmitter pack and rushed backstage. Realising that the star would almost certainly be in her second act costume by now, and would have to completely undress in order to replace the transmitter, I suggested that the stage manager should take it to her dressing room. "You must be joking," he said, "That's your problem."

I made a dash for Miss Bacall's dressing room on the first floor, but too late! Processing down the stairs was the star fully dressed for the second act with her dresser holding up the train of her ball gown. With many apologies, I explained that the sound operator thought that there *might* be a problem with the microphone and, *as* it was the first night, I would be *extremely* grateful if she would *consider* using the spare. There was a pause while I was subjected to an unnervingly icy stare. I waited for an explosion, but "Tell your soundman he will have to do better in future." was her only comment before turning on her heels and heading back up to the dressing room - which I thought was a perfectly reasonable response under the circumstances.

Pete And Dud

While all this was going on, my colleague Tony was heavily involved in rehearsals at the Cambridge Theatre for a revue that opened five days later. Entitled *Behind The Fridge* it starred Peter Cook and Dudley Moore. This was to be a short run before a successful tour of Australia and then on to America where, renamed *Good Evening*, it received Tony and Grammy awards.

Tony recalls that the director had very little real control over the rehearsals, largely because a line in the script, or a chance remark would set Peter off on another tack and a fifteen-minute sketch would flow out of his mouth as if it had been written, edited, and rehearsed for a week. The result was that Dudley became incapable with laughter while the director tried, without success, to keep a straight face.

In one sketch they discussed the modern innovation of paper panties. Peter explained, "That Mrs Entwhistle down the road, she uses these new paper panties, you know. Wonderful invention. Wonderful. And every Saturday night she sits down with her panties and a rubber". During rehearsal, for some reason this always sent Dudley into hysterics and it took some time before he was able to continue. Meanwhile, Peter filled in with further impromptu remarks that set him off again.

Tony decided to send Dudley a first night card in the form of a pair of paper panties with Good Luck written across the crotch with a rubber included in the envelope. When it came to the line, Dudley looked up at where Tony was lurking near the sound control and nearly went off again.

Peter Cook was known for liking the odd drink and a rumour went around that the first night was held up because he was drunk. The curtain did go up very late, and many people jumped to the conclusion that backstage they were trying to get Cook sober enough to perform. This apocryphal anecdote was even mentioned after his death on the radio by one of his friends, John Wells. Tony recalls that there was indeed a panic backstage, but this was caused by the failure of a projector that played a vital part in the show.

South Africa

My very good friend John Moss from my time at the Pigalle had relocated to South Africa, where he was Head of Drama for NAPAC (Natal Performing Arts Council) in Durban. He invited me out for a holiday, all expenses paid, on the understanding that I would advise on the sound for their forthcoming pantomime, *Cinderella*. He also asked me to drop by a literary agent in London and collect a script of a play that had been recommended.

Apartheid was at its height and this became evident as soon as we landed at Louis Botha International Airport. Heading for the loo, I came across my first experience of segregation. The sign on the door stated firmly: "BLANKES". Did this mean Blacks? I did not dare to go in. Later, I was to learn that Blankes meant Whites.

At the Customs desk, the official searching my baggage pulled out the script I had brought for John and started riffling through it. At first, I thought he might be some kind of theatre buff. He took some time glancing down the pages, occasionally looking up to eye me suspiciously. Eventually, he demanded in a thick Afrikaans accent, "I have to ask you. Is this script of a pornographic nature?" I was flabbergasted. "No, it's a comedy. I am bringing out for the head of NAPAC." He persisted, "Are you aware of the title?

"No, I never bothered to look at it."

He brandished the script in my face, "Look at the title," he almost shouted, "LOVE IS A FOUR LETTER WORD!"

"I think it is meant to be a joke," I replied weakly.

Still not convinced, and with very bad grace, he threw the script into the case and waved me away.

Clad in khaki shorts, knee length socks and a white short-sleeved shirt, John was waiting with his car. The heat and humidity was oppressive, especially after leaving a grey dank November in London. We drove through the bustling centre of Durban and along the seafront lined with hotels on one side and the beach on the other dotted with sunbathers and a few swimmers. Nannies in smart blue uniforms pushed prams along the promenade and we passed a bowls club with everyone wearing whites and panama hats. It could have been Eastbourne in the thirties, were it not for the palm trees and the fact that the nannies were all black.

A few minutes away from the beach, we pulled up in a quiet tree-lined road of architect-designed detached houses. As were all the others, John's house was surrounded by high walls and hedges and we entered through a locked gate. The front garden was mainly lawn plus a few shrubs and a tree groaning with great clusters of bananas. The main feature was a glistening swimming pool that beckoned seductively in the sticky heat.

Entering the house, I was greeted by John's wife Jill, a British actress and writer, and was introduced to Dorothy the maid, a rotund Zulu woman with a beaming smile. Next, I was taken upstairs to the bathroom to meet Miranda, their three year old daughter and was amazed to see her splashing about in the bath with a similarly aged girl who was black! It was Dorothy's daughter. Whatever happened to Apartheid?

It soon became clear that Dorothy ruled the roost as far as domestic matters were concerned, but I found the relationship with her employers unsettling. Her living quarters were in a krall, a small dark concrete hut tucked away in the garden, and she always referred to John and Jill as "Master" and "Mistress". It was like something out of "Gone With the Wind." On the other hand, their mutual respect and even friendship was obvious, although there were strict boundaries. For example, when I fancied a coffee one day, Jill said, "Go and ask Dorothy, but knock on the door before you enter. The kitchen is her territory."

There were to be more surprises about this segregation business. That evening John, in his capacity as Head of Drama, had been dragooned into adjudicating an amateur one-act play competition. I was invited along. There were three plays, the first two of which were entertaining and well acted. It was the third play that was the eye-opener. It was set in a little girl's Victorian bedroom where, at night, the toys came to life and acted out a story in mime. A beautiful doll, blonde hair and white lacy dress, was courted by a handsome soldier clad in a red tunic. She was flattered, but coy.

A second night, and out of the box climbs a black-faced rag doll with woolly hair and big red smiling lips. Very popular in the 20th century, it was what we all recognised as a golliwog! The beautiful doll is at first alarmed when the golliwog approaches, but he dances around and his antics make her laugh. Soon they are dancing together.

A third night. The beautiful doll and the golliwog greet each other fondly, but when the soldier appears they spring apart. The soldier draws his sword. Alarmed, the doll shields the golliwog. In a jealous rage, the soldier pushed the doll aside and runs the golliwog through. The curtain came down with the doll sobbing beside the dead body while the soldier stands back looking appalled at what he had done.

I could not believe what I was seeing. How could this entirely white audience be applauding this spectacle? At any moment, I expected a posse of policemen to burst through the doors and arrest us all. This was happening 22 years before Nelson Mandela was released from prison and democracy began to be negotiated in South Africa.

John explained that, although it was not generally known in the rest of the world, a large section of the white population was involved in a quiet revolution. In his own theatre where there used to be one performance a week reserved for blacks only, they had, without any form of publicity, simply cancelled this arrangement and allowed blacks, whites or 'coloureds' to book for any show. Another example was the public swimming pool in Durban where the management, without comment, one day removed the "Whites Only" signs.

"What many of us are hoping," John continued, "is that we can improve things step by step and avoid a possible uprising that could end in a bloodbath. Last year, we had another minor breakthrough in the theatre with a production of *Robinson Crusoe*. I had Man Friday and all the native tribe played by Zulus. This was unheard of. Blacks and whites acting on stage together! Before then, it would have been white actors wearing black make-up. The local and national press hardly mentioned it. They just reviewed it like any other show."

The following afternoon, we went to John's theatre so that I could watch the rehearsal and meet the man in charge of sound. John had to return to the office but had arranged for their driver, Joseph, to collect me at the end of rehearsal. At around five thirty, I found a car parked outside the theatre with the NAPAC logo painted on its side. Sitting at the wheel was a good-looking black man, probably in his late thirties, who jumped out and, with a flourish, opened the passenger door. I thanked him, but asked if I could sit in the front seat. "Of course," he said, grinning broadly, "whatever you prefer." During the conversation on the journey, I asked what time he finished work. "Five, six or seven o'clock, depends what is going on in the theatre."

"So what time does your day start?"

"This morning I was out at six."

At six! That was appalling. I could not believe the way these people were being exploited. "That," I said, "is a very long day. Do you always have to work those hours?"

Joseph hooted with laughter. "No, I was not working at six. I was out playing golf. It is the best time, you know. In the cool before the sun is up. The air is so good."

This totally threw me. "Do you play golf a lot?"

"Oh yes. I always keep my clubs in the boot. I really enjoy it – and I've won quite a few cups."

None of this made sense, I was out of my depth. Later, when we passed a parked police car with lights flashing and saw a black police woman handing a speeding ticket to a white driver, I finally gave up trying to get my head around how Apartheid was or was not working.

My two weeks in Durban passed quickly and pleasantly. The pantomime was spectacular with lavish costumes and scenery. John was pleased because, as in previous years during his tenure, it was a sell-out. Moreover, it was the first time anyone could remember that a musical production had not received some mention in the press about inaudibility. No news was good news and because of this, John was also able to justify to his board of governors the cost of my flight.

1973

The Amazing Technicolor Dreamcoat

Being asked by the Stigwood organisation to work on the first West End production of *Joseph and the Amazing Technicolor Dreamcoat* was the most joyous experience of 1973. It opened at the Albery (now Noël Coward) Theatre in February and ran for 243 performances.

This was the first time we dared use as many as six radiomikes, squeezing them into the narrow high frequency band then allotted to the theatre. I was anticipating problems, but not the one that actually occurred. During the first sound rehearsal, a breathless ashen-faced gentleman materialised beside our mixing desk at the side of the upper circle. "I'm the stage manager from *Godspell* " he gasped. *Godspell* was playing next door at Wyndhams Theatre. "We are in the middle of a matinee and your Joseph's voice is coming through loud and clear on our system. I'm sorry, but could you please switch him off!"

Of course, I did so immediately. Tony suggested that introducing Joseph from the Old Testament into their New Testament story might, perhaps, add a little something. Failing to see the humour of the situation, our worried friend thanked us and left. The following day, the manufacturers changed the operating frequency of the offending microphone.

Originally written for a school production, *Joseph* was a short piece with a small cast playing all the parts. The scenery and costumes were very basic and the fun was in seeing how they changed the settings by utilising a series of unlikely props and created different characters with items of clothing, beards and headgear. Towards the rear of the stage was a band of six musicians all wearing red kaftans. Joining in many of the numbers was a children's choir ranged on a three-tier rostrum to one side of the stage. For a story set in ancient Egypt, they were somewhat incongruously dressed in white surpluses. But it all added to the quirkiness and zany humour. And, of course, the music and lyrics were great.

Years later, I took two of my sons to the Palladium where we sat through the version of *Joseph* that has now become standard. Turning it into an overblown spectacle had, for me, squeezed out all the fun. They had also lengthened some of the songs and then reprised them ad nausiam, at the curtain calls. Presumably this was to give the punters their money's worth for the very expensive tickets. Even my sons, who were not around in 1973 to make comparisons, were not impressed.

In contrast to the pleasure of working on *Joseph*, we became involved with what the Americans call a real "turkey". From the little I care to recall of *Kingdom Coming*, it had a story that revolved around cryogenics; freezing bodies in the hope of bringing them back to life in the future. It died after just 14 performances and, hopefully, will never be revived.

Grease

The following month brought relief with a transfer to the West End of the successful Broadway musical *Grease*. Although we did not know it at the time, playing Danny Suko was an actor destined to become a major film star; Richard Gere. Playing opposite him as Sandy was Stacey Gregg. Later in the run, they were replaced by Paul Nicholas and Elaine Paige.

Unlike the movie version, the original stage show was conceived as a spoof of all the teenage angst films that were vehicles for early rock 'n' roll music during the 1950s. Inevitably, they would be set against a school or college background with the star-crossed lovers unable to get together through misunderstandings or because of their social differences. That is, until the big dance scene where the head of the school is scandalized and shocked by the rock music, which somehow brings the lovers together. The films would end with the stuffy school staff, despite themselves, becoming seduced by the beat of the music. Happiness all round.

To the audience in the early 70s who could remember the 50s costumes and hairstyles (greasy combed back quiffs for the men, piled up beehives for the girls), *Grease* was a wonderful send-up, and the songs with all the high falsetto, doo-wops and dingalings were hysterically funny.

Stage versions are now usually based upon the film for which three new songs were written, omitting two from the original show.

Grease opened on the 26th June at the New London Theatre (renamed the Gillian Lynne in 2018) and ran for 236 performances.

On the opening night, there was an embarrassing *contretemps* with the producer when I threatened to walk out, taking my sound operator with me. This is something I have never done before or since and, quite honestly, could never have carried out. The show must go on, and all

Namedropping in the Wings

that. Nonetheless, we had not received the substantial pre-payment agreed in the contract. Normally, one would not have worried too much, but this particular producer had a history of payment problems. The money had been due during the rehearsal period, and despite phone calls and promises that "the cheque was in the post" it had not arrived.

Half an hour before curtain up, I spied the producer heading for the lift up to the dressing rooms. He was wearing an outrageous costume that gave him the appearance of a very camp Teddy Boy. I called out, but he shot into the lift, obviously not wishing to talk. I managed to slip into the lift before the doors closed and found myself arguing about money with this vision in high platform shoes, tight black trousers, jacket smothered in sequins and an enormous wig with the shiny jet black hair. Despite my threat to sabotage the show, he pointed out that there was no way he could get back to the office before curtain up and organise a cheque. He was shortly due in the foyer to greet the VIP guests. Reluctantly, I gave in when he suggested meeting in his office the following morning to sit down calmly and sort it all out.

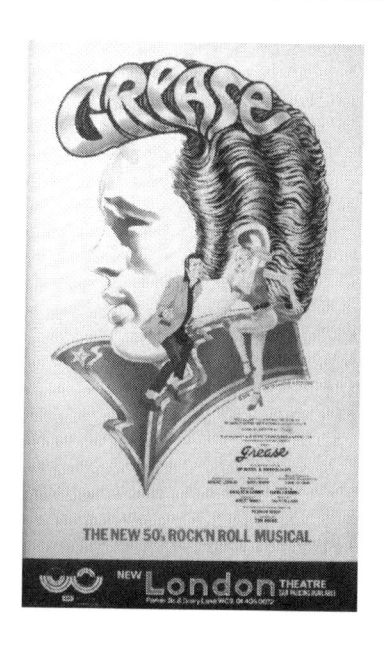

Where money is concerned, I am hopeless at negotiating, so Laurie Blackmore offered to take my place at the meeting the next day. Laurie was assistant managing director to Richard Pilbrow, and the only person in the Theatre Projects organisation who had any grip on the finances.

I was so glad he took my place, because upon his arrival he was informed that the producer was in a meeting and could not be disturbed. I might have accepted this brush-off, but Laurie's reaction was, "Too bad, I am also having a meeting." So saying, he opened the door to the inner sanctum and marched right in. Surprised, the producer demanded to know who he was.

"My name is Blackmore and I have come from Theatre Projects to collect the money you owe us."

The producer looked embarrassed in front of the others sitting around the table, which was precisely the effect Laurie intended.

"Can't you see I am in a meeting?" he blustered, "I cannot deal with that now."

Laurie's response was to pull back a vacant chair, sit down, cross his legs and announce amiably, "Very well. I shall wait."

A few minutes later, he walked out with the cheque.

When I had originally visited this office to discuss the contract for *Grease*, I found the producer studying costume designs for a forthcoming tour of a play that had been running in the West End. He had bought the set at a knock down price and, as he explained with some pride, "I am now saving money on the costumes. Actors are vain creatures and they expect the costumes to be tailor-made for them. So I have bought a load of off-the-peg clothes and paid a designer to draw them on these boards along with the names of the actors." He laughed, "It will make them feel loved, and they will never know."

Pippin

Applause ended its run and here we were again, working on our fifth consecutive musical at Her Majesty's Theatre. With sets and costumes by Tony Walton, for which he had received a Tony Award for the Broadway production, *Pippin* was a stunningly beautiful musical. Bob Fosse had also been awarded Tonys for choreography and direction, and seeing him work was always a privilege.

The piece was set in the Middle Ages with the young prince Pippin, son of Charlemagne basically searching for a meaning to his life. The tuneful score contained a couple of memorable rock ballads. Paul Jones, formerly vocalist with the Manfred Mann group and now a solo performer, played the title role. We were also treated to the thrilling voice of Elizabeth Welch, actress and entertainer who, although born in America, spent most of her career in Britain.

The show ran for nearly 2,000 performances in New York, but the London critics were less enthusiastic. Sadly, it only lasted ten weeks or so - 85 performances.

The Raymond Revuebar

A request from Paul Raymond for Robert Ornbo and me to upgrade the lighting and sound at his famous Revuebar was totally unexpected. Paul Raymond was supposed to be one of the richest men in the UK. Having made a fortune from the Revuebar, he increased his wealth by launching a number of soft-porn magazines (Men Only, Escort, Mayfair, etc.) and investing in property on a large scale.

Robert and I had both been involved with big West End musicals for some time and Robert was currently lighting an opera at Covent Garden, so working in a strip club would be a novel experience. But it was all theatre, wasn't it? And we thought it might be a bit of a laugh, which indeed it was.

Our first meeting with Mr Raymond took place in the theatre space at the club. The auditorium, all red plush and gold, probably held around a hundred people. The stage was quite small, being only some 15 feet (4.5m) square. The lighting and sound equipment was all to be upgraded for his next big production in a few week's time. To discuss the schedule, we were invited for a drink in the very crowded and noisy bar, in the middle of which was a full-size boxing ring surrounded by men shouting at two sweating fighters knocking six bells out of each other. As we pushed our way through the throng, I noticed that Paul Raymond was enjoying our expressions of surprise.

Paul Raymond

There was some studio work to be done for the shows. All the individual acts performed to their own music, which they had on cassette tapes. Most of these were terrible quality, having been recorded in their living rooms with a microphone held in front of a record player. So it was arranged that the six performers would each visit the studio bringing along their cassettes and original LPs for us to record professionally. At the conclusion of each piece of music, Paul Raymond requested an upbeat orchestral riff - da-daa! - to encourage applause at the climax of the act as bare breasts were finally revealed.

They were all very pleasant-looking ladies, not the stunning beauties that Tony and I had been eagerly anticipating. That is, apart a charming petite French girl with an abundance of blonde hair who turned out to be the star of the show. In contrast to the brash music of the fellow artistes, her recording was slow and moody, over which a man's voice could occasionally be heard seductively whispering, "Un homme - Un homme". At one point during the recording, I joked quietly to Tony, "Is he saying *"un homme - un homme"* or is it *"énorme - énorme?"*" There was a kind of tiny gasp from our French client sitting at the other end of the studio. I was convinced that I must have caused offence, but when I looked round she was smiling broadly and merely raised one rather lovely eyebrow in mock reproof.

One of the other interesting characters was a jolly but slightly dumpy little woman who, producing an LP from her carrier bag, announced in a broad Lancashire accent, "I'm using the music from *Barbarus*. That's because my act has like a Roman theme. I wear a long diaphanous robe and sandals like the Romans and, well, Barbarus was Roman, wasn't he? Anyhow," she continued, handing over the album, "I think it sounds Roman. That's the main thing. It's track three." The recording turned out to be the background score to the film "Barabbus" and Tony and I spent the rest of the session carefully avoiding the word.

As we listened to the music she enquired earnestly, "Do *you* think it sounds Roman?" We assured her that it did, which seemed to make her happy. About a minute into the piece, the music swelled. "This is where I get Slimmy out of his basket." she confided, "He's always asleep or drowsy, but soon comes to life once he's wrapped around my body." Noticing the look of puzzlement on our faces, she explained as though it was obvious, "Slimmy. He's a six-foot python. Well, as I was saying, it's the warmth of my body that wakes him up and then, of course, at the end of the act, he quite often doesn't want to go back into his basket because he's all lively. I put his tail in - and then he goes all rigid. Naughty boy. He knows the routine. People don't realise, its not all beer and skittles working with a python. Here, you'll laugh at this. There's a point in the act where I hold Slimmy way out and twirl him round and round and on one show he decided this was the moment to have a pee! He sprayed the whole audience!" She hooted at the memory.

"But that must be a constant worry," I ventured, "Presumably it could happen again."

"No, no. I've stopped his little tricks. Before each show I put a bit of sticking plaster over his little pee-hole. That does it."

With all the recordings completed, a day was set aside for Robert Ornbo to see the girls performing their acts so that he could work out the lighting cues. It was arranged that they would arrive at half hourly intervals and we were looking forward to seeing some glamour at last. We were disappointed. None of them put on - or, indeed, took off - their stage costumes. They walked in from the street, deposited handbags and shopping on the side of the stage and demonstrated their routines in whatever they happened to be wearing, mostly not even bothering to take off their outer garments. The spectacle of these women parading around the stage, miming their striptease movements to the raunchy music while wearing raincoats and plastic macs was hysterical. Because Paul Raymond was sitting with us and taking it all very seriously, we had to refrain from laughter or making silly comments, but for us, it was far more entertaining than the actual show.

Sadly, when we did get to the dress - or undress - rehearsal, the acts were for the most part, at least for me and Robert, distinctly unsexy. They were boringly formulaic and completely lacking in subtlety. The notable exception was our little French friend. Here we had a professionally choreographed piece of theatre. She moved like a dancer, and with a coquettish sense of humour, enticed the audience by not quite revealing what they wanted to see until the very end. Her strip really was a proper tease and the finale was worth waiting for.

There were two moments during the act with our friend and her python when we had difficulty controlling our laughter. The first was when the lady threw aside her "long diaphanous robe" (piece of semi-transparent gauze), pulled Slimmy from his basket and was endeavouring to wrap him around her tubby little body. Paul Raymond, seated next to us in the centre of the auditorium, was muttering to himself little words of approval such as "Good. Oh yes. Nice." until she took hold of the snake's pointed tail and pulled it up between her legs. Paul immediately jumped up and ran down the stage, shouting above the music, "No, sorry darling, you can't do that. You'll have the place closed down. Its lovely, but I can't risk it. We'll set the tape back and just do something a little... you know... different." Returning to where we were sitting, he remarked, "Powerful act, that. Powerful act."

The second incident that caused us to bite our tongues was when Slimmy had to be returned to his basket and he did, indeed, go rigid. The sight of a plump little woman, wearing nothing but sandals and a skimpy G-string, wrestling a reluctant six-foot python into a basket before cramming on the lid to keep it there is a memory to treasure.

We attended the first pubic performance, and Paul was delighted because it went down well with the punters. The running time was less than an hour, which led Robert to remark that at least it was a good deal shorter than *Pelias and Melisande* he had been lighting at Covent Garden.

There is a postscript to the Revuebar experience when, many years later, Robert was working at an opera house in Germany. One evening, when he was standing at the bar in his hotel, a shortish woman approached saying, "Hello Robert. This is a surprise. What are you doing in Germany?" For the life of him, he could not think who it was or where he might have met her. Hoping that something might click, he replied, "I'm lighting a show at the opera house. What are you up to these days?" "Oh, you know, still doing the same thing, but living here in Germany at the moment." That was no help, so he persisted, "And how's it going?" "Can't complain. But, sadly, Slimmy is no longer with me, of course." That rang some sort of bell, but out of context Robert was still baffled until he noticed her hand caressing the snakeskin handbag she had placed on the bar.

LIfe was exciting, the work fulfilling, and the Theatre Projects Group was expanding in all directions. In addition to the studio and the lighting and sound design and rental business, we were involved in the sale and manufacturing of sound equipment, audio-visual production and costume making. Richard's schedule was manic because he took the lead on consultancy projects, often having to travel abroad, whilst continually being asked to design the lighting for West End and Broadway shows. As a producer, he had two more productions in the pipeline and he was also involved with film production. *Swallows and Amazons* starring Virginia McKenna and Ronald Fraser, produced in association with EMI had just been completed.

Although we were apparently riding the crest of a wave, nobody was getting rich. Far from it. Fees for lighting and sound design were still nominal, because our main aim for this creative work was to secure long-term rental deals. In the same way, sound effects created for West End or touring shows inevitably resulted in an equipment hire contract.

Some months earlier, Richard had been talking to a former managing director of the country's leading theatre lighting manufacturing company Rank Strand, who had expressed himself amazed and appalled that an apparently successful organisation, with a reputation in the business second to none, was not making vast profits. What was needed was professional management and investment to transform this collection of talented but amateur enthusiasts into a commercially viable business. Everyone could then be paid proper salaries. In the long term, Theatre Projects would be floated onto the stock market as a public company, at which point we would all become rich. This sounded most attractive. This conversation resulted in his appointment as managing director of the Theatre Projects Group with Richard becoming chairman. Outwardly, the new MD was charming and friendly, but there was something about him I did not quite trust from the outset.

One of the first major changes he instigated was to put all the sound and lighting activities involved with live theatre into one company called Theatre Projects Services. My 90% shareholding in the now defunct sound company was transformed into 6% of shares in the new set up. As the solicitor dealing with the paperwork pointed out, it is better to have 6% of something big rather than 90% of not very much. Investment in lighting hire had been considerable during the past few years and it had grown into a profitable business.

Sadly, Laurie Blackmore who had been Richard's loyal right hand man for the past four years, handling the finances and keeping everything together during a remarkable period of expansion - without funding - felt sidelined and handed in his notice. We lost a good friend.

Another major event occurred in 1973. This one a little more personal. A recording I was supervising in the studio unexpectedly led to romance. I hit it off with the actress involved and we began to see a lot of each other during the following months and were married eighteen months later.

She happened to be an enormous fan of Lonnie Donegan, a huge star at the time, and one evening when she was due to meet me in the studio, we were alerted to her presence by a piercing shriek that seemed to be a combination of horror and delight. Walking into our little office she had come face to face with her hero, naked except for socks and underpants. He had just completed a recording session and had asked for somewhere private to change into a dress suit for a function he was attending that night. Fortunately, he had a sense of humour and was highly amused by the incident.

1974

Michael Crawford And Ghosts

1974 began with a revival of *Oh, Kay!* - a creaky 1926 musical comedy starring Amanda Barrie. With music and lyrics by George and Ira Gershwin, there were some pleasant songs including the standard "Someone to Watch Over Me", but one would not expect such a banal plot and lack of jokes from a book written by Guy Bolton and P G Wodehouse. *Oh, Kay!* occupied The Westminster Theatre for seven months.

In April, a new musical that was to make Michael Crawford a star opened in Manchester prior to its London run at the Theatre Royal, Drury Lane. Based on the play *Billy Liar* by Keith Waterhouse and Willis Hall, *Billy* had a score by John Barry and lyrics by Don Black.

Making the actors heard on the enormous set designed by Ralph Koltai was going to be a challenge. Michael Crawford did not possess a powerful singing voice and would have to rely on a wireless microphone. Being on stage for pretty well the entire show, he was concerned about the reliability factor. My suggestion, therefore, was that he should wear two transmitter packs so that the sound operator could switch over to the stand-by receiver on a different frequency if the first one failed.

He was up for this idea and I produced one of the packs specially made for Lauren Bacall. "Well," he said, turning it over in his hands, "If they were good enough for Miss Bacall, what can I say?" I explained that they were smaller than normal because it had to be hidden beneath her very skimpy costume. "So where did she actually wear it?" he enquired.

"Just here," I said, indicating my posterior, "under her left buttock."

"Yuk!" he exclaimed, throwing the transmitter back at me, "I hope it's been washed!"

I made the decision to use three more wireless microphones to be shared amongst members of the cast, including Elaine Paige who was playing one of Billy's girlfriends and sang one of her numbers on a high platform on the multi-level set. I did not dare to use more radiomikes because the more you used in those days, the less stable they became.

Both Tony Horder and I were credited on the show, because I was not available for the short try-out run in Manchester where they had a much simpler version of the scenery. Largely built with scaffolding, many of us thought that the show worked much better in this more intimate setting. If the live theatre is all about contact with an audience to tell a story, the actors' task is always more difficult if they are dwarfed by the scenery.

A large steel structure was being built on the Drury Lane stage while the show was enjoying an enthusiastic reception in Manchester. Because there were so many technical elements to be coordinated, we installed a system whereby instructions from the stage manager could be heard by the stagehands and lighting technicians via wireless headsets. Ralph Koltai requested a headset, which he wore sitting alone in the stalls watching the technical rehearsals. I assumed that he wanted to listen in on the instructions being given to the men operating the motors for the moving elements of his set, and the flymen raising and lowering other pieces of scenery. At one point, during a long and tedious day, I happened to pass him and he removed the headset, saying, "These things are marvellous. I want one on every production from now on." "Oh, good," I replied, pleased, "it's useful hearing the cues from the stage manager then." He laughed, "No, I have it switched off. Everyone thinks I am listening and concentrating, so they don't pester me with silly questions and comments. Technology. I love it!"

There was a worrying moment at the first full dress rehearsal when the orchestra struck up and nearly blasted Michael Crawford off the stage. Even when he was standing twenty feet from the front of the stage, his radiomike was picking up more band than voice. This often happens at the first orchestral rehearsal, as musicians tend to play their instruments at full volume when the score is unfamiliar, but this was a particularly large orchestra and the musical director would have to be told to moderate the sound during the vocal numbers.

I was making notes as usual when the lyric writer, Don Black, came rushing up to the sound console, shouting above the incredible din that the star could not be heard... as if I had not noticed! I yelled back that the only live microphone at the time was Crawford's radiomike, which meant that the band was too loud. Not seeming to comprehend this simple concept, he screamed hysterically: "Turn up the knob!" This was a fatuous request, so I asked: "Which knob would you like? I have about two hundred here." "I don't care." he replied, "Just turn up the bloody knob!" So saying, he turned on his heels and stormed off.

A while later, I had a discussion with the director and the musical director and we sorted out the vocal to orchestral balance. That is what rehearsals are for and, presumably, why I was employed. But this kind of exchange, although not usually quite so crass, did occur with monotonous regularity and was the main reason for eventually becoming disenchanted with my chosen career - or rather, the career that had chosen me.

Discussing this subject with American sound designer Abe Jacob, he remarked, "The trouble is, you are always at the mercy of the director, the composer or the producer all of whom think they know best. And it is amazing how often you receive comments from other people who happen to be working on the show. The fact is that people working in the theatre know two jobs: their own... and sound! Everyone is a sound expert."

Having a light voice, Michael Crawford relied entirely upon his radiomike, and the sound operator, Claire Laver, did a brilliant job making him sound good, even to the extent of dropping the fader whenever he took a large breath. Knowing that they got on well and he appreciated her skills, I could not believe it when Harold Fielding rang one morning with the same message I had heard three years before on the Tommy Steel show: *"My star refuses to perform tonight with your sound operator"*. I knew that it could not have been anything to do with Claire's technical skill, so what was the problem? Harold did not know. All he wanted was to placate his star and, to this end, insisted that I talk to Crawford before the show to assure him that there would be someone different and competent at the controls that night.

It turned out that this crisis had occurred at a point during the previous night's performance when Crawford's radio microphone had begun to break up. Claire had switched over to the stand-by system but, horror of horrors, that one failed too. There was nothing she could do from her operating position in the auditorium, but turn up the foot microphones.

Claire with Michael Crawford and the wireless microphone.

Later, when Claire visited Crawford's dressing room to explain and apologise, he gave vent to his feelings in no uncertain terms. As the failure of the equipment was in no way caused by her incompetence, she objected to the language and made it clear that she no longer wished to have anything to do with the performer or his microphones. Fortunately, Roger Norwood who had originally worked with me on *Superstar*, had operated the show for a while when I needed Claire to assist on the opening of another show. He agreed to take over until we could train up someone else.

It was with some trepidation that I knocked on the dressing room door that evening to do my bit of grovelling. Mr Fielding's star, reclining on a medical bed while being massaged, welcomed me civilly and listened as I explained how sorry I was that two separate systems had failed at the same moment, a tragic coincidence that we fervently hoped would never happen again. Crawford understood, but asked me to think about it from his point of view. Could I imagine the stress he was under, being responsible for carrying the entire show? It was because of him that the show was such a success and why they had full houses. I should see the number of fan letters he received. He could not afford to let them down. Having to be on stage eight times a week and remain on top form was an enormous responsibility.

I expressed my sympathy and appreciation of how difficult it must be for him. The equipment, I assured him, had been double-checked and Claire's deputy, who had operated the show before, was standing by at the controls. At that moment, the five-minute call came over the dressing room loudspeaker, giving me an excuse to make an exit. As I left, he was putting drops into his eyes to make them glisten under the spotlights.

It turned out that Claire was more than happy to move on from Drury Lane, not just because of the recent incident, but because of the ghost! The sound control was situated in a box at the side of the upper circle, which she claimed was haunted. Now Claire, being very practical and down-to-earth, was the last person I would have expected to contemplate the supernatural. However, she insisted that the door to the box, too heavy to be moved by a draught, would sometimes open on its own accord. A moving door she could cope with, but when spectral fingers started tampering with the controls on the mixing desk, this was beyond a joke. As she appeared to be completely serious, I asked her to explain.

"Well, I always check that everything is working before the audience comes in, then I go away for half an hour making sure that the door to the box is locked. Sometimes, when I come back I find that some of the switches and controls have been moved."

"That's impossible."

"I know, but I'm not making it up."

"How often does this occur?"

"Well, it happened quite a lot at the beginning of the run and it became incredibly annoying, so I decided to talk to it. I said, 'Look, I have a job to do here. Go away and stop bloody interfering!' After that everything was fine for a couple of weeks or so, then it started its tricks again. And so it goes on. Every so often I have to tell it in no uncertain terms to *bog off!*"

I was still not convinced. If this extraordinary story was true, I wondered why Roger Norwood had not experienced the same thing when filling in for her. So I asked him.

"Oh, yes, that box is definitely haunted. Nobody can get in when the door is locked, but somebody - or something - is always fiddling with the knobs."

Drury Lane is said to be the world's most haunted theatre; not surprising, as there has been a theatre on the site since 1663. The ghost of Charles Macklin who killed a fellow actor in an argument over a wig is said to wander the backstage corridor near the spot where it happened in 1735. Dan Leno, the music hall comedian and actor, is reported to appear in one of the dressing rooms, and there are many tales of the great clown Grimaldi (1778-1837) who is said to be a helpful apparition. Actors have reported feeling an unseen presence guiding them to the correct position on the stage to get the laugh that was missing.

One of the most famous apparitions, known as The Man in Grey, occasionally appears at the rear of the upper circle. Wearing a long grey coat and tricorn hat, he is only seen at matinees, preferring not to attend evening performances. Legend has it that he never appears at all if the show is a bummer. Obviously a spirit with taste.

During one of the performances of *Billy,* I retired to the bar for a much-needed scotch and got talking to one of the front-of-house managers. When I enquired if he believed in these stories about The Man in Grey he turned to one of his colleagues who happened to be propping up the other end of the bar, and called out, "Have you seen the Grey Man recently, Bill?" "No," came the reply, as though they were casually discussing one of the box office staff, "I haven't seen him for several weeks."

I mentioned all this to Robert Stanton, who had been the stage manager on *My Fair Lady* and he was not at all surprised.

"I was in the prompt corner running the show one night when someone tapped me quite hard on the shoulder. I was about to do a lighting cue, so I said 'Hang on a moment', but when I looked round, there was nobody there. The incident was quite unsettling, but I kept quiet about it until I heard my deputy stage manager, who often ran the show, telling one of his colleagues of exactly the same experience. We compared notes and concluded something inexplicable had definitely occurred and neither of us was mad."

Although never having actually met a ghost, I did have a near supernatural encounter at the Adelphi Theatre during *Blitz!*. After curtain down a group of us often retired to the nearby pub for a drink and a chat. One evening, realising that I had left my briefcase in the stage manager's office, I returned to the theatre and just inside the stage door two members of the lighting staff, Clinton and Jeff, were standing there with worried looks on their faces. "What's the matter?" I asked brightly, "You look as though you've seen a ghost."

"We have," replied Clinton, "At least Jeff has. We were just about to turn off the little working light at the back of the stage when it happened. We've come up to fetch a torch. We have to go back down to the stage and switch off that light. I don't suppose you would come with us, would you?"

"OK," I said tentatively, not wishing to appear a wimp.

So the three of us set off down the long stone staircase that led to the back of the stage. Clinton opened the door and we peered in. All was dark except a single 100 watt bulb on the back wall some thirty feet away.

"So what happened?" I whispered. "Well," said Clinton, also whispering, "I went across to switch off the light. Jeff was standing by the door, keeping it open so that I could see my way back, when suddenly he shouted, 'CLINTON!!!' and there was such panic in his voice that I just ran back to the door and we scooted up the stairs."

Jeff took up the story, "What I saw was this figure standing back there kind of staring at me. It looked like a man wearing a sort of cloak and he didn't seem to have feet. The lower part of him sort of faded out. It was when it started to move towards me that I shouted."

By this time, my nerves were on edge and by common consent, all three of us crept apprehensively towards the light switch with Clinton shining his torch all around. Once there, he switched off the light and we beat a hasty retreat to the safety of the lit corridor.

The following day, I sought out the theatre manager and asked if he had ever heard of a ghostly presence backstage. "Oh, yes," he confirmed, "That will be the Victorian actor William Terris. He was a very popular matinee idol and the story goes that he was murdered at the stage door by a jealous 'out of work' actor. He died in one of the dressing rooms in the arms of an actress who was also his lover. There have been a number of sightings over the years, both in the theatre and out along the alleyway beside the stage door."

It seems that every old theatre can boast of at least one ghost, but Drury Lane probably has the most. One imagines that The Man in Grey must have shown up during a matinee of *Billy*, because the show was certainly not a bummer. The Daily Express called it "the most successful British musical since *Oliver!*," while The Sunday People said it was "the brightest British musical for years... it is going to hoist brilliant Michael Crawford into the ranks of the superstars."

It occupied the Lane for more than two years with Roy Castle taking over from Crawford in the latter part of the run.

Incidentally, the opening of *Billy* was the very last time I witnessed an entire first night audience in evening dress. To see the splendid auditorium at the Theatre Royal Drury Lane a sea of men in black ties and ladies in their gowns and jewelry was an unforgettable sight and made a premiere a truly special occasion.

Hair

The month after the opening of *Billy*, I was asked by the Stigwood Organisation to work on the first West End revival of the musical *Hair*. It was to be a short run during the summer months at the Queens Theatre (now renamed the Sondheim). It was a splendid production, only slightly marred on the first night by the management not having warned a member of the front-of-house staff how the show began. The curtain went up and the company was singing the opening number when an actor, pretending to be a member of the public, strode down the aisle, shouting abuse at the cast. He had reached the middle of the auditorium when an elderly usher rushed down the aisle and grabbed him. A tussle ensued and the actor, remaining in character, began including the usher in his tirade. Finally, pulling himself away from his would-be captor he ran a few paces, turned, and ripped open the mackintosh he was wearing to reveal nothing underneath.

Being thus unexpectedly flashed, the poor usher stopped in his tracks long enough for the actor to continue down the aisle and leap on to the stage. The audience was in fits of laughter and the poor gentleman, now highly embarrassed, made his retreat, muttering darkly.

Robert Stigwood was so impressed with the standard of the production that he decided to invite the entire cast to his house after the show for a party. During the interval, he went backstage and asked the stage manager if he could organise transport. Finding a company to provide a coach at such short notice and so late at night would seem to be impossible, but impossible is what stage managers do.

Most of the cast boarded the coach, but those of us with our own vehicles were given directions to the very splendid mansion on the outskirts of London. Stigwood's staff can only have been given two hours notice, but when we arrived, there in the grand hall was an enormous table groaning with food, behind which a chef was busy carving roast chicken, ham and beef. How they had done all this in so short a time was a mystery. There must have been one almighty big freezer somewhere. Uniformed staff circulated with trays of champagne and there was a bar for any type of drink you fancied. The outdoor garden was floodlit and happily sozzled actors were soon throwing off their clothes and splashing about in the heated swimming pool.

After sampling the splendid food and knocking back a couple of drinks, it was past midnight and time to go. Unlike the actors, I had work to do in the morning. But first, needing to find the loo, I approached the elegant grey-haired gentleman guarding the baronial front door. Resplendent in black suit, grey waistcoat, white shirt with winged collar and black tie, this was obviously Mr Stigwood's butler. He pointed me in the right direction, but with a warning that there might be a queue, which indeed there was. Abandoning the whole idea I headed back. The butler, stepping forward, opened the large oak door but as I approached the threshold, he gave a discrete little cough.

"Certain gentlemen," he confided in hushed tones, "are taking advantage of the shrubbery."

Feeling a bit like Bertie Wooster, I thanked him for this interesting piece of information that, moments later, was to deliver me of much relief.

The Good Companions

The same month that *Hair* opened in the West End saw us at the Palace Theatre Manchester with the try-out of a new musical that, if the eminence of the stars and creators was anything to go by, was destined to be a sure fire success. *The Good Companions*, based on the novel and play by J B Priestley had a book by Ronald Harwood, lyrics by Johnny Mercer and a score by Andre Previn. Ronald Harwood was already an acclaimed author whose later works included *The Dresser* for the theatre and screenplays such as *The Pianist*. Andre Previn's work as a world-renowned conductor and composer is legendary, but I was most in awe of Johnny Mercer. Here was a man who had been a singer with the Paul Whiteman orchestra, duetted with the likes of Bing Crosby and Hoagy Carmichael (with whom he wrote "Stardust"), and written the lyrics for more than nine hundred published songs including "Brother Can You Spare a Dime", "That Old Black Magic", "Jeepers Creepers", "Lazy Bones. "Moon River", "The Shadow of Your Smile" and "Something's Gotta Give". The list is endless, and the fact that he was actually there added to the pressure of ensuring that his lyrics were heard.

The story of *The Good Companions* concerns the chance meeting of three disparate characters: Jess Oakroyd, a middle-aged working class Yorkshireman, a disillusioned male teacher, Inigo Jollifant and Miss Trant, a wealthy upper-middle class spinster. The trio become involved with a failing concert troupe called the "Dinky Doos" and Miss Trant decides to refloat the company with the help of Jollifant who can play the piano with Oakroyd as the practical handyman. Various adventures ensue.

Playing the leading parts were John Mills as Oakroyd, Judi Dench as Miss Trant, Christopher Gable as Jollifant and taking over from one of the cast when it moved to London was Marti Webb as Susie Dean, a member of the troupe.

Seeing John Mills singing and dancing so effortlessly was an eye-opener but, as he said, "I started life as a hoofer." His first professional West End engagement in 1929 was in a musical and he followed this with a cabaret act. Judi Dench was as wonderful as ever despite having a problem with the director.

The show was produced by Bernard Delfont (now Lord Delfont) and directed by Braham Murray. Theatre Projects was responsible for the general management. Following the Manchester opening, there was a meeting with the entire creative team where Bernard Delfont expressed himself displeased, demanding some major changes. A number of improvements were discussed and Richard Pilbrow called a rehearsal for the following morning with the cast and everyone else involved. To his surprise, Andre Previn did not turn up and it was later discovered that he was on a plane back to Los Angeles. Despite several requests during the next few weeks, he was not seen again until the day of the West End premiere.

Some alterations were made to the production, but the director seemed incapable of implementing anything dramatic enough to pull it into shape. The cast found it frustrating and even Judi Dench, renowned for her professionalism and sense of humour, began to lose patience, at one point shouting from the stage, "Give us some direction, Braham. What do you want us to *do*?"

Before one performance, I mentioned to Judi that our sound operator had been surprised on the previous night when she had sung a particular number much quieter than usual. Was she going to perform it that way tonight? She apologised and explained that she had been asked at the last moment to make the song more wistful and introspective.

"What do you think? Was it more effective?" she asked, obviously having had no comment on her performance.

"Well, it's not for me to say, and we can adjust the microphones whatever you do."

"Yes, I know all that, but which version do you prefer?"

"I thought that when you gave it more welly, it had more impact, more emotion. But that is just my reaction."

"Thank you. That," she declared firmly, "is how it will be in future."

It comes to something when one of our greatest actors has to ask the soundman for an opinion on her performance. Judi Dench later wrote in her autobiography, "Braham talked a good show, but did not have a clue how to deliver one."

The Good Companions opened at Her Majesty's Theatre. After a six month break, I was back there once again.

On first nights I tended to wander nervously around the auditorium, checking audibility on all levels and occasionally making pit stops at convenient bars. On this occasion I was walking along a corridor at the side of the stalls when I came across Richard Pilbrow perched on a short flight of stairs alongside the ample figure of J B Priestley. Richard made the introductions and invited me to join them. Priestley explained that he had been telling Richard how he had been in this very theatre back in 1931 on the first night of the play that was based on his book.

"Listen," he said, "those lines we can hear John Mills saying right now were originally spoken by a young John Gielgud on the same stage forty years ago. It's a weird experience."

Richard asked if the play had been a success. "It played here for nine months or so," he replied, "which was a pretty good run in those days."

Priestley went on to regale us with anecdotes about the production, but I cannot recall exactly what was said; just that I sat on a staircase with one of the country's literary giants talking about his past.

The musical of *The Good Companions* received mixed reviews, playing at Her Majesty's, as did the original play, for nine months.

The Beatles

There was a three week break before rehearsing another new musical that originated at the Everyman Theatre in Liverpool. *John, Paul, George, Ringo... and Bert* was due to transfer to the Lyric Theatre in London. Written by Willy Russell and based loosely on the story of the Beatles, it ran for a year and was named "Best Musical of 1974" by the Evening Standard Theatre Awards and the London Critics' awards.

There was a superb cast of then unknown actors with Antony Sher (now Sir Antony) as Ringo Starr, Trevor Eve as Paul McCartney, Bernard Hill as John Lennon and Philip Joseph as George Harrison. Much of the show's success was down to newcomer Barbara Dickson who was onstage throughout playing the piano and singing the Beatles' songs. Robert Stigwood, co-producer with Michael Codron, immediately signed her to his record label where she recorded the album "Answer Me" with the title track becoming a top ten hit. The show also led to a guest residency for Barbara Dickson on the Two Ronnies television series and the following year she had a major hit when Andrew Lloyd-Webber and Tim Rice invited her to record "Another Suitcase in Another Hall" from their forthcoming *Evita*.

There was only one spot in the show when the actors actually mimed to a Beatles recording. It was supposed to be the Fab Four getting together again for one last concert. I let rip with the sound on stage and from all around the auditorium there were recordings of girls screaming.

B A Young in the Financial Times wrote: *"When a Beatles sound was needed for dramatic purposes, it came from a recording with the Beatles miming. Half the audience did not seem to notice. They clapped like anything. Perhaps they were clapping David Collison who adroitly controls the sound, bringing the kilowatts up to danger level at the proper moment."*

Trevor Eve, Philip Joseph, Antony Sher, and Bernard Hill.

More Nudes And More Dolphins

Going from the sublime to the ridiculous, that year there was one more musical to tackle, the sixth, over which we should probably draw a thick veil. This was Paul Raymond's *Royalty Follies.* Robert Ornbo and I were once again contracted to handle the lighting and sound for a lavish production at the Royalty (now Peacock) Theatre. The show had many international artistes including a nude lady swimming with a couple of dolphins. It also featured Paul's daughter, Debbie, as the female vocalist. During the public previews, Paul had second thoughts about giving his daughter this big break. In the bar one evening, he asked Robert and me for our honest opinions.

"Is she good enough? I'm beginning to think I made a mistake putting her in the show. Tell me what you think. Should I replace her?"

Well, we both thought her pleasant to look at, and that she had a perfectly adequate, although not great, voice. Replacing her was not going to save the show. There were far more fundamental problems. So we both said that she was lovely and he was worrying unnecessarily.

The opening was a disaster and in an attempt to disassociate the show from the scathing press reviews, the *Royalty Follies* was a few weeks later subtly retitled *The Great International Nude Show.*

The big selling point, or so Raymond imagined, was that the showgirls performed totally nude for the first time in a West End spectacular. They appeared just wearing sparkly high-heeled shoes, fantastic wigs and headdresses, and nothing else. Far from being sexy, it just looked as though they had forgotten to put on their knickers. The audience stayed away in droves and the impresario lost a small fortune. But he could afford it!

Rocky Horror Show

The incredibly successful *Rocky Horror Show* had transferred from where it premiered at the Royal Court Theatre to a disused cinema in central London. Although we were not originally involved, the producer Michael White asked for my advice because he was receiving complaints about audibility. The solution was simple: reduce the ear-splitting level of the band to allow the vocals to be heard. Over a couple of nights this was achieved and Michael White expressed himself happy.

The sound operator did not appreciate my interference. He knew the lyrics by heart and relished the big thumping disco sound. I am pretty sure that the decibels crept back up again as soon as he was left to his own devices.

Jesus Christ Superstar was still running, so incredibly, for a period of four months during 1974 we had designed and supplied sound equipment for every musical in the West End.

A Brush With The Musician's Union

Among the straight plays for which we supplied sound effects that year, *A Streetcar Named Desire* was memorable for falling foul of the musicians union. Produced by Bernard Delfont at the Piccadilly Theatre, it starred Claire Bloom as Blanche DuBois, Morag Hood as Stella Kowalski, Martin Shaw as Stanley Kowalski and Joss Ackland as Harold Mitchell. The whole production had rave reviews with many plaudits for the leading lady. Tennessee Williams attended a performance and declared, "I am absolutely wild about Claire Bloom."

The director, Ed Sherrin, had asked me to supply various street noises and other sounds of life in a New Orleans tenement block, including some authentic jazz music to be heard as though coming from a distant radio. When a commercial recording is copied, it is necessary to obtain permission from the Mechanical Copyright Protection Society and if it is to be played in public, further permission must be obtained from the Performing Rights Society. Both organisations then levy royalties for their members the songwriters, composers and publishers. In this instance, we duly filled in the applications as usual, so were surprised when the musicians union came up with an objection. They stated that the reproduction of recorded music in a theatrical production was not permitted, insisting that five musicians should be employed to play the music live at every performance.

This was, of course, nonsense and Ed Sherrin asked for a meeting to discuss the situation. The union official arrived at the theatre and restated their case, but he had the wind taken out of his sails when the director said,

"O.K. So find me five musicians in London capable of playing authentic New Orleans Jazz."

Obviously, this was not feasible and so as not to completely lose face, the union finally agreed that the recording could be used so long as a live pianist was employed to play along with it.

A musical arranger was commissioned to listen to the recording and write a suitable piano score. An upright piano was hired and installed in the wings. But when played in a rehearsal, it was far too loud and sounded ridiculous. At my suggestion, the piano was moved to a dressing room where we could use a microphone to control the level and blend it in with the recording. This proved to be more satisfactory.

During one of the previews, Ed Sherrin asked for the level of the piano to be taken down a little, which he said was an improvement. A little while later, he said, "What if you take it down a touch more?" I adjusted the fader again. "Yes, that's even better." He listened for a moment, considering, then, "What if you fade it out completely?" I obliged. "That's it," he said, "Plot that. But let it remain a secret just between the two of us."

The pianist turned up every night, donned a headset to hear the jazz recording, waited for the cuelight from the stage manager and then played the music that had been especially scored for him - and nobody ever heard a note.

1975

Stagesound

Under our new managing director's expansion plans, Theatre Projects acquired Stagesound Limited, formerly the leading sound company in the British theatre. Since the death of its founder ten years earlier, it had gone into decline and was now in the hands of the receiver. Once having offered me employment on the grounds that I could never compete with such an organisation, I now found myself running it.

The purchase of Stagesound included a building in Langley Street and an adjacent building in Mercer Street in the centre of Covent Garden, only a stone's throw from the TP (Theatre Projects) offices in Long Acre. Mercer Street became the base for the lighting hire company and a retail shop. Langley Street housed the expanding sound hire company and our fledgling manufacturing business under Sam Wise. After designing and building a mixing desk for our new voice-over studio, Sam went on to develop a version for the hire department. It was the first ever affordable mixing desk that was truly modular. Designed specifically for theatre use along with an equally ground-breaking intercom, it soon attracted a broader interest and this led to setting up a manufacturing and sales business.

Sam later developed a much more sophisticated console for Pinewood Studios. It was used for dubbing many major films, including several *James Bond* and all the *Superman* movies until 1999 when it was sold to a studio in Japan.

A Little Night Music

Tony Horder and I had by now worked in every one of the 36 West End theatres, some of them several times. It always gave us a buzz to be allowed to walk through any stage door merely by mentioning the magic words "Theatre Projects". Although most of my time was taken up with consultancy projects and managing the new sound manufacturing business, I managed to fit in three more major musicals that year.

The first was another Theatre Projects co-production with Hal Prince of Stephen Sondheim's *A Little Night Music*. Directed by Hal, it starred Jean Simmons, Joss Ackland and the wonderful Hermione Gingold who, when Richard Pilbrow introduced me to her, commented, "I don't really *like* microphones, you know. They make one sound so *unnatural*." I replied that some of the cast would benefit from a little help, but assured her that the amplification would be extremely subtle during her numbers as she did not really need it. And this was far from false flattery. Trained in the theatre, she certainly knew exactly how to project her voice to the very back of the auditorium.

A Little Night Music opened at the Adelphi Theatre on the 15th April 1975 and ran for 406 performances. During the run, Virginia McKenna and Angela Baddeley took over from Jean Simmons and Hermione Gingold.

Jeeves

From a professionally produced and slickly directed musical with a wonderful score, we move on to a piece of theatre that turned out to be severely lacking in these qualities.

I was excited when Maurice Fournier announced that Bernard Delfont was producing a new musical based on the P G Wodehouse character Jeeves, Wodehouse being my favourite author. With a book and lyrics by Alan Ayckbourn, music and lyrics by Andrew Lloyd-Webber, and an excellent cast headed by David Hemmings, it had all the elements of a major hit. Tim Rice was originally on board to write the lyrics but, perhaps wisely, he backed out before the project was properly under way.

The first run-through I attended in a rehearsal room with lighting designer Robert Ornbo was encouraging. David Hemmings was totally believable as the well-meaning but goofy playboy Bertie Wooster, and Michael Aldridge superbly inhabited the unassumingly loyal and sagacious character of his valet Jeeves. There were some pleasant tunes and the whole company performed with gusto. Admittedly, it was far too long and there were a few dull patches, but this is not unusual for a new musical at this stage of rehearsal. There was time for cuts and sorting out the scenes that did not work.

Or so we thought.

The show opened at the Bristol Hippodrome in March for a two-week try-out and the first night ran for an agonising four and a half hours!

Eric Thompson, he of the children's television show *The Magic Roundabout*, was the director. An experienced actor and television presenter, this was his first foray into directing a major musical and the task seemed to overwhelm him. During rehearsals, he merely tinkered with the script, cutting short pieces of dialogue here and there when what was required was major surgery.

I remember being in a pub with Robert Ornbo one lunchtime when worried members of the cast including David Hemmings were agreeing about scenes that should be cut and how the plot could be altered to improve the story. It was all so obvious, why could the director and the production team not see it? One hoped that Hemmings, who had a lot riding on the success of this, his first musical, would insist on the changes. But he was far too nice. Everybody on that production was nice and nobody wanted to upset Eric Thomson because he was so nice. One would have thought that experienced writer and director Alan Ayckbourn would have intervened, but he is also terribly nice.

Unfortunately, producer Bernard Delfont was not in evidence. Had he been there to witness the chaos, there would surely have been fireworks. He had entrusted the production to a colleague, a most likeable and charming man, but not one who relished confrontations or making tough decisions. He was too nice.

Eric Thomson made a few more small, but mostly meaningless, adjustments, but by the end of the Bristol run the musical was still running approximately 3½ hours.

During rehearsals and previews at her Majesty's in London, Eric continued to tinker with the action. Sitting at the production desk in the stalls using a microphone to make suggestions to the actors, he was surprisingly relaxed, seemingly unaware of the parlous state of the show. His air of serenity might have been due to the amount of white wine he was consuming throughout the long days.

Bernard Delfont must have attended a run-through because four days before the London premiere, Eric was removed as director. Alan Ayckbourn took over and did his best to pull together this shambles of a show in the short time available. He managed to reduce the running time to 2¾ hours - still far too long.

In a desperate bid to reduce the running time, one major cut was implemented. Poor Betty Marsden was informed only two days before the opening night, that her character, Aunt Dahlia, had been written out of the script. This did shorten the show a bit, but also made nonsense of parts of the story.

The reviews of *Jeeves* were universally damning. In the Daily Mirror it said, "The sight of a British musical falling flat on its face is not a pretty sight, although a fairly familiar experience in the theatre. But I never expected *Jeeves* to be so dreary, unfunny, untuneful and so woefully staged. Directed by Eric Thompson, it hardly seems possible that he had a hand in this clumsy production."

The Times critic was slightly kinder, "*Jeeves* is a modest, well-written, unspectacular piece in the musical comedy tradition: everything stops when somebody gets a song, and Eric Thompson's production generally inhabits small areas of the stage and shows no flair for company animation."

Jeeves played for just ten previews and thirty-eight regular performances before closing. Replacing *The Good Companions*, it was my seventh musical in that wonderful theatre. Since *Fiddler on the Roof* in 1967, I had designed the sound on every production in Her Majesty's for the previous eight years, barring a six-month break after *Pippin*.

Twenty-one years after the ill-fated production of *Jeeves*, Alan Ayckbourn directed a radically revised version at the Stephen Joseph Theatre he ran in Scarborough. With a new title, *By Jeeves*, it transferred to the Duke of York's Theatre in London for a 12-week season. A positive audience reaction led to the show being transferred to the Lyric Theatre in Shaftesbury Avenue where it remained for another six months. Stephen Pacey played Bertie Wooster with Malcolm Sinclair as Jeeves.

Dad's Army

Towards the end of the year, there was another musical for Bernard

Delfont. *Dad's Army*, based on the hugely popular television series, included most of the original cast. It played for two weeks at the Forum Theatre in Billingham before opening in London on the 4th October at the Shaftesbury.

One of my main memories of Billingham was a moment during a rehearsal on stage. As part of the plot, the Home Guard were putting on a concert in the village hall, which gave the leads a chance to do their party pieces. When it was John Le Mesurier's turn as Sergeant Wilson, he performed the song *A Nightingale Sang in Berkeley Square*. The orchestra was not there for that rehearsal, so with just a piano accompaniment he half talked and half sang the lyrics as though wistfully recalling a sad occasion. Cast and crew stopped what they were doing. It was so unexpectedly haunting and magical. When the last notes died a way, there was silence. You could hear a pin drop. Then the director shouted from the stalls, "Thank you, John. Very good." which somehow seemed inadequate.

When we came to the dress rehearsal with the small pit orchestra, in place of the simple piano accompaniment, Le Mesurier's quiet reflective rendition of the song had to battle against the totally unsympathetic noise of electric keyboard, trumpets, trombone and drums. Lighting designer Robert Ornbo and I were appalled and Robert grimaced at the director sitting next to him at the production desk. Obviously, theses awful orchestrations had to be cut, but not a bit of it. The director seemed to have no comprehension of why everyone had been so moved in the previous rehearsal. It was on these occasions that one longed for a director with the sensitivity of Hal Prince or a producer with the theatrical flair of Harold Fielding.

Next up was Arthur Lowe as Captain Mainwaring, who came on wearing a long brown fur coat and a battered straw boater. He was being Bud Flanagan from the famous wartime comedy duo, Flanagan and Allen, with Ian Lavender in a smart suit and tie playing Chesney Allen. Together they sang *Hometown,* one of their many popular songs from the 1940s. Bud Flanagan had, of course, recorded the theme tune for the television series, *Who Do You Think You Are Kidding, Mr Hitler?*

Lance Corporal Jones, Clive Dunn, performed an act he had perfected at the Players theatre in London where he was a regular performer. The Players presented Victorian music hall and Dunn marched on to the stage dressed as a soldier in black trousers and red tunic to sing a medley of comic songs of the period. To tell the truth, the songs were not that funny and as the show was over-running, after the first few performances, Bernard Delfont insisted that the act was cut. This did not go down well with the actor and he threatened to walk out unless his spot was reinstated, probably imagining that his presence was vital to the show's success. The producer did not back down so Mr Dunn left the show. A few scenes were rewritten and even without him the audience reaction remained enthusiastic.

Presumably swallowing his pride, he was back on stage for the London opening. He tended to appear for the curtain calls with his arms outstretched as though he was the star of the show but, surprisingly, the biggest burst of applause every night was not for him or, indeed, for the wonderful performances of Arthur Lowe and John Le Mesurier, but were for Ian Lavender playing Private Pike.

The personalities of most members of the cast were very similar to their stage personae. I particularly noticed this after the final rehearsal in Billingham. A group of them were standing on the side of the stage discussing what they were going to do after the premiere the following evening. Ian Lavender was worried that the hotel restaurant would be closed by the time they returned, and John Le Mesurier was saying, "It's impossible. Everything in Billingham seems to be shut by ten thirty. I really have no ideas, I'm afraid." At that point, Arthur Lowe bustled up to the group and demanded to know what was going on. Le Mesurier explained, "We were just discussing, Arthur, what on earth we were all going to do about eating after the show. You see, everywhere in Billingham..." With a wave of his hand, Arthur Lowe stopped him talking.

"Don't worry about that. It's all in hand. My wife has found a suitable venue. I have booked a table and there will be a taxi for those of you who do not have transport."

Having sorted that out, he marched off leaving the little group to disburse, all muttering gratefully.

I cannot believe that during all the time I spent with the oldest member of the cast who played the character of Private Godfrey, that I never asked him about one of the most celebrated stage effects in the annuls of theatre for which he was responsible. Apart from being an actor, Arnold Ridley wrote film scripts and plays, including the fantastically successful play, *The Ghost Train*, produced at the St. Martin's Theatre in 1925 before transferring to the Garrick.

The undoubted star of that show was the ghostly train itself. Never seen by the audience, the effect was created with lighting and sound. This was, of course, way before the use of recordings. Later, when researching my book on the history of theatre sound, I discovered how it was done. A variety of items were employed, including a garden roller pushed over wooden slats on the stage floor, a galvanized iron tank and a side drum both hit with padded mallets, a side drum stroked with wire brushes, a bass drum hit with sticks, a metal thunder sheet, a compressed air cylinder to make a hiss and another fitted with a train whistle, a tubular bell, a milk churn and two electric motors. As the train passed, which happens three times in the play, a visual effect of light from carriage windows was added. This was achieved by passing long strips of plywood cut with a series of square holes in front of two spotlights.

The overall effect, created by a team of ten carefully orchestrated stagehands, stunned and thrilled the audiences. Another fact I discovered was that the phenomenal success of the play spawned the idea of the spooky ghost train ride we now take for granted in funfairs.

The opening night of *Dad's Army* in London went without incident, but there was one big surprise. Towards the end of the Flanagan and Allen sequence, Arthur Lowe and Ian Lavender, with Ian's hand on Arthur's shoulder, strolled off stage in time to the music just as Flanagan and Allen used to do, and then they strolled back on for the final verse. Only, it was not Ian Lavender with his hand on Arthur's shoulder this time, it was actually Chesney Allen. Along with many members of the audience who remembered the war, I found myself choking up. Bud Flanagan had been dead for seven years, but his eighty-one year old partner was still going strong.

Following a five month run in London, *Dad's Army* set off on a seven month national tour.

Pilgrim

We went straight from the opening of *Dad's Army* to London's Roundhouse where *Pilgrim* had its premier eleven days later.

I had great hopes for this musical. A few months earlier, we recorded a demo in our studio of the score composed by Carl Davis. The orchestrations were most unusual; featuring, as far as I can recall, mainly woodwind and strings. This was something completely novel for a musical, and I was looking forward to recreating this extraordinary sound in the theatre. But it was not to be.

As tends to happen in the theatre, everything changed. The director, in his wisdom, decided to engage a rock musician, with no theatrical experience, to completely change the orchestrations. It became electric guitars, keyboards, horns and drums. Why Carl was persuaded to accept this, I will never understand.

Pilgrim failed.

Bernard Miles

Sir Bernard Miles instigated the building of the Mermaid Theatre in the City of London and ran it for many years. He telephoned one day requesting a meeting in the theatre to discuss a problem with their Christmas show. They were in the final stages of putting on *Gulliver's Travels*, written, designed and directed by Sean Kenny.

When we met at the back of the auditorium during a rehearsal, Sir Bernard complained, "I can't hear the actors. We are going to need a sound system."

Possibly talking myself out of business, I replied, "But this is a small theatre. Surely they could speak up a bit."

"You would think so, but the trouble with these young actors is that they don't seem to be taught projection these days. But you are right, I'll go and have a word."

So saying, he walked down to the stage, stopped the rehearsal and gathered the company around him. I was then treated to a demonstration of a properly trained stage voice. Although the cast had been acting their socks off during the bit of rehearsal we had witnessed, I had been unable to understand much of what was being said, but when Bernard spoke to the cast in a conversational voice, with his back to me, I could hear every word at the very back of the theatre.

Rehearsals continued and, despite Bernard's pep talk, we eventually agreed to install microphones, although this is never the answer to poor diction. Amplifying garbled speech just makes for louder garbled speech.

Bernard Miles

There was another occasion at the Mermaid when we were asked to record a poetry recital one Sunday. The readers were the unlikely trio of Bernard Miles, Robert Graves and Spike Milligan. There were two performances and after the first, Bernard said that it had gone well, but perhaps they should all go for a little refreshment and discuss how to make the next reading a little slicker. Milligan's reaction was, "You go and get slicker if you want, but leave me out." Spike always preferred a bit of jeopardy in his performances.

1976

Summoned To The Palace

1976 was the 200th anniversary of the signing of the Declaration of Independence when the American colonies severed their political connection to Britain. To mark the event *The 1776 Exhibition* was mounted at the National Maritime Museum in Greenwich. Apart from providing background sounds for some of the tableaux in the exhibition, we were involved in the creation of a time capsule containing an assortment of present day artefacts to be reopened a hundred years hence in 2076.

One of the items in the capsule was to be a recreation of the somewhat stilted interchange in St. James's Palace between King George III and the first American Ambassador to Great Britain. This was after the Treaty of Paris in 1784 when the United Kingdom finally acknowledged the Americas to be "free, sovereign and independent states." The current US ambassador was to record the speech of his predecessor, and I was privileged to be allowed into his official residence, Winfield House. This is an extraordinarily imposing mansion in Regent's Park set in twelve acres of grounds, the second largest private garden in central London after Buckingham Palace.

It was then on to Buckingham Palace where Prince Charles had agreed to speak the lines of his ancestor.

At the time, The Troubles in Ireland were at their height with several devastating bombing incidents in London. The city was on "red alert". Even pubs and restaurants had people manning the doors to check bags for weapons and explosives. One imagined, therefore, that security for the Royal Family would be incredibly tight. Driving down the Mall, circumnavigating the Queen Victoria monument and turning through a gate in the railings in front of the Palace was a surreal experience.

Just inside the gate, a single unarmed policeman was lurking inside a little green hut. He emerged when he saw the car and I informed him that I had come to make a recording with Prince Charles at six thirty. He consulted the clip-board he was carrying.

"No, I have no record of that down here," he said, "What's it all about then?"

There had obviously been a breakdown in communications and I was now concerned that I would not be allowed in. My explanation about recording the Prince for an exhibition could well be a complete fabrication, but he seemed satisfied.

"What you need to do," he said. "is drive up to that small door in front of the palace on the right. You can leave your car there. Then go in and the man at the desk will sort you out."

Following orders, I duly parked the car as instructed, opened the boot and took out a tape recorder and a large black holdall containing microphone and cables, either of which could have contained an explosive device, and entered the building. The reception desk was deserted. After a wait of some minutes, I considered wandering into the palace with my "bomb" to try and locate someone. Time was getting on. The Prince would shortly be arriving from Greenwich where he was taking a Lieutenant's course at the Royal Naval College, and I knew that he could only spare a few minutes for the recording. He was fitting me in before attending an official banquet given by the Queen.

Fortunately, a gentleman materialised behind the desk and politely asked me to state my business. He made a phone call, and a short while later a tall and frightfully smart young man appeared, introducing himself as Equerry to his Royal Highness. We had less than twenty minutes to prepare for the Prince's arrival, so I was whisked up to one of the enormous State Rooms with windows looking out on to the Mall. There was a certain amount of traffic noise and I asked if there was not somewhere a little quieter. The only rooms available away from the traffic were at the rear of the Palace facing the garden. This meant hurrying down to the ground floor, crossing a large quadrangle at the centre of the building, then once inside again, heading for a grand staircase where a group of soldiers in splendid red uniforms and silver helmets were practising a fanfare for the forthcoming occasion. Finally, we entered another splendid State Room looking out on to the enormous garden. No traffic noise, but the place was awash with clocks of all shapes and sizes; ornate long case clocks, fantastical ormolu mantle clocks, highly polished wooden wall clocks - you name it - and all ticking away merrily.

"So many clocks!" I exclaimed.

"These," explained the equerry, "are just a small sample of the timepieces gifted to the Queen by visiting Royals and dignitaries. Some poor person has the task of keeping a record of all these clocks and hundreds of other gifts. His task is to ensure they are on show the next time whoever gave them is invited."

This was all very interesting, but His Royal Highness was about to arrive. There was nothing for it but to set up the equipment and hope that a background of ticking clocks would be considered an ingenious concept for a time capsule.

The most illustrious voice-over artist I was ever likely to record made his entrance and, following brief introductions by the equerry, took his place at the table and expressed himself ready. He spoke a few words into the microphone so that I could set a recording level and then read the short speech, which in essence was the King George III indicating "what is done is done and we all have to make the best of an unfortunate situation."

When I commented that His Highness had completed the script perfectly in one take, he gave me an old-fashioned look.

"Well don't sound so surprised!"

I quickly explained that the American Ambassador required three attempts before managing an acceptable recording." The Prince raised his hands and chuckled as if to say, "What else would one expect from an amateur?"

He was obviously keen to get away, but I begged him to wait while I replayed the tape to ensure there were no technical faults. I ran the tape backwards at double speed and the moment he heard the high-pitched gobbledegook, he joined in with a very good imitation of Peter Sellers doing the voice of Bluebottle in the Goon Show. It was well known that he was a great fan.

Recording successfully completed, the Prince took his leave and wandered off to join his mother for a spot of dinner and a cosy chat to fifty or more guests, most of whom would be complete strangers. What a nightmare.

Side By Side By Sondheim

I received a call from a young producer called Cameron Mackintosh. He was putting on what turned out to be his first success both in the West End and on Broadway. They were in previews at the Mermaid Theatre with a revue called *Side By Side By Sondheim*, featuring songs from the composer's musicals. Apparently, Mr Sondheim was in London working with the cast and was not happy with the sound. This was an emergency. Could I come to the theatre that evening?

I was busy in the studio and only managed to see a bit of the show that night. It was a delightful little piece with Millicent Martin, Julia McKenzie and David Kernan singing the songs to a piano accompaniment while Ned Sherrin, who also directed, tied the whole thing together with an amusing and informative narration. With a cast of four plus piano in a small theatre, it was not a huge challenge, so I agreed to replace the equipment they were using the following day.

There being no spare sound operators available at such short notice, I found myself in the hot seat. There had been no time for any rehearsal and I had only seen a few minutes of the show the night before. Although I was given a script to follow, much of the show came as a surprise.

As the first half ended, I saw Stephen Sondheim heading up the aisle towards the mixing desk at the back of the auditorium. I made ready to explain that the mixing would become much smoother once I had completed a show and had a chance to make a proper cue sheet, but before I could offer any excuses, he grasped me by the hand, saying: *"Thank you so much. I can now hear my lyrics."*

Not only a genius, but a fine gentleman.

Side by Side by Sondheim had a short run of 59 performances at the Mermaid before moving to Wyndhams Theatre and then to the Garrick. In all, it had a total of 806 performances before Cameron co-produced it on Broadway with Hal Prince who persuaded the American Actors Equity Association to allow the original British cast to transfer with the show.

The production opened on the 18th April, 1977 at the Music Box Theatre, transferring later to the now-demolished Morosco. Between the two Broadway venues, it ran for a total of 390 performances. It is one of the few shows to have the distinction of its entire cast nominated for Tony Awards (Best Featured Actors and Best Featured Actresses in a Musical).

Stars At The Palladium

While transferring *Side by Side* to the Garrick, we were preparing for a major event at London's famous Palladium Theatre with two of the most celebrated stars in the world. Julie Andrews was to perform for two weeks with a one-woman show backed by a male chorus, followed by one of my all-time heroes, the incredible Bing Crosby.

Richard Pilbrow knew Julie Andrews from when she was married to Tony Walton and I had met her during the production of *She Loves Me*. The couple had parted in 1967, and she was now married to Hollywood director Blake Edwards. Julie had asked Richard to design the lighting for her show and I was responsible for the sound.

A few days before the opening, Richard and I attended a private run-through in a rehearsal room with just the director and a pianist. Julie was wearing a white shirt and black tights and I remember finding her incredibly sexy, the more so because of her tremendous sense of fun. Before we began, she explained her original idea for starting the show.

"Imagine this big orchestra on tiered rostrums at the back of the stage. The curtain rises and they strike up with a medley from *Mary Poppins*, then I appear from high up at the rear of the auditorium and float down towards the stage - on a wire - with my umbrella and Mary Poppins costume. The audience is amazed. When I reached the stage, I head towards the drummer, slam into him, and we would both disappear in a tangle of arms and legs behind the rostrum. How's that for an entrance?"

The director interjected, "I had to veto that idea. This is not Julie's image. I can imagine some of her fans being quite upset."

"I still think it would be *great*," she replied, "but never mind. Let's get on."

We then sat spellbound as she performed a stream of her world-renowned songs, but when she was a few bars into "The Hills Are Alive...", she stopped and complained to the director.

"Oh God, do I really have to sing this one?"

"Well, yes," he replied, "The audience is going to be disappointed if you leave it out."

"Really?" She sounded disheartened.

Then turning to Richard and me, "What do you guys think?"

I cannot remember what Richard said, but I replied quite truthfully, "When you sang those first few words, the hairs on the back of my neck stood up."

She shrugged. "That settles it then. We leave it in."

With a fixed smile on her face and performing all the correct movements and gestures, she sang for us "The Sound of Music" from beginning to end, but ever so slightly off-key. It had us all in stitches. I just wish the audience could have seen it.

Following Julie's two-week sell-out, tickets were similarly like gold dust for Bing Crosby who appeared with co-star Rosemary Clooney and wife Kathryn Crosby.

His voice was a few tones lower than in his younger days, but still sounding completely effortless, with unbelievable breath control. During that very hot summer, at the age of 73, he was on stage for most of the two and a half hour show. Even when not performing, I am told that he remained in the wings every night to watch Rosemary Clooney's set.

The performance ended with a thirty-five minute medley of his old hits. He only sang a verse and chorus of each one so there must have been well in excess of thirty instantly recognisable songs. Several equally memorable numbers were sadly cut during the rehearsal because of the time constraint.

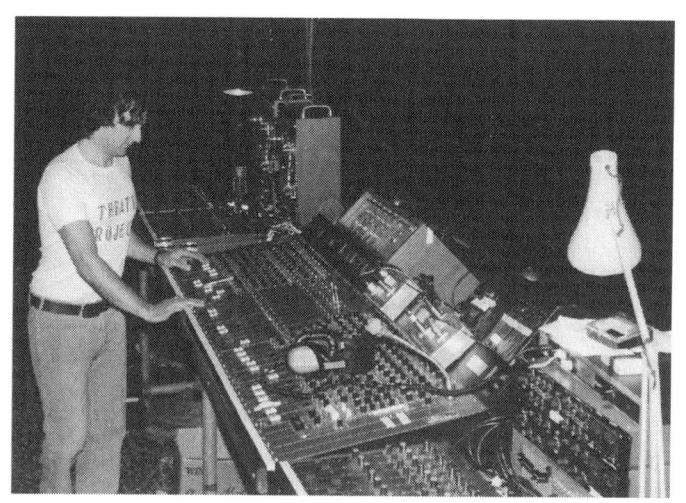

Michael Moor adjusting the sound balance
of the orchestra during rehearsals.

The concert was part of Crosby's celebration of 50 years in show business, during which time he became the most successful radio and recording artist in history. During his career he became equally popular for his films (61 movies) and appearances on television. From 1934-1954 he dominated American entertainment. His recording of "White Christmas" alone sold in excess of 50 million worldwide, a figure that no other singer has approached.

Back in the early 1930s, microphones were only just beginning to be used by band singers. Bing's mellow baritone voice was ideally suited to the limited capability of the microphones and loudspeakers of the period and he developed an intimate style of singing that became known as "crooning'.

In 1948 he invested $50,000 in the American company Ampex to improve the quality of tape recorders and make them suitable for the broadcast and recording industries. This led to him being the first person to tape record his radio shows.

I feel fortunate to have been involved in what turned out to be one of this great star's last public appearances. A year later, he died of a heart attack on a golf course in Spain. Fit and in good voice right up to the end, this is probably the way he would have wished to go.

Bing Crosby

There was a third star in the Palladium season following Crosby. This was Andy Williams. I was not directly involved as he had his own soundman. Rather than fly over a whole sound system for the two weeks, it was agreed that he could use ours. Upon his arrival, the first thing he did was produce a Real Time Analyser. This is a hand-held meter that highlights any troublesome frequencies that are being intensified by the acoustics of the auditorium and/or by the loudspeakers themselves. With a graphic equalizer - sophisticated tone control unit - it is then possible to smooth out these frequencies to obtain a more natural sound.

Or that is the principle.

We had been using graphic equalizers for some time, but Real Time Analysers were relatively new and too expensive. We were still relying on our ears, making small adjustments until satisfied that a warm and natural sound had been achieved. So it was with great interest, and not a little envy, that we watched our American friend change all our equalizer settings. To my ears, the result was very hard and strident, but he seemed happy so we left him to it.

Unfortunately, the newspapers the following morning were extremely critical of the amplification system at the Palladium. One critic even wrote a half page open letter to the producer complaining of "the appalling treatment of one of America's finest singing stars."

I was astonished to receive outraged telephone calls from the producer's office and from the manager of the theatre both demanding to know what I was going to do about this disaster. The theatre manager seemed unable to comprehend that the solution was not in my hands. When I finally got him to agree that everyone had been entirely happy with the sound quality for Julie Andrews and Bing Crosby, I went on to explain how the person in control of the mixing desk had the ability to change the quality of the sound. It was the same as the man in charge of the lighting who was able to make the stage look bright or dim and vary the colour from warm pink to cold blue. I suggested that he talked to Mr Williams's sound designer as it was entirely out of my hands. He said that he would certainly do this and concluded the conversation by saying, "Never do this to me again!".

Sometimes, you just cannot win.

Another Stinker

Kenneth Tynan had been a successful theatre critic for The Observer newspaper before being appointed by Laurence Olivier as literary manager for the National Theatre Company. During the 1960s, the sexual revolution was at its height and being a strong opponent of theatre censorship, Tynan persuaded a number of well-known writers to contribute to his nudist revue *Oh! Calcutta!* It opened in New York in 1969 with a successful London production following a year later.

Carte Blanche was an attempt to create a sequel to this success. His stated aim was "to have the audience sexually aroused without feeling ashamed or manipulated". He also wanted to "raise the standards of eroticism."

Richard Pilbrow had become friendly with Kenneth Tynan whilst lighting shows at the National Theatre. He now suggested that Richard should co-produce *Carte Blanche* with Michael White who had been the producer of *Oh! Calcutta!*. It sounded like a potential winner, so Richard agreed. It was only later when it became clear that Tynan was determined to increase the more sadistic and kinky aspects of the show that Richard became concerned.

Clifford Williams, who had been responsible for many RSC and West End productions had also worked on *Oh! Calcutta!* and was now engaged to direct *Carte Blanche*. On the first day of rehearsal he announced that he wished to have a private chat with the cast and everyone else, including the stage management, was banned from the rehearsal room until further notice. However, during this period the stage manager received an urgent phone call from the production office that required an immediate decision from Clifford Williams. Despite the director's instructions, she felt it was her duty to interrupt the "private chat", so she knocked on the door and entered the rehearsal room. To her surprise and slight embarrassment, she was confronted with the sight of the director standing stark naked in front of a fully dressed cast all regarding him with some bemusement.

She was later informed by one of the actors that the director was demonstrating that nobody should be embarrassed about their bodies. He was giving a pep talk that might have been relevant in 1970 when preparing for *Oh! Calcutta!* when theatre censorship in England had been abolished for less than two years. Six years on, it was no longer a big deal. In fact, some of the cast had actually been in *Oh! Calcutta!* and others had also appeared in shows with nude scenes. Moreover, they had all known exactly what they were in for when they signed up. So the last thing they were expecting was for their director to present himself bollock naked before them in order to make a point about nudity. Fortunately, nobody laughed out loud.

During the run-throughs in the theatre prior to opening, I kept being given instructions to increase the volume of the small pit orchestra consisting of electric guitars, keyboards, brass and percussion. This is a sure sign that a show is not working. People often mistakenly imagine that making it louder will somehow make it more exciting. The noise level I was being forced to create in the theatre came home to me one evening when I accompanied Robert Ornbo to the Coliseum before going on to a run-through of *Carte Blanche*. He had designed the lighting for a production of Wagner's *Die Walküre* and wanted to check some adjustments he had made to the first scene.

One seldom has the chance to hear the glorious sound of eighty or more musicians playing live and I waited with some anticipation as the conductor raised his baton. When the moment came, the quality and lushness of what I was hearing was wonderful, but I was surprised at the lack volume. Then I realised that my ears had become acclimatised to the raucous racket I had managed to create with six musicians up the road in the Phoenix Theatre.

Carte Blanche opened on the 30th September and despite being savaged by the press, managed to run for ten months, presumably because some members of the public were intrigued by the lurid publicity.

I do not consider myself a prude but I did find the whole voyeuristic enterprise extremely unpleasant. And I was not alone. During run-throughs in the theatre, there was one particular scene where the entire production team, including the director, would walk out of the auditorium leaving Kenneth Tynan to relish the spectacle in solitary splendour from his seat at the front of the stalls.

Opening Of The National Theatre 25th October 1976

Fourteen years after the National Theatre Company was formed and moved in to its temporary home at the Old Vic, the big new concrete building on the South Bank opened, despite the fact that it had yet to be completed.

Outside in the pouring rain, a large crowd turned up to be entertained by bands, fireworks and a carnival. Inside, it was a star-studded occasion with a fanfare to announce the arrival of the Queen accompanied by Prince Philip to unveil a commemorative plaque. The royal party and members of the Great and the Good then moved into the Olivier theatre where the former artistic director Laurence (now Lord) Olivier welcomed visitors with a reference to Henry V (one of his most famous film roles): "It is an outsize pearl of British understatement to say that I am happy to welcome you at this moment in this place." They were then treated to a performance of Goldoni's *Il Campiello,* a comedy featuring pandemonium in a poor Venetian piazza.

Many people thought this an odd choice to launch our National Theatre. Kenneth Tynan is quoted as saying, "it was perverse to the point of madness." Most of the critics were unkind. The Sunday Times thought it was "an empty dish to lay before the Queen."

National Theatre opening - Peter Hall welcomes the Queen.
Lord Olivier standing behind.
Royal Collection Trust / © Her Majesty Queen Elizabeth II

We lesser mortals were in the Lyttleton auditorium, the second of three theatres in the complex. The building of the smaller Cottesloe had yet to be completed. Lord Olivier's welcoming speech was relayed to us by closed circuit television. We were then treated to a performance of Tom

Stoppard's *Jumpers* with Michael Horden. It was always a joy to see Michael Horden, but I have to confess I had little idea what the piece was about.

Following the curtain calls of *Jumpers*, there was another fanfare as the Queen and Prince Philip entered the Lyttleton auditorium to hear a speech from the reigning artistic director, Peter Hall, in which he mentioned having just witnessed two remarkable events: A British architect applauded to the echo and Laurence Olivier standing on the Olivier stage.

Despite not fully appreciating the play, the whole occasion was tremendously exciting. Part of why I failed to get to grips with the text could have been due to the theatre's poor acoustics. One had to really concentrate to grasp what the actors were saying. Having said that, the Lyttleton acoustics were not as bad as in the Olivier.

One day when the theatre was under construction and the massive ceiling panels had just been installed, I was puzzled because they did not appear to be correctly angled to reflect sound from the stage. I am not an acoustician, but I had learned a bit about the subject over the years. At the time, we happened to be working with the world-renowned American acoustician Russell Johnson on the planning stage of Nottingham's Royal Concert Hall.

He was keen to have a look at the National Theatre building so I offered to take him along. When we walked into the Olivier auditorium, he looked up at the ceiling and said one word: "WRONG!"

He was then appalled to discover that these acoustic panels could not be adjusted. They were firmly welded in place.

A great deal of the blame has to be laid at the door of the architect Denys Lasdun. During the design process for the building, Richard protested that the ceiling was too high for angling the spotlights from the lighting bridges. He was told that it could not be changed because the acoustic consultant had stipulated the height. After the theatre opened, Richard finally met the acoustician who bemoaned the fact that his ceiling reflectors were far too high to be effective because, according to the architect, Richard had insisted on this height for his lighting. If Denys Lasdun has not deliberately kept all the consultants on the project apart in order to retain control, the theatre would have had better acoustics and improved lighting.

Not long after the opening, Peter Hall, who had replaced Laurence Olivier as artistic director, told me that they were receiving a load of complaints from the public about inaudibility. He continued, "I recently called a meeting with the architect and his acoustician about this and all they could say was that the acoustics were *'within specification.'* What on earth does that mean?"

"Nothing," I replied, "it's meaningless."

"Exactly. The fact remains that people have difficulty hearing. I was recently shown a letter written by a female member of the company in which she wrote, *'The only way to be heard in the Olivier is to move down stage centre and SHOUT. The only problem is that Dame Peggy Ashcroft or Sir Ralph Richardson have always got there before you!'*"

When Richard Eyre took over as artistic director in 1987, he decided to install a complex American acoustic enhancement system. Resident sound designer Paul Groothuis advised against this costly installation, warning that lots of distant microphones relaying actors' voices to banks of small loudspeakers within the auditorium would be a case of garbage-in-garbage-out. He was proved right.

The next artistic director, Trevor Nunn, asked Paul if there was a solution. The answer was yes, but only if he was given the funds and - big question mark - if the actors could be persuaded to wear radiomikes. It was put to the company who were, in general, not happy with the idea. However, once leading actor Sir Ian McKellan declared that he would agree if it meant that he could be understood in the far corners of the auditorium, the rest fell in line.

Not all the actors were comfortable with the situation, but there was no comment from the public until two years later when someone informed the press. An outcry ensued at the very idea of the finest actors in the country having to resort to microphones, and critics began to write about the "unnatural sound" at the National Theatre. Paul Groothuis was invited to appear on the BBC's 'Today' programme where he was initially given a tough time by a couple of critics. But his detractors had the wind taken out of their sails when he reminded them that regular mention of the Olivier Theatre's audibility problems had ceased since introducing the enhancement system - and that was two years before. They only noticed the microphones now (or thought they did) because they had been told about them. The National Theatre continued with the vocal reinforcement and soon everybody forgot about it.

The third auditorium, the Cottesloe (now renamed the Dorfman), was finally completed a year after the opening of the National Theatre. As a cost-cutting exercise, this empty space beneath the Olivier Theatre had been "mothballed"; but as a condition of accepting his appointment as artistic director, Peter Hall had insisted that the studio theatre should be reinstated.

Much to the great annoyance of the architect, Peter asked Richard Pilbrow to come up with a design. With senior TP consultant, Iain Mackintosh, a concept for an adaptable performance space was conceived. Peter Hall later wrote in his autobiography: "The Cottesloe proved to be the most flexible and, to many, the most interesting of our three theatres."

Becoming An Author

Richard Pilbrow had published a very successful book introducing the basic principles of lighting design for amateurs and professionals entitled "Stage Lighting". My book "Stage Sound" attempted to do the same for someone wanting to learn about sound. As the only book covering the subject in such detail, it proved popular, particularly in America, and a revised edition was published in 1982.

Pre-computers, publishers printed books from a master on film. When my publishers merged with another company, the original films of the text were lost during the move from one building to another. Consequently, they were unable to print any more copies. I only discovered this fact when a number of people contacted me complaining that the book was not available.

South Africa Again

My old mate John Moss, head of the Natal Performing Arts Council (NAPAC) had persuaded his committee to invest in upgrading their sound system and, following my apparent success in making the actors heard in their pantomime three years earlier, I was invited to design the sound for the 1976 Christmas show. This was the Vivian Ellis musical I had worked on at the Arts Theatre Club: *Listen To The Wind*. So 1976 ended very pleasantly working with friends on a delightful show in the sunshine.

1977

Serious Opposition

Incredibly, during the past twelve years or so we had enjoyed an almost clear run as sound designers on West End musicals. Manchester-based Ian Gibson had recently come to London with a couple of transfers, and in 1969 a new company, Theatre Sound and Light, had been credited with sound design on *Promises Promises*, but had done very little since. But now things were beginning to change.

Founded a few years before by two audio technicians at the Royal Opera House, Autograph Sound had not really bothered us until the Broadway hit, *A Chorus Line,* came to London in 1976. The director/choreographer Michael Bennett brought with him the Broadway sound designer Abe Jacob. Autograph was engaged to supply the equipment and this major production at the Theatre Royal Drury Lane put them firmly on the map. Autograph was eventually to become the major player in the West End with their own team of sound designers.

Denmark

Most of my time was now taken up with managing our manufacturing company and design work on new theatres. My colleague Tony was running the recording activities. Live theatre, which was where I felt at home, was taking a back seat. Occasionally, there were opportunities to get away from the desk and drawing board, and one of these was prompted by a Danish gentleman seeing my book "Stage Sound" on a stall at Heathrow airport.

Sven Clausen was the head of production of a charming theatre in the town of Aalborg. They produced at least two musicals a year and despite the efforts of their Head of Sound, they always had problems with audibility. Sven made contact and invited me to visit Denmark to make recommendations.

Built in 1878, the theatre had only 870 seats, 500 in the stalls and 370 in the balcony, and appeared to have excellent acoustics. I suggested replacing the loudspeakers and advised how they should be positioned. This was agreed and back in London we arranged to have them shipped out. I thought that was the end of the matter, but far from it, as will become clear later.

Musical Nightmare

There have been a number of occasions when I was forced to take over a show under difficult circumstances and the most nightmarish of these was a musical called *Fire Angel*. It did bring me back to my favourite theatre after a two-year break, but this time with a sense of foreboding. Produced at Her Majesty's Theatre in March 1977, *Fire Angel* was a rock musical based on Shakespeare's *Merchant of Venice*. Probably not the best of ideas.

It all started, as these things usually do, with a phone call; this time from musical director Anthony Bowles with whom I had enjoyed a good relationship on *Jesus Christ Superstar*. He sounded desperate.

"We have just started public previews and the sound is disastrous. We can't open like this. We need your help."

"When does the show open?"

"In four days."

"Four days! I'm sorry, but that's not possible. If I were to become involved, I would want to install our own equipment and there just isn't enough time."

"Will you at least come and see the show and give an opinion? You might have some helpful suggestions. We are at our wits' end."

That evening I sat through the show and was grateful that we had taken no part in it. Following the performance there was a meeting with Anthony Bowles and the producer, Ray Cooney, at which I was unable to come up with anything constructive that might improve matters with the current set-up.

"Alright," said Ray Cooney, "What would you do if you were starting from scratch?"

"For a start, I would be using our own equipment with different loudspeakers and different microphones. One of the main problems is that you will never achieve a full-bodied rock sound with wireless microphones buried within the costumes. This is why we used hand-held cable microphones in *Superstar*."

"Right. So we change the microphones." said Ray Cooney.

"It is not as easy as that. Most of the numbers would have to be restaged. The cast have to learn where and when to pick up and replace the microphones, and movement is restricted because of all the cables."

"We have to do something," moaned Anthony Bowles, "I can't open with a show sounding like this."

Then came the question I was expecting and dreading.

"You can see the dilemma we are in," said Ray Cooney. "It's desperate. So we are asking you... will you take over? You can have whatever you want. I don't care how much it costs."

A producer has to be pretty desperate to utter those words!

"Money is not the problem," I explained, "It is the lack of time. How can we possibly install an entire sound system and introduce hand-mikes and then have someone restage all or parts of every number in the show? The premiere is only three nights away. I'm sorry, but it just can't be done."

Anthony Bowles spoke again, "We understand all that, but tell us honestly, if you did have a go would the sound be worse than it is now?"

That put me on the spot.

"I sincerely hope not, but I have no idea if the boys in the hire department could put together all the equipment we need tomorrow, and then be willing to spend most of the night rigging it in the theatre. And, of course, we cannot make a start until the present company has removed all their gear after the show."

There was another ten minutes of arm-twisting and emotional blackmail before I finally agreed to the inevitable.

The heroes in our hire store spent the next day assembling all the equipment including forty-six microphones for the cast and orchestra including six hand-held and six radiomikes.

That evening we loaded our equipment into the theatre while the other company was getting theirs out. Embarrassing for all concerned. As I carried a loudspeaker across the stage, I was amused to overhear a comment from one of the stage crew, "Here comes Theatre Projects. We'll be alright now."

We worked through the night and by lunchtime the following day, everything was up and running in readiness for the rehearsal scheduled for the afternoon. I was fortunate to have Claire Laver once again at the controls. A deputy had been arranged to stand in for her at *Jesus Christ Superstar* where she was currently working.

The rehearsal got off to a bad start. Valuable time was lost because the orchestra refused to play until some of their microphones had been repositioned.

Finally, we were ready to begin rehearsing the first musical number with the new hand microphones. The director, Braham Murray (responsible for the ill-fated *'Erb* and *The Good Companions*) did not seem to understand the urgency. Each time we arrived at a new number he wasted time discussing the re-staging with the cast when what was needed was decisive direction.

We only had two hours with the orchestra and it was obvious by the time the musicians stopped for their break, that we would never get through the show. I had a word with Anthony Bowles and he insisted that the director should allow me to take charge of the rehearsal.

From then on, we cut from number to number with me on stage instructing members of the cast what microphones to use, where to pick them up, when to put them back, even where to stand. The cast seemed to appreciate some positive decisions. Even so, we reached the end of the orchestral session before several pieces had been restaged and, of course, the musicians downed their instruments and departed. For the remainder of the show, it was a matter of arranging the use of microphones with the cast and hoping for the best.

Under the extremely fraught conditions, Claire had not had time to write down all the microphone levels, but this was not a worry because she had an incredible memory. From experience, I knew that one could discuss the mix on any item in a show and she would be able to tell you the exact levels of any fader.

But then came the bombshell: a message at the stage door stated that the deputy operator for *Superstar* was ill and could not make it. This meant that the only person who could possibly mix *Fire Angel* that night was me.

Before she had to leave for the Palace Theatre, Claire was only able to write down some very basic notes on which microphones were used in each number. I would have to follow the script to see when and who was about to sing. It did not help my nerves to be told by the producer that this last preview before the first night was incredibly important as it was to be attended by radio disc jockeys and other important people from the music industry.

Adrian Paul, a member of our exhausted crew contemplating
the array of controls I would be operating that evening.

The lighting designer later told me that just before curtain up he saw me looking so sickly white that he wondered if I would survive the performance. I was surrounded by three mixing desks linked together to handle the forty-six microphones. There were no computers in those days, so the large array of faders and knobs all had to be controlled manually. I had only seen the show once, never had a rehearsal and was relying on the script to discover what was going to happen on stage next. No wonder I looked ill.

Somehow or other, the cast remembered to pick up the right microphones and I managed to open the faders on time. The overall balance could certainly have been improved but, at least, the lyrics were now audible. Even the radiomikes worked. But when the final curtain came down I was a total wreck.

Over a very large scotch in the company manager's office, the producer was effusive in his praise and gratitude for "saving the day". He promised to employ me on every one of his shows in the future.

I may have saved the day, but I did not save the show. It was savagely attacked by the critics. In a newspaper interview some years later, Ray Cooney said, "I once did a musical called *Fire Angel* and put £100,000 into it. The show ran for three weeks and I lost the lot."

Time passed, and when I heard that Mr Cooney was about to produce another musical, I rang his office to talk about equipment and sound design. Despite several attempts, he was never available. The contract was awarded to a rival company.

Charming.

Working on another show some months later, one of the stage crew, who was obviously a bit of a wag, gave me a laugh. He was sporting a T-shirt emblazoned with the slogan: *FIRE ANGEL - WORLD TOUR*

A Brush With Max Bygraves

I could hardly believe my ears when Tommy Elliott, production manager for the Stoll Moss organisation, called one morning to explain that he had a major crisis on his hands and was begging a favour.

"My Star is refusing to do any more performances unless the theatre sound system is replaced."

Oh no! Not again!

I knew Tommy well as he had been production manager on *Company* and we had worked together on several other shows. I could see that his "star" had placed him in an impossible situation and I did not want to let a friend down. Besides, as owners of ten major West End theatres, the Stoll Moss Group was rather important.

I should have learnt my lesson with *Fire Angel* but, once again, I was having my arm twisted. It was obviously out of the question to do anything for that evening's performance, but I reluctantly agreed to see if anything could be achieved for the following day. Relieved, Tommy said that with that promise, he was sure that he could persuade his Star to perform that night.

The good news was relayed to the lads in the hire department and once again they were ready to install a complete rig overnight in one of the largest West End Theatres, the Victoria Palace. That afternoon, we had a brief orchestral rehearsal before launching blindly into the evening performance.

The star was Max Bygraves, a comedian who had transformed himself into a major recording artist with several gold "sing along" discs to his name. As far as he was concerned, as he stressed when we were introduced, the sound was the most important element in the show. The show was called *Swingalongamax* - would you believe?

With the trusty Claire once again at the controls, all went remarkably well that night. After the performance, his only request was for much more foldback; i.e. loudspeakers placed on stage so that he could hear himself. It appeared that Mr Bygraves liked to hear a lot of his own voice. So, we installed a large column loudspeaker each side of the proscenium pointing at the stage.

The format of the show was that Bygraves came on for a thirty-minute spot in the first act, and then there was a long gap while other artists performed. He did not reappear until the second act when he ended the show with another thirty-minute session.

During the next performance after Mr Bygraves had completed his first stint, I was informed by one of his assistants that his boss wanted me to join them in the circle bar. "Only," he added with a grin. "Don't expect him to actually buy you a drink!"

When we entered the bar, the Star was sitting alone at a table looking worryingly despondent. I was mightily relieved when he began by saying that the general sound quality was good and went on to ask what I would like to drink. Thanking him, I opted for a gin and tonic. There was a pause.

"The thing is," he said with a sigh, "if I cannot hear myself clearly, it affects my performance. I really need more foldback. A big orchestra makes so much noise you can't hear yourself. It's almost impossible to sing."

Refraining from mentioning that Julie Andrews and Bing Crosby did not suffer from this problem, I said that we would boost the foldback in the second half. He seemed happy with that, but went on to tell me how he had started as a comedian, but was now a recording artist selling millions of records and this is why everything had to be right so he could perform at his best. He rambled on for some time in this manner and I began to wonder if I would ever get the drink. Eventually, giving me a knowing look, his assistant went to the bar and ordered the gin and tonic. At the end of the show, as there were no further notes I presumed that our job was done, but I decided that it would be politic to show my face at one more performance.

The following night, Mr Bygrave's assistant told me that I was once again summoned to the bar again with the warning, "I'm afraid he won't be in a good mood." I was surprised. Nothing had changed since last night.

"Didn't you notice that when Max made his first entrance and the spotlight hit him at the top of the staircase the applause was not quite as enthusiastic as usual?" I had not noticed. "Well, I can tell you, that has definitely put him in a grump."

Sure enough, there he was in the bar, slumped in a chair with a look of utter depression on his face.

"It's no good," he complained, "I can't sing if I cannot hear myself. You have to turn the foldback up. Way up!"

This concerned me as the amount of level we were pumping through these speakers was already affecting the overall quality of sound. I tried to explain.

"I do understand, but we can already hear the sound from those speakers in the auditorium and any further increase will be seriously detrimental to what is being heard by the audience."

The unexpected retort was an angry, "I sing for ME! Turn it UP!"

To which there could be no answer.

Although I was far from happy with the result, I went backstage during the second act and was given the thumbs up when he came off briefly between songs. I thought we had cracked it, but apparently not. At the end of the show, when the entire cast was on stage taking their bows, Mr Bygraves stepped forward and signaled for the orchestra to stop playing. Then, to sixteen hundred bemused people, not to mention the performers and musicians, he made the following announcement:

"You have all probably noticed that the sound system in this theatre is pretty poor. Something like the end of the pier at Skegness. Well, those people responsible," he pointed us out, "sitting up there at the side of the balcony, they always say it is impossible to tune a sound system without an audience. So I am going to sing a song with all you lovely people and give them a chance to get it right."

There followed a discussion with the musical director and a rustling of musical parts in the orchestra pit until, finally, they struck up with one of his most popular songs, "Tulips from Amsterdam". It went something like this:

> *When its spring again I'll bring again*
> MORE FOLDBACK *from Amsterdam*
> *With a heart that's true I'll give to you*
> *Tulips* AND A BIT MORE BASS
> *I can't wait until the day you fill*
> THAT'S BETTER *arms of mine*
> *Like the windmill keeps on turning*
> TRY SOME TREBLE *keeps on yearning...*

And so it went on for several verses. Finally, he expressed himself happy and brought the song to a conclusion with a flourish. There was wild applause from the audience, pleased to have witnessed something extra for their money. The cast, on the other hand, had been left standing like lemons the entire time with most of them struggling to maintain even a sickly grin.

In the dressing room afterwards, Max Bygraves just commented, "I hope you didn't mind me sorting out the foldback like that, Dave, but it was really the only way." My somewhat stiff reply was, "We did find it rather embarrassing and I would have preferred some warning." But he shrugged this aside, saying that it had all been worth it.

Not one of my most pleasant evenings in the theatre.

Return To Canada

I had designed a permanent sound system for the O'Keefe Centre in Toronto incorporating a large mixing console designed and built in-house by Sam Wise. He and I travelled to Canada to supervise the installation and make sure that it all worked.

The O'Keefe Centre has an enormous auditorium holding 3,212 seats, so a very high standard of amplification was vital. It all had to be ready for a concert given by Cleo Laine with her husband Johnny Dankworth and his orchestra. Sam and I spent the first half of the show moving around the auditorium making notes and then adjusting the controls. In the second half, we continued our wandering and listening, and at one point found some empty seats and sat down for a while. Twenty minutes later, we realised that we had been enjoying the wonderful singing of Miss Laine and had forgotten why we were there. So it must have sounded all right. A couple of days later, she was followed by the great American singer, Johnny Mathis. He had travelled all his own equipment, but his sound designer decided to use what we had installed and expressed himself pleased with the result.

While we were still working on the installation, there had been a concert given by the Carpenters. They also travelled their own equipment and I was intrigued at the set-up. They had an enormous 'foldback' mixing console positioned in the wings for controlling banks of loudspeakers around the stage, whereas the man operating the desk at the rear of the stalls for the auditorium sound had a much smaller console. I was able to wander round the stage during a rehearsal and one was simply bathed in a glorious blending of the orchestra and Karen Carpenter's wonderful voice. I have never heard anything like it. Sadly, what the audience was hearing was not nearly so impressive. I discussed this with the Carpenter's touring soundman and he was perfectly frank.

"It's simple. The artistes pay the bills and if they are happy, they'll use you again on the next show."

Back to London and a revival of *Hair* for a second summer season. Once again on the first night there was a lavish party at Robert Stigwood's mansion.

That year my wife and I moved from London to Oxfordshire with our two sons; Mark who was nearly two and Dominic nine months. We had bought an idyllic thatched cottage in the wonderfully name village of Kingston Bagpuize; a move that was to have unfortunate repercussions later. We had hardly moved in when there came a call from Denmark. It was Sven Clausen.

"Well, David, we have installed the loudspeakers you recommended and as you were so confident they would work, we would like you to be here when we use them for the first time on our Christmas musical."

In other words, put your money where your mouth is!

1978

The Soundman Is Deaf

The Christmas production at the Aalborg Teater was a musical version of the Hans Andersen fairy tale *The Tinderbox* with music by a talented Danish composer who went by the name of Fussy - pronounced Foosie.

The change in pressure as the aircraft landed had caused my ears to block up again. Sven sent me to a specialist who managed to restore most of my hearing but recommended that at least one more session was needed to complete the process. The following day was the all-important sound rehearsal in the theatre with the cast hearing the orchestra for the first time. That morning, the theatre's artistic director, the big boss, enquired about my hearing.

"One ear is working perfectly thank you," I replied, "the other still needs a bit more work." He looked worried.

"But we have the sound rehearsal this afternoon."

"That's alright," I said, "I'm going to do it in mono."

He gave me an old-fashioned look, wondering for a moment if I was being serious, then announced with a smile, "Good. And we pay you half the fee."

The performance was of course in Danish but, surprisingly, one soon forgot that. Assessing audibility was exactly the same as if it had been in English. Some of the lyrics sounded a little difficult to sing with their tortuous vowel sounds and when I mentioned this to one of the actors, he replied, "You are right. Some people say that Danish is not a language, it is a disease of the throat."

Everybody in the theatre spoke perfect English, many without the trace of an accent. Sven and his wife could even assume a Scottish accent or talk "posh" English. One of the actors actually greeted me in broad cockney with "allo Dave, me ol' cock sparrer, how're yer diddlin?"

Working in a State subsidized theatre in Denmark is a refreshingly collaborative affair with seemingly no class distinctions between the actors, musicians, stage management and crew. They are all deemed to be making an important contribution. At a dinner given after the first night, everyone who worked on the show was invited and I noticed the head flyman and the leading man sitting next to each other chatting merrily away; a sight you would never see in the British theatre.

The show was a great success, the audience was able to hear the actors, and it became the first of five musicals at the Aalborg Teater for which I had the enormous pleasure of designing the sound.

Bruce Forsythe

Back in London there were preparations for two major musicals scheduled to open within days of each other. The beginning of March saw us at the Palace Theatre Manchester for the pre-London opening of *The Travelling Music Show*, a vehicle for the television presenter and all-round entertainer Bruce Forsythe. Without much in the way of a story, it was more of a revue than a traditional musical, providing an opportunity for Forsythe to demonstrate his considerable singing, dancing and comedic skills. During the first few performances in Manchester, there were problems with the scenery with either the wrong backcloth being flown in, or some other item getting stuck. Bruce Forsythe was notorious for ad-libbing and he took full advantage of these situations. The audience loved it and in my opinion they were by far the most enjoyable performances of the show.

Kismet

The following week we were back in London setting up *Kismet*. Originally a big hit on Broadway in 1953, it had been repeated two years later in London with Alfred Drake reprising the starring role. *Kismet* had music and lyrics by Robert Wright and George Forrest with much of the music adapted from the works of Alexander Borodin.

This revival, managed for an American impresario by Theatre Projects, opened at the Shaftesbury Theatre on the 21st March. It had positive reviews, but towards the end of May box office receipts were not particularly good. Richard Pilbrow decided to nurse it through the summer by reducing the running costs. One of the first items looked at, of course, was the rental bill for the audio equipment. The musical director had always disliked the idea of amplifying his orchestra and, despite the fact that I had spent many hours of rehearsal time fine-tuning the orchestral balance with the two creators, he queried the necessity of microphones. He even suggested that with the strong voices we had in the cast, they did not need amplifying either.

It was decided to carry out a test. At the next matinee performance, with a deputy conductor in charge of the orchestra, the musical director, the musical arranger, and Richard gathered at the rear of the circle. We had the sound system switched off for the overture and the musical director expressed himself totally happy. The man who had arranged the orchestrations, however, disagreed strongly, "Can you hear the oboe? Can you hear the harp? No. We might just as well send them home."

I was asked to have the mikes faded in and, reluctantly, the MD had to concede that, although subtle, it was a much better balance when you could hear all the instruments.

The curtain went up and when the two leads began to sing a duet, the MD, who had never listened to the show in the auditorium announced triumphantly. "I can hear them perfectly without the microphones!"

"But the microphones are on," I countered. "These loudspeakers provide a very natural sound."

"Can you fade them out?" asked Richard.

We gently pulled back the faders and the voices faded down until they no longer could be heard clearly above the orchestra. Richard turned to me with a look of astonishment.

"My dear chap, we have been working together for nearly twenty years and, do you know, this is the first time I have really understood exactly what you do!"

I am still not sure how much of a compliment that was, although he did have a twinkle in his eye when he said it.

The sound system was left intact, and although some cost savings were made in other areas, the show came off a few weeks later.

Sometimes people can have short memories. A few months after *Kismet* had closed, I was discussing with Richard the trend for musicals becoming unnecessarily loud with audiences no longer able to hear the natural human voice. Performers should not have to rely on all this equipment. Richard agreed, citing *Kismet* as a case in point.

"We were able to cut half the sound system because it was not contributing very much...!"

The day following the first night of *Kismet*, *The Travelling Music Show* was being set up at Her Majesty's with the opening exactly one week later. It played there for four months before setting off on a national tour. It was my eighth and last musical in that theatre.

Not Much Fun Anymore

In order to make us all more businesslike in Theatre Projects, one of our new managing director's plans was to "incentivise" the work force. This was to be achieved by setting budgets and turnover targets for each division within the group. To my mind, there seemed to be a major flaw in that concept. That kind of financial control might be appropriate for a manufacturing company, but it was surely not appropriate for a theatre design and rental business. One could not plan for how many shows independent producers might mount in any one year, and how many of these might come our way or, indeed, how long the shows might run. Targets were fine in theory.

A worrying factor of becoming 'businesslike' was the escalating central management costs including the salaries of the managing director and his secretary, plus a new financial director with an expanding accounts department. This was in addition to the ongoing expense of running the office with receptionists, telephones, etc.

These costs were apportioned to the various "profit centres", creating a great deal of resentment within middle management who had no control over this whatsoever. With the pressure to meet budgets, they became more concerned about the turnover in their own operations than cooperating with other departments. Richard's original concept of a group of enthusiasts working happily together for the common good began to dissipate.

I discovered one day that we were contracted to design and supply equipment for a new musical that I knew nothing about. This had never happened before and when tackled, the manager of the hire department said he could not afford my intercompany charge-out rate. Apparently, I had become part of the central management costs. I checked with the head of the lighting hire department and discovered that he had the same concern about Richard, the leading lighting designer in the country.

Apart from the folly of not exploiting Richard or my reputation for marketing purposes, setting an hourly rate was ludicrous. Like all the other designers, we did not charge for the hours we worked, we simply carried on working until the job was done, even if this meant working through the night, which it often did.

What the old guard at TP totally understood was that our success in gaining lucrative rental contracts relied heavily upon our team of lighting designers and, in the case of sound hire upon the fact that I had been designing the majority of West End musicals for years. It is true that fees were modest - £1,000 for lighting a show was at the top end – and there were no royalties in those days. The biggest fee I ever received was £400 for *Superstar*. This was why our managing director did not view design as a satisfactory profit centre. Over the months, it became increasingly obvious that he was less than enthusiastic about our unique group of talented lighting designers and, no longer feeling appreciated, they gradually drifted away. Most of them became freelancers with the majority doing very well. In fact, royalties were now being paid to lighting designers on the more prestigious musicals and two of them were lucky enough to hit the jackpot, becoming millionaires. This was something our MD did not see coming!

Robert Ornbo remained with the company, continuing to light operas for Covent Garden, the Coliseum and several opera houses abroad, and every year generated sizeable rental contracts from lighting the Royal Tournament and the Edinburgh Tattoo.

My good friend Tony Horder had resigned the previous year when he married a nice French lady and took himself off to live in Paris. With its set hourly rates, the recording studio was another activity viewed as a stagnant business, and Tony had been constantly harassed and pressured to increase profits. This could not happen without much needed investment for advertising and updating the technical facilities, but that was not forthcoming. He was forced to cut overheads and the biggest expense, although possibly the greatest asset, was our studio engineer. The lucrative demo recordings of the Swinging Sixties had come to an end and we were no longer recording music for the National and Royal Shakespeare Theatres following the debacle with the Musicians Union, so Tony had the unpleasant job of making our friend Michael Moor redundant.

Money, however, was being poured into all the sales and hardware activities. Apart from manufacturing sound consoles and intercoms, we were now producing our own brand of architectural lighting. We had also acquired Rank Strand Electric's lighting hire division for London and the south of England, making Theatre Projects the largest lighting rental operation in Europe.

Richard was heavily involved with theatre and film production and the consultancy business now had ongoing projects around the world. This meant that he was out of the country a great deal. Every time he returned home he was given brilliant news of the company's growing commercial success. This, despite the fact that all this spending had caused a serious cash crisis.

With the TP Group continuing to expand, the bank manager was happy to lend money, but it really was not a good time to borrow. A string of crises had plagued the British economy for most of the 1970s and we were about to hit what was called 'The Winter of Discontent' in which numerous public sector workers staged strikes. Interest rates soared and by the end of the year, the bank rate had reached an impossible 17%.

I was not a director of the main board, but I knew what was going on and I could not comprehend the madness of borrowing vast sums of money when we were constantly spending more than we were making. Eventually, I aired my concerns to Richard, adding that I was convinced the MD did not understand theatre and was heading us all in the wrong direction. Moreover, he had created such an unpleasant atmosphere in the company that I no longer wished to be a part of it. The only option open to me was to resign.

As you can imagine, this came as a bolt out of the blue and we had a long heart to heart over lunch. He refused to accept my resignation and we agreed a compromise. As most of my time was now spent consulting on new theatres and concert halls, I would now work from home and only come into the office two days a week. This way, I would avoid contact with the MD who had little to do with the consultancy business. Although this was another fee-based activity of which he did not approve, both Richard Pilbrow and Dick Brett, managing director of TP Consultants, were fiercely protective of this little empire and did not allow any interference.

Things had changed so much during the past five years. We were no longer a 'family', a bunch of theatre enthusiasts all bustling along together. But perhaps that is inevitable when a company expands to the extent that one hardly knows some of the employees.

1979

Strange Bedfellows!

Robert Ornbo and I were invited by a Dutch producer to work on a new musical to premiere in the Carre Theatre in Amsterdam. We arranged to be in Holland on a Sunday evening to be fresh for the equipment fit-up on Monday morning and a technical rehearsal in the evening. Tuesday and Wednesday were public previews with the opening night on Thursday. What could go wrong?

We arrived at Gatwick airport to find the flight to Amsterdam was delayed by fog. An hour after the scheduled take-off time, it was still delayed and the fog was thickening. There were no announcements about the flight.

"Let's go and make a nuisance of ourselves", suggested Robert, "It will at least pass the time." So we marched up to the British Airways enquiries kiosk where Robert thumped the counter and demanded to know when our plane was going to take off. The poor girl behind the desk had no idea, so Robert insisted that she should contact Traffic Control or the Met Office or someone who could give us an answer. Several phone calls later and the general consensus was that nobody had a clue.

Walking around Gatwick airport for the umpteenth time to while away the hours, we passed the restaurant. "Why don't we stop for a meal?' I suggested. Robert's reply was, "I'm not hungry yet, but look, there's the airport chapel. Let's go and have a chat with the vicar."

"You can if you like, but I'm not going in there."

"It will pass the time and could be interesting. I'm going to have a look"

So saying he headed into the chapel, to emerge a short time later with a bemused look on his face.

"There's a fellow in there praying."

"Well that's hardly surprising. It's probably our pilot."

When we did decide to go for a meal there was a queue, which meant standing in line for half an hour to get a table. Just as we were settling down and were looking forward to a juicy steak and the bottle of claret we had ordered, our flight was called. Hastily, we found the waiter, cancelled everything and headed for departures. Almost immediately, there was another announcement stating that the previous one had been made in error. The flight was still on hold.

That did it.

"Right. Who are we going to attack?"

A lady in uniform happened to be standing behind a nearby counter doing nothing. "She'll do," said Robert and startled her by demanding to see who was in charge of operations at the airport. "There must be a manager or something. We are appalled at being kept hanging around for hours with no information about our flight. This is not acceptable. Who is in charge?"

The woman explained that there were men in peaked caps sitting in some lofty place, but this was strictly out of bounds. However, the sight of Robert puce-faced and practically frothing at the mouth (he was a good actor) was obviously more frightening than the peaked caps, so she scurried off to see what she could do. After a while, a smartly uniformed young man put in an appearance to offer us a ticket for some free drinks. But if he thought that the prospect of a couple of rounds of scotch would get him off the hook, he was much mistaken. We now suspected that our airplane was not even at Gatwick and, following some harsh interrogation, he admitted that this was indeed the case. He also had to confess that the plane, being fogbound in Paris, was very unlikely to leave for England until the following day, a fact they must have known for some hours. We demanded that our luggage be brought to us immediately from wherever it was being held.

"I am sorry, sir. That is not possible until the flight is officially cancelled."

At this, Robert exploded with me joining in with the verbal assault. Flailing arms and banging counters soon produced a result. A porter was summoned and instructed to go down to wherever the luggage was stored and prise our bags from the pile.

We booked two of the few remaining seats for a flight in the morning and arranged for a local hotel that night. By the time we left for the hotel, there had still been no announcement about the non-existent flight, and the other passengers were still sitting around on uncomfortable seats or propping up the bars.

At the airport the following morning there was still quite a bit of mist hanging about. So we were straight in with the desk thumping to quickly discover that there was no likelihood of anything taking off for several hours. We cancelled our tickets – another minor rumpus – and telephoned the office to say that we were returning to London and needed immediate land/sea transportation to Amsterdam. By the time we arrived at the office it was too late to get the boat to Holland. The only route possible was a boat from Dover to Zeebrugge and then catch a train. The secretary in the office said that from Zeebrugge to Amsterdam was only a couple of inches on the map, so it should not take long. We leapt into a taxi and headed for Waterloo station.

Having made it to the boat in time, I decided that we should get some local currency for a hotel in Zeebrugge and the rail fare. I located the Bursar's office and asked to if he could exchange some pounds. This was, of course, before the invention of the Euro. The man replied, "No problem. Which denomination of currency would you like?" Geography not being one of my strong points, I was acutely embarrassed to have to ask, "What country are we going to?" He gave me a very old fashioned look before replying, "I believe we are sailing to Belgium, sir".

That night on the boat we did get our steak and bottle of wine and then Robert remembered that he should have phoned his wife. The startled Telegraph Officer, when we eventually tracked him down in his cubbyhole, had a plate of egg and chips on his apparatus and we agreed to return in twenty minutes when he had finished his pudding. Rose Ornbo was most surprised to receive a phone call from the middle of the North Sea when, if all had gone to plan, we should have been finishing a technical rehearsal in Amsterdam.

We arrived at the port of Zeebrugge at one o'clock on the Tuesday morning. It was cold, wet, foggy and completely deserted. Leaving Robert sitting on a suitcase, I walked some distance towards the town. All the buildings were closed and dark, but eventually I located a hotel and managed to raise a night watchman. He said the hotel was full, which seemed unlikely, so I pretended not to understand. Finally, my appalling French wore him down and he grudgingly admitted that there was one room available with a double bed. Done.

Fifteen minutes later, I returned with Robert and the baggage and we were shown to our room. A short while later found the two of us edging nervously around a small French double bed like a pair of middle-aged virgin honeymooners. Robert coughed nervously.

"Which side of the...um...do you like to sleep?"

"I really don't mind. I mean, I usually sleep on this side, but", I added hastily, "it really doesn't matter." A wave of relief unknotted Robert's brow.

"No, that is good. I like the other side. We are compatible."

There followed polite mutterings about who should go into the bathroom. I insisted that he should go first. Having completed our ablutions, I was amused to note that we had both donned fresh pairs of pants.

Some moments after we had both climbed into bed and switched out the lights, I felt the bed beginning to shake. Then there came a series of high-pitched strangled sounds. Various wild thoughts raced through my mind until I realised that my bedfellow was having an uncontrollable fit of giggles. Hysteria is contagious and we were soon crying with laughter at the thought of the two of us clinging to opposite side of a bed at two in the morning…. in Zeebrugge!

Information from the hotel receptionist a few hours later, revealed that the "two inches on the map" entailed a taxi ride across town, a dash for the only train that morning to the border, and then an hour's wait for another train to take us across Holland.

Having set off from home at lunchtime on Sunday, we eventually arrived at five o'clock on Tuesday evening. There was just time to check into our hotel before attending the first public preview of the musical where the lighting was hit and miss and the sound required serious attention.

The Dutch producer was reasonably sympathetic regarding our story, but was understandably vexed that we had missed the vital fit-up and technical rehearsal. The director/choreographer, Paddy Stone, was the only one who found the story of our misfortune hugely enjoyable.

Fortunately, during the next two days prior to the opening, we managed to redeem ourselves. The lighting was beautiful, the sound was pleasant and the show was such a success that it was revived for the following two seasons. There were obviously no hard feelings as I was invited back twice. Sadly, I was not available on either occasion because of other commitments.

The Threepenny Opera

I did, however, ensure that I could be in Denmark for the start of a special season celebrating one hundred years of the Aalborg Teater. The production was to be Kurt Weill's *The Threepenny Opera* and no expense was spared. They had engaged the British director Clifford Williams and set designer Ralph Koltai for the occasion. I knew Clifford, of course, from the dreaded *Carte Blanche* and Ralph from *Billy* and we had also crossed paths at the Royal Shakespeare Theatre where both of them were associates.

It was a novel experience for me when the musical director actually asked my opinion regarding the sound of the orchestra. I suggested that it could be more brittle and spikey - technical terms that he seemed to understand - and everyone agreed that, as a result, it became more like the original 1930 recordings with Lotte Lenya. This type of cooperation would never happen at home. I would be told in no uncertain terms to mind my own business.

A minor backstage crisis occurred during rehearsals when Sven received a phone call from Ralph Koltai's wife announcing that she was arriving unexpectedly that afternoon. Sven had to pass on this information to Ralph who was staying in a rented flat in Aalborg with his girlfriend. We all knew that Ralph had a complicated love life; in fact, at one show we worked on, he invited both his wife and his current girlfriend to the premiere with the wife sitting in the stalls and the girlfriend in the circle. He arranged to meet his wife in the stalls bar during the first interval, having coopted the services of the company manager to escort the girlfriend to the circle bar, saying that Ralph was very sorry but he was dealing with problems backstage. Then the procedure was reversed for the second interval. He got away with that one, so I was intrigued to see how he would deal with the present situation.

When informed by Sven that he only had a matter of two or three hours, he hardly turned a hair. "You go to the airport and meet my wife and I will make sure that the other woman leaves. Don't worry."

How was he going to arrange that? Simple. He returned to the flat, generated a blazing row with the girlfriend, who packed her bags, ordered a taxi and left for the airport. When Sven met the wife coming off the plane, he saw the other woman in a queue at the check-in desk. He hoped they would not recognise each other. Meanwhile, Ralph was happily working away in the theatre, seemingly unconcerned.

The production was splendid, altogether a most enjoyable experience and I was delighted to be invited back later in the year to work on their production of *Showboat*.

These brief excursions to Denmark were almost my only contact with the live theatre around that time. Being heavily committed to the sound manufacturing business and theatre consultancy, I had given up pestering producers for jobs in the West End. As it turned out, this was bad timing. The previous year had seen the opening of *Evita* and when Abe Jacob was brought over from America to design the sound, he demanded a large fee plus a royalty deal. This set a precedent for British sound designers and one or two who became involved with Cameron Mackintosh or Lloyd-Webber musicals were to become very rich indeed. But as Richard was often heard to say, "I did not come into the theatre to make money and, in this, I have succeeded beyond my wildest dreams."

1980

Worrying Times

The Theatre Projects Group now had seven companies employing over a hundred people. Borrowings were alarmingly high and TP was making a loss. Despite this, the management team remained confident that with all this growth there would eventually come profits.

TP Consultants was busier than ever, and I had to spend long days at the drawing board or at meetings with architects. The Barbican Theatre and the Royal Concert Hall in Nottingham, both with complex sound systems, were soon to open, as was the Derngate Theatre in Northampton. There were major projects in Canada with an Arts Centre incorporating two theatres and a concert hall in Calgary, and another theatre in Edmonton. There was a multi-purpose sports/concert hall in Kuala Lumpur plus several other projects in the pipeline.

Cameron Mackintosh

Despite the workload in the consultancy company, I did manage to fit in a couple of "proper" jobs. The first was another trip to Aalborg for a production of *Oliver!* for which they recreated the original Sean Kenny set. To my surprise Cameron Mackintosh turned up for the opening. He had acquired the rights to the musical and staged a revival in London two years earlier. Productions were now being mounted in many countries and Cameron had a clause in the contract whereby any theatre wishing to put on a production had to pay for him to attend the first night, which is one way of seeing the world.

At the traditional dinner for the company after the premiere, Cameron complemented me by grandly announcing that it was the best sound he had heard of any production of *Oliver!* so far. To which some wag shouted out to much laughter, "You ought to take it up as a profession, David!" Ignoring the interruption, Cameron went on to add, "I only have one note for you about the sound." For some reason, this comment caused a great deal of hilarity amongst the well-oiled group of actors, and I never did receive that note.

Director Larry Oaks thanking everyone after the first night of Oliver! Sitting next to him, Cameron Mackintosh listens.

Son et Lumiére

The other welcome escape from the drawing board was an invitation to write and direct a *Son et Lumière* in Plymouth Cathedral as part of the city's celebrations for the 400th anniversary of Francis Drake circumnavigating the globe; great scope for incorporating lots of music and sound effects and an opportunity for friend and ex-TP lighting designer, Bob Bryan, to work his magic. Bob was now head of lighting at the Glyndebourne Opera House.

I managed to cast the television newsreader and presenter Richard Baker as the narrator who, in my script, was constantly interrupted by the ghost of Drake who wanted to add his point of view. Drake was played by Leo McKern at his rumbustious best and we had great fun in the recording studio. Richard Baker was so good and pleasant to work with that I used him on two future projects.

My concept for the ghost was that his voice would appear from different positions in the Cathedral and each time he spoke a spotlight hit a pillar or wall on in that vicinity. As the show progressed, the lights gradually took the shape of a man until, right at the end of the show Drake actually appeared standing beside the altar. This was achieved by employing an old theatrical trick called Pepper's Ghost. Using a carefully angled large piece of glass to reflect a projected image, the figure of Drake magically appeared.

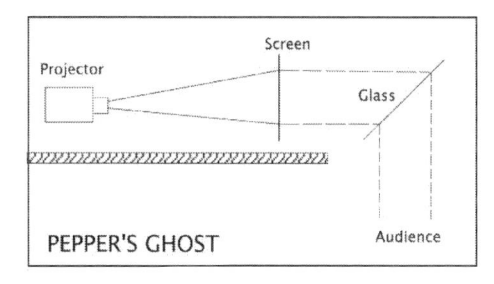

```
                        Screen
         Projector        |
           ┌─┐       ─────┼────
           │ │────────    │   /
           └─┘            │  / Glass
                          │ /
         ▓▓▓▓▓▓▓▓▓▓▓▓▓▓▓▓▓▓▓▓
                          │
                          │
         PEPPER'S GHOST   Audience
```

I am reminded of a *Son et Lumière* in Birmingham Cathedral for which I had created the sound track some years earlier. There was a meeting with the head of music to discuss recording the organ and choir. His office within the Cathedral had his name on the door followed by the letters FMW. Supposing that this was some kind of qualification, I asked him what they stood for. "Ah yes," he said. "It goes back to when we were having some building work done on the outside of the cathedral. I was strolling past the workmen one day, chatting to the Dean, when from high up in the scaffolding someone shouted, 'Watch your language everybody, here comes the fucking music wallah!' The Dean was highly amused, so I'm afraid the epithet has stuck."

1981

Where Has All The Money Gone?

Despite a ridiculous amount of borrowing during the past five years or so, Richard Pilbrow was informed once again that TP had run out of money. Where had it all gone? Bank interest had remained high, peaking at 20% in June 1981, so further borrowing would lead the group into even more debt. The answer Richard came up with was to approach the head of a venture capital company in the City who agreed to invite a select group of investors to buy shares in the company in a private placement. This resulted in six financial and City institutions becoming shareholders, contributing a capital injection of £800,000. It also meant that Richard had to raise a substantial sum of money himself in order to retain a much-reduced shareholding.

The MD was now able to continue his expansion plans. One of these was to purchase a Dutch lighting company to provide a base in the growing European market; an acquisition that was to become a major disaster.

Some months later, a rock-and-roll lighting company, currently in the hands of the receiver, was acquired and turned out to be another drain on resources.

The sound manufacturing business needed funding in order to realise its obvious potential. With finance arranged by the venture capital company, it was floated off as a completely separate company with TP having a shareholding. However, the new company only ever received half the promised money. Theatre Projects kept the other half by levying administration charges and costs. This resulted in the eventual failure of the enterprise with managing director Sam Wise, who had invested in shares, losing all his personal savings.

Always needing to generate income, our managing director negotiated an unusual deal with Cameron Mackintosh, currently producing a new musical with a very large lighting rig. Normally we would give a substantial discount on a West End show in order to obtain the rental contract, but there were rumours that this one was a turkey. Cameron was therefore offered an extraordinary contract whereby he would be charged the full list price for the first few weeks of the run, after which he would have to pay absolutely nothing. TP would receive a much-needed chunk of money to help with the ever-present cash flow crisis, and when the show failed, as was inevitable, the equipment would be returned to be hired out again. Cameron accepted the offer. After those first few weeks, he had free lighting equipment for the whole of the 21-year run of his little production. It was called *Cats*.

Final Meeting With A Great Talent

During a rehearsal at the Apollo Theatre for a musical entitled *I'm Getting My Act Together And Taking It On The Road* co-produced by Richard Pilbrow, I was surprised to see Lionel Bart enter the auditorium. He had nothing to do with the show but had dropped by to see his friend Diane Langton who was playing the lead. I had not seen him for twenty years, but when he spotted me, his face lit up with a big smile and he came over to give me a hug saying, "Dave! How are you doing? I'm really glad to see you. I'm working on an interesting project at the moment. I need to talk to you about it." At this point, the director hissed at us to be quiet and Lionel whispered, "I'll catch up with you later." He never did catch up, so the interesting project will forever remain a mystery.

Emerging from years of depression following the failure of *Twang!*, Bart returned once more into the public eye in 1986 when he received an Ivor Novello Award for his lifetime achievements.

He continued writing songs and themes for films, but his only real success was with a song for an Abbey National Building Society TV advertisement. Called *Happy Endings*, he was featured playing the piano and singing to a group of children.

In 1994, Cameron Mackintosh who owned the rights of *Oliver!*, staged a revival at the London Palladium and contracted Bart to do a few rewrites, for which he was given a share of the profits. Lionel Bart died in 1999 aged 68.

1982

Elizabeth Taylor

Tommy Elliott from Stoll Moss called again. Not with a crisis this time, but with a request for something that went against my principles. He wanted me to install microphones for a play. I knew that they amplified drama in some of the Broadway theatres, but it had always been my opinion that if actors did not have the ability to make themselves heard in a play, they were in the wrong profession.

However, Tommy explained that they were bringing over an American production of *Little Foxes* starring the hugely famous film star Elizabeth Taylor. It was a limited run, just seventeen weeks, and the producers knew that with Elizabeth Taylor in the lead role it would sell out. Therefore, although not really suitable for drama, they had booked the largest theatre available. This was the 1,550-seater Victoria Palace where we recently had the pleasure of 'rescuing' Max Bygraves.

Concerned that there would be adverse criticism if it was thought that Miss Taylor could not perform without microphones, I took great pains to create the most unobtrusive amplification possible. However, it was not the star who was the problem. She was totally at home on the stage and her vocal clarity was impressive. The difficulty was with some of the other American actors, one or two of whom were more used to working in television and had not bothered to master the technique of playing to a large audience. Apart from a lack of projection and poor diction - swallowed consonants - everything was directed towards the stalls so that the people in the two balconies only ever saw the tops of their heads.

When the director kept asking for the microphone levels to be increased, I warned him that the London critics were likely to be unkind if it became too obvious. Could the actors not be asked to speak up - and perhaps look up? The director passed these requests on to the cast, but the worst offender did not agree.

"There is nothing I can do about it. My voice is in the baritone range and *everybody* knows that deep voices just don't travel. We need the mikes turned up." Unfortunately, the director lacked authority and after that extraordinary statement, we did reluctantly increase the level of amplification - and still nobody in the balconies could understand what that actor was saying.

During the interval of the first public preview, I was informed by the stage manager that Miss Taylor wished to see me. With some trepidation I knocked on her door and entered the star dressing room. It had been decorated in lavender, her favourite colour. She apologised for bothering me, but was keen to know what it was sounding like at the back of this large theatre. Could she be heard? Should she speak up? I replied that apart from the gentleman with the "voice that did not travel" - at which she laughed - it was pretty good. "Now that we have an audience," I continued, "I am making improvements, checking the stalls and the balconies and making notes so that my sound operator can fine-tune the loudspeakers on each level."

"Do you have a wireless intercom to talk to your sound operator?" she asked, "Because I have a set you are quite welcome to borrow. It will save you having to keep running up and down."

We did not possess radio communication, so I gratefully accepted the offer. She explained that her intercoms were a godsend because she was able to keep in touch with her secretary back at the hotel and inform her chauffeur when to bring round the limousine. It must have been a powerful system and would have been broadcasting on a totally illegal frequency. But what the hell!

Elizabeth Taylor's arrival in this country caused a flurry of media excitement, especially when her equally famous and (twice) former husband, Richard Burton, turned up at her 50th birthday celebration at a London nightclub. Her current marriage was said to be floundering and Burton had recently separated from his wife, so there was a great deal of speculating about whether she and Richard would get together again - for a third time.

Despite all this notoriety and attention, backstage and in rehearsals she behaved like any other actor concerned with putting on a good show. Eminently professional, always approachable and easy to talk to, behind all that charm there was undoubtedly a razor-sharp mind. I think I fell under the spell.

Elizabeth Taylor in *Little Foxes*.

Another Royal Occasion

The 3rd March saw the Queen open the Barbican Centre in London with a great deal of pomp and ceremony. More than 3,500 people arrived for the celebrations, which culminated in a spectacular fireworks display over the Centre's lake. With a cinema, library, conference facilities, concert hall for the London Symphony Orchestra and two theatres for Peter Hall's Royal Shakespeare Company, it was the largest complex of its kind in Europe. We attended the RSC's inaugural production in the main theatre, upon which TP Consultants had been working for thirteen years.

1983

Crisis Upon Crisis

The recent large injection of cash to Theatre Projects had already run out and the year-end figures were not looking good. Through the venture capital company, another £800,000 was raised from investors with a rights issue. All the finance experts and professional management members of the board did not appear concerned about profits. They were still convinced that continued expansion would soon make the group a valuable enough asset to go public and make a killing.

Despite this confidence, Richard's gut feeling was one of unease. Although theoretically in charge as the chairman, he felt outnumbered. So, to give him some backing, he asked me to become a director of Theatre Projects Limited, the TP Group's parent company.

Now that I was on the main board and doing my best to keep an eye on things when Richard was out of the country, the wonderful plan of distancing myself from company politics by working three days a week at home fell apart, and driving to and from Oxfordshire nearly every day aggravated a problem I was having with my back.

Longer periods away from the family did not help my marriage, which was already under strain. In an attempt to find a solution, we sold the thatched cottage in Kingston Bagpuize and bought a small flat in London and a modern house in a village near to the school the two older boys, Mark and Dominic, attended. Their younger brother Robin was still only three.

In May, I had a pleasant interlude in Denmark designing the sound for the musical *Anything Goes*. It was to be the last time I had the pleasure of working with my Danish friends. Their in-house soundman and his assistant were now perfectly capable of handling future shows.

Upon my return, I was completely taken aback when my wife proposed that we should split up. I had not realised that the marriage had deteriorated to that extent. Discussions took place about my moving permanently to the London flat.

With the pressure of work, the tensions at home and the hours spent in the car, my back became steadily worse until I finally ended up in hospital undergoing an operation. Unfortunately, the procedure did not go according to plan. It was not the 100% cure promised by the surgeon. I remained in hospital for another three weeks in some discomfort while the nursing staff tried various treatments to improve the situation.

One afternoon during this period, Roger Norwood, who was now running the recording studio, appeared at my bedside. He was looking incredibly depressed.

"I'm really sorry for bothering you when you are not well, but I felt that someone should tell you what has happened. This morning I was informed that the studio is to be closed at the end of the week and that I and the two remaining staff will be made redundant. I would have spoken to Richard Pilbrow if he was in the country, but they have timed this when he is working in Japan and you are in hospital."

I was devastated. It made no sense. Money had been poured into setting up an audio-visual business and now there was to be no audio. But what could I do? Not yet able to walk properly and with problems at home and the ever-worsening situation within the company, there was little fight left within me. This was just another nail in the coffin.

It took another six weeks after leaving hospital before I was back at my desk, although still not able to walk properly. Eventually, I discovered a wonderful chiropractor who managed to get me upright and moving normally.

At the next Group Board meeting I attended, we were informed that the year-end figures for 1983 were anticipated to show a healthy profit. Was this some good news at last? Sadly not. Despite the optimistic forecast, when Richard returned from yet another trip abroad, he was horrified to be informed that the Group had run out of money - again! The MD showed him figures to prove that the situation was in hand and told him not to worry. But this time he did. He engaged a management consultant to appraise the whole operation.

After two months of going through the financial records and interviewing all the directors and other key personnel, the consultant produced an overwhelmingly damning report regarding both the future of the group and the management who were running it.

Not knowing what to do, Richard turned to his American friend Wally Russell who was running the TP Consultants office in Los Angeles. Wally was an experienced and tough businessman who had for some years been President of a large commercial operation, Strand Lighting USA. He agreed to fly over for a week to discuss what action should be taken. He stayed for six months.

Wally Russell

After a few weeks of detective work and delving through a mountain of files, Wally came up with a devastating report.

Moving the lighting hire division to a new warehouse in Nine Elms had cost £50,000 more than budgeted, acquiring a loudspeaker manufacturing business had cost £33,000 more than budgeted, and there was another £50,000 loss in the Dutch subsidiary. Extended credit of £60,000 to an unreliable producer of a musical had to be written off, and the lighting sales shop had lost £28,000. The acquisitions of the bankrupt Stagesound company and the failing rock and roll lighting business both lost money. There had been an enormous investment in a video studio, which had failed because the man in charge installed all the wrong equipment before hurriedly resigning.

And so it went on.

Wally's report remained classified for the time being, but the management must have been apprehensive. One morning Richard arrived in the office to find an envelope on his desk. It was a letter of resignation from the financial director - effective immediately!

Boardroom Drama

A special meeting of the board was called to which our managing director arrived, all smiles, oblivious of the drama about to unfold. Richard began by announcing that he was handing over the meeting to Wally who had a serious announcement about the management of the Group. One of the board members suggested that in order to have a frank conversation, perhaps both Richard and the managing director should leave the room. As soon as they had departed, Wally gave a summary of his findings to the alarm and consternation of the shareholders. He concluded with the warning that the whole enterprise was on the brink of collapse and required immediate drastic action.

There followed twenty minutes of subdued discussion before Richard and the managing director were invited to return.

Wally announced that the board had unanimously agreed that they had lost all confidence in the managing director. Consequently, he was invited to resign.

For a long moment there was silence while this piece of devastating news was digested. Then, apparently accepting the situation, he rose and headed for the door; but before making his exit he turned angrily to protest that the decision the board had made was entirely unfair, he had been totally loyal to the company, worked day and night, and everything he had done was to further the... At which point he choked up and was unable to continue. Wally asked one of board members to escort the distraught man from the building, making sure he took with him only his personal belongings.

Richard, looking completely shattered, stated that he felt equally responsible for the debacle and wished to tender his resignation as chairman. This was unanimously rejected.

The meeting concluded with another bombshell. I was appointed managing director.

The City accountants, Thompson McClintock, were appointed to advise us. One of their senior partners, Michael Haines, informed Richard that it would be perfectly feasible to sue the auditors for producing incorrect financial reports and their insurance would likely pay for any damages awarded. A large amount of money might be recovered, but the case could take years going through the courts. Other individuals who were culpable did not have sufficiently deep pockets to be worth going after.

"The alternative," he advised, "is to move on. The essence of the company, its reputation and its ideals are intact. Turn your back on the past and get on with your life."

We discussed the way forward. It was obvious that Richard's main interests were in theatrical production and consultancy - designing theatres for the future. The decision was made. We would concentrate on these activities. Thus I began the process that was to take up much of my time for the next three years; closing or selling off all the other companies and activities within the group and generally downsizing.

Too often this meant having to inform friends and colleagues that they no longer had a job.

Three weeks after the momentous events in the boardroom, Richard had to fly to the States for a meeting in the City of Dallas. He had been appointed consultant for the design of their new multi-million dollar multi-theatre arts centre; thus confirming that concentrating on the consultancy company had been a wise decision.

1984

Sculduggery In Holland

Two months after the fateful board meeting, Richard received an unexpected phone call from a junior employee in the Dutch company. The man was very nervous about calling the chairman of the Group, but thought he should know that Theatre Projects B.V. was about to be put into receivership by the local VAT office. All the assets were to be sold by auction and there would be no company, no equipment and no records of what anybody had been up to.

Wally Russell took an early flight the following morning, having arranged to meet one of Holland's leading lawyers. Unannounced, they walked into the TP office in Haarlem and informed an astonished managing director that he was suspended and had to leave the building immediately. They then proceeded to the VAT office where the lawyer made it clear that the company was wholly owned by Theatre Projects in England, so putting the Dutch company into liquidation and arranging the sale of assets was totally illegal.

That having been sorted, they visited the company's bank manager, who turned quite pale when recognising one of Holland's most famous lawyers. He denied all knowledge of any liquidation but unfortunately for him, there happened to be a file from the VAT office on his desk marked "Theatre Projects B.V."

Neither the VAT man nor the bank manager were prepared to talk about any discussions they might have had with Dutch or English representatives of Theatre Projects. The suspended managing director later received a jail sentence.

By the second half of the year, the remains of the group had stopped losing money and we were beginning to trade positively. With financial advice from Thompson McLintock, Richard devised a new business plan, "The Way Forward". A board meeting was called. It began with the representative from the venture capital company making an announcement that stunned everybody. He claimed that the investors had no confidence in the plan and would not support it. He was therefore resigning. With that, he stood up and walked out.

Our professional advisors, Thompson McClintock and our lawyer were speechless. The man who was the principal link with our City investors had just abandoned us.

We could not proceed with the plan and the only option was to sell our biggest remaining asset, the profitable lighting and sound rental business. Subsequently, a deal was reached with the Samuelson Group, a major equipment supplier to the film industry.

Leonard Bernstein Approves

Meanwhile, nothing daunted, Richard was busy producing another show. He saw a brilliant production of *West Side Story* at the Haymarket Theatre in Leicester, and decided to take it on a short tour before bringing it in to Her Majesty's Theatre. This was to be the first revival of the show since the 1958 London premiere in the same theatre.

The revival enjoyed a successful run from that May until September the following year, producing much-needed income. It was to be my tenth and last musical in that lovely theatre.

When Leonard Bernstein, the composer of *West Side Story*, happened to be in London, he attended a performance and was full of praise when meeting the cast after the show. Before going backstage, he took time to approach the sound control at the rear of the auditorium to give the sound operator a broad smile and big thumbs up. I was not there at the time, but I like to take some of the credit for that gesture.

It was also that year when my wife and I were finally divorced. It had been a remarkably amicable process, except for a brief spell when lawyers became involved. I was living a bachelor life once more in a newly built houseboat on Taggs Island, on the Thames near Hampton Court.

Hazards of the Job

By now, I had been working in the theatre pretty well non-stop for thirty years. The pleasure and excitement of being employed for one's creative talents was why we all did it. But there was a downside. It often involved a great deal of stress. This, and the long hours, had taken a toll on some of us in Theatre Projects. There were failed marriages and difficulties with various health problems.

Some of my colleagues struggled with alcohol, and being a lighting designer seemed to be particularly hazardous in this respect. You would arrive in a theatre or opera house, and immediately have to establish a rapport with the crew with whom you were going to be working during the next few days. They are probably tired from taking down the previous show, and should they take against you for some reason, your life could become a misery.

Starting off by treating the crew to a round of drinks in the local bar is one way of breaking the ice and getting everyone on your side. During the long hours of rigging the lanterns, focussing, and plotting cues, often late into the night, rather than wasting time with lengthy meal breaks, it is back to the pub for a bevy or two and a sandwich. Even during rehearsals when the cast is given a break, there are usually adjustments to be made before they return, so there is only time to visit the pub for a quick one... or possibly two.

Another reason the designer might feel the need for a bracer is when the director turns up to see the lighting for the first time. After all the hours of technical work have been completed, the fear is that the director might be unhappy, or even appalled, with the result. Happily, the designer's artistic endeavours normally fulfill or even exceed the director's expectations. In which case, the director might well wish to express his or her gratitude in the theatre bar.

Sound designers work similar long hours, but are not so reliant upon the in-house theatre technicians. The installation is usually handled by the designer's own crew or by a company with whom they are familiar. However, there is still the pressure of getting the job done within the time allowed, and to the entire satisfaction of a whole raft of people including the director, the composer, the lyricist and the producer.

1985

Too Many Balls In The Air

While I was in the office dealing with general management and a few consultancy projects, Richard was once more jetting around the world. In China, the Ministry of Culture had asked him to give a series of lectures on theatre architecture and technology in the Academy of Drama in Beijing. Although everything he said had to be translated, it must have gone well because at the end of his visit he was escorted to the Forbidden City to be shown three theatres that were not open to the general public. When they entered the lavish auditorium of the Emperor's personal theater, his host declared, "You are the first Westerner ever to have been in this theatre."

In September he was in Canada for the triumphant opening of the Calgary Arts Centre with its concert hall and two theatres, for which I had designed the sound. We had been working on this project for the past three years. I was sad to miss the sparkling gala concert for which Richard designed the lighting. The Centre was deemed a great success with the music critic for the New York Times describing it as "The best music hall in the Western hemisphere."

Back home in London, Richard and Iain Mackintosh, a director of the consultancy company, had the idea of transferring the National Theatre's incredibly successful production of *The Mysteries* to the West End. Based on the Wakefield Mediaeval Mystery Cycle, this was a trilogy of plays that ran for nine hours and could be seen on separate nights, or as a single all-day performance. Richard and Iain presented the plays in the dilapidated Lyceum Theatre that had not seen a theatrical production for years. It was a magical experience but, sadly, failed to attract the public in sufficient numbers.

He was then asked to light a play at the National Theatre. While all this was going on, he was planning two more theatre productions for the following year, plus working on a massive project for ICL Computers. This was to design, produce and direct a huge industrial show to tour the country. For this million pound plus project he came up with an ingenious stage with motorized elements incorporating masses of lighting, sound and projection. Over the Christmas break, when he should have been relaxing, he had a meeting with the man who was assisting on the scheme to discuss the budget.

And then he collapsed.

1986

Collapse Of Stout Party

On the 2nd January, there came a call from Richard's wife Molly. Richard was in a bad way. He could not sleep, he could not think straight. He was panicking about the seemingly insoluble problems in the company and overwhelmed at the thought of all his commitments. He was in a deep depression and obviously needed professional help.

I had heard of a private hospital in Roehampton, just outside London, called The Priory. Specialising in stress and other mental disorders, it was often mentioned in the press because so many celebrities sought treatment there. I made a booking and drove him and Molly to this white Gothic Mansion sitting in large grounds in South West London. Richard, hardly aware of what was going, had accepted that we were taking him somewhere for medical help. But when he hauled himself out of the car and spied a woman in a white coat standing at the front door, he said accusingly, "You've brought me to a funny farm!"

The lady doctor showed him to a very pleasant bedroom and took away his keys and credit cards, saying, "You won't be needing these." Then after a short consultation, he was given a cocktail of drugs and was out for the count for two days.

It took two and a half weeks before he realised that his brain had stopped churning and he was able to start thinking rationally. The doctors agreed to let him out on "day release", so he was able to attend meetings with Hal Prince and Cameron Mackintosh regarding *The Phantom of the Opera,* for which he was to design the lighting.

We had kept everything ticking over while Richard was out of action, but he was soon back in the office, full of enthusiasm for the next project.

Wally Russell had returned to the States and, before his breakdown, Richard had persuaded Professor Anthony Field to leave his post as financial director of the Arts Council to take control of the still very flaky financial situation at TP. He brought with him his assistant, David Pelham, of whom there is more to tell later.

Hal Prince rang to say that there were concerns with the script of *Phantom*, and they were postponing the opening date. This was disastrous news because it meant that Richard would not be available to light the show as it clashed with the ICL Computers event.

Richard now had an agent who had negotiated a good fee for *Phantom* plus a 0.75% royalty of box office receipts. As this was to include future productions around the world, the royalties would literally have made him millions... and would still be rolling in!

It was the young ex-TP lighting designer who Richard recommended for the job who hit the jackpot.

Frankie Howerd Again

Following the launch of the ICL tour, Richard produced a British production of the hit Broadway play called *I'm Not Rappaport*. Sir Paul Scofield was cast in the lead. There was a major crisis on the pre-London tour after a disastrous opening in Birmingham. What was meant to be a comedy was played to complete silence. Scofield panicked and decided that he was not capable of playing the part and refused to continue. Fortunately, he was persuaded back and the London opening was a triumph. It played to capacity for the six months contracted run, making serious and much needed money for Theatre Projects.

Some time during the previous year, Richard and I were having lunch in a restaurant when Frankie Howerd walked in. He came over for a chat and, not unnaturally, the subject of *A Funny Thing Happened on the Way to the Forum* came up. He suggested that it could be a good time for a revival. He was still in excellent shape and would be happy to take it on again. Richard agreed to give it some thought.

The decision was made to go ahead with *A Funny Thing* when finance was raised from some American backers. Larry Gelbart, who had co-written the original book with Burt Shevelove, agreed to direct and the show's composer Stephen Sondheim came over to help. It opened in Chichester to favourable press reviews, but failed to attract the public when it moved to the Piccadilly Theatre in London.

It was twenty years since Frankie Howerd had first played the part and he no longer possessed the vitality for such a taxing role. He was also missing the cast of supporting actors and comedians from the original, who had all been stars in their own right. *Forum* closed after only six weeks. As if this was not bad enough, the American backers welched on their contract and failed to send the money. The loss was more than twice the profit from *Rappaport* and plunged TP into yet another crisis.

Michael Haines from the accountants Thompson McClintock used to drop by occasionally, unpaid, because he was fascinated to see us all busying away as if we had not a care in the world. He once laughingly remarked, "I don't believe you theatricals. Here you all are, working your socks off with none of you accepting the fact that the company was six feet under a long time ago. It is dead, but you just won't lie down."

We did now have to accept that we were teetering on the edge of collapse. At Michael Haines' suggestion, it was agreed that the way forward was a management buy-out of the Consultancy company. It had always strived to remain isolated from the general chaos, and was currently working on a number of lucrative contracts in this country and abroad.

Part of this process would involve closing down the TP Group with what little was left within it. To this end, a liquidator was brought in to dispose of the remaining assets and deal with the creditors.

A Fairy Tale!

The following anecdote also appears in my book *Are We Driving Up The Right Riverbed?* which describes the trials and tribulations of trying to build a house in Spain. Nevertheless, it is part of my theatrical story and seems a good enough reason for repeating it here.

The production of *The Tinderbox* musical in Denmark had been such a highlight that in my spare time (!) I had been attempting to adapt the story for an English audience. Watching the children totally engrossed in the narrative, it had been noticeable how they tended to lose interest when anyone started to sing. So my version omitted all the songs.

Without any great expectations, I showed the script to Richard Gill, founder of the very successful Polka Children's Theatre in Wimbledon. He was one of my long-term clients for whom we had created many sound effects over the years. To my great surprise, Richard said that he liked the script and would like to put it on. To my even greater surprise, he suggested that I should direct it. This was a new departure for me, but I thought "Why not?" and arranged for my annual holiday to coincide with the scheduled rehearsal period.

The Hans Christian Andersen story of *The Tinderbox*, as you might know, is all about a poor soldier and his quest for treasure involving encounters with dogs with eyes as big as saucers, eyes as big as dinner plates, and eyes as big as millstones. And, of course, there is a beautiful princess.

I had written the part of the Princess as a feisty young girl who had tantrums and argued a lot with her long suffering parents – not your usual run-of-the-mill fairytale princess - and one of the actresses auditioning for the role, Alison Neil, really entered into the character, shouting, grimacing and jumping up and down with rage. It was very funny, just as I had hoped, and I determined to give her the part. The decision, you have to believe, was in no way swayed by the fact that during the audition she innocently enquired from the stage:

"Who wrote this script? It really is very good."

I discovered later that Alison had worked at Polka Theatre several times before and it was entirely possible that someone had told her who was the author – a possibility she has always stoutly denied.

Scene from the Tinderbox - Polka Children's Theatre 1986

Rehearsals were fun and, judging by the reaction of the children, the show was a success. Towards the end of the four-week run, I plucked up courage and asked Alison if she would care to accompany me to the first night of a West End play at the Young Vic, explaining that it was being produced by Theatre Projects. I was not at all confident that she would wish to spend time with some divorcee with three children who was a good twenty years her senior. So I was more than delighted when she accepted. Of course, her decision might have had something to do with the fact that, as an actress about to be out of work, making friends with someone involved with a West End production company could be a smart move. I had so far omitted to mention the fact that we were on the brink of going bust.

At the end of our first date, we exchanged telephone numbers. However, the relationship could well have ended at this point. By error, the number I gave her was wrong. This she discovered when ringing to thank me for the evening, concluding that this might have been a deliberate ploy to prevent further contact. Not being one to give up that easily, she worked her way through permutations of the number until eventually succeeding. During the ensuing conversation, I recalled that she had been intrigued by my living on a houseboat and suggested that she might like to visit the following weekend and see it for herself. However, the offer was declined with some excuse about a younger brother arriving home from a year-long trip to Australia. A likely tale, I thought; the not unexpected brush-off. Fortunately, the following week I managed to pluck up enough courage to give it one more go. This time she accepted.

After that, as much time as possible was spent together, although opportunities were limited because dealing with the continuing crisis in the office involved long working days. This usually meant Alison driving from her flat near Woolwich to the houseboat on Taggs Island, a journey of up to an hour and a half. So when my old mate Tony Horder offered us his house in Spain for a holiday, we jumped at the opportunity. Shortly after that memorable holiday, we moved in together, eventually tying the knot in 1992. All these years later, we are still happily married, thanks to Richard Gill and Polka.

1987

Anthony Hopkins Is Not Pleased

While the liquidator went about his business, life went on as usual and I became involved in an exhibition sponsored by the National Museum of Cardiff. It was based upon the life of an important Welsh historian known as Gerald of Wales, clerk and chaplain to King Henry II of England. For one section of the exhibition we required someone to record the voice of Gerald for an audio-visual. I was expecting to employ one of the excellent voice-over artistes we often used, but somehow the client had managed to persuade Anthony Hopkins to be our Gerald.

I hired a studio in the West End and all went reasonably well. Anthony Hopkins became annoyed with himself when he made the odd fluff, but I told him not to worry as it could easily be edited later. It was only a four-minute piece and at the end of the session, which took less than twenty minutes, I thanked him for a splendid recording and he went happily on his way.

The following day when I played the edited tape to the designer of the exhibition, one of his assistants who happened to be Welsh queried the pronunciation of the word "Cymru", the Welsh word for Wales. Born and bred in Port Talbot, surely Mr Hopkins would not have made a mistake. But he had. The word had been pronounced "Cumroo" when it should have been "Cumree".

There was nothing for it, but to ask him back to re-record that sentence. To put it mildly, the actor was not at all pleased when the exhibition organiser contacted him. At the time, he was working long days at the National Theatre rehearsing *Anthony and Cleopatra* with Judi Dench, and he only agreed to come to the studio if someone picked him up in a taxi first thing in the morning and took him back to the theatre in time for his ten o'clock rehearsal.

Because it was early in the morning when he re-recorded the line with the offending word, his voice sounded tired and hoarse. I asked him if he would kindly do another take using a lighter tone. This he attempted. Then, getting to his feet, said, "Is that OK? I have to go now."

Unfortunately, it was by no means OK. It did not match the speed and lightness of the original, which had been recorded in the afternoon. I suggested that we should play the earlier recording back to him on a headset so that he could pick it up when we got to the line in question and we would "drop in" to record mode. Hopefully, in this way he would be able to match his previous delivery.

It took a while to set this up and he was becoming increasingly impatient, so his first attempt at recording the line sounded somewhat irate. With some trepidation, I asked him to repeat the process. It was still not on the button and, although I could see that he was having difficulty keeping his temper in check, I had to beg him to try just one more. Fortunately, it was a good take. I think he would have exploded if I had made any further comments on his performance.

Later, when the audio-visual was set up in the Museum of Wales, the exhibition designer asked if he could have a viewing. It was a very simple audio-visual with Gerald of Wales, as voiced by Anthony Hopkins, reminiscing about his childhood and the successes and disappointments of his later life with relevant images projected onto the screen in a scenic setting. It was not a particularly wonderful script, but there is something magical about that warm mellifluous voice and the gentle Welsh accent that can be very moving. At the end of the four-minute sequence, the designer had tears running down his cheeks. Perseverance in the recording studio had paid off.

Horse Racing Across America

From a small slide show to the biggest exhibition I ever worked on. This was to be a major feature in the American National Museum of Racing in Saratoga Springs, which was being entirely redesigned and renovated.

The initial request was to produce an audio-visual presentation on the subject of horse racing across America in their Hall of Fame. The client was anticipating a multi-projector slide show, but horses are all about the beauty of movement, so my proposal was for a wide-screen movie film. The big blank wall behind the stage in the Hall of Fame would be covered with a slightly curved screen 40 feet (12m) wide and 10 feet (3m) high. I called the film "Race America". The client thought this a wonderful idea and agreed the sizeable budget. It was only then that I discovered a slight flaw in my plan. There was no film stock and no camera lens available to produce a picture that was half as wide again as Cinemascope.

The leading film equipment company was Samuelsons, to whom we had sold our lighting and sound rental business. I had met the chairman, Sydney Samuelson, during the negotiations so was able to seek his advice. His immediate reaction was that what I was proposing was not feasible with existing equipment, and was a bad idea anyway. Knowing absolutely nothing about film, I tentatively suggested, "How would it be if we shot the film using a wide screen camera, but only showed the middle section when projecting it in the theatre? Surely we could blank off the top and bottom of the picture."

"You would only be showing about half of the image and the quality would be terrible," he replied.

Nothing daunted, I argued, "But surely films are shown that wide on big screens. True, you see the entire picture, but the quality of the middle bit remains the same, doesn't it?"

He thought for a moment before conceding, with a broad grin, that I was right. "I still think it's crazy, but I'll tell you what we'll do. I'll get our company in Los Angeles to supply two 70mm cameras with the view finders marked with lines so that your cameramen can see what they are supposed to be shooting."

That sorted out the technical side. I now needed to find someone who, unlike me, had some idea of how to organise the making of a film. By a stroke of luck I found the ideal person; Tony Horder's ex-wife Stephany Marks, who was one of the BBC's top television producers. She happened to be free for the short period of shooting and agreed to be my co-producer. This really meant that she would be completely in charge of everything.

Me trying to look professional with Steph laughing in the background.

Steph brought in an experienced director, Keith Cheetham, organised an American film crew and set up an incredibly tight schedule with shooting locations across the US. Three hectic but exciting weeks were spent visiting the leading racecourses across America. Steph also hired a practice racetrack with a set of starting gates and a dozen horses and jockeys, so that we could film close-ups of horses racing from all angles. For this, she managed to hire a special buggy with a long boom that could place the camera in the thick of the pack alongside the jockeys.

Namedropping in the Wings

Apparently, it belonged to Clint Eastwood.

Back in London in post-production, the director sometimes chose to have the unusually wide screen split into several different moving pictures, at other times it would burst into a 40-foot wide image of horses thundering towards you. Of course, I made sure that the audience was engulfed in glorious sound with loudspeakers behind the screen and all around the room.

Split images on forty-foot wide screen.

The following year saw the grand opening ceremony of the splendidly refurbished museum. We were greeted by the President of the museum, Whitney Tower, a horseracing journalist related to the fabulously wealthy Vanderbilt family. To cut the ribbon, he introduced Paul Mellon, one of the richest men in America. Noting in his speech that the fund-raising for the refurbishment had not yet reached its target, Paul Mellon presented Whitney Tower with a cheque to cover the shortfall - just a million dollars or so!

At the banquet that evening I was seated next to an elegant and charming lady who invited me to visit her museum next time I happened to be in New York. I imagined that she was perhaps a director or a senior curator, but I later discovered that she was referring to the Whitney Museum of American Art, founded by Gertrude Vanderbilt Whitney to whom she was related. They owned it!

The film was received with enthusiastic applause by an audience consisting entirely of wealthy racehorse owners and other aficionados of the sport. The racing section in a New York paper stated:

"An incredible 15-minute film is being shown at the National Museum of Racing, Saratoga Springs. In the renovated Hall of Fame, RACE AMERICA captures the sights and sounds of a day at the races like you have never seen before. If this film does not get your blood pumping, go see your cardiologist."

In 2020 the museum was once again updated, but our film, *Race America,* had been enjoyed by the public for the previous thirty-one years. Not a bad run.

1988

Back To Reality

The liquidator finally wound up the old TP, and a restructured consultancy company was formed. Although it had the same name, Theatre Projects Consultants Limited was a brand new company, but with a thirty-one year track record. It was owned by the original directors plus Wally Russell and financial director Anthony Field. Richard Pilbrow moved to America where there was a boom in the building of theatres and arts centres, and he continued to light shows on Broadway.

Richard is one of the most extraordinary and charismatic figures I have had the joy and privilege of knowing. Totally driven, yet with a gentle unassuming manner, he has enriched the lives of so many people - not least my own.

Under his leadership, we changed the face of lighting and sound in the UK and then went on to influence theatre design and technology around the world. Despite receiving many awards and accolades from his peers during a distinguished career, he retains his self-deprecating sense of humour and is always excited about what tomorrow will bring. He loves to foster the next generation and I have so often seen him enthusing about a young lighting designer's work, when we all know that he could do it himself so much better.

At its height, the Theatre Projects Group had the biggest lighting and sound operation in Europe, a recording studio, a video suite, a theatrical costumiers, a photographic business, a shop in Covent Garden and manufacturing facilities for audio equipment and display lighting. Meanwhile, Richard was spearheading the world's most successful theatre design/consultancy business. Somehow, he also found time to win awards for lighting in the West End and on Broadway while producing more than thirty West End shows, the movie *Swallows And Amazons* and a television series on popular music. He did achieve his dream, but the irony is that while we were all having an exciting and fulfilling life, nobody ever got rich.

Richard and Molly Pilbrow at our house in 2019

Theatre Projects Consultants continues to be leaders in the field. In 2020 the company had fifty employees with offices in London, New York, Paris, Connecticut, Denver and Shanghai, and had worked on 1,500 projects in 80 countries.

As for me, once the old TP had finally been consigned to history, I was yearning to get back to something more creative than sitting at a drawing board and having arguments with architects about where the loudspeakers could be installed.

There was no possibility of returning to being a sound designer in the theatre, having been out of the loop for far too long. I may have started the ball rolling, but technology had moved on and there was now a clutch of talented and successful people handling all the big shows. In fact, in 2011 the Association of Sound Designers was formed. At last count, it boasted more than seven hundred members. Heaven knows what they all do!

However, an opportunity presented itself to take my theatrical experience in a completely different direction. For some reason, the more unusual requests for our expertise always ended up on my desk, and one of the oddest was from the head of tourism at Hastings Council. They owned some caves on the West Hill in Hastings on the south coast, and were inviting us to prepare a feasibility study, concept and detailed budget to turn them into a visitor attraction.

This was just up my street. Following some research, my proposal was for an exhibition on smuggling, which was rife in that area during the 1700s. Anthony Field's assistant, David Pelham, prepared some figures to show the financial viability of the scheme and we presented it to the council.

Although it was greeted with enthusiasm, they did not have sufficient expertise or funds to pursue the project themselves, so they asked if we could recommend a private operator who might be interested in taking it on. I discussed this with David Pelham, who was shortly to be out of a job, and we surprised our client by suggesting that we would like to be considered.

David put together a financial prospectus that was sufficiently positive to attract an investor. A new company was formed with me as managing director and David as financial director to design and manage historically themed attractions. It was called Adventure Projects.

A Smugglers Adventure opened in 1989 and over the next few years the company acquired three more attractions in Hastings, including an audio-visual show at the Castle, a "Quasar" laser tag game on Hastings pier, and a large aquarium. We also ran a model railway exhibition in York. All of these employed theatrical effects with the technical installations (lighting, sound, video, etc.) brilliantly handled by my friend Roger Straker who used to run the TP rental department.

Smugglers Adventure: Paying out after a good night's work.

Adventure Projects also designed and installed visitor centres for other clients. Among these, Newhaven Fort was awarded "Visitor Attraction of the Year" by the South East England Tourist Board, as was the Smugglers exhibition in a previous year.

Twenty years on, in 2008, there was an approach out of the blue from a gentleman who seemed bent on acquiring every aquarium in the country. He already owned three and was keen to add ours to his portfolio. I was seventy-one at the time, and as he was also offering to purchase all our other Hastings attractions, we accepted the deal. After all, how often does someone knock on your door wanting to buy a load of tanks full of fish?

For a few years, I continued to create visitor attractions and produce videos for anyone who asked. My book *The Sound of Theatre* was published in 2006. It still seems to be the only book describing the history of theatre sound in the western world. It was particularly well received in America and might have been why the United States Institute for Theatre Technology decided to present me with an award for "Distinguished Career in Sound Design". Thus proving that if you write a book about something, everybody thinks you are an expert!

2007: Presented with a USITT award in America.

During the 1960s to the 1980s, during a period of vast change, I was fortunate to have been at the forefront of theatre sound in the UK; starting out using 78 rpm gramophone records for sound effects and ending up with radiomikes and digital technology.

One link still remains with the theatre in that my wife, under her stage name of Alison Neil, has for many years been writing and performing one-woman shows based on famous or notorious characters, which she performs up and down the country. To keep up with demand, new plays have to be offered every couple of years or so and I have the great pleasure of being allowed to direct them.

And guess who creates the sound effects...

Every effort has been made to ensure that images reproduced in this book are properly credited. We apologise for any errors or omissions and will endeavour to correct these in any reprints.

Namedropping in the Wings

My West End Musicals

1961	The Pub Show	Comedy
1962	Blitz!	Adelphi
1963	A Funny Thing Happened on the Way to the Forum	Strand
	Half a Sixpence	Cambridge
	Pickwick	Saville
1964	Maggie May	Adelphi
	She Loves Me	Lyric
1966	On the Level	Saville
	Ad Lib (Larry Adler/Libby Morris)	Fortune
1967	Fiddler on the Roof	Her Majesty's
	The Four Musketeers	Drury Lane
1968	Sweet Charity	Prince of Wales
	Cabaret	Palace
1969	Mame (Led by Antony Horder)	Drury Lane
1970	Kiss Me Kate	Coliseum
	'Erb	Strand
	The Great Waltz	Drury Lane
	Meet Me In London	Adelphi
1971	Tyger	Albery Theatre
	Oh Kay!	Vaudeville
1972	Company	Her Majesty's
	Applause	Her Majesty's
	Jesus Christ Superstar	Palace
	Trelawney	Prince of Wales
	I and Albert	Piccadilly
	Tom Brown's Schooldays	Cambridge
1973	Joseph and the Amazing Technicolor Dreamcoat	Albery
	Kingdom Coming	Roundhouse
	Pippin	Her Majesty's
	Grease	New London
1974	John Paul George Ringo & Bert	Apollo
	The Good Companions	Her Majesties
	Billy	Drury Lane
	Hair (Revival)	Queens
	Royalty Follies	Royalty
	Rocky Horror Show (Re-mix)	King's Road Theatre
1975	Jeeves	Her Majesty's
	Dad's Army	Shaftesbury
	A Little Night Music	Adelphi
	Pilgrim	Roundhouse
	Gulliver's Travels	Mermaid
1976	Side by Side by Sondheim	Mermaid
	Side by Side by Sondheim	Wyndhams

	Julie Andrews Show	Palladium
	Bing Crosby Show	Palladium
	Carte Blanche	Phoenix
1977	Fire Angel	Her Majesty's
	SwingalongaMax	Victoria Palace
	Hair (Revival 2)	Her Majesty's
1978	Kismet	Shaftesbury
	Travelling Music Show	Her Majesty's
1981	I'm Going to Get My Act Together And Take It On The Road	Queens
1984	West Side Story (Revival)	Her Majesty's
1986	A Funny Thing Happened on the Way to the Forum (Revival)	Piccadilly

Musicals designed by Antony Horder in The West End

1969	Danny La Rue at the Palace	Palace
	Phil the Fluter	Palace
1970	Carol Channing and Her Ten Stout-Hearted Men	Drury Lane
	Jacques Brel is Alive and Well and Living in Paris	Duchess
1972	Behind the Fridge	Cambridge

Names Dropped

Ackland, Joss	341, 345
Adams, Lee	302-303
Adler, Larry	216
Albery, Bronson	274
Albery, Donald	61, 67, 70-71, 74, 79, 131, 141, 143-144
Albery. Ian	72-73, 90, 142,
Aldridge, Michael	346
Allen, Chesney	349, 352
Andrews, Julie	188, 197, 360-362, 364
Aronson Boris	230
Arden, John	221-222
Arnold, P.P.	273
Ashcroft, Peggy	126, 370
Atwell, Winifred	14
Ayckbourn, Alan	345-348
Bacall, Lauren	303-305, 325
Baddeley, Angela	345
Bahl, Bob	181-183, 234
Barker, Ronnie	49, 189
Barr, Ida	129
Barry, John	325
Bart, Lionel	131, 133-134, 141-142, 193, 195, 201, 204, 206-207, 209-210, 405-406
Barton, John	156
Bass, Alfie	229-230
Bassey, Shirley	107, 253
Bateson, Timothy	53-54
Baty, Robert	25-29, 31, 33-35, 37-38, 40, 48, 50, 62-64, 133, 147, 271
Baxter, Stanley	251
Baylis, Lilian	155
Beckett, Samuel	51, 54
Bennett, Alan	247
Bennett, Michael	167, 285, 373
Bennett, Tony	107-108
Bentine, Michael	255
Bernstein, Leonard	418
Bishop, Jack	70, 76-79, 135
Black, Don	325, 327
Blackmore, Laurie	317, 324
Blair, Lionel	110, 233, 251, 254
Blair, Joyce	254
Bloom, Claire	341
Boch, Jerry	221, 228
Bogarde, Dirk	49
Bolt, Robert	202
Booth, James	204

443

Borge, Victor	258
Bowles, Anthony	81, 297, 374-377
Brett, Richard	240, 393
Britten, Benjamin	17-18, 23
Brook, Peter	274, 276-278
Brown, Georgia	201
Bruce, Brenda	59
Bryan, Bob	402,
Bull, Peter	53
Burnett, Al	107, 110
Burns, George	98
Burton, Richard	20, 155, 223, 409
Bygraves, Max	379-381, 383-384, 407
Caron, Leslie	61, 74, 118, 125-127
Carpenter, Karen	384-385
Channing, Carol	264-265
Charles, HRH Prince	355-358
Cilento, Diane	79-80
Clausen, Sven	373-374, 385-387, 399-400
Clooney, Rosemary	362
Codron, Michael	81, 85-86, 339
Coe, Peter	158, 160, 189, 191, 194, 231-232, 272, 292
Cogan, Alma	107
Cole, Nat King	110
Company	285-291
Connery, Sean	79, 254-255
Cook, Peter	137, 306-307
Cooney, Ray	375, 379
Corbett, Ronnie	204
Craig, Wendy	123
Craven, Gemma	301
Crawford, Michael	325-329, 333
Cribbins, Bernard	63-64
Crosby, Bing	335, 360, 362-364
Cuka, Frances	76
Dandridge, June	63-64
Daneman, Paul	53
Dankworth, Johnny	384
Danvers-Walker, Bob	256
Davis, Joe	120
Davis, Carl	352-353
Davis, Sammy	107-110, 114-116, 189, 192-194
Delfont, Bernard	107, 159, 195, 198, 200-201, 206, 209, 304, 336, 341, 345-347, 349-350
Dench, Judi	126-127, 155, 244-245, 336-338, 429
Derbyshire, Delia	215
De Valois, Ninette	255
Dickson, Barbara	339
Donald, James	70

Donlan, Yolande	211
Dotrice, Roy	126, 292
Drake, Alfred	58, 388
Duttson, Pembroke	25-26, 28
Duffell, Bee	91, 93
Dunn, Clive	350
Eckstein, Billy	183
Eddington, Paul	247
Edinburgh, HRH Duke of	187
Elizabeth, HRH Queen	172, 197, 241, 356-357, 367-369, 410
Elkins, Hillard	190-193
Elliot, Denholm	45-46
Elliott, Marianne	120
Elliott, Michael	116-119, 128, 152, 155, 260-261
Elliott, Tommy	285, 379-380, 407
Ellis, Mary	47-48
Ellis, Vivian	49, 372
Evans, Edith	155
Eve, Trevor	339
Eyre, Richard	370
Fazan, Eleanor (Fiz)	79, 81, 86, 117, 128, 133, 141, 150
Fernald, John	36, 42-43, 46, 62
Ffrancon-Davies, Gwen	126
Field, Anthony	423, 435, 437
Fielding, Harold	249, 261, 263, 267, 269, 291-292, 327, 329. 349
Flanagan, Bud	349-350, 352
Fosse, Bob	231, 318
Forrest, George	388
Forsythe, Bruce	387
Fournier, Maurice	195, 198-201, 204, 206, 209, 303, 345
Gable, Christopher	336
Gascoigne, Bamber	81
Gelbart, Larry	209, 425
Gere, Richard	315
Gibson, Ian	273, 294, 373
Gielgud, John	126-128, 155, 247, 338
Gill, Richard	426, 428
Gingold, Hermoine	345
Good, Jack	273
Gordon, Bernard	80, 86, 89
Gormé, Eydie	107
Goudsmit, Lex	229, 230
Gough, Michael	41
Grainer, Ron	79, 215
Graves, Robert	354
Gregg, Stacey	315
Griffith, Hugh	57, 59-60
Groothuis, Paul	370-371
Guthrie, Tyrone	154

Haigh, Kenneth	195
Hall, George	117-118
Hall, Peter	36-37, 40-42, 44-46, 49, 51-55, 58-62, 67, 70, 72-74, 80, 89-90, 94-96, 98, 101, 117-119, 123, 125-126, 156-157, 201-202, 243, 368-371, 410
Harnick, Sheldon	188, 221-222, 228
Harrison, Rex	196-198,
Harwood Ronald	211, 335,
Hawkins, Peter	256
Hay, Pamela	273
Hemmings, David	18, 345-346
Hill, Bernard	339
Hobson, Harold	53-54
Holloway, Stanley	197
Holm, Ian	126-127
Hood, Morag	341
Hopkins, Anthony	429-430
Horden, Michael	253, 369
Horder, Antony	133, 147-152, 158, 162, 200, 211-213, 237, 239, 246-248, 252-253, 255, 258-261, 263-264, 266, 270-271, 292, 301, 306-307, 313, 320, 326, 344, 372, 391-392, 428
Howard, Trevor	260-261
Howerd, Frankie	164-165, 424-425
Humphries, Barry	195
Hurry, Leslie	72
Hutchinson, Leslie (Hutch)	14
Hutton, Betty	107
Jackson, Gordon	61
Jacob, Abe	293, 301, 327, 373, 400
Jaques Brel is Alive....	269-270
James, Polly	302
Jeans, Isabel	70, 72, 74
Jeffrey, Peter	126
Jeffries, Lionel	70, 91, 94, 96-97
Jenkins, Anne	37, 62, 67, 79, 131, 133
Johnson, Russell	369
Jones, Disley	81
Jones, Paul	318
Jones, R.G.	77-78
Joseph, Philip	339
Karlin, Miriam	50
Karloff, Boris	110
Kedrova, Lila	244
Kendall, Bryan	121
Kennedy, John	173
Kennedy, Robert	224-225
Kenny, Sean	137-138, 141-142, 158-160, 162, 170, 175-177, 180-181, 183-184, 195, 198-199, 231, 233-236, 238, 254-255, 353, 401

Kernan, David	358
Knight, Esmond	260-261
Knight, Michael	234
Koltai, Ralph	325-326, 399-400
Kossof, David	70
Kotcheff, Ted	196
Laine, Cleo	384
Langton, Diane	405
La Rue, Danny	251
Lasdun, Denys	240, 369-370
Laughton, Charles	98
Lavender, Ian	349-350, 352
Laver, Claire	248, 327-329, 376-378, 380
Lawford, Peter	110
Lawrence, Steve	107
Le Mesurier, John	255, 349-350
Lee, Christopher	61
Lee, Peggy	107-108
Lehmann, Beatrix	59-60
Leighton, Margaret	123
Listen to the Wind	49-50, 81, 372
Little Foxes	407-409
Little, George	230
Littlewood, Joan	204-206, 208-209
Littler, Emile	246
Lloyd-Webber, Andrew	293, 297, 300, 339, 345
Loren, Sophia	111
Love, Bessie	45
Lowe, Arthur	349-352
Lynn, Vera	135, 149-150
Mackerras, Charles	79-80
Mackintosh, Cameron	358-359, 400-402, 405-406, 423
Mackintosh, Iain	371, 421
Madame Tussauds	216-220, 223-226,
Maggie May	193, 195-196, 198-201
Mame	249-251
Mann, Jack	166, 172, 267, 286-288, 304
Marks, Stephany	429
Marsden, Betty	347
Mathis, Johnny	384
Martin, Millicent	358
Maughan, Susan	263
Mayo, Paul	45
McGoohan, Patrick	61, 118
McKellan, Ian	371
McKenna, Virginia	323, 345
McKenzie, Julia	358
McKern, Leo	57-58, 90, 93-94, 97-98, 259, 403

Mellon, Paul	433
Messel, Oliver	206
Mercer, Johnny	335
Miles, Bernard	353-354
Milligan, Spike	104, 354
Mills, John	336, 338
Mitchell, Yvonne	41
Moreno, Rita	188
Moor, Michael	253, 296, 298, 362, 392
Moore, Dudley	306-307
Morris, Libby	216
Morris, Mary	48
Moss, John	106, 130, 307-312, 372
Mourning Becomes Electra	46-49
Muggeridge, Malcolm	54, 223
Munshin, Jules	94, 99
Munderloh, Otts	231
Murray, Braham	261, 336-338, 377
My Fair Lady	63, 123, 196-198, 213, 331
Neil, Alison	426-428, 439
Nicholas, Paul	298, 315
Northen, Michael	120
Norwood, Roger	298, 328, 330, 412
Nunn, Trevor	370
Oddie, Bill	254
Oh! Calcutta!	274, 365-366
Oh, Kay!	325
Oliver!	132, 138, 158, 195, 201, 333, 401-402, 406
Olivier, Laurence	11, 155, 167-168, 170-171, 189, 240-241, 253, 365, 367-370
On The Level	215-216
Ornbo, Robert	186, 188, 230-231, 285, 318-319, 321, 340, 346, 349, 366, 391, 394-398
Othello	152, 273
O'Toole, Peter	11, 247
Owen, Alun	195
Page, Patti	107
Paige, Elaine	315, 326
Parkinson, Bill	72-73
Patrick, Nigel	248, 255
Peacock, Trevor	261
Pears, Peter	17-18
Percy, Esmé	57
Pelham, David	420, 434
Phillips, Frank	135
Phillips, Leslie	215, 255
Phillips, Siân	126
Pickwick	158-162, 189

Namedropping in the Wings

Pilbrow, Richard	89, 120-122, 124, 128, 131-132, 141, 143, 146, 163, 165, 167, 172-174, 186-189, 203, 209-210, 212, 219, 221-222, 226-229, 240-244-245, 260, 267, 274-278, 288-291, 323-324, 337-338, 345, 360-361, 365, 369-371, 388-393, 404-405, 411-418, 435-436
Pilbrow, Molly	274-276, 278, 288-290, 423, 436
Pilbrow, Viki	121, 165-166, 172-173, 188, 228-229, 240, 245, 274
Pilgrim	352-353
Pippin	318
Pleasance, Donald	43
Plowright, Joan	61
Plummer, Christopher	126, 253
Porter, Eric	126
Powell, Peter	79
Previn, Andre	335, 337
Priestley, J.B.	335, 338
Prince, Hal	163-164, 166-167, 172-174, 188, 226, 244, 285-287, 345, 349, 359, 423-424
Proby, P.J.	273
Prowse, Juliet	231, 251
Race America	431-434
Race, Steve	20
Raymond, Debbie	340
Raymond, Gary	188
Raymond, Paul	318-319, 321-322, 340
Redgrave, Michael	155
Redgrave, Vanessa	128
Rice, Tim	293, 297, 300, 339, 345
Richardson, Ian	126
Richardson, Ralph	155, 370
Riddle, Major	176-177, 184
Ridley, Arnold	351
Rigg, Diana	126
Roberts, Rachel	195-196, 198, 201
Robbins, Jerome	226-228
Robinson, Edward G	225
Rocky Horror Show	341
Rogers, Anne	188
Rogers, Clodagh	262-263
Rogers, Ginger	249-251
Ross, Edmundo	110
Rowbottom, George	170
Routledge, Patricia	63, 80
Rowland, Toby	94
Rowlands, Patsy	80
Royalty Follies	340
Russell, Ken	223
Russell, Wally	413, 417, 423, 435
Russell, Willy	338

Saint-Denis, Michel	128
Saint Joan	33-35, 40, 155
Sallis, Peter	61, 188, 244
Samuelson, Sydney	431
Sargant, James	217, 224-225
Schlesinger, John	302-303
Schneider, Alan	65-67
Scofield, Paul	424
Secombe, Harry	96, 104, 158-162, 231-233
Sellers, Peter	94-100, 102-105
Shankar, Ravi	255
Share My Lettuce	81-86
Shaw, Martin	341
Shaw, Robert	64
She Loves Me	172-174, 189, 221, 360
Sher, Antony	339
Sherrin, Ed	341-342
Sherrin, Ned	359
Shevelove, Burt	163, 209-210, 425
Shufflewick, Mrs	129
Shuman, Mort	270
Side by Side by Sondheim	358-340
Siffre, Labbi	253
Simmons, Jean	345
Sinden, Donald	157
Slade, Julian	63-64
Smith, Maggie	49-50, 82, 84, 86, 155
Sondheim, Stephen	163, 165-167, 285, 287-288, 290, 345, 358-359, 425
South	44-46
Spot, Jack	115-116
Spragg, Bill	76-77
Stanley, Kim	90
Stanton, Robert	197, 213, 331
Steele, Tommy	158, 261-263
Stephens, Robert	123
Stigwood, Robert	293-295, 313, 333-334, 339, 385
Straker, Roger	296, 438
Stritch, Elaine	288-290
Stripp, Dave	256, 259
Strouse, Charles	191, 303
Suzman, Janet	157, 253
Swallows and Amazons	323, 436
Sweet Charity	231, 264
The Alchemist	152, 154
The Battle of Trafalgar	217-222
The Burnt Flowerbed	57-58
The Boyfriend	223-224
The Cherry Orchard	125-128
The Comedy of Errors	63-64

The Curse of the Daleks	256
The Devils of Loudun	125
The Duchess of Malfi	125
The Fantasticks	189
The Four Musketeers	231-233
The Gates of Summer	70-75
The Ghost Train	351-352
The Good Companions	335-338
The Great Waltz	267-269
The Immoralist	41-43
The Midnight Family	46
The Mysteries	421
The Physician's Folly	17-23
The Pub Show	128-129
The Rules of the Game	43-44
The Ruling Class	247
The Threepenny Opera	399-400
The Thwarting of Baron Bolligrew	202
The Travelling Music Show	387, 389
The Turn of the Screw	18
The Tinderbox	386-387, 426-427
The Waltz of the Toreadors	59-61
The Wars of the Roses	156-157
The Wrong Side of the Park	123
Trelawney	301
T. Rex	254
Twang!	204-210, 405
Two Stars for Comfort	260-261
Tyger	273
Tarbuck, Jimmy	129
Taylor, Elizabeth	90, 223, 407-409
Thompson, Eric	257, 346-348
Thompson, Neville	170-171, 293-295, 300
Thorndyke, Sybil	155
Toff, Benn	25, 62
Topol	228-230
Tower, Whitney	433
Toye, Wendy	215
Tutin, Dorothy	70, 72, 126
Twiggy	223-224
Tynan, Kenneth	53, 210, 365, 367-368
Walton, Bill	132
Walton, Tony	163, 188, 318, 360
Wannamaker, Sam	90-92
Warner, David	157, 201
Watts, Charlie	279-281
Watts, Shirley	279-281
Wells, John	239, 307
Wells, Orson	61-62

Welch, Elizabeth	318
West Side Story	165, 418
White, Michael	341, 365
Whittington, Dick	217-218
Wigzell, Peter	71-72
Wilkinson, Mark	257
Williams, Andy	364
Williams, Clifford	365-366, 399
Williams, Kenneth	35, 61, 81-86, 91
Windsor, Barbara	204
Winter, Mark	251
Wise, Sam	296, 344, 384, 404
Wolfit, Donald	155, 210-212
Wood, John	94-96, 101
Woodthorpe, Peter	53
Woolfenden, Guy	156, 225, 235, 257-258
Wrede, Caspar	117, 119
Wright, Robert	388
Wyngarde, Peter	35
Zuleika	79-81

ABOUT THE AUTHOR

In 1962 David Collison received the first poster credit for sound in the theatre and went on to become the first person to be called a Theatre Sound Designer in the UK. Among his many innovations was the introduction of the first mixing desk in the West End for the Stephen Sondheim musical "Company" in 1974.

During the 1970s and 1980s, he worked on more than fifty West End musicals including Fiddler on the Roof, Cabaret, Sweet Charity, A Funny Thing Happened on the Way to the Forum, Mame, A Little Night Music, Grease, Company, Applause, Joseph and the Technicolor Dreamcoat and Jesus Christ Superstar.

He was Sound Designer for the Royal Shakespeare Company under Sir Peter Hall and for the National Theatre Company under Sir Laurence Olivier. As a sound consultant with Richard Pilbrow's company, Theatre Projects, he designed permanent sound systems for theatres and concert halls in the UK and around the world, including the National Theatre of Great Britain.

In 2007, David Collison received the USITT Harold Burris-Meyer Distinguished Career in Sound Design Award.

His book, *Stage Sound*, with a foreword by Sir Peter Hall was published in 1976 with a second edition in 1982. Describing the basic components of a sound system, the creation and use of sound effects, plus information on sound reinforcement for musicals, it was welcomed as an important handbook for both amateur and professional theatre technicians, and a vital reference for drama schools and colleges.

His next book, *The Sound of Theatre* was published in 2008 and republished in paperback in 2020. He has also written *Are We Driving Up The Right Riverbed?* (a true account of his and his wife's adventures trying to build a house in Spain).

David is married to actress Alison Neil, renowned for writing and performing her one-woman plays. They live in the Forest of Dean with a Yorkie called Monty.

ALSO BY DAVID COLLISON

Stage Sound
Published by Cassell 1962, reprint 1976, second edition 1982

"A remarkably concise and balanced presentation of the craft of theatre sound."
Educational Theatre Journal (USA)

"The section on sound effects is one of the best ever written."
Sightline

The Sound of Theatre
Hardback published by Plasa Limited in 2008
Paperback/eBook by Entertainment Technology Press in 2020

"Endlessly interesting. The whole book is such an informative and generous record of its subject."
Hal Prince – Broadway Producer and Director

"It is the most comprehensive book on this subject yet produced, and is likely to remain a standard reference for years to come."
The Stage and Television Today

Are We Driving Up The Right Riverbed?
Published by Kindle Publishing Services in 2017
Amazon Verified Purchasers:
"A wonderfully written true story."
"Could not put it sown. One of my best reads."
"A truly enjoyable rollercoaster of emotions."
"I was so sorry when the book came to an end."

davidcollisonsound.com

Namedropping in the Wings